Campaigning for Justice

Stanford Studies in Human Rights

Campaigning for Justice

Human Rights Advocacy in Practice

Jo Becker

Stanford University Press
Stanford, California

Stanford University Press
Stanford, California

Printed in the United States of America on acid-free, archival-quality paper.

Library of Congress Cataloging-in-Publication Data

Becker, Jo, author.
   Campaigning for justice : human rights advocacy in practice / Jo Becker.
      pages cm. — (Stanford studies in human rights)
   Includes bibliographical references and index.
   ISBN 978-0-8047-7450-5 (cloth : alk. paper)
   ISBN 978-0-8047-7451-2 (pbk. : alk. paper)
      1. Human rights advocacy—Case studies. 2. Human rights—Case studies.
I. Title. II. Series: Stanford studies in human rights.
JC571.B425   2012
323—dc23
                                                                2012010567

Contents

Foreword

CAMPAIGNING FOR JUSTICE: HUMAN RIGHTS ADVOCACY IN PRACTICE is a much-needed antidote to the perceived gap in the literature between human rights theory and the practice of human rights advocacy. The book demonstrates that ideas about human rights and the contemporary world are deeply connected with forms of practice and institutional shifts within international and transnational communities and that case studies of individual actors within these broader movements are a singular source of experiential knowledge and insight. Jo Becker is a longtime staffmember at Human Rights Watch with years of global experience in human rights advocacy, reporting, and monitoring. She draws from this considerable experience on the frontlines of international human rights practice in a wide-ranging study of organized advocacy campaigns, developments in the UN monitoring system, the politics of accountability within international criminal law, and the role of new forms of media in creating a "curious grapevine" of information about human rights violations that transcends—and transgresses—the boundaries of nation-states. Her book is meant to be used in multiple ways: as a source of new information about contemporary human rights practices; as a guide to the lives and experiences of people caught up in ongoing struggles for human rights and accountability; and as a deeply felt reflection on the pitfalls and potential ways forward for activists in the midst of conflict, resistance, and movements for social justice.

Her book is organized around profiles of human rights advocates and is structured in such a way that the lessons learned from these diverse experiences can be used by others who wish to participate in future campaigns. The writing and presentation are accessible, and the book speaks to a growing constituency that desires more grounded perspectives on human rights, both within academia and beyond. The book is not a simple how-to manual; rather, it is an informed overview of current human rights practices anchored in illustrative lives and institutions. What is so indispensable about *Campaigning for Justice* is the way Becker distills her many years at the forefront of highly visible human rights campaigns and interviews with dozens of other experienced activists to identify the most promising areas of human rights advocacy for the future. Despite what critics might say about the politics of human rights and the strategic manipulation of international law by particular nation-states, Becker's book paints an optimistic picture of the role of human rights and the people who have dedicated their lives to a more just world. As she puts it, the "human rights movement is full of . . . examples of innovative partnerships, skillful messaging, strategic interventions, and persistent organizing," and her book serves as a signpost for those who would carry on the fight for human rights with understanding and creativity.

Mark Goodale
Series Editor
Stanford Studies in Human Rights

Campaigning for Justice

ADVOCATES WITHIN THE HUMAN RIGHTS MOVEMENT have had remarkable success in establishing new international laws to address egregious abuses, securing concrete changes in government human rights policies and practices, and transforming the terms of public debate in order to bring new human rights issues squarely onto the global agenda. Yet too often, the strategies that human rights advocates have employed to achieve these goals are not broadly shared or known. While the human rights movement has grown exponentially over the past few decades, the practitioners who are on the front lines of advocacy rarely take time to document their efforts or analyze for a broader audience why their tactics have succeeded or failed.

This book explores the strategies behind some of the most innovative human rights campaigns and exciting victories of recent years. It delves into local, regional, and international advocacy efforts to discover how advocates were able to address seemingly intractable abuses and secure concrete advances in human rights. For example, how did families in Libya organize to demand accountability for a prison massacre despite intimidation by security forces and laws prohibiting human rights activity? How did a small group of advocates mount a global campaign to win an international treaty banning the use of child soldiers? How did African and international groups ensure that former Liberian president Charles Taylor stood trial for alleged war crimes? How were advocates able to use YouTube, Twitter, Facebook, Internet blogs, satellite feeds, and an online television station to bring global attention to Tibet during the 2008 Beijing Olympics?

The human rights movement is full of such amazing examples of innovative partnerships, skillful messaging, strategic interventions, and persistent organizing that have highlighted new issues, empowered victims, changed attitudes, and resulted in new policies and practices. The eleven case studies featured in this book are but a sample of the wealth the movement has to offer. Drawing on interviews with dozens of experienced human rights advocates, the examples selected for this volume focus on four strengths of the human rights movement: the development of new international legal standards; the use of the United Nations system and its mechanisms on behalf of human rights; efforts to ensure accountability for human rights abuses and bring perpetrators to justice; and the emergence of broad new alliances and the use of new technology.

Some of the human rights movement's most significant recent victories have been the adoption of new international legal standards, including treaties to abolish anti-personnel mines (1998), to establish the International Criminal Court (1999), to prohibit the use of child soldiers in armed conflict (2000), to protect the rights of persons with disabilities (2006), and to abolish the use of cluster munitions (2008). These campaigns have established new models of organizing that are increasingly accepted as the norm. For example, the International Campaign to Ban Landmines created a new model of partnership between non-governmental organizations (NGOs) and "like-minded" governments and established a precedent for treaty negotiations outside of the traditional venue of the United Nations. The successful effort to achieve the 2006 Convention on the Rights of Persons with Disabilities was marked by unparalleled organizing and involvement by persons with disabilities. Their insistence on "nothing about us without us" ensured their presence at the table and active involvement in the negotiations. Many of these new treaties have been ratified at astonishing rates, winning broad acceptance in just a few years, thanks in large part to persistent pressure from the campaigns that worked for their adoption.

Part I of this book provides an in-depth look at two campaigns for international standards. Chapter 1 examines the global campaign to stop the use of child soldiers. During an intense two-year period, a coalition of human rights and humanitarian organizations worked with allied governments to organize an ambitious series of regional conferences, engage influential policymakers, establish the extent of child soldiering, and mobilize public support and national campaigns in more than thirty countries in its successful effort to win a UN treaty banning the participation of children in armed conflict.

Chapter 2 details efforts by domestic workers and their allies to win new global labor standards to protect the rights of tens of millions of women and girls. Domestic workers—which include housekeepers, maids, nannies, and others working in private households—form one of the world's largest but most vulnerable sectors of employment. Examples of organizing by domestic workers in Tanzania and the Philippines illustrate how national-level mobilization built a base for a successful global effort that reached fruition with the adoption of a new international labour convention in 2011 to ensure decent work for domestic workers.

Part II takes a closer look at UN human rights bodies and their mechanisms. The United Nations is a significant locus of human rights activity and offers advocates myriad opportunities to advance human rights norms and influence the policies and practices of member states and other actors. Human rights advocates have used the UN Commission on Human Rights and its successor, the Human Rights Council, to bring attention to both thematic and country issues, to secure agreements to begin drafting new treaties, to establish special mandates to monitor human rights, to initiate commissions of inquiry, and to secure resolutions sanctioning human rights abusers. Advocates work closely with some forty-five UN special procedures, including special rapporteurs and expert groups that monitor both country situations and themes including torture, extrajudicial executions, violence against women, and the rights to health, education, and housing.

The UN's premiere human rights body, the Human Rights Council, was established in 2006 to replace its discredited predecessor, the Commission on Human Rights. Chapter 3 examines a series of successful annual campaigns to ensure that the new Human Rights Council avoided the failures of the commission, which had become co-opted by countries with abysmal human rights records in order to protect themselves and other abusers from criticism and scrutiny. By bringing together dissidents and civil society in Belarus, Sri Lanka, Azerbaijan, and other candidate countries with respected international figures such as Václav Havel, Desmond Tutu, and Jimmy Carter, a cross-regional coalition was able to influence the votes of UN member states and defeat the election of some of the world's worst human rights abusers to the council.

Between 2000 and 2010, the number of UN special rapporteurs nearly doubled, offering human rights advocates greater opportunities to provide information and input for the rapporteurs as they conducted country visits, sent governments communications regarding human rights violations, and prepared reports and recommendations on how governments could better promote and protect human rights. Chapter 4 explores collaboration between human rights NGOs and special rapporteurs, highlighting three particular cases. In the Philippines, a visit by the UN special rapporteur on extrajudicial executions, coupled with pressure from national and international NGOs, helped prompt a dramatic decline in extrajudicial executions. In Brazil, a country mission by the special rapporteur on adequate housing was used by NGOs to launch a renewed campaign on behalf of land rights for *quilombos*, the descendents of African slaves. In Jordan, where national organizations had repeatedly called for the closure of a detention center known for torture, a country visit by the special rapporteur on torture prompted the government finally to shut the facility. In each case, the visit of the special rapporteur was able to reinforce the NGOs' demands and serve as a catalyst for stronger action.

Human rights advocates have also used the UN architecture to bring underrecognized human rights abuses to light and to establish new mechanisms to ensure sustained and systematic action to address them. Chapter 5 details a nine-year effort by children's rights organizations to spotlight the myriad ways that children are subject to violence and to demand a stronger international response through the United Nations, first through an in-depth global study to document the horrific scale of such violence and then by securing the appointment of a high-level UN representative to work with UN member states and agencies to implement the study's recommendations and take meaningful action to prevent and to end violence against children.

Part III addresses efforts to seek accountability. Increasingly, the human rights movement has focused on accountability for human rights abuses and mechanisms to bring offenders to justice, deter future abuses, and provide victims with redress. Special courts and tribunals, including the International Criminal Tribunal for the Former Yugoslavia (established in 1993), the International Criminal Tribunal for Rwanda (established in 1994), and the hybrid Special Court for Sierra Leone (established in 2000) have prosecuted and convicted scores of individuals responsible for some of the worst abuses of recent armed conflicts. A watershed 1998 agreement between states created the International Criminal Court as a permanent venue to prosecute individuals responsible for war crimes, crimes against humanity, and acts of genocide.

Prior to the 1990s, few believed that world leaders could be held personally criminally responsible for gross human rights abuses. With high-profile indictments of former heads of state, including Augusto Pinochet of Chile and Hissène Habré of Chad, the prosecution of former Peruvian president Alberto Fujimori , and ICC-issued arrest warrants for Sudanese president Omar al-Bashir, Libyan leader Mu'ammar Gaddafi, and the former president of Cote d'Ivoire, Laurent Gbagbo, even the most powerful began to realize that their positions could not shield them from possible prosecution should they trample the rights of their people.

In 2003, when the Special Court for Sierra Leone indicted Charles Taylor, then the president of Liberia, for alleged war crimes in Sierra Leone, Taylor sought refuge in Nigeria. Chapter 6 outlines how more than three hundred African and international NGOs formed a "Coalition Against Impunity" to keep Taylor's case on the international agenda and use multiple pressure points to ultimately gain his transfer to the Special Court for Sierra Leone to stand trial.

The movement for accountability has been profoundly influenced by family members who have organized to demand the truth about the fate of loved ones who have been disappeared, tortured, or massacred. Prominent examples include women in Latin America such as Las Madres de Plaza de Mayo in Argentine, Comadres in El Salvador, and the National Coordination of Guatemalan Widows (CONAVIGUA) in Guatemala. More recently but less well-known, a group of families in Libya undertook unprecedented activism to seek the truth regarding a 1996 massacre of more than twelve hundred prisoners. Chapter 7 outlines how years before the Arab Spring, they defied a virtual prohibition on human rights activity to hold demonstrations, file lawsuits in domestic courts, make complaints to UN bodies, and publicize their demands in their quest to learn the fate of their loved ones and hold those responsible to account. Their efforts led Libya's top leadership to acknowledge the massacres, notify families that their loved ones were deceased, offer financial compensation, engage in dialogue with representatives of the families, pledge investigations, and tolerate independent public demonstrations for the first time in forty years. The families' activism also helped spark the 2011 uprising that eventually brought down the Gaddafi regime.

Chapter 8 highlights the efforts of three international NGOs—Amnesty International, Human Rights Watch, and International Crisis Group—to halt massive civilian casualties during the final months of the civil war in Sri

Lanka between government forces and the rebel Liberation Tigers of Tamil Eelam (Tamil Tigers) and their subsequent efforts to establish an international investigation of alleged war crimes by both sides. The chapter details ongoing efforts that have yet to bear fruit and the significant obstacles they face, including the Sri Lankan government's single-minded determination to destroy a so-called terrorist organization at any cost and the tacit support from other governments for its victory.

Part IV explores the impact of new media and new alliances in human rights advocacy work. Emerging technologies are transforming the human rights movement, as a new generation of activists increasingly uses Twitter, Facebook, Internet blogging, and other new media to raise awareness of human rights issues and mobilize new constituencies to action. Chapter 9 describes the innovative use of new technologies by Students for a Free Tibet in its campaign to spotlight China's human rights violations in Tibet during the 2008 Beijing Olympics. The group staged high-profile direct actions during the lead-up to the Olympic Games and during the games themselves and used new media to reach a global audience with its message, ensuring that Tibet was an ongoing theme of Olympic media coverage and putting the lie to China's claims of progress on human rights.

On many human rights issues, communities most directly affected by abuses are the driving force in shaping and leading advocacy efforts on their own behalf, often overcoming threats, isolation, and marginalization to do so. Chapter 10 compares efforts by lesbian, gay, bisexual, and transgender activists in Nepal and Jamaica to confront homophobia and antigay violence. In Nepal, court challenges and engagement with a dynamic political process brought extraordinary advances, including a Supreme Court decision decriminalizing homosexual conduct and affirming equal rights for all LGBT citizens. Nepal even began to promote itself as a gay-friendly tourist destination. In Jamaica, the country's leading LGBT organization was able to build a broad coalition of support and create public debate regarding the rights of LGBT persons. An international "Stop Murder Music" campaign was hugely successful in bringing global attention to violent, antigay lyrics in Jamaican dancehall music, forcing the cancellation of hundreds of concerts, and prompting several leading performers to sign pledges promising to stop performing homophobic songs. Sustained engagement with the Jamaican police virtually ended police participation in violent attacks against members of the LGBT community.

The strongest human rights advocacy efforts are based on broad and diverse partnerships—sometimes between unlikely allies—united around a single goal. Chapter 11 details a dynamic grassroots campaign in California to challenge the sentencing of juvenile offenders to life in prison with no possibility of parole. The campaign brought together a diverse coalition including members of the religious community, youth, law professors, family members of the incarcerated, family members of murder victims, and former law enforcement officials. In its effort to change state law, the campaign managed to gain the support of the 30,000–member state's prison guards' union, a powerful political force known for its "tough on crime" stance. The campaign generated hundreds of visits to state legislators and thousands of phone calls and letters in an effort that came only one vote short of passing new legislation that would provide juvenile offenders sentenced to life without parole an opportunity for review and possible release.

In addition to the eleven case studies explored here, this book also provides a series of profiles, one accompanying each chapter, to lend insight into the lives of some of the individuals at the center of these campaigns. Some of the profiles are about activists, and others are about individuals who have suffered the human rights abuses described. Some are both. These personal stories show how human rights abuses profoundly affect people's lives, what motivates people to become activists, and why they persist in their struggle, despite tremendous obstacles.

Many of the individuals profiled never intended to become activists. They began other careers—for example, one as a computer scientist, one as a journalist, another as a gemologist—but once exposed to human rights abuses, they became passionate advocates for justice. Some became advocates as a result of intensely personal experience—such as the Libyan seeking justice for the brother who was massacred at Abu Salim prison, or the young woman who survived years of exploitative child labor to become a national leader for domestic workers. Their stories depict the diversity among human rights advocates, and their reflections illuminate both the frustrations and the rewards of human rights work.

Before turning to the case studies and profiles, it is important to note that most of the tactics and strategies of the modern-day human rights movement are not new. Today's human rights advocates stand on the shoulders of the slavery abolitionists of the eighteenth and nineteenth centuries, the civil rights movement of the mid-twentieth century, and other social movements that have transformed society in profound and unalterable ways. Exploring this rich history is beyond the scope of this book. Interested readers can find resources on the history of the human rights movement and social activism in the Further Readings section at the end of this volume.

While virtually all the tools human rights advocates use—from press releases to lobbying meetings with government officials to public demonstrations—have been used before in many other contexts, there are new lessons to be learned from how these tools have been applied to human rights issues; the way advocates have been able to navigate the United Nations to advance the human rights agenda; the development of innovations and the adaptation of traditional advocacy strategies to a rapidly changing world environment; and the explosive growth of civil society and its potential for powerful new alliances and partnerships on behalf of human rights.

This book gives preference to cases where advocates have been able to win victories and advance the cause of human rights, even in modest ways, in order to illuminate campaigns that have been effective and can offer lessons for others. The reality of human rights work, however, is that despite their best efforts, advocates may work on an issue for years without discernible progress. Often external factors, such as powerful governmental interests, are simply insurmountable. This book also attempts to explore the considerable challenges that human rights advocates encounter in their work. Each chapter examines the elements that contributed to a campaign's success, as well as barriers to progress. Not every case study presented here ends in triumph. Some have failed to achieve their goals, at least in the short-term. Regardless of outcome, each story provides valuable lessons, and in many instances, tremendous inspiration. These accounts provide a window into the way that human rights advocates conduct their work, their real-life struggles and challenges, the rich diversity of tools and strategies they employ, and ultimately their courage and persistence in advancing human rights.

PART I

Campaigns for New Human Rights Standards

Chapter 1

Campaigning to Stop the Use
of Child Soldiers

The mayi-mayi took twelve girls and ten boys from my village. I was fourteen. Some
were younger, between ten and thirteen. Everyone went to the front, even the little
ones. . . . It was terrible—you would be whipped if you did something wrong. Once, I'd
been ordered to carry some bananas but they were too heavy so I left some behind.
As a punishment, I was tied by my arms and feet and given twenty lashes with a rope.

—Joseph, recruited by government-allied militia
in the Democratic Republic of Congo[1]

FIGHTING FORCES HAVE USED CHILDREN as soldiers for millennia, but the
phenomenon escalated with the end of the Cold War and the prolif-
eration of armed conflicts in the 1990s. By the end of the decade, an
estimated three hundred thousand children under age eighteen were participating in more than thirty armed conflicts raging around the globe.[2]
Their ranks included children as young as eight recruited into paramilitaries in Colombia, teenage boys picked up off the street in Burma and forced
into the national army, and girls kidnapped from their homes by the Lord's
Resistance Army in Central Africa for use as soldiers and sex slaves.

Some child soldiers are forcibly recruited and compelled to follow orders
under threat of death. Others, their lives devastated by poverty or war, join
armed groups out of desperation. As society breaks down during conflict,
children are often left with no access to school, driven from their homes,
or separated from their families. Many perceive armed groups as their best
chance for survival. Others join to avenge abuses against their family, or are
lured by promises of a good salary or education. Most child soldiers are adolescents, but some are as young as eight years old. Many are female. In conflicts in the Democratic Republic of Congo, Nepal, Uganda, Sri Lanka, and
elsewhere, more than 30 percent of child soldiers were girls. Girl soldiers are

often trained and deployed into combat, but also subject to sexual exploitation or forced to become the sex slaves of commanders.

Child soldiers may start out as porters, cooks, or messengers, but too often, they end up on the front line of combat. Considered "dispensable," child soldiers are sometimes pushed into the most hazardous roles—going into minefields ahead of older troops, or being used for suicide missions. Those who survive and are released or escape often face huge hurdles

Profile: Khin Maung Than

Khin Maung Than was on his way home from visiting some relatives in Rangoon one day when he was stopped by police at a checkpoint.[1] The police asked him for his identity card, but at age eleven, Khin Maung Than was too young to have one. When he couldn't produce an ID card, the police told him, "You'll have to go to jail for six years." They took him to the police station where they gave him another choice: "You can go to jail, or you can join the army." Khin Maung Than said, "They could see that I was only eleven, but if the police give a boy to the army, they can get pocket money from the army and thirty kilos of rice. They gave me from 8 a.m. until the afternoon to decide. I didn't want to go to jail for six years, so I agreed to join the army."

In Myanmar, also known as Burma, a military junta has controlled the country since 1962. The government maintains one of the largest armies in Southeast Asia, primarily to control the civilian population, to supervise forced labor on roads, dams, and other large infrastructure projects, and to fight against ethnic opposition forces. Children are routinely recruited to meet the army's quotas for new recruits.

After Khin Maung Than agreed to join the army, he was sent to a training camp, where he was often beaten. He said, "Once I couldn't run as fast as the others because I was small, so I arrived late and was beaten. One time I was beaten for quarrelling with my friend. Sometimes they beat us in the face not so hard, but sometimes they used a stick and it was very painful." He sometimes cried at night. A sympathetic captain told him that after his training was over and he was sent to a battalion, someone would send him home to his family. Khin Maung Than said, "I believed him." In fact, he never saw his family again.

Khin Maung Than experienced his first combat when he was only twelve. On patrol, his section encountered a group of opposition forces. His section leader ordered them to take cover and open fire. "I was too afraid to look," he reintegrating into civilian society. Many have little or no education, no marketable job skills, and emotional and psychological problems stemming from their experiences. Some have been forced to commit atrocities against their family or neighbors, creating significant social stigma and sometimes outright rejection from their home communities.

As recently as the year 2000, international law allowed fighting forces to recruit children as young as fifteen years old and send them into warfare.

said. "So I put my face in the ground and shot my gun up at the sky. I was afraid their bullets would hit my head. I fired two magazines, about forty rounds. I was afraid that if I didn't fire the section leader would punish me." Over the next year, he experienced combat about twenty times.

His most difficult experience was the day his unit captured a group of fifteen unarmed women and children in opposition territory. The unit captain reported back to headquarters that they had captured the women and children and asked what to do. The order that came back over the radio was to kill them all. "They took some of the women's clothing and used it to blindfold them. Then they took them away in a line to a little gully some distance away and made them stand in a line along the slope. Then six of the corporals loaded their guns and shot them. They fired on auto. I saw it. I felt very bad because there were all these people in front of me, and they killed them all. Their bodies were left there. After the mothers were killed, they killed the babies. Three of the privates killed them."

When he was fourteen, Khin Maung Than decided he could no longer tolerate life in the army. Although he knew that punishment for desertion could be a long prison sentence or even death, he fled and was able to escape across the border into Thailand. Although he no longer had to endure the brutal life of the army, his life was precarious. Without documentation, he was forced to work illegally, risking deportation if he was picked up by authorities. Throughout his ordeal, he had no opportunity to contact his family. Even after his escape, he said, "I fear my mother and sister are crying, because they don't know where I am or what is happening to me." But he didn't dare go home. If he were returned to Burma, he believed the likely punishment would be at least ten years in jail.

1. Author interview, March 2002, Thailand. Name has been changed.

This standard was an anomaly within accepted children's rights standards. In the 1980s, governments negotiated the Convention on the Rights of the Child (CRC), a comprehensive children's treaty that protected children under the age of eighteen from exploitative labor, torture, and other abuse.[3] The treaty had become the most widely ratified human rights treaty in history. However, its universal protections included a glaring exception. Instead of setting eighteen as the minimum age for military recruitment or participation in armed conflict, it adopted a lower age of fifteen, based on the 1977 additional protocols to the Geneva Conventions.[4]

In the mid-1990s, governments agreed to try to redress the discrepancy and raise the minimum age for recruitment and participation in hostilities. Instead of amending the original Convention (which would require agreement by two-thirds of ratifying states), however, governments believed it would be more realistic to negotiate an optional protocol. Such a protocol would have the status of a treaty, but it would not be legally binding on a country unless the government specifically chose to ratify it. In 1994, the United Nation's Commission on Human Rights established a working group, open to any UN member state, to negotiate such an optional protocol.

Governments began a series of annual negotiations in Geneva, but by 1998, negotiations floundered as it became clear that governments that had long used under-eighteens in their national armed forces, notably the United States and United Kingdom, were not willing to support a new standard that conflicted with their national practice. According to Martin MacPherson, a legal advisor for Amnesty International, "We were up against a major opponent, namely the US and the Pentagon, that showed very little flexibility on the issue and took a very hard line."[5] US laws dating from 1917 allowed seventeen year olds to volunteer for the US armed forces with parental permission.[6] Even though their proportion of the total active-duty US armed forces was very small, the armed forces typically deployed these young recruits as soon as their basic and technical training was complete, including for combat. In the early 1990s, seventeen-year-old US soldiers fought in Somalia, Bosnia, and the 1991 Gulf War.[7] The UK had an even bigger problem: it allowed sixteen year olds to join the armed forces and serve in combat roles, and a much larger proportion of its soldiers were under eighteen.

The United States argued that the most significant problem was the recruitment of children under fifteen in violation of existing international standards and that adopting an age of seventeen for recruitment and participation in armed conflict had "a greater potential to secure consensus among the members of the General Assembly." In demarches to other capitals, the United States said it could not accept eighteen as the minimum age for either voluntary recruitment or participation in armed conflict. Advocates of an eighteen-year age standard responded that in countries where children commonly lacked age documentation, a legal age of fifteen allowed commanders to recruit even younger children of twelve or thirteen without undue scrutiny, and that military expediency did not justify adopting lesser protections for children facing the dangers of warfare than for children at risk of other forms of exploitation.

Although the United States was the most vocal opponent of the new treaty, a handful of other states initially supported its position. Of the fifty governments that participated in the 1998 negotiations, seven—Bangladesh, Cuba, Israel, Korea, Kuwait, Pakistan, and the UK—joined the United States in supporting a minimum age of seventeen for participation in armed conflict. Some of these states, however, attempted to distance themselves from the hard-line position taken by the United States. Four of these states, including the UK, stated that they would not block an agreement that set an age of eighteen. Forty-one explicitly supported eighteen as a minimum age for participation in armed conflict. In the face of US intransigence, however, governments reached an impasse. Unable to reach agreement, they adjourned the session three days early.

Following the failed 1998 session, nongovernmental organizations (NGOs) that were following the negotiations decided that a global campaign was necessary to mobilize the political will needed to overcome the objections of the United States and its allies to conclude a strong treaty. "We had done as much as we could as individual NGOs," said Rachel Brett, a human rights lawyer working for the Quaker United Nations Office in Geneva.[8]

The Campaign

In May 1998, representatives of six nongovernmental organizations met in Geneva to form the Coalition to Stop the Use of Child Soldiers. At its first meeting, the fledgling coalition agreed on a specific goal: the adoption and implementation of an international standard setting eighteen as the minimum age for any recruitment (whether forced or voluntary) or participation in armed conflict. This became known as the "straight-18" standard.

The organizations forming the new coalition included both human rights and humanitarian groups—Amnesty International, Human Rights Watch, International Federation Terre des Hommes, Jesuit Refugee Service, the Quaker United Nations Office (Geneva), and Save the Children. Even prior to the first meeting, the Quakers secured $50,000 in seed money from the Canadian government to hire the coalition's first coordinator, Stuart Maslen, a veteran organizer who had worked with the International Campaign to Ban Landmines.

The coalition knew it had limited time to influence government positions before negotiations resumed. It embarked on an ambitious campaign to influence the course of the negotiations on the optional protocol, including publishing new research, organizing a series of high-profile regional conferences, supporting advocacy by national coalitions, and cultivating alliances with sympathetic governments. Maslen secured additional funds from sympathetic governments to hire a small staff, while the organizations that formed the coalition's new steering committee committed both funds and substantial staff time to push the coalition's agenda forward. The steering committee met several times a year to shape the coalition's strategy, inviting participation by UNICEF, the International Committee of the Red Cross, and the International Labor Organization.

At the campaign's genesis, knowledge of the child soldiers issue among the public and even policymakers was low. The coalition produced a basic briefing booklet geared to diplomats, NGO activists, and the public, stressing the scale of the child soldier problem, the short- and long-term negative impacts on the lives of children, and the inadequacy of existing international standards. Coalition volunteers soon translated the booklets into a dozen different languages. The Red Cross and UNICEF sent them to all of their field offices. The coalition also quickly established a website, produced posters, advocacy videos, and worked to place stories in the mainstream media.

Maslen's experience with the landmines campaign had convinced him that regional organizing needed to be a priority. "You want to coalesce the regional groups," he said. "When you have the Africans speaking with one voice, saying that 'this is a problem and we want you to do something,' it's very hard for the West to do nothing. The regional conferences were mind-numbingly difficult in terms of organization and funding, but were the right way to go."[9] The coalition organized a series of regional conferences for representatives of governments, civil society, and UN agencies to share information about the use of child soldiers in the region and strategies for preventing child recruitment and addressing the demobilization, rehabilitation, and reintegration needs of former child soldiers. A critical element of each conference was the negotiation of a public declaration that was adopted by participants at its conclusion, expressing the principle that children under age eighteen should not be recruited or used in warfare and addressing regional aspects of the issue. Although the declarations were not binding, they were used to bolster the commitment of governments to the "straight-18" principle and to generate momentum toward a strong optional protocol. Sympathetic governments agreed to host the conferences and issued invitations to ensure strong representation from other governments in their region.

Mozambique hosted the first conference in April 1999 for the African region. More than 250 individuals from thirty African countries attended, including officials from twenty-five African governments and observers from supportive governments outside the region.[10] On the opening day of the conference, the coalition released a new report, providing a country-by-country survey on the use of child soldiers in Africa. In addition to a press conference in Maputo, the report was released at coordinated press conferences in London, Geneva, Bonn, Paris, and New York, generating substantial media coverage. On the final day of the conference, participants adopted the Maputo Declaration, unequivocally condemning the use of child soldiers and calling for legal standards and measures at every level to prohibit any military service by children under the age of eighteen. During the conference, nearly a dozen African countries made public their commitment to ratify the African Charter on the Rights and Welfare of the Child, the only regional treaty that set eighteen as the minimum age for recruitment and participation of children in armed conflict. Janet Mukwaya, the Ugandan minister of gender, labor, and social development, spearheaded the pledge effort supported by the International Save the Children Alliance. In large part because of these additional commitments, the African Charter went into force just a few months later, on November 29, 1999.

At the conference, NGOs from the region selected three NGOs—the African Forum for Child Welfare, the African Network for the Prevention and Protection Against Child Abuse and Neglect (ANPPCAN), and Defense for Children International/African Region—to help coordinate follow-up to the conference in the region and to be represented in the coalition's steering committee.

Only three months later, the coalition held its second regional conference, hosted by Uruguay in Montevideo for the Latin American region. One hundred participants from twenty Latin American countries participated, including government representatives from Argentina, Bolivia, Brazil, Chile, Costa Rica, Ecuador, Guatemala, Mexico, Panama, Paraguay, Peru, and Uruguay. The research report released at the beginning of the conference highlighted the recruitment of children into both state forces and nonstate armed groups in Colombia, Peru, Paraguay, and Mexico, and the ongoing challenge of reintegrating former child soldiers in El Salvador, Guatemala, and Nicaragua. Like the Maputo conference, the Montevideo conference also resulted in a strong declaration condemning the use of child soldiers and any recruitment of children under the age of eighteen. NGOs attending the conference agreed to form a regional NGO network to follow up the conference and its recommendations, led by NGOs from Colombia, Uruguay, and Guatemala.

The most contentious of the conferences was the third, held in Berlin in October 1999 for the European region. While the vast majority of countries in Africa and Latin America supported the "straight-18" position, key European countries, based on their national law and practice, rejected the age of eighteen as the minimum age for participation in armed conflict. Joschka Fisher, Germany's minister of foreign affairs, opened the conference, and representatives from the previous regional conferences presented the Maputo and Montevideo declarations. One hundred and eighty participants attended from thirty-five countries. More than sixty journalists covered the conference.

Negotiations on the Berlin declaration for the conference were difficult, and delegates continued consultations late into the night before the final day of the conference. The conference ended with a declaration that called for the swift adoption of international law prohibiting all participation in armed conflict of children under eighteen years of age. However, a small number of states—notably Austria, France, Germany, Luxembourg, the Netherlands, and the United Kingdom—refused to support language calling for a prohibition on recruitment of under-eighteens. The UK also announced its intention to continue its policy of recruiting girls and boys from sixteen years of age and deploying them from age seventeen. In a statement delivered at the final session, the coalition noted its disappointment in the outcome and called upon governments in the region to "lead by good example, not by double standards."[11] The coalition also acknowledged notable progress in the region, particularly action by several European governments to end the military recruitment of children into their armed forces, including the Czech Republic, Denmark, Finland, Norway, Spain, and Portugal.[12]

Despite the controversial nature of the conference, organizers were encouraged. "For me, the European conference was one of the turning points," said Rachel Brett, a cofounder of the coalition and representative of the Quaker United Nations Office. "Until then, it wasn't clear that European governments saw sending under-18s into combat as unacceptable. At the conference, it became clear that they recognized that."[13] The Berlin conference was also important in solidifying the German government's support for a prohibition on the participation of under-eighteens in armed conflict. One of the organizers, Andreas Rister of Terre des Hommes Germany, reflected, "The conference was a point of prestige for the government. It got enormous media coverage. The issue was at a very high level in Germany at that time."[14] By the end of 1999, government representatives and NGOs from more than one hundred countries had participated in the first three regional conferences.

Few studies had been published on the use of child soldier prior to the 1990s, and none had systematically attempted a global survey of the issue. Maslen made the publication of new research a priority for the coalition: "The importance of research shouldn't be underestimated. Just presenting governments with information and facts is sometimes more powerful than we think. We sometimes overestimate governments' ability to do their own research."[15] Relying on documentation from its members, UN, media, and other sources, the coalition published a series of regional reports documenting the national legislation, policies, and practices relating to the recruitment and use of child soldiers in each country. Published to coincide with each of the coalition's regional conferences, the reports provided a basis for discussion at the conference and a means of gaining media attention. In its first regional report on Africa, the coalition also posited a global estimate—three hundred thousand—of the number of child soldiers actively participating in armed conflicts around the world. This figure was repeated hundreds of times by major media, governments, and UN sources as evidence of the severity of the problem.

The coalition's US-based members researched data produced by the US military to refute the contention that prohibiting the participation of under-eighteen's in armed conflict would hurt US military readiness. It accessed US armed forces reports showing that less than one-quarter of 1 percent of active duty US forces were age seventeen. According to Rachel Stohl, a member of the US national campaign, "We were able to counter their argument with the US military's own data to help support our case. That data was without question, so it made it easier for the US to look at their own policies."[16]

The coalition received a major boost in October 1998, when UN Secretary General Kofi Annan announced a new policy requiring that UN peacekeepers be at least eighteen years old, and preferably at least twenty-one. In announcing the policy, the secretary-general made explicit links to the child soldiers issue, saying, "This decision has been taken as an additional measure in the organization's efforts to promote the rights of the child . . . and to ensure that the organization's use of uniformed personnel is an example for police and military forces worldwide."[17] Human Rights Watch's advocacy director for the European Union, Lotte Leicht, had secured support for the position from the UN under-secretary general in charge of peacekeeping operations, Bernard Miyet, convincing him that such a policy would both guarantee more experienced soldiers for UN peacekeeping operations and also be a valuable contribution to the global effort to end the use of child soldiers.

In August 1998, Save the Children successfully won a public commitment from all five foreign ministers of the Nordic countries to achieve an optional protocol establishing eighteen as the minimum age for both recruitment and participation in armed conflict. Meanwhile, Human Rights Watch approached former US president Jimmy Carter and former Costa Rican president Oscar Arias for their support. The former presidents sent a joint letter to other former heads of state and government asking them to sign a public statement supporting the optional protocol. Former world leaders from sixteen countries signed onto the statement, including Nelson Mandela, Mikhail Gorbachev, Shimon Peres, and Helmut Schmidt. To coincide with the formal launch of the coalition, President Carter authored an op-ed on child soldiers for *USA Today*, the largest-circulation daily newspaper in the United States, drawing on his experiences with the armed conflict in Liberia, when thousands of children had been recruited to fight as soldiers.[18]

As a result of the regional conferences, regional bodies such as the Organization of African Unity (OAU) and European Parliament took strong positions against the use of child soldiers. Following the Maputo conference, the government of Mozambique submitted the Maputo Declaration to the Organization of African Unity Council and Assembly of Heads of State and Government, meeting in July 1999. The body endorsed the declaration and called on its member states to adopt and promote norms prohibiting recruitment and use of children under eighteen years of age.[19] After the adoption of the Berlin Declaration, the European Parliament called on EU member states to support the adoption of an optional protocol to "outlaw" the recruitment and use of children under eighteen in armed conflicts."[20] The coalition also approached other influential figures and bodies to lend their support through statements, including the World Council of Churches and World Veterans Association.[21] In September 1999, the UN secretary-general urged member states to support the proposal to raise the minimum age for recruitment and participation in hostilities to eighteen in a report to the UN Security Council on the protection of civilians and to accelerate the drafting of the optional protocol.[22]

In October 1999, the International Committee of the Red Cross issued a "People on War" report, based on consultations in seventeen countries worldwide regarding attitudes on the laws of war.[23] One of the survey questions was: "At what age are young people mature enough to be combatants?" Ninety-three percent of respondents worldwide responded with an age of at least eighteen. Thirty-five percent replied "21 or over."[24] The coalition used these results in its public education efforts to illustrate the popular support from all regions of the world for a higher age for participation in armed conflict.

The coalition believed that domestic pressure was needed in as many countries as possible in order to convince governments to engage in the negotiations for the optional protocol and to press for the strongest standards possible. Members of the coalition encouraged their national chapters and other NGO partners to mobilize and form national coalitions. Within just a couple of months of the coalition's founding, coalitions had been established or were being explored in Canada, Denmark, Finland, Germany, Mozambique, the Netherlands, Norway, the UK, and the United States. By 2000, national coalitions were active in more than thirty countries, conducting public awareness activities and working to secure support from their governments for a "straight-18" position. Some national coalitions emerged out of the regional conferences. For example, the Montevideo conference prompted the formation of a national coalition to stop the use of child soldiers in Colombia, the country in the region with the largest incidence of child soldier use. The Colombian coalition included a dozen local and national NGOs and undertook an ambitious program of advocacy, education, and monitoring designed to prevent recruitment of children by both guerilla forces and government-linked paramilitaries and to press the government to take more effective action on the issue.

In the United States, the US Campaign to Stop the Use of Child Soldiers brought together more than sixty religious, human rights, humanitarian, youth, and other organizations. Campaign members repeatedly met with State Department and the Pentagon to discuss the issue. After State Department representatives told campaign representatives that they had "not heard from Congress" on the issue, the campaign employed a variety of tactics to engage lawmakers. The campaign organized briefings on child soldiers with the Congressional Human Rights Caucus, arranged individual meetings for senators with child soldiers, and enlisted members of Congress to introduce resolutions, make floor speeches, and write joint letters to President Clinton.[25] To address Pentagon concerns about military readiness, the campaign organized a letter to President Clinton signed by thirty-seven retired US military officers stressing that excluding seventeen-year-old service members from combat operations would not harm US national security and urging the United States to end its opposition to the optional protocol.[26] During the lead-up to the final negotiations, the campaign partnered with Working Assets, a progressive telephone company, to generate thirty thousand calls to the White House urging the United States to support the optional protocol.

The coalition worked to build a cross-regional group of governments that supported the "straight-18" position to share information and develop common strategies. Beginning with the coalition's first meeting in May 1998, the steering committee met regularly with representatives from these states in Geneva to discuss the course of the negotiations on the protocol, positions being taken by various states, and how to achieve the best result. According to Martin MacPherson, a legal advisor for Amnesty International and one of the coalition's founders, "This 'friends' group was absolutely vital. We were able to exchange information, discuss what the issues were going to be, and what kind of flexibility there might be. It made sure all the sympathetic governments would speak with one voice."[27] By 1999, this core group included Canada, Denmark, Ethiopia, Finland, Japan, Mozambique, Norway, Portugal, South Africa, Sweden, and Switzerland.

In January 1999, governments held only one day of discussions, agreeing that there was little prospect for progress on the optional protocol. The coalition had encouraged its government allies to support a short session in order to buy more time to build support for its campaign. By the following year, some governments were pushing for a conclusion to the negotiations. Rachel Brett reflected, "We felt we had the momentum on our side, but others also recognized that and were prepared to stop the process. Less positive governments also felt the momentum and determined that they would finish the process and hold the line."[28]

In January 2000, fifty-two governments met in Geneva for what was widely expected to be the final round of negotiations on the optional protocol. The outcome was uncertain, as the United States was still opposed to setting eighteen as a minimum age for participation in armed conflict. The coalition considered this position as its "red line" and had agreed that any age lower than eighteen for participation in hostilities would be unacceptable.

The coalition geared up for a final push during the negotiations. It issued a press release and held a press conference on the opening day of negotiations, singling out the United States for criticism and noting the overwhelming support of other UN states for an eighteen-year age limit for participation in armed conflict. Members of Terre des Hommes held a vigil outside the main gates of the United Nations, and the coalition mounted a child soldiers photo exhibition inside the UN building itself. The coalition issued daily updates on the negotiations, sending these to all national coalitions and posting them on its website.

On the third day of negotiations, a large majority of government endorsed eighteen as the minimum age for participation in hostilities. Germany made a particularly strong intervention, stating that this was an issue where they could not compromise. "This is where the German coalition had done a really good job to build domestic pressure," said Brett.[29] The coalition issued another press release, noting the overwhelming support and again criticizing the United States for its opposition. Only four countries—the UK, Kuwait, Egypt, and Singapore—shared the US position, though only the United States seemed prepared to block consensus on the minimum age of participation in hostilities. The *New York Times* noted the isolation, saying that the United States "found itself with few allies" under a headline "US Fights Tide on a Move to Raise Military Service Age."[30] On the defensive, the head of the US delegation stated to the plenary, "We reject the assertion that support for 18 should be a litmus test for whether a country cares about the fate of its children."[31]

In a dramatic turnabout, the United States changed its position during the second week of negotiations and agreed to join a consensus on setting eighteen as the minimum age for direct participation in hostilities. Later, it became known that Secretary of State Madeleine Albright had appealed to the joint chiefs of staff for a top-level review of whether the armed forces could accept an eighteen-year-old limit. She was afraid that the protocol would be agreed without US support, creating a "third strike" following the US refusal to join both the 1997 Ottawa Mine Ban Treaty and the 1998 Rome Statute creating the International Criminal Court.

The US agreement paved the way for consensus on the final text of the protocol. It set eighteen as a minimum age for direct participation in hostilities and for any conscription or forced recruitment. It also set eighteen as the minimum age for any recruitment (whether forced or voluntary) by nonstate armed groups. However, it set a lower age for voluntary recruitment into government armed forces, requiring states simply to "raise the minimum age for the voluntary recruitment of persons into their national armed forces from that set out in article 38, paragraph 3, of the Convention on the Rights of the Child" (which stipulated fifteen). It required states to enter a binding declaration stating their minimum age for voluntary recruitment and to outline the safeguards that were in place to ensure proof of age, parental permission, and that the decision to enlist was informed and made voluntarily.

The United States asked for a final concession—allowing states that had signed but not ratified the Convention on the Rights of the Child itself to ratify the protocol. Such a provision would allow the United States to become party to the optional protocol, even though it was the only state other than Somalia that had failed to ratify the Convention. Some states balked, arguing that states should not be allowed to ratify an optional protocol without ratifying its parent treaty. But ultimately they agreed. The governments concluded their negotiations and protocol was adopted formally by the UN General Assembly on May 8, 2000.

In May 2000, the coalition organized an Asian regional conference in Kathmandu, Nepal, with 150 government and NGO representatives from twenty countries, including conflict-ridden areas such as Aceh in Indonesia, northeastern Indian states of Jammu and Kashmir, and northeastern Sri Lanka. The Kathmandu Declaration called on states to ratify the new protocol and implement it in their national laws. The coalition's final regional conference was held for the Middle East in April 2001 in Amman, Jordan. Like the others, the Asia and Middle Eastern conferences also identified regional NGOs to help coordinate follow-up and participate in the coalition's activities.

After the adoption of the protocol, the coalition began a global ratification campaign. In September 2000, when the General Assembly convened for its Millennium Assembly, the coalition organized a special event in New York attended by heads of state, foreign ministers, and other government representatives to indicate their support for the new standard. National coalitions began ratification campaigns, including letter-writing and other advocacy to urge their governments to swiftly ratify the protocol.

Between 1999 and 2010, at least twenty countries adopted or amended their national legislation to raise their minimum age of voluntary recruitment to at least age eighteen.[32] Some governments increased their recruitment age even in the middle of armed conflict. In early 2000, the government of Sierra Leone announced government policy raising the minimum age for bearing arms from seventeen to eighteen, formalizing it in law in 2007. The government of Colombia, engaged in a thirty-year civil war, adopted new legislation in December 1999 prohibiting all recruitment of children under age eighteen and discharged more than six hundred children from the army and more than two hundred from other government forces. In early 2003, the National Security Council of Afghanistan established a new minimum recruitment age of twenty-two.

The protocol also influenced changes in military deployment practices, even from some of its initial opponents. Both the United States and the UK ratified the protocol, taking steps to end the deployment of underage soldiers to combat arenas. After the United States ratified the optional protocol in December 2002, each branch of the armed services issued new policies excluding seventeen-year-old members of the armed forces from combat duties. This was the first time the United States changed its own practices in order to support a new emerging international standard; in the past, the

United States had only signed onto treaties that were already consistent with its own policies, or entered reservations in order to carve out exceptions for any practices that were not in compliance with the treaty. In 2008, the US Congress adopted legislation requiring other governments to adhere to the standards of the protocol to be eligible to receive US military training and assistance.

By the end of 2000, 75 states had signed the protocol. By mid-2012, 147 governments had ratified the optional protocol. Of those, 96—a full two-thirds—had made a voluntary declaration setting at least eighteen as their minimum age for voluntary recruitment, essentially endorsing the "straight-18" standard.

Lessons Learned

The protocol was not an unqualified success. The coalition was unable to reach its aim of a "straight-18" standard, and ultimately accepted a compromise that allowed the voluntary recruitment of children under age eighteen by government forces. According to Maslen, the coalition's first coordinator, "The fact that there are states still out there that recruit at less than 18 is a matter of regret. It's problematic. For child soldiers, you have to create a very clear line. Under no circumstances should children be in the armed forces."[33] In addition, the protocol created a double-standard for government forces and nonstate actors, prohibiting all voluntary recruitment of children under age eighteen for nonstate armed groups, but not for government forces. Some participants in the process believed that holding nonstate actors to a higher standard than states was both legally and morally problematic.

Nonetheless, the campaign achieved far-reaching and significant outcomes. It established a new global standard in international law, prohibiting the participation of children in hostilities during a time when child soldiers were engaged directly in dozens of conflicts worldwide and bringing the age for conscription, forced recruitment, and participation in armed conflict in line with other accepted child protection standards. It raised the profile of an issue that had previously received little attention and helped muster greater international efforts to end the use of child soldiers. It prompted changes in practice by both government and nongovernmental forces and legislative reforms by nearly two dozen governments. "The significance is huge," says Brett. "What it establishes in essence is that the armed forces of your country are not exempt from the rules of protection of children. That was a huge step from when we started."[34]

The coalition faced a number of hurdles in achieving the new legal standards set by the optional protocol. One obstacle was that governments opposing a "straight-18" protocol held disproportionate weight during the negotiations. The coalition estimated that more than one hundred governments had national laws and policies that would enable them to support the "straight-18" position. But because they already had high standards, many of these states believed they had little at stake and, as a consequence, did not participate in the negotiations, particularly if they had understaffed missions in Geneva. In contrast, opponents of the protocol had a clear vested interest in influencing the negotiations in order to preserve their perceived national interests and were very active.

While relatively few UN member states allowed children under eighteen by law to participate in armed conflict, a much larger number of states allowed for voluntary recruitment at a younger age, typically at age seventeen. Those that accepted under-eighteen volunteers included not only the United States and the UK, but also other powerful European states. Ultimately, the coalition was not able to muster consensus for an age of eighteen for voluntary recruitment and was forced to drop one of its demands to achieve a final agreement.

The number of "straight-18" government allies that worked actively with the coalition was quite small. Brett reflected:

> It was a great group that worked really hard. The problem was that they were all relatively small, sometimes very small, without a significant amount of weight. They didn't have much weight compared with what we were up against. What we were up against was not only the US, but in practice there wasn't EU support for the straight-18 position. While the EU is traditionally seen as a standard setting group, in this case, they certainly weren't there. And there was little support from Asia, because they didn't see it as an issue.[35]

Maslen agreed that the campaign would have benefited from the participation of stronger, more influential states. "You need heavy hitters who are willing to be out front to scream and shout, who are willing to have their foreign minister out there to speak out."[36]

The pace of negotiations meant that the coalition only had a couple of years to build sufficient support and momentum to achieve its desired result.

An unanswered question is whether the coalition could have convinced governments to extend the negotiating period in order to have more time to reach its goals. Reflecting on the campaign's timetable, Maslen believed it could have been desirable and possible to go on for another year.[37] MacPherson, however, was skeptical that the coalition could have slowed down the negotiation timetable.[38]

The coalition set an extremely ambitious agenda, which included three major regional conferences and research reports in barely more than six months. Maslen, the first coordinator, said, "One of the problems was we crammed so many regional meetings into such a short period of time." He recalled traveling to Montevideo to plan the Latin American conference: "Our contact in the Foreign Ministry asked me how many people we had in our secretariat, and when I answered, he said, 'You seriously think you can organize a conference?' Our staff were pulling all-nighters to put the research together. We shouldn't expect that. One lesson could have been to space the conferences out a bit more."[39] The small staff worked itself to exhaustion, and Maslen resigned after less than a year and a half. The Asian regional conference, originally scheduled for 1999, was postponed until 2000, after the protocol's adoption.

Several key elements helped facilitate the campaign's success. First, the coalition had a clear and compelling message. The use of children as combatants aroused strong public sympathy, and opponents found it difficult to counter the argument that children in armed conflict should receive the same protections that international law provided other vulnerable children. The coalition's "straight-18" position was readily adopted by all of its members and was easy to communicate: no recruitment and no participation in armed conflict before the age of eighteen. MacPherson said, "No one could misunderstand the straight-18 position. It was very easy to campaign on. Especially since 18 was often the age of majority, the minimum age to join the police, for drinking alcohol, etc, it was difficult to argue that it was justifiable to send under 18s into combat."[40] Stohl agreed:

> As compared to many issues, at a superficial level it's a pretty easy one. No one is going to campaign against you and say, "No, I want child soldiers." That's different than a lot of policy issues where there are clear pros and cons. It makes the issue more salient for policymakers. . . . Also, this is a human rights treaty, but it also affects national defense and national security

policy. In this particular case, it's very clear and easy to explain why stopping the use of child soldiers helps a government's national security and doesn't hurt it.[41]

A second key element was the role of national coalitions in solidifying governmental positions on the optional protocol. Particularly in Europe, the domestic pressure built by national coalitions in a number of countries influenced those governments to adopt strong positions and make clear that on key points—particularly the minimum age for participation in hostilities—they would not compromise. This was especially important when these states engaged with the United States and the UK. Their message was, "because of domestic pressure, we can't back down." According to Brett, the shift in US position was important, but "even if the US hadn't moved, I believe we would have gotten 18 for participation anyway, because within the EU, there was a strong enough stance. Other EU countries would not have agreed to a lower age. The US was really pretty isolated."[42]

A third factor behind the coalition's success was the multipronged nature of its strategy. It used multiple fora—including its regional conferences, press events, the Organization of African Unity, European Parliament, International Labor Organization, and other bodies—to repeatedly raise its message and gain support for its goals. By securing support from a wide range of influential individuals—from the UN secretary-general, former military officers, former world leaders, and sitting foreign ministers—the coalition was able to build influence and credibility. Taken together, its activities created a strong sense of momentum toward a strong optional protocol.

Multipronged efforts were also important at the national level. According to Rachel Stohl, a steering committee member for the US campaign: "One of the reasons the US campaign worked is that we didn't put all our eggs into one basket. There was a media angle, a Congressional angle, a national campaign angle in terms of people calling into the White House and their congressional offices, face-to-face meetings with high-level officials. It wasn't a one-pronged strategy. We had a lot of activities all focused on one goal."[43]

A fourth factor, external to the coalition's activities, was timing. The negotiations on the optional protocol were happening in the wake of negotiations for the Rome Statute for the International Criminal Court (1998) and the Landmine Ban Treaty (1997). The United States had not supported either process and had taken a lot of political heat for its outlier status. The Clinton administration did not want to be seen as a spoiler for yet a third time in just a few years, particularly on an issue such as child soldiers. According to Stohl, "The US needed a victory. They needed to show that they were willing to work within [these processes]. It was the waning days of the Clinton administration, so politically they had less to lose. It was a nice confluence of events."[44] In addition to outside pressure from the US Campaign, sympathetic officials were working inside the State Department, the Pentagon, and the National Security Council to push for a policy review to allow the United States to support a strong optional protocol. The result was that just prior to the final round of negotiations, the joint chiefs of staff agreed that the Defense Department could live with the proposed new standards.

As another example, Germany was one of the governments that took a strong stance on eighteen for participation, indicating during the final negotiations that it would not change its position. According to Andreas Rister of Terre Des Hommes Germany, that position was a combination of public pressure and timing. The final negotiations were taking place during the 'Red-Green' German government,[45] when Joschka Fisher of the Greens was foreign minister. "So in that sense, it was the right moment. The German government was very interested and knew that the German public was very interested, so we had a bit of luck about it. The child soldier issue was something where if you were on the wrong side, you could be unpopular, so it was easy for them to be on the right side in that historical moment."[46]

Finally, the coalition benefited from its diverse membership, which paired strong research and advocacy organizations like Amnesty International and Human Rights Watch with humanitarian organizations that operated rehabilitation and reintegration programs for former child soldiers in conflict-affected countries, such as Save the Children, International Federation Terre des Homme, Jesuit Refugee Services, and World Vision. As a result, the coalition could utilize established advocacy channels and respected research and also provide persuasive evidence from programs on the ground regarding the undeniable harm caused children by serving as soldiers. According to MacPherson, "The campaign's biggest strength was that it brought together such a large number of NGOs, including human rights, humanitarian, and child rights groups. It was a very credible coalition because the partners were recognized for their expertise. It was also one of the first big campaigns that managed to bring in the international organizations—UN agencies and the International Committee of the Red Cross."[47] Brett agreed that a strong combination of diverse groups was one of the factors most critical to the campaign's success. "It was a combination of the different groups and that we worked very well together and with a lot of confidence in each other."[48]

Reflecting on the significance of the campaign's achievements a decade after the protocol's adoption, Brett said, "It has been huge. It is now the norm. We shifted the debate, our little band of sisters and brothers. What a small group of NGOs and a small band of governments achieved, it is quite remarkable."[49]

Chapter 2

Organizing for Decent Work for Domestic Workers

The ILO Convention

I started to work at twelve years old. Since then, I never saw my family. Homesickness is my greatest enemy. My mother only saw me when my employer finally told her where I was working in Manila. They did not allow anybody to see me because they always beat me. I always wanted to tell my parents how difficult my life was, but there was no chance . . .

—*Diwata, Philippines*[1]

You don't achieve progress from one day to the next, but over a long period of many years, with a lot of commitment from colleagues. . . . Before we were vulnerable and invisible; but with the new law now people are aware of us.

—*Migueline Colque, domestic worker activist from Bolivia*[2]

AN ESTIMATED FIFTY TO ONE HUNDRED MILLION PEOPLE,[3] a vast majority of them women and girls, are employed in private homes as domestic workers.[4] They carry out many of the most essential tasks for the household, including cooking, cleaning, doing laundry, shopping, and caring for children and elderly members of the employer's family. In some countries, domestic work accounts for nearly 10 percent of total employment, providing an important income source for women and their families. For example, the International Labor Organization (ILO) estimated in 2004 that Indonesia alone had an estimated 2.6 million domestic workers,[5] while Saudi Arabian households employed an estimated 1.5 million domestic workers.[6] A large flow of women who migrate between countries for domestic work, including from Asia to the Middle East, also generates billions of dollars in remittances for their countries of origin.

Despite the importance of domestic work to individual households and to national economies, domestic workers are subject to a shocking array of labor and criminal abuses, and their work is often unprotected and unregulated. Cultural norms that devalue "women's work" mean that domestic workers are often regarded as "helpers" rather than employees who are entitled to basic labor rights. Governments, in turn, consider domestic work part of the informal sector and often exempt domestic workers from the national labor laws that apply to other workers, leaving them without legal rights to a minimum wage, overtime pay, rest days, annual leave, workers' compensation, or social security. Exclusion from key labor protections places many domestic workers at the mercy of their employer regarding the terms of their employment.

Many domestic workers are grossly underpaid and forced to work unrelenting hours, seven days a week for months or even years on end. They may be expected to be "on call" around the clock, for example, to feed or care for infants during the night. ILO studies found that in Kuwait, domestic workers worked an average of seventy-eight to one hundred hours per week, while in Nepal, a survey of 378 child domestic workers found that 374 reported working more than twelve hours a day.[7] They are often paid a small fraction of what their counterparts earn in the formal sector. In Indonesia, for example, one study found that child domestic workers typically made 1/10th of the normal minimum wage.[8] Some employers withhold wages as a strategy to prevent the worker from leaving or finding other work, or make illegal or arbitrary deductions from their salaries. Migrant workers in particular are often forced to forego months of wages to pay unregulated recruitment fees. In Kuwait City, embassies of labor-sending countries received more than ten thousand complaints from domestic workers in 2009 for nonpayment of wages, excessive working hours, and physical, sexual, and psychological abuse.[9]

A large number of domestic workers live in their employer's home, where isolation and power imbalances between the worker and employer place them at heightened risk of physical, sexual, and psychological abuse. Domestic workers have reported physical violence by their employers ranging from slaps to severe beatings using implements such as shoes, belts, sticks, electrical cords, and household tools. Sexual abuse is also a risk: in Guatemala, one study found that one-third of domestic workers interviewed had been subject to unwanted sexual approaches or demands from men associated with the household.[10] An ILO study in El Salvador found that for child domestic workers, sexual abuse was the second most common reason cited for leaving a position.[11] In the worst instances, domestic workers are subjected to forced labor and trafficking. Some domestic workers are locked in their employer's house and ordered not to leave, or threatened with substantial fines if they fail to complete their contract. In many countries, employers commonly confiscate the passports or work permits of migrant domestic workers, leaving the worker vulnerable to arrest and deportation if they try to escape.

Trade unions in Brazil and Chile began organizing domestic workers as early as the 1920s; in most countries, however, domestic workers typically were unorganized and not represented by traditional trade unions throughout the twentieth century. Existing unions prioritized the formal sector, where workers were easier to organize and higher wages yielded higher union dues. Organizing domestic workers was also very difficult, due to domestic workers' isolation and lack of time off. By the 1990s, however, domestic workers were forming their own associations, unions, and networks in countries such as South Africa, the Philippines, Indonesia, and Namibia as well as across Latin America. They advocated for their rights, challenged social stigma, and pressed for labor protections through national legislation, and eventually, they demanded an international convention to protect their rights globally.

Emerging domestic worker associations and unions provided their members with support, skills training, and avenues to organize and speak out about their grievances. They pushed for better working conditions and, in some cases, succeeded in winning national legislation to protect their rights. For example, in both Bolivia and Peru, laws were passed in 2003 to strengthen labor rights for domestic workers. In Kenya, the 2007 Employment Act included domestic workers, ensuring them a minimum wage, eight-hour working day, and twenty-eight days of annual leave. In 1994 in South Africa, the Labor Relations Act was expanded to cover domestic workers, and a minimum-wage law was introduced for domestic workers in 2000.

This chapter first explores strategies employed in the Philippines and Tanzania to advocate at the national level for the rights of domestic workers. It then turns to the successful global effort by domestic worker organizations, trade unions, NGOs, and allied governments to achieve the first international labor treaty specifically protecting the rights of domestic workers worldwide.

Philippines

By various estimates, between 600,000 and 2.5 million Filipino women and girls are employed as domestic workers within the Philippines.[12] In addition, tens of thousands of women leave the Philippines each year for employment abroad as domestic workers. In 2009, Filipino migrant workers, mostly women, sent home US$19.8 billion in remittances, 16 percent of the country's gross domestic product.[13] The government estimates that Filipina domestic workers are employed in at least fifty countries worldwide.[14]

Domestic workers in the Philippines were often referred to with derogatory terms, such as "muchacha" (girl), "katulong" (help), or "inday" ("provincial," implying the worker is illiterate). Advocates decided that they would challenge the stigma domestic workers faced by challenging such terms. "People find it very annoying, accusing, and judgmental when we just focus on abuses [against domestic workers]. So we focused our advocacy on challenging the names that domestic workers are called," said Cecilia Flores-Oebanda, founder and president of the Visayan Forum, one of the leading organizations working on behalf of domestic workers in the Philippines.[15] Advocates promoted the term *kasambahay* (companion in the home) as an alternative term that connoted respect. "The name triggers a debate about the role of the domestic worker in the life of the employer, in the home," said Flores-Oebanda.[16]

Visayan Forum organized demonstrations and rallies of domestic workers to heighten their visibility and raise awareness of abuses. The group felt that initially mass mobilization was effective. It gave domestic workers a voice and demonstrated that a so-called unorganizable group could, in fact, be organized. Over time, however, advocates decided they needed to change their strategy. Flores-Oebanda reflected, "We sometimes found that it was counter-productive. Employers stopped allowing domestic workers out of the house to participate in rallies. Employers were viewing Visayan Forum as enemies; we didn't get support and the government didn't want to engage with us. So instead of being productive, our strategy was unproductive."

The organization began to focus instead on engagement with key stakeholders, including churches, schools, and employers of domestic workers. The group began to reach out to churches, particularly parish women's groups, to establish Sunday programs to facilitate dialogue among employers of domestic workers and to create a forum for sharing of experiences by domestic workers themselves. By encouraging the parishes to run the programs, dialogue regarding domestic worker issues became more accepted within local communities. By 2010, programs were supported by about eighty churches nationwide, both Catholic and Protestant.

The organization also began approaching school administrators to set up activity centers for domestic workers and special curricula for child domestic

Profile: Lilibeth Masamloc

Lilibeth Masamloc was born in a poor tribal community in the southern part of the Philippines.[1] Raised with twelve brothers and sisters, she said that "money was always tight. We never had enough. My parents could barely scrape by to send us to school." She started working on a farm when she was eight years old, and when she was thirteen, a cousin convinced her to go to Davao City to work as a domestic worker. Lilibeth had finished elementary school and hoped that in the city she would be able to pursue secondary education.

During the next few years, she had four different employers. The first paid her only 800 pesos (roughly US$18) a month, but often withheld her wages for "mistakes" that she made. Lilibeth said, "I was a first timer in the city and didn't know anything about operating electric appliances. I stayed in the house all the time because I was afraid I would get lost. I didn't even dare to ask my employer to send me to school. I felt that they would not allow it." After a year, the first employer moved to the United States and passed Lilibeth off to her siblings, leaving Lilibeth responsible for taking care of three households for the same salary. "I cleaned three houses, cooked for two families, washed all their clothes and did all their errands," she said. "At night I ironed their clothes until 11 p.m." Exhausted, she sought another employer.

She hoped the third employer, a doctor, would treat her better, but she was wrong. She was never allowed to leave the house and not allowed to use the telephone. One night, after a disagreement, her employment was terminated, and at 8 p.m. at night, she was turned out of the house. Her fourth employer was the worst of all. After working for them for three months, they started a new business, a mini-videoke bar and eatery. Lilibeth was expected not only to carry out all the household chores but also to work in the new business, serving food and liquor to the customers, cooking and washing dishes, often from 10 p.m. until 4 a.m. She often got only three hours of sleep a night and endured verbal and psychological abuse. Lilibeth said, "There were times that I wanted to end everything by committing suicide, when my employers don't respect me as a human and degrade my dignity."

Despite the punishing hours she worked, Lilibeth managed to attend school on Sundays, her day off, paying for tuition out of her own salary. With the help of a guidance counselor at school, Lilibeth was referred to Visayan Forum, an NGO that works for the welfare of domestic workers and trafficked women and children. She was also introduced to SUMAPI, an association of domestic workers. She said, "Through SUMAPI, I was given a thorough orientation about the rights of the child and the domestic worker. I never even imagined that domestic workers could form associations and have programs for fellow domestic workers. Before that, I didn't have the faintest idea that I, too, have rights."

Lilibeth became active in SUMAPI, conducting trainings for other domestic workers in schools and advocating for better working conditions. She eventually left domestic work to work with SUMAPI and Visayan Forum, becoming the Davao chapter president of SUMAPI, and in 2009, at age twenty-one, the national president. Visayan Forum helped to support her further education, allowed her to complete college with a degree in social work.

Lilibeth now coordinates SUMAPI's national activities and serves on the technical working group for the Domestic Workers Campaign in the Philippines. She routinely meets with legislators in the Philippines to advocate for national legislation for domestic workers and the ILO Convention. She says, "I like to do lobbying because I can represent the issue and what we want to the legislators. I give a face to the organization, to SUMAPI. I always look at my own story and how Visayan Forum helped me to transform my life. The legislators now recognize me as a representative of domestic workers and find time to talk to me."

Lilibeth attended the final negotiations of the ILO Domestic Workers Convention in Geneva in 2011. In what she described as a "once-in-a-lifetime opportunity," she was selected as one of five NGO representatives to address the plenary of delegates. She urged them to adopt specific provisions for child domestic workers, saying, "We have been ignored and lived in the margins of society for so long. Now is the time to protect us."

She says, "The thing that motives me to work for this sector is that it is my own issue. I experienced my own suffering when I worked as a domestic worker. . . . Now, I look at my hardships from a different and more positive perspective. I am thankful that I struggled early in life because the difficulties I faced transformed me into a stronger and better person."

1. Author interviews and email correspondence, May 2010 and June 2011.

workers that would enable them to attend school on Sundays, their typical day off, and eventually earn their diploma. According to Flores-Oebanda:

> Schools are an entry point for employers. School teachers and officials can speak to both the domestic workers and the employers and can act as mediators. In their classes, some teachers allow space for child domestic workers to talk with each other about issues, and we also come to educate them about their rights. We engage on rights awareness, how to report abuse, how to spot symptoms of abuse in fellow classmates, etc. The first line of defense is the child domestic workers themselves, and teachers became a support network.[17]

By 2010, approximately four thousand child domestic workers were attending school each year, and Visayan Forum was working with partners to expand the programs.

Beginning in 1995, Visayan Forum helped domestic workers organize themselves, by providing support for the first domestic workers' union in the Philippines, called SUMAPI.[18] By 2011, the union had eight thousand members with chapters throughout the country. For many domestic workers, contact with SUMAPI helped to break their sense of isolation. Lilibeth Masamloc began working as a domestic worker when she was thirteen years old, but was able to access educational programs run by SUMAPI and Visayan Forum and eventually was elected SUMAPI's national president. She said:

> I never even imagined that domestic workers could form associations and have programs for fellow domestic workers! Through the trainings and activities given by SUMAPI, I was enlightened about the rights and privileges of a domestic worker. Before that, I didn't have the faintest idea that I, too, have rights. . . . SUMAPI serves as my second family. My fellow domestic workers understand me and help me through dark times.[19]

In the mid-1990s, Visayan Forum began working for national legislative change by promoting a "Magna Carta" for domestic workers (called the *Batas Kasambahay*). The bill addressed issues of minimum wage, regular rest days, mandatory registration and contracts, social security protection, provision of education, and better working conditions. Advocates organized consultations in different regions of the country to generate support for the bill, organized special events and demonstrations, and gathered one million signatures supporting swift passage of the *Batas Kasambahay*. Support for the bill among the public was extraordinary: in 2005, a survey by the Social Weather Station, a well-respected polling organization, found that half of all household heads were aware of the bill, and that 87 percent supported it. Among those who were familiar with the bill prior to the survey, 96 percent of respondents supported the bill.[20]

The bill passed the Senate in 2007, but failed to be adopted by the House of Representatives. It was derailed by presidential impeachment proceedings and other postponements. In 2010, a new Congress was elected. Cecilia Flores-Oebanda said, "We will start over, just as we did ten years ago. We told them [legislators] that as long as we don't have a law for domestic workers, you will see us every year until we die, so they might as well pass it."[21] In 2010, the bill again passed the Senate, and domestic workers and their advocates pushed to build support in Congress. Lilibeth Masamloc visited several members of Congress every month to talk about the bill on behalf of the domestic workers in SUMAPI. "I think it's very promising now. I'm optimistic that this year we will have the national law," she said in June 2011.[22]

As the *Batas Kasambahay* encountered political delays, Visayan Forum adopted a complementary strategy of pushing local ordinances that included key provisions from the *Batas Kasambahay*. Between 2008 and 2010, six cities adopted such ordinances, and two more had drafts in the pipeline. The ordinances set a minimum age for domestic work and put in place registration systems for domestic workers and mechanisms for monitoring and dispute resolution. Two of the ordinances included budgets for implementation.[23]

Reflecting on the extent of progress, Flores-Oebanda said, "It took us about 15 years since we started, but domestic work is now a major issue in the Philippines and in the world. Our second biggest success is that now everyone in the Philippines uses the term 'kasambahay.' We have a wide range of programs created by multiple stakeholders so that domestic workers can readily access help. We've also had success in local policies and engagement with the policymakers."[24]

Tanzania

In Tanzania, thousands of women and girls migrate from poor rural areas to Dar es Salaam and other urban areas to work as domestic workers. A large number of domestic workers enter the workforce before the age of fifteen; in urban areas, studies found that up to one-third of all working children were engaged in domestic labor, usually because of family poverty.[25] Children also were recruited by agents that then trafficked them to neighboring countries such as Kenya, or as far as the UK or Saudi Arabia. A 2004 survey by the Kivulini Women's Rights Organization found that 43 percent of child domestic workers in Tanzania worked sixteen to nineteen hours a day, but were paid less than US$15 per month. Half received less than US$8. Florence Rugemalira of Kivulini reported that their interviews found high incidence of physical, sexual, emotional, and economic violence against child domestic workers. "Three-quarters [of the children] would choose not to do this work if they had the choice, and most would not want this for their own children."[26]

Concerted organizing on domestic workers in Tanzania began around 2000, led by the Conservation, Hotels, Domestic and Allied Workers Union (CHODAWU), established in 1998, and local NGOs including Kivulini and the Kiota Women Health and Development Organization (KIWOHEDE). The groups established help centers for domestic workers in receiving areas of the country, opened vocational training centers in sending areas, conducted awareness-raising through the media and in rural communities, and worked with local leaders and government officials to create child labor committees and to promote stronger legal protections for domestic workers.

Vicky Kanyoka, the former director for women and organization of CHO-DAWU, said:

> The children are often taken from their homes by agents with promises like "she will work and send you money" or "she will be going to school." . . . First we had to create public awareness about the consequences of child labour. I was interviewed on TV so the message would reach all over the country. I used vivid cases of what happens to child domestic workers. Then we held aware-ness-raising meetings in the rural communities where the children come from, in collaboration with local government officials, village committees and other leaders.[27]

As in the Philippines, CHODAWU and other groups working on domestic workers found that it was important to engage a wide range of stakehold-ers, particularly at the community level. CHODAWU would first approach officials at the district level to discuss the issue and then, together with dis-trict officials, would approach key leaders in local villages, including social workers, teachers, cultural workers, the village chairperson, and influential women, traditional leaders, and faith-based organizations to discuss the issue and establish local child labor committees. The committees worked to identify neighborhoods where children were most likely to be recruited (for example, those without access to electricity, water, health care, or education) and to develop an action plan. By 2010, dozens of committees has been established in seven districts. According to Kanyoka,

> Each community produces a strategic plan, working out who can tackle what. Teachers check school registers to find out who is not attending. The youth say who among their friends are missing; they sometimes help identify the bus-stops and train stations through which children have been taken. This helps the police track the agents. This mapping has been so good. It has been an eye-opener even to local politicians to see what is happening on the ground to children. It has helped influence local governments to increase the budget to the areas where children are most vulnerable.[28]

The committees also developed and recommended local by-laws to local governments. For example, in some villages, by-laws were adopted to encourage parents to keep their children in school by levying fines, such as a chicken or a goat, against parents who sent their children to work in the city.[29]

CHODAWU sought to address both the push factors that sent girls into domestic work, as well as abuses they faced in urban areas. To address the family poverty and lack of economic opportunities that often drives children to domestic work, CHODAWU, with the support of the ILO, began to establish vocational skills training centers for children aged fifteen to eighteen, to offer courses in skills such as tailoring, batik, carpentry, welding, cooking, professional cleaning, candle making, and handicrafts. One of the centers was established with strong community support in Singida. The response was overwhelming. Parents began to write to their children working as domestic workers in urban areas to encourage them to return home to take the courses. Many children did so. An ILO assessment of the program found that "the involvement of parents to withdraw their own children is something that is very innovative. In other circumstances, this work is usually done by civil society organizations which are few and do not have the capacity to bring back as many children. . . . The act of involving parents in the withdrawal process had a dual effect; first of all, reunification with family, and secondly, children were coming back to a better alternative."[30] By 2006, CHODAWU was running seven such training facilities, which had served some twenty-five hundred children, three-quarters of them girls.[31]

CHODAWU and KIWOHEDE also set up help centers in Dar es Salaam in order to assist domestic workers, primarily children, who have experienced abuse or have not been paid salaries and lack the financial means to return home. The centers take in approximately four thousand children per year and provide counseling, vocational training, legal aid, family reunification, and other services. Titus Mlengeya, the national chairman of CHODAWU, believes that the help centers serve to empower domestic workers:

> As a union associated with domestic workers, [CHODAWU] has a role to play to ensure that its members are not mistreated. But you cannot protect them if they themselves are not made aware of their own situation, if they have no confidence in the fact that they are human beings and deserve to be treated the same way as everyone else. . . . If we do not act at this level, they will continue to be disrespected, to receive extremely low wages, and this new generation of domestic workers will develop within the context of mental and material difficulties, which is no good for the future.[32]

Kivulini also works with elected street leaders to respond to reports of abuse and conducts advocacy with members of the police to help them respond appropriately to violence against domestic workers. Florence Rugemalira of Kivulini says, "When a worker is abused, the police see it as a 'private' matter. This is especially the case when the work is done for distant family members, aunts or cousins, etc. We are trying to convince the police that abuse of a domestic worker is a criminal offense. However, those who are responsible for enforcing laws are themselves often the employers of domestic workers!"[33]

CHODAWU engaged actively with the Ministry of Labor regarding labor law and policy. It campaigned to have domestic work recognized in the 2004 Employment and Labor Relations Act and participated in a minimum-wage board set up by the ministry to conduct a study and make proposals regarding the minimum wage for various sectors. Through these processes and negotiation with the government and employers, CHODAWU helped secure a new law mandating a minimum wage for domestic workers equivalent to US$60 per month. A new National Employment Policy adopted in 2008 also included domestic workers in Tanzania's social insurance scheme.

According to Mlengeya, prior to the new minimum-wage law, many domestic workers were paid only five or ten dollars a month. Following the adoption of the law, CHODAWU also worked to publicize the new wage. "The families who have access to the media know that there is now a law that obliges them to apply this wage, but most people have not yet heard about it.

Our duty as a union is to help spread this awareness, in the same way that it is the government's duty to enforce the law."[34]

Reflecting on the impact of their efforts with child domestic workers in particular, Kanyoka identified one of the key achievements as a shift in attitude by parents and children regarding domestic work in the cities. "Now they realize that the child may get HIV/AIDS, and come back with nothing." She also cited active engagement by local and village governments in the issue and a greater recognition of the importance of education, including the allocation of additional resources for schools.[35]

The Push for an International Convention for Domestic Workers

In 2006, the FNV trade union confederation in the Netherlands hosted the first international conference in Amsterdam for domestic worker organizations and their supporters. Sixty representatives from national domestic worker associations and unions, international trade unions, and other groups met to discuss actions being taken around the world by domestic workers to organize themselves. The conference also laid plans to develop an international domestic workers' network and to explore the possibility of establishing global standards to protect the rights of domestic workers through a new International Labor Organization convention.[36]

Initially, not all domestic worker groups believed that pursuing an ILO convention was worth the time or intensive effort that would be required. At the 2006 conference, a leader of the domestic workers' union in Namibia said, "ILO conventions take five to ten years to achieve. For domestic workers in hardship, this is a long process. . . . I don't believe in a long process; I want to know what we are going to do now."[37] Others, however, saw it as an opportunity for mobilizing, for promoting domestic workers' organizations and their agendas, and for establishing international standards that could influence individual governments to improve their national laws and policies to protect domestic workers.

At the same time, international concern was growing over the issue. Beginning in 2000, Human Rights Watch began publishing a series of hard-hitting reports exposing abuses against domestic workers, particularly migrants and children.[38] Migrant Forum Asia, Anti-Slavery International, the Labor Solidarity Center, UNIFEM, and the ILO all carried out work on the issue. UN experts began raising concerns about abuses against domestic workers,[39] and the media began publishing exposés of particularly severe cases of employer abuse against individual domestic workers.

The ILO—the leading international organization responsible for protecting the rights of workers and developing and monitoring global labor standards—had been very slow to address the specific conditions of domestic workers.[40] Despite a 1948 resolution regarding the conditions of employment of domestic workers,[41] and another in 1965 recognizing the need for global standards to protect the rights for domestic workers,[42] until 2011 the ILO still did not have a single binding treaty specifically addressing the millions domestic workers worldwide or their unique circumstances of employment. In contrast, the ILO had adopted sixty-five separate instruments relating to the rights of an estimated 1.2 million maritime workers.[43] In total, the ILO had adopted 188 separate labor conventions (which have the status of legally binding treaties), and 199 nonbinding guidelines known as recommendations through its unique tripartite negotiating process, involving workers, employers, and governments.

Following the November 2006 Amsterdam conference, follow-up meetings were quickly held with trade unions and the ILO to discuss the proposal for a new domestic worker network and an ILO convention. The International Union of Food, Agricultural, Hotel, Restaurant, Catering, Tobacco and Allied Workers' Associations (IUF) agreed to support the development of the new International Domestic Workers' Network (IDWN). The International Trade Union Confederation (ITUC), the main international trade union body, representing 176 million members worldwide, and ACTRAV, the ILO office supporting workers, agreed to begin pressing for an ILO convention specifically addressing the rights of domestic workers.

In October 2007, the ITUC called on all of its member trade unions to seek support from their governments for an ILO convention for domestic workers.[44] In March 2008, the ILO's worker members formally proposed that the ILO's executive body, known as the Governing Body, place decent work for domestic work on the agenda of the 2010 International Labor Conference and begin the process of developing a new international labor instrument on domestic workers.[45] The Governing Body accepted the proposal, with the workers and a strong majority of governments expressing support.[46]

The ILO has a clear, step-by-step process for developing new standards that generally takes three years, including intense negotiations among the ILO's members—workers, employers, and governments—during the annual

International Labour Conference. The process begins with the International Labor Office preparing a "law and practice" report that surveys existing laws and practices by member states. For the report, NGOs submitted research they had conducted on working conditions for domestic workers and the impact of discriminatory laws that excluded domestic workers from the labor protections available to other workers. The International Labor Office also reviewed national legislation from seventy-two countries, representing more than 80 percent of the world's population. It found that 40 percent of the countries did not guarantee domestic workers a weekly day off, and 50 percent did not impose a mandatory limit of normal hours of work.[47] The report concluded that domestic work is "undervalued and poorly regulated, and many domestic workers remain overworked, underpaid and unprotected."[48] It noted that one of its most important findings was that conditions for domestic workers did not improve without concerted action to improve the legislative framework.[49] It recommended that ILO members adopt international labor standards to regulate and protect domestic work. The report also included a questionnaire about key issues—including the form of the instrument and key provisions—that was distributed to all ILO members for response.

Domestic workers and their allies began mobilizing to influence the positions of ILO members that would be participating in the negotiations. At stake were two key issues: whether the new instrument would take the form of a legally binding convention (or simply a nonbinding "recommendation" to give guidance to ILO member states), and whether it would guarantee the rights that domestic workers had long been denied.

Domestic worker groups at the national level held meetings to identify key demands for the instrument and to engage with their trade union confederations and national governments. For example, the Philippine Campaign on Decent Work for Domestic Workers held a series of three consultations among domestic workers, government representatives, trade unionists, and NGOs in 2009, aimed at developing a unified Philippine position on the ILO domestic workers' instrument. In August of that year, a National Domestic Workers Summit brought together more than three hundred government, trade union, domestic worker, and civil society representatives to discuss the proposed ILO instrument and the domestic worker agenda in the Philippines.

In countries such as Tanzania and South Africa, domestic worker unions pressured their Departments of Labor to respond to the ILO questionnaire and support a convention. "We put lots of pressure on the government to respond to the questionnaire," said Myrtle Witbooi, secretary general of the South African Service and Allied Workers Union.[50] In Tanzania, Vicky Kanyoka said that the union used the reforms that had been achieved at national level to argue for government engagement in the ILO process. "We said, the Tanzania government already recognizes domestic workers in the law, so it is important for the government to support the Convention."[51]

Domestic worker groups, with the International Trade Union Confederation and the ILO, held regional and international preparatory meetings in the Asia-Pacific region, Latin America, and Europe to strategize and develop action plans for the 2010 International Labor Conference. A September 2009 meeting in Mexico City, for example, involved representatives from eleven Latin American and Caribbean countries and included a press conference highlighting domestic workers' conditions and their most urgent demands.[52] Migrant Forum Asia also held consultations in the Philippines, Indonesia, Cambodia, Singapore, and India, as well as online consultations in order to mobilize its members and partners and develop coordinated advocacy strategies on behalf of the convention.[53]

The International Domestic Workers Network and its regional coordinators provided information and resources and facilitated communication with national-level groups. The network published a "platform of demands," articulating key provisions that should be included in the instrument, including freedom of association and the right to collective bargaining, written employment contracts, the right to a minimum wage, daily and weekly rest periods, protection from harassment and abuse, access to social security and medical services, freedom of movement, and provisions regarding occupational health and safety, and implementation and enforcement measures.[54] The ITUC prepared recommended responses to the ILO questionnaire and circulated them among national trade unions, while international NGOs, such as Human Rights Watch and Anti-Slavery International, provided "model responses" to governments regarding the questionnaire, met with government representatives to the ILO during a series of advocacy trips to Geneva, and wrote letters to national ministers of labor regarding the importance of the proposed instrument.[55]

A critical issue for domestic workers was that they be able to speak for themselves and be represented as part of the official workers' delegations to the negotiations. In countries including the United States, Kenya, Bolivia, Brazil, Jamaica, Mexico, Canada, Nepal, Italy, and the UK, domestic workers won spots in their country's official delegation to the International Labour Conference.[56] Other unions included representatives who were involved directly in organizing domestic workers.

An early victory was apparent in March 2010, when the ILO issued its second report summarizing the responses of ILO members to the questionnaire about the proposed instrument for domestic workers.[57] ILO members from more than one hundred countries had responded, including approximately seventy-five governments, one hundred twenty-five worker groups, and twenty-three employer associations. As expected, virtually all worker groups supported a binding convention, while employers preferred a nonbinding recommendation. Among governments—which hold half of the votes among ILO members and are therefore decisive—a surprising two-thirds stated their support for a binding convention. However, of concern was that moderate countries including the UK, the Netherlands, Switzerland, New Zealand, and Canada all expressed a preference for a nonbinding recommendation.[58]

When the first round of negotiations finally began at the 2010 International Labour Conference in Geneva, interest was overwhelming. More than five hundred delegates and NGOs attended, including domestic worker organizations from around the world. Many of them attended as formal members of their country's delegations. During opening statements, the employers' representative warned that global standards could result in job losses if employers were unable to meet the requirements and were forced to dismiss domestic workers.[59] The workers' representative countered that clear rules would promote a more robust labor market and would allow employers to compete for workers on the same basis.[60] More than twenty governments took the floor to make opening statements. While some stated that the issue needed more study or argued that a nonbinding recommendation was the best approach to address situations that varied widely from country to country, many stated their position in favor of a binding ILO convention. Each such statement met with applause from workers and NGOs. South Africa elicited the most enthusiastic response when it took the floor to announce that the entire fifty-four–member African group was supporting a binding convention accompanied by a recommendation.

Several nongovernmental organizations were also given the opportunity to give opening statements. One of them was delivered by Vicky Kanyoka of Tanzania on behalf of the International Domestic Workers Network and the IUF. She said, "We have been waiting for this moment for a very long time," and she described the challenges facing domestic workers, as well as some of the advances made in some countries. Describing progress in her own country, she cited the steps that had been taken by the government to include domestic workers under the labor law and to provide domestic workers with minimum wage and social security protection. She said, "What do these examples mean? That this is not just something for the rich, developed countries. Even poor countries like my own can do it. It is a question of commitment to the principle of decent work for all."[61]

Some members had argued that the content of the instrument should be discussed before any decision was made about its form. However, in a move that surprised most delegates, on the third day of negotiations the employers called for a roll-call vote on the form of the instrument. The vote was specifically on a proposal from the Indian government that the instrument take the form of a nonbinding recommendation. The amendment was defeated. The employers voted as a bloc in favor of the amendment, while the workers voted unanimously against it. The decisive votes were cast by governments: sixty-one rejected the amendment, while only fourteen supported it. Four abstained.[62]

The vote was the first significant hurdle of the negotiations and determined that the instrument would be a legally binding convention accompanied by a recommendation. Domestic workers were ecstatic. "We are making history!" blogged Jill Shenker, the lead organizer for the US-based National Domestic Workers Alliance. "This means that we are closer than ever before on assuring international standards for domestic workers will be established."[63]

In long negotiations during the week that followed, delegates agreed on key provisions for the convention. Many of these addressed domestic workers' long-standing demands. For example, delegates agreed that domestic workers should be entitled to minimum-wage coverage, to a weekly day of rest, to payment at least once a month, and to hours of work and overtime compensation on an equal basis with other workers. They agreed that workers should have the freedom to negotiate whether to live in their employer's household, should be free to leave the house during their time off, and should be entitled to keep possession of their identity documents. They agreed that domestic workers should have clear terms and conditions of employment, preferably in the form of a written contract, access to the courts and dispute-resolution processes, and protection from harassment and abuse. They agreed that each government should regulate private employment agencies and set a minimum age for domestic work in line with other sectors, and that domestic work by children should not interfere with their education. They also agreed that domestic workers were entitled to freedom of association and the right to bargain collectively.[64] NGOs such as Human Rights Watch met with key government delegations throughout the negotiations regarding specific provisions, advocating for or against particular amendments and sometimes providing specific wording. In several cases, governments put forward amendments based on language that had been provided by NGOs.

Governments that advocated strongly on behalf of domestic workers included Argentina, Australia, Brazil, South Africa, the United States, and Uruguay. Some, such as Brazil, South Africa, and Uruguay, drew from their national experiences and the impact of efforts to strengthen legal protections for domestic workers in their own countries.

Domestic worker groups, including both NGOs and unions, organized a range of activities in Geneva during the negotiations, including a poster exhibit and an evening of speeches and musical performances celebrating domestic workers. During one demonstration on behalf of Swiss domestic workers advocating for minimum-wage coverage, the Asian Domestic Workers Network unfurled a giant apron sewed from thirty-eight hundred patches, each made by a domestic worker expressing their demands for labor rights. Anti-Slavery International brought five young domestic workers from Togo, India, and Peru to speak with ILO delegates about their experiences working as children.

Following the first round of negotiations in 2010, domestic workers and NGOs continued national and regional efforts to build support for the convention. They lobbied their national governments and employers' organizations. The International Domestic Worker Network and the ITUC held regional consultations in Indonesia, South Africa, and Brazil and an international strategy meeting in Geneva. Migrant Forum Asia held additional consultations, including in Bangladesh and Singapore. The European Trade Union Confederation successfully pushed to get a European Parliament resolution adopted supporting the convention and urging European countries to ratify it. Human Rights Watch continued to meet with government representatives in Geneva, submitted possible amendments to supportive government for the final negotiations, and held discussions with employers' representatives, who continued to oppose a binding convention.[65]

Excitement was high in June 2011 when ILO members convened for the final negotiations. During the course of ten days, nearly five hundred representatives of governments, trade unions, and employer groups debated the provisions of the proposed convention and recommendation, often negotiating until 9:30 or 10 at night. Throughout the negotiations, trade unions, domestic worker groups, and NGOs continued to meet with individual government delegations and employer groups, and they held briefings and events to push for the strongest possible text. Although employers attempted to remove or weaken a number of key provisions, such as domestic workers' rights to compensation for working "on-call" or overtime, nearly all of the rights that had been agreed the year before were retained. The number of governments supporting the convention grew, as Bangladesh and the Middle Eastern Gulf countries made a dramatic shift toward supporting rights and protections for domestic workers, and others, such as Indonesia and the Philippines, became more outspoken.

When ILO members completed the negotiations on June 10, 2011, the room erupted with applause. Afterward, domestic workers gathered to reflect on the historic moment, to cheer, dance, and sing. Myrtle Witbooi, the trade unionist and former domestic worker from South Africa said, "If someone had told me forty-five years ago that we would be here today, I would not have believed it. We do not have to be slaves anymore. But the fight is not over. We need to go back home. We need to campaign. We need to be sure that what we vote for is implemented. We must not rest until our governments ratify the Convention. We cannot be free until we free all the domestic workers."[66] Vicky Kanyoko from Tanzania said that she felt very emotional when the convention was adopted. But like Witbooi, she also looked at the victory as part of a continuing struggle: "I feel very proud that our energy had such a good impact. But now, this is the beginning of the job. Ratification and implementation is another challenge waiting for us."[67]

On June 16, 2011, the ILO Convention Concerning Decent Work for Domestic Workers was officially put to a vote in the International Labor Conference. It was adopted by an overwhelming margin, with 396 members voting in favor of adoption, 63 abstaining, and only 16 voting against. Only one government—Swaziland—voted against adoption of the instrument.

Lessons Learned

Advocates for global standards for domestic workers faced obstacles both within and outside their movement. Initially, many employers groups and governments resisted the push for a binding convention. Governments such as the UK argued that many ILO conventions adopted in recent years had achieved a very low rate of ratification and that it would undermine the credibility of the ILO to adopt additional conventions that might not be widely ratified.[68] Both employers and some governments argued that existing conventions were sufficient to protect domestic workers, that conventions should not be sector-specific, or that it was impossible to adopt global standards that would be relevant to the widely divergent social, economic, and cultural conditions across countries. An employer group from Pakistan argued that in developing countries, regulation of domestic work would rob many poor people of the opportunity to make even a meager living.[69]

Other governments recognized domestic work as a historically neglected sector of employment, particularly given the large numbers of workers involved and that more than forty years had passed since the ILO first recognized the need for global standards for domestic workers. Increasing rates of international migration for domestic work, high-profile cases of abuse against migrant domestic workers, and growing documentation of the general vulnerability of domestic workers to abuse provided a convincing case for stronger regulation.

To become an effective advocacy movement, however, domestic workers needed to organize. In many countries, domestic workers found it extremely difficult to form unions. SUMAPI, the domestic workers' union in the Philippines, found that the same factors that made domestic workers prone to abuse also hindered union organizing, citing domestic workers' relative invisibility, mobility, low levels of education, lack of information on protection mechanisms, and low self-esteem stemming from society's bias and low value attached to domestic work.[70] A domestic worker organizer in Mexico described the hurdles: "It is not easy. We are not trained as professionals; many of us have worked in private homes for fifteen-twenty years, since we were children, and so we have had few educational opportunities; we do not necessarily have the basic organizing skills. However, we are convinced that we have to win back our rights and it is through our activities that we grow and learn how to organize and defend the rights of our members and friends."[71]

Domestic workers found little interest or active resistance from traditional unions. Unions used to organizing factory or office-based workers often placed low priority on organizing workers in the informal sector and believed it was not worth their time or resources. Because domestic workers' wages are typically so low, their union dues were often insufficient to keep unions functioning. In Namibia, one of the first countries in Africa to have a domestic workers' union, the union was forced to disband in 2003 due to lack of funds. Union membership rates were 1 percent of monthly wages, which typically amounted to only N$3 (US$0.50). According to a union leader, "We raised these problems in the national federation, asking if another union would take domestic workers under its umbrella. No one wanted us except the farmworkers, who said they understood."[72] The two unions later merged.

Domestic workers and their allies won greater recognition of their rights through a long and persistent struggle. In particular, several factors made the negotiation and adoption of the Domestic Workers Convention possible. Fundamental to the success were efforts by domestic workers to mobilize and empower themselves through the organization of domestic worker groups and unions. Fledgling groups found creative methods to reach out to other domestic workers, approaching them in parks on their days off, going out early in the morning when domestic workers were buying bread, visiting night schools where domestic workers might be attending classes, and using informal networks and word of mouth. To empower their members and build their own capacity, many domestic worker groups organized training and awareness-raising sessions. In the absence of support and capacity from traditional trade unions, NGOs often played a supportive role, providing shelter, legal assistance, and other services, as well as conducting advocacy and supporting domestic workers' efforts to organize themselves.

Although few countries had active domestic worker associations or unions prior to 1990,[73] organizing gained momentum through the 1990s and 2000s. By 2010, trade unions for domestic workers or domestic worker associations were active in at least forty-four countries and regional networks of domestic worker groups had been established in Latin America and the Caribbean (1998) and in Asia (2004).[74] The emergence of these groups raised the profile of domestic worker issues and prompted national-level reforms, while the creation of regional and international networks such as the International Domestic Workers Network allowed domestic worker groups to share experiences across borders and begin organizing at an international level.

A second key factor was the strategic alliance between the domestic worker groups and the International Trade Union Confederation. The ITUC's decision in 2007—prompted by the 2006 Amsterdam conference of domestic worker groups—to push for an ILO convention on domestic work at the ILO governing body was a key turning point. Once the governing body agreed to place a standard-setting process on the ILO's agenda, the prospect of an international convention provided a galvanizing focus for domestic worker groups around the globe. They were able to build on the momentum they had created through national-level change in laws and practices to pressure their governments and trade unions to adopt global standards that would have far-reaching international impact.

A third factor was the strategic advocacy by domestic workers and their NGO allies with individual governments, both to push for legislative reforms at national level and to seek support for the international convention. Adoption of laws at the national level built momentum for the convention and helped show that legal reform to protect domestic workers was possible. At the 2010 International Labor Conference, governments that had a tradition of organizing by domestic workers or progressive legislation emerged as champions for global standards for domestic workers. For example, Brazil, South Africa, and Uruguay were outspoken on behalf of strong protections for domestic workers and often drew on their national experience and legislation in their statements during the negotiations. The United States, despite having relatively poor legal protections for domestic workers, also had strong organizing by domestic worker groups and emerged as a major ally due to progressive positions taken by the Obama administration. "It's not a coincidence that Brazil, South Africa and the United States are so strong [in the negotiations]," said Jill Shenker, lead organizer for the National Domestic Workers Alliance. "There has been a lot of organizing by strong domestic worker unions in each of those countries for a long time."[75]

The impact of national-level advocacy for the convention became clearer as the negotiations progressed. Countries such as Indonesia, the Philippines, and Bangladesh became more vocally supportive of the convention due to domestic pressure by domestic workers and their allies. Lobbying by South African and Canadian workers resulted in support from their employer counterparts. International NGOs helped complement these national-level efforts by meeting with dozens of government representatives in Geneva, contacting ministries of labor, and working with a handful of allies on specific amendments to the convention.

Fourth, advocates found that it was important to engage with all actors in the process, including the employers. The employers group was initially strongly opposed to a binding convention, and many participants in the process believed that the group—representing one-quarter of voting members—would either vote as a bloc against the final convention or abstain from the vote. Although some felt that it was not worth the time to seek their support, Human Rights Watch pursued constructive engagement with employer representatives during a two-year period through a series of meetings and written communications. During the final negotiations, Human Rights Watch representatives briefed the entire employers group regarding its research findings on abuses by private employment agencies. The organization's advocates believed that its continuous engagement helped influence a shift by employers. In the final vote, nearly half of employer representatives voted in favor of adopting the convention.

A final element was the growing body of research—generated by NGOs, the ILO, and high-profile media stories—that illustrated without a doubt the protection deficit and shocking abuses that domestic workers experienced. Although the employers' group initially argued that more research was necessary before the ILO should undertake negotiation of a legally binding instrument, in the face of overwhelming documentation, nearly all members of the ILO accepted that domestic workers were vulnerable to abuse and needed stronger legal protections in order to ensure decent working conditions. Solid research from multiple sources of widespread labor and criminal abuses helped many ILO members conclude that the time was finally right to adopt binding labor standards for domestic workers.

Two strategies commonly used in advocacy were not particularly effective in influencing the convention. One of these was the use of the media to highlight the negotiations on the ILO convention and to put pressure on states. While the media had increasingly produced stories about extreme abuses against individual domestic workers, or new research reports on the topic during the years leading up to the negotiations, few journalists were interested in covering the negotiations themselves. Second was the use of public demonstrations or other direct actions. Although some domestic worker groups organized public events during the convention negotiations in Geneva, government and employer representatives to the ILO indicated they had little impact on the discussions.[76] The real action was in the negotiating room itself and in the individual capitals where positions were being decided.

The combination of a young but strategic international domestic workers' movement; sympathetic government, trade union, and NGO allies; positive momentum created through national-level reforms; and a recognition of the need for stronger global protections for domestic workers finally converged. The result was the first international labor treaty specifically addressing the rights of the largest sector of working women and girls in the world. Many challenges remained: the vast majority of the world's domestic workers remained outside the scope of domestic workers' groups and unions; it remained to be seen how many governments would ratify the new treaty; and even once ratified, enforcement of the new standards would be difficult. However, the convention represented a groundbreaking achievement. It created clear legal standards that governments would be expected to meet, provided domestic workers and their allies with a powerful new advocacy tool, accelerated the process of national-level legislative reform, and represented an unequivocal affirmation of domestic workers' rights to respect and equal treatment under the law.

PART II

UN Human Rights Bodies and Mechanisms

Chapter 3

Defeating the Election of Human Rights Abusers to the UN Human Rights Council

The campaign has a multiplying effect, by ensuring that other, better countries are elected, but also discouraging abusive states from running. Now they'll think twice before exposing themselves to embarrassment.

—*Lawrence Moss, NGO Coalition for an Effective Human Rights Council*[1]

WHEN THE UN GENERAL ASSEMBLY created the Human Rights Council in 2006, governments and NGOs sought to create a preeminent intergovernmental body that would protect and promote human rights around the world, while avoiding the flaws that had fatally discredited its predecessor, the UN Commission on Human Rights. The commission had increasingly become known not for advancing human rights, but rather as a body co-opted by countries with abysmal human rights records in order to protect themselves and other abusers from criticism and scrutiny. Countries had used their membership to defeat resolutions criticizing human rights violations by their own and other governments and to dismantle special procedures that had been created to monitor practices in countries with a history of poor human rights records.

In contrast, when the General Assembly created the new council, it specified that its members should "uphold the highest standards in the promotion and protection of human rights" and "fully cooperate" with the new council.[2] While members of the previous commission had usually been selected by their regional groups and rubber-stamped by the UN Economic and Social Council, new council members were required to win the affirmative vote of an absolute majority of UN member states (97 votes out of the 193 UN member states) as well as successfully compete against other candidates from their region.

The Human Rights Council is responsible for promoting universal respect for human rights, addressing specific violations of human rights, including gross and systematic violations, appointing experts to monitor the human rights practices in specific countries and around particular themes, and assessing the human rights records of individual UN member states. While the old commission had met just once a year for a six-week session in Geneva, the new council was to meet for three sessions a year, totaling at least ten weeks. It has the authority to hold special sessions to address human rights crises, and in 2007, it established a "universal periodic review" that subjects every UN member state to a peer review of its human rights practices every four years.

For human rights advocates, the Human Rights Council offers significant opportunities to shine a light on issues that require international attention and create pressure on governments to end human rights abuses. The council's country-specific resolutions can be a potent tool for censuring violators, as even the most abusive governments are sensitive to their international reputation and seek to avoid public condemnation of their abusive practices. Advocates promote council resolutions and debates on particular themes in order to promote emerging areas of human rights or to reinforce existing ones, including the rights of women, children, migrants, and other vulnerable groups. In 2011, for example, the Human Rights Council established special commissions of inquiry to investigate human rights violations in Syria, Libya, and Cote d'Ivoire and adopted nearly ninety resolutions addressing a dozen specific country situations, as well as thematic issues including migrants, climate change, the death penalty, violence against women, and the right to water and sanitation.

The council, like the preceding commission, also has the authority to create and renew country and thematic mandates, which include special rapporteurs that monitor and report on human rights practices in a particular country or around a specific right. The creation or renewal of a country mandate signals that the country involved has serious human rights problems and is widely perceived as carrying a significant stigma. NGOs routinely provide documentation of human rights abuses to special rapporteurs, who may then include it in their official reports to the full council. By early 2012, the council had established thirty-five thematic special rapporteurs, experts, or working groups, and ten country-specific rapporteurs or experts.[3] Five of these mandates were created in 2011, including new positions to focus on Syria and Cote d'Ivoire, a new working group on transnational corporations and business enterprises, an independent expert on the promotion of a democratic and equitable international order, and a special rapporteur on the promotion of truth and justice.

The negative influence of abusive governments in the Commission on Human Rights had shown that the membership of the new Human Rights Council would significantly impact its effectiveness. As the new council was being debated in the General Assembly, NGOs advocated for specific criteria that all new members should be required to meet, including ratification of core human rights treaties, timely reporting to UN treaty bodies, cooperation with UN experts and special rapporteurs, implementation of the recommendations of UN human rights bodies, and dedication to improving respect for human rights in their respective countries. In creating the Human Rights Council, the General Assembly set two key standards for membership: full cooperation with the council and upholding the "highest standards" in the promotion and protection of human rights.[4]

The new council was established with forty-seven members, distributed geographically and serving three year terms.[5] Each year, one-third of the council members would be elected or reelected by ballot, requiring a majority vote of General Assembly members.

Campaigning to Defeat Human Rights Abusers

After the creation of the Human Rights Council, a broad-based international coalition of NGOs came together to help ensure that elections for the council resulted in the selection of member states that would actively promote and protect human rights, rather than simply seek to shield their own practices from international scrutiny. According to Dokhi Fassihian of the Democracy Coalition Project, "Governments knew the commission had failed. They knew that governments weren't always running for the best reasons and that the council couldn't afford to fail again. . . . One of the biggest achievements with the new council was the competitive election process. It gave us an opportunity to really work to make sure that the best countries won."[6] Beginning in 2007, the NGO Coalition for an Effective Human Rights Council ran successful annual campaigns to defeat some of the worst human rights violators from election to the Human Rights Council, including Belarus, Sri Lanka, and Azerbaijan.[7] It engaged NGOs from across regions, international figures including former heads of state and

Nobel Peace Prize winners, and NGOs from within the countries concerned to highlight the abusive human rights records of candidate countries and vocally oppose their election to the Human Rights Council on the grounds that they did not meet General Assembly's requirements for Human Rights Council membership.

2007: Belarus

In 2007, Belarus ran for election to the Human Rights Council despite a history of gross and systematic human rights abuses. Just a few months earlier, the UN General Assembly had adopted a resolution expressing deep concerns over a litany of abuses, including the country's failure to hold free and fair elections, arbitrary use of state power against opposition candidates, routine harassment and arrest of political and civil society activists, harassment and detention of journalists, implication of government officials in the enforced disappearance or summary execution of opposition politicians and journalists, and the closure of civil society organizations.[8]

In March 2006, the president of Belarus was reelected to a third term with more than 80 percent of the vote in an election that the Organization for Security and Cooperation in Europe concluded failed to meet standards for democratic elections. The government had severely persecuted leaders of opposition parties both before and after its March 2006 national elections. It harassed opposition candidates and campaign workers, and it sentenced political party leaders to jail for participating in protests.

The government stifled both freedom of the press and association by criminalizing adverse media coverage, refusing to investigate or prosecute the murder of journalists, and curbing the right to peaceful assembly through criminal code provisions, and violently dispersing, arresting, and fining peaceful protesters. In 2004, the Parliamentary Assembly of the Council of Europe accused high-ranking Belarusian officials of involvement in the disappearances of the former interior minister, the prime minister, electoral commission chairman, and an independent journalist.

Fassihian said, "When we realized Belarus was running, we asked our partners in the region to talk with local organizations and dissidents in Belarus to ask them to make a decision about how they wanted to work with us."[9] Civil society groups in Belarus made a decision to actively oppose Belarus's candidacy. They wrote several joint letters and some individual dissidents in prison even wrote letters that were smuggled out.

The NGO coalition initiated a "No on Belarus" campaign. It argued that Belarus "does not come close to meeting the requirements" for membership on the Human Rights Council and that Belarus failed both of the council's key criteria of upholding the highest standards of human rights and fully cooperating with the council. The coalition pointed out that Belarus had refused to allow the UN special rapporteur on the human rights situation in Belarus to visit the country and stated that this fact alone "should be sufficient to deny Belarus a seat on the council."[10] The special rapporteur had noted the "absolute refusal to cooperate on the part of the government of Belarus," including its refusal of all visit requests, of all efforts to constructive dialogue, and of any governmental response to the rapporteur's conclusions and recommendations.

The NGO coalition circulated the letters from Belarus organizations and dissidents to UN member states and set up a website that highlighted Belarus's poor human rights record and contrasted its pledges for its Human Rights Council membership with its actual practices. It urged individuals and organizations to send faxes and emails to their country's UN ambassador to vote against Belarus in the council elections. Three weeks before the vote, the coalition mobilized some forty human rights and democracy organizations from around the globe to send a joint letter opposing Belarus's candidacy to all UN ambassadors. The letter highlighted Belarus's extremely poor human rights record, its failure to cooperate with special procedure mandate-holders, and the findings of the various European and UN bodies that had condemned human rights abuses by Belarus. It concluded that the election of Belarus would damage the credibility not only of the Human Rights Council but of the General Assembly.

The coalition engaged former Czech president Václav Havel, who issued a statement ten days before the vote stating that Belarus's human rights record was deteriorating rather than improving, and that even Belarusians working in human rights organizations rejected the candidacy of their own country. Havel said that he considered Belarus's candidacy to the Human Rights Council "to be a mockery of the efforts of all liberal-minded Belarusians and the international community to achieve free and democratic conditions in the country."[11]

Initially, Slovenia and Belarus were running unopposed for two Eastern European regional seats on the council. Members of the coalition worked with supportive UN member states to identify additional candidates. Just two days before the election, urged by the United States, Bosnia and Herzegovina declared its candidacy. The United States, France, UK, and Canada coordinated outreach to some 150 member states, urging them to support Bosnia and Herzegovina's election. According to Lawrence Moss, a member of the coalition representing Human Rights Watch, "The US, the UK, and France did a lot of heavy lifting in capitals around the world, the kind of heavy lifting that is difficult for us to do. Their influence was pivotal. But we created a lot of

Profile: Dokhi Fassihian

Dokhi Fassihian joined the Democracy Coalition Project in 2005, just as the Human Rights Council was being negotiated.[1] "It's not a perfect process," she says. "But a lot has been achieved, and it's important for people to understand that we have an international human rights system that can be strengthened even more."

Dokhi studied international affairs and Middle East studies in college and as a graduate student. As an Iranian, she had a particular interest in Middle East issues and served as the executive director for the National Iranian American Council before joining the Democracy Coalition Project. "I never planned human rights as a career," she said. "But I've really loved it, working on the international human rights system."

After the Human Rights Council was established in 2006, Dokhi helped to create a global network of international and regional human rights organizations to coordinate advocacy at the Human Rights Council. She believes that there have been concrete results. "Watching it evolve, it's come a long way. The Council is responding to human rights emergencies, which we didn't really have before. Recently, when the Libyan and Syrian governments were cracking down on protesters, the Security Council couldn't act on either of those issues, and it was the Human Rights Council that took the lead." She readily acknowledges weaknesses in the system, noting, "The process can be strengthened, but we need to build the political will to strengthen it."

As part of her work, she collaborates with dozens of local human rights partners in various countries around the world. "The best part of my job," she says, "is to work with human rights defenders all over the world. It's an incredible experience to work with people on the front lines. The biggest lesson I've learned is to defer to them and not to simplify human rights situations. Defer to them and support them the best you can."

noise about how Belarus was inappropriate and that created space for Bosnia to come in."[12]

During the May 17, 2007, elections, Belarus was defeated by a large margin. Slovenia easily won election with 168 votes. In a second round of voting, Bosnia and Herzegovina won 112 votes, while Belarus received only 72—falling far short of the absolute majority required for election.

At the Democracy Coalition Project, she was deeply involved in the campaigns to defeat abusive countries from election to the Human Rights Council. "The election victories were exciting and fun, especially the first one, because it was precedent-setting." She also led a successful campaign to establish the first country rapporteur at the UN Human Rights Council on Iran. The victory surprised some observers. "Everyone thought it would be very difficult, because for the first two years, the Human Rights Council seemed intent on cutting the country mandates. We had lost Cuba, Belarus, and the DRC. Getting a new special rapporteur on a country was considered very difficult if not impossible."

During her work, Dokhi also found herself fighting on behalf of her own organization. The Democracy Coalition Project applied for official NGO consultative status at the UN, but after a three-year struggle, the Committee on Non-Governmental Organizations, which was dominated by countries like Cuba, Russia, and Sudan, voted down their application because of the organization's vocal criticism of abusive states. "We were working against the idea that governments could silence NGOs," she said. After being rejected by the committee, Dokhi lobbied members of the UN's Economic and Social Council (ECOSOC) directly to overrule the committee's recommendation and approve the application in 2009.

The most challenging part of human rights work, she finds, is that "Things are just slow. You can't expect victories every day. The impact of your work isn't easily measurable. Sometimes it's hard for you to see the result until many years later. You may be frustrated because of lack of leverage, or because most governments care less about human rights than about other issues. The lack of leverage and the slow progress can be frustrating. But if you have a broad, decade-long perspective, you can step back and see progress."

1. Author interview with Dokhi Fassihian, July 28, 2011.

2008: Sri Lanka

In 2008, six Asian governments—Bahrain, Japan, Pakistan, South Korea, Sri Lanka, and Timor Leste—competed for four seats for the Asian region on the Human Rights Council. The NGO coalition consulted with civil society groups in Bahrain, Pakistan, and Sri Lanka regarding their views on their countries' candidacies. In Bahrain, civil society groups couldn't decide what to do. Some wanted to oppose the candidacy, while others wanted to use it as leverage to try to get improvements in human rights from the government. In Pakistan, which had a new government, civil society groups decided that they wanted to push their government for reforms as part of its candidacy. They wrote letters to the government outlining their demands. The government agreed to some of them, and the groups decided not to oppose Pakistan's bid for the council. In Sri Lanka, civil society groups deliberated for several weeks before they decided to oppose Sri Lanka's candidacy. According to Moss, "We waited until they came to a decision about the campaign before launching the international campaign. We wanted them to go first. But for them it was tough. Opposing their own government's candidacy was not an easy matter."[13]

Sri Lankan government forces had been implicated in a wide range of serious human rights abuses, including hundreds of extrajudicial killings and enforced disappearances, widespread torture, arbitrary detention, and complicity in the recruitment of child soldiers. In 2007, hundreds of people were detained under emergency regulations that gave the government broad powers of arrest and detention without charge. The regulations were used to conduct mass arrests of ethnic Tamils and to detain journalists, political opponents, and human rights activists. Between January 2006 and June 2007, more than eleven hundred new disappearances or abductions were reported, the vast majority Tamils. The rate of new cases reported in 2007 to the UN Working Group on Enforced and Involuntary Disappearances was the highest in the world.[14]

When Sri Lanka first was elected to the council in 2006, it pledged to implement recommendations from UN bodies. However, it failed to do so. It ignored the recommendations of UN human rights experts, obstructed their work, and publicly attacked UN officials who were openly critical of the government. Senior Sri Lankan government officials accused the UN High Commissioner for Human Rights, the UN undersecretary-general for humanitarian affairs and a UN special advisor for children and armed conflict of being "terrorists" or terrorist sympathizers.

The NGO coalition kicked off the campaign with a letter from the Sri Lankan-based NGOs, urging member states to reject Sri Lanka's bid for reelection. The Sri Lankan NGOs said that during Sri Lanka's tenure on the council, it had "presided over a grave deterioration of human rights protection" and had "used its membership in the Human Rights Council to protect itself from scrutiny."[15] They argued that rejecting Sri Lanka's bid for council membership would help to hold the Sri Lankan government "accountable for the grave state of human rights in the country."[16] A week later, the coalition sent UN ambassadors a letter signed by twenty national and international NGOs urging them to withhold their vote for Sri Lanka. Days before the election, a group of eighty-four Asian NGOs signed an open letter issued by the nongovernmental Asian Human Rights Commission, stating that "a vote for Sri Lanka is a vote for disappearances, widespread torture, extrajudicial killings and impunity. It is a vote to undermine the Human Rights Council and therefore a vote against victims of human rights the world over."[17]

The coalition successfully engaged Nobel Peace Prize winners Desmond Tutu, Jimmy Carter, and Adolfo Pérez Esquivel, who each published op-eds or statements about the council elections during the weeks leading up to the vote. Archbishop Tutu published a commentary in *The Guardian* of London, stating that Sri Lanka's human rights abuses "are among the most serious imaginable," and that "a government which tortures and kidnaps its own people has no place on the world's leading human rights body."[18] Pérez Esquivel, who won the Nobel Peace Prize in 1980 for his opposition to disappearances, extrajudicial killings, and torture by the Argentine military government, compared the history of his own country to the abuses committed by Sri Lankan government forces. In a commentary in *Página 12* in Buenos Aires, he said, "As Latin Americans know all too well, there are few crimes more horrible for a government to commit than summarily removing its own citizens from their homes and families, often late at night, never to be heard from again. . . . Latin American governments can do a great service to the people of Sri Lanka by rejecting their government's candidacy for the Human Rights Council."[19] Despite aggressive campaigning by the Sri Lankan government and its ambassador to the UN in New York, Sri Lanka failed in its bid for reelection. On May 21, 2008, the General Assembly elected Japan with 155, Bahrain with 142, South Korea with 139, and Pakistan with 114 votes. Sri Lanka received 101 votes. The coalition issued a public statement welcoming the results. "We applaud UN members for rejecting an abusive state which has used its position on the Human Rights Council not to promote human rights, but to protect itself and other violator states from scrutiny," said a coalition spokesman. "The defeat of Sri Lanka this year, and of Belarus last year, will help discourage other human rights violators from seeking or winning election to the council."[20]

2009: Azerbaijan, China, Cuba, Russia, Saudi Arabia

A challenge faced by the coalition in each election for the Human Rights Council was that many regional groups chose not to run competitive slates. Instead, the number of candidates often was equal to the number of available seats, virtually guaranteeing the election of each state running. In 2009, only twenty governments ran for the available eighteen seats, with competitive elections in only two of the five regions—Eastern Europe and Africa. Nevertheless, the coalition took public positions against the reelection of five members of the Human Rights Council: Azerbaijan, China, Cuba, Russia, and Saudi Arabia. Of the five, only Azerbaijan and Russia were running in competitive elections, competing with Hungary for the two seats available in the Eastern European region.

The coalition criticized the failure of regional groups to mount competitive elections, saying that UN member states should have the opportunity to select the best human rights proponents that each region had to offer. A spokesperson for the Asian Forum for Human Rights and Development said in a public statement that "the lack of real choice in so many regions suggests that many countries have gone back to putting politics and vote trading ahead of human rights and an effective Human Rights Council."[21]

The coalition included the Western group in its criticism. During the Bush administration, the United States had shunned the Human Rights Council, in part because of the council's repeated criticism of Israel. Once Barack Obama was elected president, many NGOs urged the United States to reverse its position and reengage with the council. Human rights advocates welcomed the decision by the United States to run for election in 2009, but were concerned when New Zealand withdrew its candidacy after the US announcement, leaving a noncompetitive slate. The United States, Belgium, and Norway ran for three seats open in the Western group.

On its website, the coalition highlighted human rights concerns in Azerbaijan, China, Cuba, Russia, and Saudi Arabia. In China, the coalition cited government harassment and prosecution of human rights defenders, repression of ethnic Tibetans and Uighers, sanctions on journalists, the use of administrative detention and "re-education-through-labor," and forced confessions and torture. It named Cuba as "the one country in Latin America that represses nearly all forms of political dissent," utilizing harassment and arbitrary arrest and detention against journalists and dissidents. It cited concerns in Russia including restrictions and attacks on civil society, abuses in the North Caucasus, racism, xenophobia, and abuse of migrant workers. In Saudi Arabia, the coalition highlighted systematic violations of the rights of women, unfair trials and arbitrary detention of thousands of people, and curbs on freedom of expression and association.[22]

The coalition focused attention on Azerbaijan in particular, highlighting its harassment and intimidation of journalists and human rights defenders, torture and ill-treatment in police custody, and detention of political prisoners. In Azerbaijan, criticizing the government could bring physical attacks, exorbitant fines, or criminal charges. In 2008 alone, there were forty-nine incidents involving physical or verbal assaults against journalists. Only eleven of the cases were investigated by the government, and only one brought to trial. Several journalists were convicted on terrorism and other spurious charges for reporting government abuses and were sentenced to up to ten years in prison.[23]

A month ahead of the elections, a group of some twenty Azeri human rights and democracy advocates, professors, lawyers, and journalists wrote to members of the UN General Assembly, urging states to withhold their vote from Azerbaijan. They said that in the three years that Azerbaijan had served on the Human Rights Council, "the human rights situation has gotten worse, not better." They addressed their own precarious situation in the country: "We, as journalists and human rights defenders, face a constant risk that the government will bring politically motivated criminal or civil charges against [us]. Harassment, intimidation, and physical attacks on civil society have become common. Torture in detention is widespread. The government's unwillingness to address and prevent these abuses means near-total impunity for the perpetrators and lack of justice for us."[24]

Approximately five weeks before the election, coalition members began meeting one-on-one with ambassadors and other government representatives to the UN in New York to discuss the records of candidate states and why they should withhold their votes from the five countries identified by the coalition. By the time of the elections, the coalition had met individually with ninety-two governments. A week before the election, members of the coalition wrote to UN member states, highlighting Azerbaijan's attacks on press freedom, harassment and intimidation of human rights defenders and trade unionists, the detention of political prisoners, and the widespread use of torture in police facilities and prisons.[25]

The day before the election, the *New York Times* ran an op-ed from Václav Havel, the former president of the Czech Republic, highlighting the flawed elections and lack of competition. The op-ed was widely read, circulated, and quoted, including by the news media. "Imagine an election where the results are largely preordained and a number of candidates are widely recognized as unqualified," Havel said. "Any supposedly democratic ballot conducted in this way would be considered a farce."[26] Drawing on his own experience, he said, "Like the citizens of Azerbaijan, China, Cuba, Russia, and Saudi Arabia, I know what it is like to live in a country where the state controls public discourse, suppresses opposition and severely curtails freedom of expression. It is thus doubly dismaying for me to see the willingness of democracies in Latin America and Asia to sit by and watch the council further lose its credibility and respect."[27] In the May 12, 2009, election, Azerbaijan suffered a humiliating defeat. With only eighty-nine votes, it failed to even reach the ninety-seven–vote threshold that was necessary for election. As expected, the other targets of the campaign—China, Cuba, Russia, and Saudi Arabia—were all reelected, although Saudi Arabia, China, and Cuba came in at the very bottom of their respective regional slates. The coalition put out an immediate statement following the election. It lauded the result on Azerbaijan, which it called "a wake-up call" to Azerbaijan to improve its record and a hopeful sign to Azerbaijani human rights defenders. The statement also highlighted the African group's first competitive elections, calling it an important milestone.

The coalition continued to draw attention to the lack of competition in key regions, arguing that if there had been competitive elections, China, Saudi Arabia, and Cuba could have been defeated, particularly since the election's secret ballot could shield states from reprisals from powerful states such as China. A spokesperson from Corporación Humanas Centro Regional de Derechos Humanos y Justicia de Género criticized Latin American countries for allowing Cuba to "stroll into the council with no reforms or concrete steps toward change."[28]

The elections received extensive international news coverage, in part because of the United States' first-time election to the council. Spokespersons for the coalition were frequently quoted, and the lack of noncompetitive slates was repeatedly highlighted. Apart from the United States, the countries most often mentioned in the media reports were those that the coalition had cited for their appalling human rights records. For these states, the many negative media references were painful and embarrassing, despite their election victories.

Lessons Learned

The campaign achieved remarkable success by defeating three abusive governments for election, shining a spotlight on violations by governments that ran unopposed, and challenging the practice of noncompetitive elections. The campaign also created a deterrent effect for abusive governments considering running for election. In 2010, Iran announced that it would run again. But as soon as the coalition launched a new campaign opposing Iran's candidacy, supported by Iranian groups and notable figures including Iranian Nobel Peace Prize laureate Shirin Ebadi, Iran withdrew its bid. In 2011, pressure from the United States and a broad range of NGOs prompted Syria to withdraw its candidacy shortly before the elections. Despite its victories, however, the coalition faced a number of barriers, including lack of cohesion among local and regional NGO partners, vote trading by UN member states, and particularly, regional blocs that refused to mount competitive elections.

In the case of Azerbaijan, Sri Lanka, and Belarus, local NGOs were unified in their opposition to their countries' election to the Human Rights Council, but as noted in other cases such as Bahrain, local NGOs could not reach agreement about what position to take regarding their government's candidacy. When Egypt ran in 2007, the same year as Belarus, local NGOs were also not able to reach a consensus about what position to take. When Cuba ran in 2009, Cuban NGOs and dissidents were strongly involved in the campaign opposing Cuba's candidacy, but regional Latin American NGOs were reluctant to get involved. According to Fassihian, "It was really frustrating. In part the regional groups weren't going to beat up on Cuba because of the politics surrounding the embargo. They didn't see the value of getting Cuba off the council. Cuban organizations were so disappointed when Cuba was reelected. They had worked really hard and dissidents on the inside had really put their lives at risk. They were like, 'What happened?'"[29]

At the United Nations, member states have a long practice of promising each other votes for various positions in exchange for backing for other posts or votes on issues. This was a continuing problem during the elections for the

Human Rights Council. During each campaign, vote trading was common, and many governments were pressured to reveal their intentions and pledge their votes to particular candidates. While the coalition urged governments as a matter of national policy to support competitive elections and not trade votes, few did so. As of 2011, only Mexico and the United States had made a public commitment not to trade votes or disclose their voting intentions for the Human Rights Council.

One of the campaign's biggest challenges was member states' reluctance to compete with each other and the decisions by regional groups to put forward closed slates. Some states argued that competitive elections for the Human Rights Council should be avoided because they are too "humiliating" or "traumatic" for states who are defeated. For example, in 2008, Spain lost election by only one vote after several rounds of voting. Such defeats are considered particularly difficult after a state invests significant resources in their campaign or are the only state not elected in a region. Advocates saw little improvement in achieving more competitive slates as the campaign progressed from year to year. "We're definitely on a bad trajectory," said Dokhi Fassihian. "From what we're seeing, it's getting worse and worse."[30] Moss agreed and reflected that in some ways the campaign was a victim of its own triumphs. "In 2008, we killed Sri Lanka's bid. But the price of our success was a closed slate in Asia the next year." He also pointed to the negative impact of the United States's unopposed run in 2009: "Let's not underestimate how damaging the US running unopposed was to our argument for competitive slates. The US was always a big proponent of quality of membership on the council. And running unopposed was completely unnecessary for the US to get elected."[31]

Campaign activists said they would continue pushing for competitive slates, and when abusive governments announce they are running, they would advocate for other states with better records to submit their candidacies. Advocates discovered this often involves working far in advance of a particular election. For example, to create a competitive slate in Asia in 2009, Asian NGOs lobbied Nepal and Maldives, urging them to put their candidacies forward. However, the initiative was too late as the Asian group had already made its decision in December 2008 regarding its slate.

Despite the hurdles they faced, the campaign was able to have a demonstrable impact on the votes of UN member states and the overall dynamic of the elections to the Human Rights Council. According to Fassihian, "We used a combination of civil society opposition, campaigning, and the competitive slates, and the abusers were defeated."[32]

Active engagement from NGOs within the countries concerned was at the heart of the campaign's strategy, and ultimately, its success. Coalition members believed that the positions, letters, and statements from national civil society and dissidents had profound impact and made the campaign much more credible. "If we were asked why we were opposing some candidates and not others, we would respond that the campaign was supporting the wishes of local civil society," said Dokhi Fassihian. "We told diplomats that if civil society was opposing the candidacy of their own country, that member states should also consider opposing that candidate."[33] According to Elizabeth Sepper, another coalition member representing Human Rights Watch, the letters from local NGOs were particularly influential. "Ambassadors are more convinced by voices from within those countries than they are from us saying the same thing."[34] Maintaining a cross-regional coalition was extremely helpful to avoid accusations of Western imperialism.

A second important aspect of the campaign was op-eds and statements from respected international figures. Pieces from Václav Havel, Desmond Tutu, Jimmy Carter, and Adolfo Pérez Esquivel published shortly before the elections were widely read and discussed among UN diplomats. Moss felt that the statements had a particularly powerful impact in the campaign against Sri Lanka in 2008: "The media stuff was really important. Sri Lanka spent a couple million dollars on their campaign. Their foreign minister came to New York a couple of times to lobby and their ambassador really put himself into it. But what really killed their bid in the end was the trifecta of Desmond Tutu, Jimmy Carter, and Adolfo Pérez Esquivel."[35]

A third important strategy was to highlight abusive states regardless of whether they were running for a contested seat. Prior to 2009, the coalition only campaigned against countries running in competitive elections. However, in 2009, it made the strategic decision to campaign against China, Cuba, and Saudi Arabia, who were all running in noncompetitive elections. Coalition members agreed that it was important to campaign against such states, since campaigns that only targeted states running in competitive fields would create a disincentive for states to support competitive elections. Elizabeth Sepper said that some states claimed that China had engineered a noncompetitive Asian slate in large part to try to escape criticism on its own record. She said, "That says to me that we made the right decision to campaign against them. China never thought they wouldn't be reelected, but they put resources into their campaign because we made them nervous."[36]

The coalition's vocal criticism of clean slates also "hit a huge nerve, especially with the Western Europeans," said Sepper. "Everyone was talking about it at the UN. It had huge media impact. Every journalist picked up on it because we hammered this point. Some of the wires made it a centerpiece of their reporting."[37] Even with closed slates, the campaign created a deterrent effect that may discourage some of the most abusive states from running. For example, Moss observed an effort in the African region: "If not to put the best foot forward, at least to not put the worst foot forward, for example by allowing Sudan or Zimbabwe to run."[38]

Fourth, the documentation the coalition provided on abusive states was particularly valuable to the campaign, particularly when presented in one-on-one meetings. Several representatives said they were surprised at the shallow knowledge that many UN ambassadors had regarding the human rights records of candidates for the Human Rights Council. Dokhi Fassihian participated in dozens of individual meetings with UN diplomats during the campaigns. She said:

> The missions are just not able to keep up with the human rights developments in all these countries so many of them appreciate it when you come in to talk with them. Sometimes they know generally, but they didn't know the extent of what was happening. But when you sit down with them and go over it all, some of them go "wow." You can feel it sometimes that it's very new information for them. You can see that you've changed their perspectives and that they are going to go back and do what they can to influence positions at the capital level.[39]

One African government told a coalition member that they had changed several of their votes at the last moment as a specific result of the coalition's advocacy and the materials it had provided.[40] Other governments praised the coalition for providing profiles on five countries during the 2009 election and encouraged it to profile all of the candidates, not only those that the coalition opposed.

Summing up the effect of the campaign, one coalition member reflected:

> Letters from dissidents, letters from civil society from within the country, that has probably the most powerful impact. But that alone is probably not enough.

It's important to have those take the lead, but it's important to have the global human rights community support them. Different governments react differently. Some governments don't take their own civil society groups very seriously but will listen to the international NGOs. . . . All of the components of the campaign are important—the public figures, the statements from civil society, the one-on-one meetings. It all came together.[41]

The campaign was not able to prevent all abusive governments from election to the council, and closed slates plagued their efforts. The continuing weaknesses of the council election process were highlighted again in 2011, when Syria ran for election as part of a closed Asian slate of four countries. During the months leading up to the election, the Syrian government carried out a brutal crackdown against peaceful antigovernment protesters who had taken to the streets in cities across the country during the Arab Uprising. Government security forces killed hundreds of protesters and arbitrarily arrested and detained hundreds more. In late April, the Human Rights Council sharply criticized the Syrian government, condemning the use of lethal violence and asking the High Commissioner for Human Rights to investigate. Scores of NGOs wrote to governments, urging them to call on Syria to withdraw its bid. The US government also led a diplomatic push to block Syria's candidacy. Less than two weeks before the scheduled election, Syria finally withdrew, with Kuwait taking its place on the ballot. For many NGOs, however, the fact that a country could be censured by the Human Rights Council one month and be on the ballot for election to the body the next was a travesty. A representative from the Heritage Foundation in Washington asked, "Do we really have to wait until a government is gunning down its own citizens in the streets before its membership on the council is deemed unacceptable?"[42]

Despite some progress, the Human Rights Council continued to be plagued by many of the weaknesses of its predecessor. Abusive countries that were elected continued to protect their own records and shield other abusers, as illustrated by the elimination of several country-specific special rapporteurs and the May 2009 Human Rights Council resolution that failed to recognized government abuses during the Sri Lankan war. An Amnesty International researcher working on Sri Lanka said, "We see the Human Rights Council not fully recovering from the faults and weaknesses of the commission. We need to be cautious of putting too much confidence in this body given that it is susceptible to voting blocs that can counter human rights for their own self-interest."[43]

Working within the constraints of the election process, however, the coalition effectively raised the stakes for membership in the council with demonstrable results. It combined the assets of local NGOs and civil society who spoke powerfully and credibly regarding the abuses of their own governments, international NGOs who were able to deploy advocacy personnel for intensive lobbying of UN missions in New York, and international public figures who gained significant attention to the elections through personal statements in influential media outlets. It signaled to other governments that continued vote trading and noncompetitive elections would be met with criticism. It kept some of the worst human rights abusers off the council, deterred others from running, and put all governments on notice that they would not be able to run for election to the Human Rights Council without significant public attention to their human rights records.

Chapter 4

Working with UN Special Rapporteurs to Promote Human Rights

I always said to NGOs and to governments that I have no power at all, and my impact would depend entirely on how much my findings and recommendations resonated with civil society and parts of government. . . . special rapporteurs by definition aren't in a position to follow-up, so we hope that we have civil society strong enough to do so.
—*Philip Alston, special rapporteur on extrajudicial, summary or arbitrary executions*[1]

SOME FORTY-FIVE INDEPENDENT EXPERTS and working groups monitor human rights for the United Nations. Under the auspices of the UN Human Rights Council, these "special procedures" address country situations such as Burundi, Myanmar, Somalia, and Syria, and an expansive range of themes, including torture, extrajudicial executions, extreme poverty, violence against women, the right to education and to food, and the human rights of migrants.[2] In 2010, the special procedures conducted field missions to forty-eight countries, issuing reports of their findings and recommendations for action by the governments concerned.[3] On the basis of information received from NGOs and others, in 2011 they sent governments in 131 countries more than six hundred urgent appeals or other communications regarding alleged human rights abuses.[4]

The fundamental purpose of the special procedures is to monitor and report on human rights violations and to recommend ways to promote and protect human rights. The first special rapporteurs were established in the 1980s to respond to civil and political rights violations. The Commission on Human Rights (predecessor to the Human Rights Council) created the mandate for the special rapporteur on extrajudicial, summary, or arbitrary executions in 1982, the special rapporteur on torture in 1985, and special rapporteur on freedom of religion in 1986. In the 1990s, the commission created a series of mandates focusing on specific country situations, including special rapporteurs for Myanmar, Somalia, Sudan, Cambodia, the Occupied Palestinian Territories, and Haiti.[5]

From 2000 to 2011, the number of special procedures more than doubled, as UN member states created twenty-four new mandates. In contrast to the previous two decades, where special procedures focused primarily on country situations and civil and political rights, many of the new mandates stressed economic, social, and cultural rights (including the right to housing, food, health, and water) and emerging issues such as human rights and transnational corporations and the protection of human rights while countering terrorism. Increasingly, governments refused to establish new mandates focused on individual countries, with only two such mandates created between 2000 and 2010—on Burundi and the Democratic People's Republic of Korea. The trend against country mandates appeared to turn in 2011, when an additional three were created—on Syria, Iran, and Cote d'Ivoire.

By January 2012, ninety countries had issued "standing invitations" to the UN's special procedures, indicating a commitment to accept a request from any thematic special procedure for a visit.[6] In cases where no standing invitation had been issued, special procedures sought specific invitations from the government concerned before making visits to assess human rights conditions. Typically, special rapporteurs make one or two field visits each year. The Office of the High Commissioner for Human Rights in Geneva provides limited staff support; the special rapporteurs are not compensated, ostensibly to ensure their autonomy; and few have more than one staff assistant.

The Brookings Institution conducted an in-depth study in 2010 to assess the work of the special procedures and the impact of their activities on the implementation of human rights norms.[7] The assessment identified a number of challenges and shortcomings to the system, including states' resistance to cooperating with the mechanisms, back-room deals to select experts that are not always well-suited to their mandates, and chronic underfunding. Brookings' overall assessment, however, was that the system of special procedures represents one of the most effective tools of the international human rights system. The study concluded that the experts are "catalysts for rights," by shaping the content of international human rights norms, shining a light on states' compliance with these norms, and influencing the behavior of states.[8]

The Brooking study found that among the strategies used by the special procedures, country visits were the most effective in creating change. Such visits establish facts, identify violations, and recommend appropriate remedies. When conducted skillfully, they can motivate key actors both inside and outside government—including government officials, politicians, civil society, and the media—to take up and act on key human rights issues. In contrast, the study concluded that communications from the special procedures—letters of allegation and urgent appeals—serve an important role in establishing a written record of victims' complaints and in limited cases, generate positive outcomes, but are generally ineffective.[9]

The special procedures rely on nongovernmental sources for the vast majority of their information on human rights abuses and for particular guidance in conducting country visits. According to Manfred Nowak, the special rapporteur on torture, "We would be lost and totally ineffective without NGOs."[10]

This chapter explores examples of collaboration between NGOs and special procedures that resulted in concrete human rights improvements, including a dramatic decline in the rate of extrajudicial executions in the Philippines; a national campaign and subsequent government agreement to address housing rights for Quilombos communities in Alcântara in northeastern Brazil; and the closure of the Al-Jafr detention center in Jordan because of its routine use of torture.

Extrajudicial Executions in the Philippines

In the Philippines, government security forces have killed hundreds of people suspected of belonging to "front" organizations for the Communist Party of the Philippines and its armed group, the New People's Army. According to Karapatan, a Philippine NGO, at least 1,205 individuals were killed in extrajudicial executions between January 2001 and July 2010.[11] The victims included clergy, students, members of political parties and civil society organizations, union activists, journalists, and agricultural reform activists. Victims of extrajudicial killings were shot by gunman while in their homes, traveling by car or motorcycle, or walking down the street. In many cases, the victims had no involvement in New People's Army operations, but had been placed on lists of "communist sympathizers" by members of the military based on their involvement with local civil society groups.

Rates of extrajudicial killings increased after President Gloria Macapagal Arroyo took office in 2001 and often took place in the context of the military's counterinsurgency operations against the New People's Army. Major General Jovito Palparan, who commanded counterinsurgency operations in Eastern Visayas and Central Luzon, denied direct responsibility for the killings, but called them "necessary incidents" and publicly noted that the executions were "helping" the armed forces by eliminating individuals who opposed the government.[12]

In 2006, President Arroyo declared an "all-out war" against the New People's Army, which was believed to have some seven thousand fighters. She gave the armed forces of the Philippines two years to eradicate the group, which government officials said posed the "most potent threat" to the Philippines' national security. That same year, the rate of extrajudicial executions rose sharply. Local NGOs estimated that 235 people were killed in 2006, nearly double the rate of killings during the years between 2001 and 2004.[13]

Domestic and international criticism over the killings mounted, prompting President Arroyo to establish the Task Force Utig, an investigative body of the Philippines National Police charged with solving ten specific cases, and a commission headed by a former Supreme Court Justice, Jose Melo, to investigate extrajudicial killings more generally. However, when the Melo Commission issued its report in early 2007, President Arroyo initially refused to release it publicly. The commission concluded that while extrajudicial executions were not part of a "sanctioned policy," evidence pointed to elements within the military, including General Palparan, as responsible for the killings by tolerating and even encouraging them.[14]

In February 2007, Philip Alston, the special rapporteur on extrajudicial, summary, or arbitrary executions conducted a field mission to the Philippines to investigate the killings and the government's response. Cookie Diokno, a local activist with the Free Legal Assistance Group, said, "We invited all the groups to a meeting to discuss his visit and what we were going to do. Everyone understood the possible impact it could have. No one was naïve enough to believe the killings could be solved, but we believed his presence and investigation could put a spotlight on the killings."[15] Alston and his team traveled to Manila, Baguio, and Davao City, meeting with government officials and civil society representatives from across the political spectrum and interviewing dozens of witnesses to extrajudicial executions. Civil society organizations advised Alston on places to visit and provided him with detailed dossiers on 271 extrajudicial killings. During the mission, he and his team conducted interviews with witnesses to fifty-seven incidents involving ninety-six extrajudicial executions.[16]

Alston concluded that perpetrators of the killings, primarily members of the military, intentionally targeted leftist leaders, used torture and interrogations of others to ascertain the leaders' whereabouts, and conducted vilification campaigns in order to create a culture of fear in the community. In a press statement at the end of his mission, he said that the impact of the killings "intimidates vast numbers of civil society actors, it sends a message of vulnerability to all but the most well connected, and it severely undermines the political discourse which is central to a resolution of the problems confronting this country."[17]

Alston also documented killings of journalists and the operations of a death squad in Davao City, which shot and stabbed suspected criminals, street children, and gang members, often in broad daylight. Between 1998 and 2007, civil society groups documented more than five hundred killings attributed to the death squad.[18] According to Diokno, "Before, no one was talking about the killing of common criminals in Davao. We call ourselves a democratic society, but we are not. There are some categories of society that it is okay to get rid of. What I appreciate is that Alston brought forward the fact that you can't kill someone regardless of who they are. He also placed on the table the responsibility of the government to do something about it."[19]

Shortly before leaving the Philippines, Alston met with President Arroyo. He said that she asked him, "What can I do?" Alston said he told her, "It's very simple. Just tell the armed forces to stop killing. You have to send a message."[20] He repeated the point in a public press conference in Manila, telling the media, "I would like a statement from the very top, from the President, from the Secretary of Defense, and certainly from the [armed forces] chief of staff saying that extrajudicial killings will not be tolerated."[21] He also pressed the government—successfully—to release the Melo report. Alston sharply criticized the armed forces of the Philippines, saying it remained "in a state of almost total denial" regarding the killings. He found that the perpetrators enjoyed virtual impunity. Witnesses to killings were systematically harassed and intimidated, and no one responsible for any of the killings of leftist activists had ever been convicted. Only six cases involving journalists had resulted in convictions.

Alston's press conference at the end of his mission generated enormous media coverage in the Philippines. According to Diokno, "The most significant element of Alston's visit was his quotes to the press. He had tremendous impact with the media. The average Filipino has lost faith in government, police, and other authorities, so the media is a very powerful force and really shapes public opinion. The extensive media coverage was tremendous. People began to see the killings in a different light, it became a real issue in the country. The government had no choice but to respond."[22]

Alston issued an interim report in March 2007, shortly after his mission, and a final report in April 2008. He recommended that the government act

---

Profile: Renaldo "Naldo" Labrador

Renaldo Labrador was a thirty-nine-year-old farmer who lived near Davao City in Mindanao. He was known to his friends and family as "Naldo." With his wife Leonisa, he had a ten-year-old son and two younger daughters, aged four and eight. He was also a member of the local Paquibato District Peasant Alliance (PADIPA), a chapter of the Peasant Movement of the Philippines.

On September 3, 2010, Reynaldo spent the day driving a passenger motorcycle. After arriving home, he rested upstairs while his daughters ate dinner and his wife did laundry. Around 7:30 p.m., two men approached the house. Leonisa recognized one of the men as Berto Repe, a member of CAFGU, the Philippine paramilitary force. The men told Leonisa that they had a document that they wanted to give to Reynaldo. Leonisa offered to give it to him, but the men insisted on delivering it to Reynaldo themselves.

Leonisa said that Repe made a sign to her ten-year-old son, drawing his finger across his mouth, to tell him to stay quiet. The other man then went upstairs, where Reynaldo was resting. "Then I heard three gunshots," said Leonisa. "My son went and saw his father with blood all over him. My children and I left the house, calling to our neighbors for help."[1]

Meanwhile, the gunmen escaped. When Leonisa returned to the house later, she found the note the assailants apparently had intended to deliver to Reynaldo. It said, "Demonyo ka! Hiposon ka!" [You are evil! You will be dealt with!] She gave the note to the police, and several witnesses identified Repe as one of the men involved in the killing.

to eliminate extrajudicial executions from its counterinsurgency operations, direct all military officers to stop making public statements linking political or civil society actors to armed insurgent groups, and ensure a significant number of convictions in extrajudicial execution cases.[23]

Alston's visit appeared to catalyze progress, most notably a dramatic drop in the rate of extrajudicial killings. Local NGOs documented one hundred killings in 2007 and ninety in 2008, compared to two hundred thirty-five in 2006, the year before Alston's visit.[24] In July 2007, the chief justice of the Supreme Court organized a national summit on extrajudicial killings and forced disappearances. The summit was the first official initiative to bring all branches of government and civil society together to discuss extrajudicial executions. The National Commission on Human Rights

After Reynaldo's murder, KARAPATAN, an NGO working to stop extrajudicial executions, lobbied the local government to act on a recent spate of killings. Their activity resulted in a hearing by the city's Human Rights Committee less than a week after Reynaldo's death. KARAPATAN reported, however, that soldiers visited Reynaldo's family before the hearing to intimidate them and dissuade them from participating.[2] Fearful of further reprisals, Leonisa decided to move her family away from the area. A month later, soldiers visited the house again, asking neighbors where Leonisa and her children were.

Members of the New People's Army killed Berto Repe in November 2010. As of mid-2011, the other assailant responsible for Reynaldo's death had not been identified.[3]

1. Human Rights Watch interview with Leonisa Labrador, Davao City, Philippines, March 10, 2011, cited in Human Rights Watch, "No Justice Just Adds to the Pain": Killings, Disappearances and Impunity in the Philippines (New York: Human Rights Watch, 2011), 34.

2. KARAPATAN, KMP Member Shot to Death in Front of his Wife in Paquibato District Davao City, Philippines, September 17, 2010. Available at http://www.karapatan.org/node/385 (accessed July 25, 2011).

3. Human Rights Watch, "No Justice Just Adds to the Pain": Killings, Disappearances and Impunity in the Philippines, 33–35.

began an independent investigation of the death squad in Davao City. Several senior military officers, including the armed forces chief of staff, made public statements affirming human rights and pledged to hold members of the military accountable for violations.[25] Between 2007 and 2009, several individuals were convicted for extrajudicial killings, including a former police superintendent.[26]

In an April 2009 follow-up report, Alston noted the dramatic reduction in the number of extrajudicial executions of leftist activists and other steps forward, but expressed concern regarding the government's failure to implement many of his recommendations. He said that while continued rates of extrajudicial executions were significantly lower than before, they remained a "cause for great alarm." He particularly highlighted an increase in the numbers of death squad killings in Davao City, where as many as twenty-eight murders took place in the first month of 2009 alone, stating that the situation had "significantly worsened."[27] The month after Alston issued his follow-up report, President Arroyo ordered the Department of the Interior and Local Government and the police to "get to the bottom" of the Davao death-squad killings.[28] The police chief, Jesus Verzosa, instructed local police chiefs to investigate those implicated in the killings, and in 2010, the office of the ombudsman ordered the preventative suspension of twenty-six police officers for their failure to stop alleged death-squad killings while serving as station commanders. The National Commission on Human Rights conducted public hearings on the death squads, and the chairperson promised to investigate the killings "for as long as it takes."[29]

Alston cited NGOs as essential actors in carrying out his mandate. "I couldn't have done half of what I did without them. At every stage, as soon as I agreed on a mission to a place, the first port of call would be both local and international NGOs."[30] In the case of the Philippines, Alston spent approximately half of his mission meetings with NGOs from across the political spectrum and credited the extensive and high-quality documentation on extrajudicial killings that he received from civil society groups as enabling him to produce a report that was much more detailed than any of his previous reports.[31] He said, "It was a pretty amazing mission in terms of information. . . . I received incredibly detailed dossiers from NGOs on both the left and the right. They are very sophisticated. From the days of martial law they have been honing their arts. As a result, I brought back three to four feet of files, and had a better database than anyone in the Philippines."[32] His mission also built on growing pressure brought by outside governments. Filipino groups had been meeting with diplomats from Europe, Canada, and Australia to discuss the extrajudicial killings.[33] As a result, the issue was being raised with the Philippine government at high levels by foreign governments.

Although extrajudicial executions remained a serious problem in the Philippines, Alston's field mission, statements, and reports, coupled with growing international pressure, prompted both government action and tangible improvements. Alston said, "It was clear that I was able to leverage the public role of a UN rapporteur and the timing just happened to be right. As a result, there was a very big impact on government policy in the Philippines."[34]

Land Rights of *Quilombos* Communities in Brazil

In Brazil, more than thirty-five hundred *quilombos* communities are found across the country, consisting of descendents of African slaves that were brought to Brazil for forced labor during the colonial period. The communities have occupied and managed their land collectively for more than a century, relying on community-based agriculture, fishing, and the use of natural resources for their livelihood. For the *quilombos*, the land and its resources also represented a critical aspect of social and cultural cohesion.

In 1986, the Brazilian government began forcibly evicting members of *quilombos* communities in Alcântara, a municipality in the northeast of the country, to make way for a space launch center. Nearly 1,350 people were forcibly relocated from the Alcântara *quilombos*. Most received neither financial compensation nor title to their new lands. Although the federal Land Statute required that Brazilians forced to resettle by the government would be given thirty hectares of land, the relocated *quilombos* families were given only fifteen hectares of land. In other parts of Brazil, *quilombos* communities faced displacement by farmers, mining companies, hydroelectric power plants, and other infrastructure projects.

In 1988 a new Brazilian constitution guaranteed the *quilombos* communities property rights over the territories they had traditionally occupied,[35] and a 2003 federal decree established a process to identify, demarcate, title, and register the lands.[36] Despite these legal protections, the titling process was lengthy and complicated. Between 1995 and 2009, *quilombos* communities filed 1,054 applications, but the government awarded only 106 land titles.[37]

To resist evictions and advocate for their land rights, *quilombos* representatives from every state formed the National Coordination body for Quilombos Communities (CONAQ). Local *quilombos* communities worked with local and international NGOs and reached out to national and international human rights mechanisms for support in advocating for their rights.[38] In 2001, many of the affected *quilombos* communities and their NGO supporters presented a petition to the InterAmerican Commission on Human Rights, setting out allegations of human rights abuses by the government of Brazil and the government of Maranhao against the evicted *quilombos* members. In 2003, the Centre on Housing Rights and Evictions (COHRE), an international NGO based in Geneva, carried out a joint mission to Alcântara with Brazil's National Rapporteur on the Right to Adequate Housing and Urban Land. During the mission, the National Rapporteur held a public hearing with the affected communities. COHRE also worked with local NGOs to produce a report on the situation, which they launched later that year during a national meeting of *quilombos* communities.[39] It also shared information regarding the *quilombos* with UN special rapporteurs, especially Miloon Kothari, an Indian architect who served as the UN special rapporteur on adequate housing as a component of the right to an adequate standard of living.

In late May and early June of 2004, Kothari conducted a field mission to Brazil, visiting both rural and urban areas across Brazil, including *quilombos* communities in Alcântara and one of the resettled communities. The National Rapporteur and Brazilian civil society groups organized seven civic forums during Kothari's visit, including a public hearing in Alcântara with representatives of *quilombos* communities, NGOs, and reporters. During Kothari's visit, COHRE and the National Coordination of Quilombos Communities (CONAQ) launched a national campaign calling for official land titles for all *quilombos* communities. As one of the campaign's first activities, civil society groups, national and international NGOs signed a joint declaration on the human rights of Alcântara's *quilombos* communities. COHRE described the statement as a "manifesto" against the forced evictions and for the *quilombos* communities' right to land and adequate housing.[40]

Kothari issued his report in February 2005. Based on his interviews with resettled *quilombos* members, he concluded that the relocation sites constituted "a flagrant example of short-term solutions becoming a long-term problem." He found that while the *quilombos* inhabitants had been self-sufficient in their traditional community where they had access to fishing and fertile land, once resettled, they had become dependent on the government. He stated that relocation could only be justified in rare cases and must be done in full consultation with the affected communities. In his recommendations, he urged the government to follow international law and the human rights provisions of the Brazilian constitution in addressing the housing and living conditions of the *quilombos* communities.[41]

Shortly after Kothari's visit, Brazil's president issued a decree establishing an interministerial working group for the sustainable development of the municipality of Alcântara.[42] A subgroup of the working group was to specifically focus on the environment, housing, and land issues. Kothari noted the development in his report, asked to be kept informed of the new working group's progress, and urged it to respect the entitlements of the *quilombos* communities and avoid any further forced evictions.[43] In 2005, the Interministerial Working Group held a seminar in Alcântara to discuss sustainable development of the municipality. During the event, federal government officials stated that there would not be any further forced displacement of local communities, and that in the exceptional case in which it might be necessary, it would be carried out in compliance with national and international human rights law.[44]

COHRE urged other special rapporteurs with mandates related to the *quilombos'* plight to take on the issue. In 2005, the UN special rapporteur on contemporary forms of racism, racial discrimination, xenophobia, and related intolerance, Mr. Doudou Diéne, conducted a field mission to Brazil. In his 2006 report, he highlighted violent attacks and death threats against *quilombos* and made a series of recommendations, urging the government to conduct a census to assess *quilombos'* living conditions, to ensure better security for the communities and their leaders, and to guarantee *quilombos* with adequate food, health care, housing, and education. He also urged the government to "proceed urgently with recognition and handing over of property titles to *quilombos*."[45] During Diéne's visit, COHRE launched another report on the forced evictions and violations of the right to adequate housing.[46] In 2010, COHRE again engaged the special rapporteur on the right to adequate housing regarding a legal challenge to the 2003 decree regulating the granting of land titles to *quilombos* communities. The special rapporteur in turn issued a statement affirming the *quilombos'* rights to have access to land and natural resources.[47]

In July 2010, Brazilian President Lula da Silva signed the Statute of Racial Equality, which guaranteed the right to preservation of *quilombola* customs and the creation of special sources of public financing for *quilombola* communities and codified their property rights as set out in the 1988 constitution. While *quilombos* leaders and their allies felt some progress had been made, many felt frustrated that the pace was far too slow. Just before the Statute of Racial Equality was signed, one *quilombos* advocate said, "Look, we don't have many advances. We have a Constitution from 1988 where the right to title of *quilombola* territories was guaranteed. We are now in 2010 and are still debating how to carry out these procedures."[48]

An academic who has worked with *quilombos* communities in Alcântara agreed that progress was "precarious" but nonetheless believed that the role of the special rapporteurs had been helpful: "[Kothari's] report became part of a series of international allies and international pieces of evidence that *quilombos* have been able to marshal, along with court cases, ILO Convention 169,[49] and a series of international and institutional precedents that people have been able to mobilize locally. It has been helpful to social movements in Alcântara and probably has moved the ball forward."[50]

Torture in Jordan's Al-Jafr Detention Center

In Jordan, prison guards and other officials used torture against detainees in the country's prisons and detention facilities. Allegations included torture by the General Intelligence Directorate against terrorism suspects, by the Criminal Investigations Department to extract confessions during routine criminal investigations and against detainees in Jordan's prisons and pretrial detention facilities, including the Al-Jafr Correction and Rehabilitation Centre, an isolated facility located in the desert 250 kilometers from Amman.

Jordan's National Center for Human Rights issued several reports from 2004 through 2006, citing beatings and torture in Jordan's rehabilitation centers, and sent a memorandum to the prime minister demanding legislative and procedural measures to combat torture.[51] The organization received more than two hundred and fifty complaints of torture against government security forces in 2004 and seventy complaints of torture and mistreatment from detainees during 2005. In two periodic reports focusing on prison conditions in Jordan, the center specifically cited torture at Al-Jafr and recommended that the facility be closed immediately.[52] A local NGO, the Liberties Committee, also recommended that the Al-Jafr center be shut down. During visits to six different prisons in 2005, the Liberties Committee found conditions at Al-Jafr to be particularly bad. The organization reported that "inmates complained of general beating and insults and of being asked to kiss the ground of the prison [and] . . . to take off their clothes and have cold water poured over them."[53] Amnesty International also reported repeatedly on torture in Jordan.[54] The organization provided information to the special rapporteur on torture, Manfred Nowak, urging him to conduct a mission to Jordan and visit the Al-Jafr facility.[55]

In December 2005, Nowak requested a visit to Jordan. The Jordanian government responded with an invitation in April 2006, and the visit took place in June 2006. Nowak met with senior government officials, including the minister for foreign affairs, the minister of justice, minister of interior, and director of the public security directorate. He also met with the National Center for Human Rights, NGOs, and lawyers and visited six detention facilities, including Al -Jafr. Nowak concluded that the practice of torture was widespread in Jordan, that there was a general lack of awareness of the seriousness of torture, and that there was "total impunity" for torture and ill-treatment in the country.[56] No Jordanian official had ever been prosecuted under Jordan's penal law for torture, and all the heads of security forces and detention facilities that Nowak visited denied any knowledge of torture, even when presented with substantiated allegations.

Nowak singled out Al-Jafr in his report as a "punishment center," where detainees were routinely beaten and subjected to physical punishment that amounted to torture. At the prison, which had a capacity of 320 inmates, Nowak conducted private interviews with sixteen detainees. He reported that "virtually every detainee described the treatment meted out by prison staff in Al-Jafr as humiliating and brutal."[57] Staff beat prisoners with electrical cables, tree branches, and water pipes; hung prisoners upside-down with a stick under their knees in a position called *farruj* ("grilled chicken"); hung prisoners for long periods of time from the wrists tied to metal rings in a wall; and forced prisoners to eat food from a guard's shoes.[58] Prisoners described a "welcoming committee" of up to twenty officers that would force newly arrived detainees to strip to their underwear and then beat them for long periods with batons and electrical cables while the detainees were still handcuffed. The officers would revive detainees that lost consciousness with cold water and then beat them again.[59]

"Al-Jafr was one of the worst places I've seen," said Nowak. "It was pure intimidation and punishment."[60] Based on his findings, Nowak recommended that Al-Jafr be closed and that criminal charges be brought against the director of the facility and other officers responsible for torture. Pressure mounted as Amnesty International published a report on torture in Jordan a month after Nowak's visit,[61] and the National Centre for Human Rights published its fourth periodical report on conditions in Jordan's prisons, stating that the number of torture violations found by the organization during a May 2006 visit to Al-Jafr required "an immediate and urgent closing to this prison."[62] In December 2006, just as Nowak was finalizing his report to the UN Human Rights Council, King Abdullah issued a directive to the government ordering the closure of Al-Jafr.

Lessons Learned

In Jordan, the Philippines, and Brazil, local and international NGOs had documented human rights abuses, published reports, and worked to bring violations to the attention of policymakers prior to the involvement of the special rapporteurs. These efforts had already achieved incremental progress, including the initiation of investigations into extrajudicial executions in the Philippines and Brazil's federal decree establishing a process to grant title to *quilombos* for their lands.

In each of the three cases, the visit of the special rapporteur was able to reinforce the NGOs' demands and serve as a catalyst for stronger action. In the Philippines, Alston's visit, together with continued pressure from national and international NGOs, helped prompt a dramatic decline in the rate of extrajudicial executions. In Jordan, where national organizations had repeatedly recommended the closure of the Al-Jafr detention center, Nowak's visit to Jordan finally prompted the government to shut the facility. In Brazil, Kothari's visit helped contribute to a government pledge not to carry out any further relocation of *quilombos* communities and was used by NGOs to launch a renewed campaign for *quilombos* rights.

The Brookings study identified six factors that facilitate positive impact by the special procedures: the credibility of the United Nations; the quality of the special procedures' research, analysis and recommendations; freedom of the media to report on the special procedures' activities; the level of attention by the UN country team and relevant UN agencies; the willingness of the relevant government to cooperate with the special procedures; and the ability of victims' groups and local and international NGOs to communicate their grievances and conduct follow-up advocacy.[63]

As an outside voice representing the United Nations, special rapporteurs are often able to bolster the ongoing efforts of national and international civil society groups and gain attention for human rights issues in a way that local civil society cannot. Paulo Sérgio Pinheiro, a former special rapporteur on Myanmar and Burundi, said that "governments and civil society tend to attribute greater powers to special rapporteurs than we actually have and, at the same time, underestimate the moral authority conferred by the job."[64] In the Philippines, for example, NGOs had a very adversarial relationship with the government on the issue of extrajudicial executions. According to Cookie Diokno of the Filipino NGO FLAG, "To have someone from the UN come in and make these statements was very, very helpful to push the human rights agenda forward."

Manfred Nowak identified NGOs as by far the most important source of information in planning his missions. His typical practice for a fact-finding mission was to collect all relevant NGO reports ahead of a mission and to request updates just before his trip, including recommendations for specific detention facilities to visit and specific issues to focus on. Once arriving in the country, he would meet with local NGOs a day before meeting with government officials, in order to get last-minute information. Based on the information they provided, he would often decide at the last minute where to make unannounced visits of detention facilities. "Without NGOs," he said, "my missions would not have been impossible, but they would be much more difficult."[65]

Mara Bustelo, coordinator of human rights and economic and social issues at the Office of the High Commissioner for Human Rights, reflected that national NGOs not only provide special rapporteurs with detailed information and access to victims and witnesses but also play a critical role in helping special rapporteurs craft specific and sophisticated recommendations based on their analysis and knowledge of the local situation. She also highlighted the important link between national and international NGOs. "One factor that comes through loud and clear is that a presence in

Geneva makes a difference, even if it is just one person working as a volunteer," she said. "For national and local NGOs, it makes all the difference to have contact with an international NGO that is savvy on these issues who can help guide and facilitate. To have those intermediate actors is a powerful mechanism for providing contacts and suggestions for Special Rapporteurs on where to go on mission, and to connect on the ground at the national level."[66] For example, in the Brazil case mentioned in this chapter, COHRE played an important facilitation role between Kothari and national Brazilian NGOs and worked with Brazilian NGOs to maximize the impact of Kothari's field mission.

Interviews with special rapporteurs and the cases examined in this chapter suggest a number of strategies for local human rights advocates that want to work effectively with special rapporteurs. A first step is to provide the special rapporteur with documentation of violations in a particular country, and the reasons why he/she should conduct a country visit. Once a visit is scheduled, a second step is to provide detailed guidance regarding specific places or facilities and particular aspects of human rights violations the special rapporteur should investigate and to identify victims and witnesses for the special rapporteur to interview, in particular new cases that have not been previously investigated. Advocates can maximize the special rapporteur's visit by organizing civic forums or other public meetings where affected individuals speak publicly with the special rapporteur about human rights abuses, or by launching new reports or campaigns and publicizing them with the media. Advocates may consider providing suggestions for the special rapporteur's meetings with government officials and for the recommendations for his/her report, based on their knowledge of the local situation. Finally, when feasible, advocates should plan to use the special rapporteur's report and recommendations for follow-up advocacy with relevant officials, the UN country team, and the media. Local NGOs that do not have experience with the UN special procedures might consider partnering with an international NGO that has previously worked with special rapporteurs and can provide advice.

The impact of special procedures is a topic of constant debate. Many governments are reluctant to invite special rapporteurs to examine their human rights conduct and do not respond to requests for a visit or delay their response. Only 35 percent of the communications sent by special procedures in 2010 resulted in a reply from the government concerned.[67] In his final report as special rapporteur on extrajudicial executions, Philip Alston noted that during the six years of his mandate, mission requests were sent to fifty-three countries, but that 70 percent either did not respond at all to the request, or failed to approve a visit.[68] Nowak believes that fact-finding missions are most likely to have impact when the government is willing to consider outside criticism. "If I manage to establish a good diplomatic relationship with a government that is willing to accept my criticism and willing to change something, and there is some pressure via the media and the public, that helps. So in choosing countries, I try not to select the worst, but those where I feel there is a government that is willing to change or is willing to use me for an objective external assessment."[69]

Not surprisingly, the pressure from special rapporteurs and their partners—as in other examples in this volume—often achieves only limited results. Five years after Alston's visit to the Philippines, for example, the rate of extrajudicial executions remained much lower than it had been before his visit.[70] However, dozens of civilians were still being killed each year, and little progress had been made on impunity. By mid-2011, only seven extrajudicial killing cases had been successfully prosecuted, resulting in the conviction of twelve defendants. Not a single conviction involved anyone who was an active member of the military at the time of the killing.[71] This may indicate that curbing new killings was easier for the government than implicating members of its own military for previous crimes.

Even in cases where a special rapporteur is able to influence change, governments are often reluctant to credit a special rapporteur's visit or recommendations with its actions to address human rights violations. For example, Jordanian authorities told Manfred Nowak that their decision to close Al-Jafr had nothing to do with his mission and that they had plans to close it down anyway.[72] However, the timing of the King's directive to close the center with Nowak's report to the UN Human Rights Council seems to indicate that Nowak's strong criticism, added to that of national and international NGOs, played a role in the government's decision.

On their own, special procedures rarely have the clout or the resources to create significant change in human rights practices. In concert with other forces and actors, however, they can serve as effective catalysts for reform. Mara Bustelo reflected that "in the best case scenario, special procedures add to existing pressures. We can't reasonably ask them to be more than that. At most, they play into a strategy and events that are already taking place."[73] Special rapporteurs and NGOs can play effective, mutually reinforcing roles on behalf of human rights. NGOs can provide special rapporteurs with critical information, strategic advice regarding the priorities and logistics of a mission, suggest recommendations, and conduct follow-up advocacy. Special rapporteurs, by contrast, can provide the moral authority of the UN, an international platform and spotlight, and access to senior policymakers. Together they may be able to achieve change that neither can achieve alone.

Chapter 5

Creating a New International Priority

Ending Violence Against Children

No violence against children is justifiable; all violence against children is
preventable. There should be no more excuses. . . . None of us can look children in
the eye if we continue to approve or condone any form of violence against them.

—*Paulo Sérgio Pinheiro, independent expert to the
secretary-general on violence against children, 2006*[1]

AFTER THE CONVENTION ON THE RIGHTS OF THE CHILD was adopted
in 1989, three issues dominated the arena of children's rights during
the 1990s: child labor, sexual exploitation, and the impact of armed
conflict on children. New transnational coalitions and networks formed,
including the Global March Against Child Labor, the Coalition to Stop the
Use of Child Soldiers, and ECPAT International (End Child Prostitution,
Child Pornography, and Trafficking of Children for Sexual Purposes). These
global movements helped drive the development of additional legal norms,
including the ILO Worst Forms of Child Labor Convention, adopted in 1999,
and two optional protocols to the Convention on the Rights of the Child: one
on the involvement of children in armed conflict, and another on the sale of
children, child prostitution, and child pornography, both adopted in 2000.

Other human rights abuses against children—though pervasive—failed to
gain the same level of attention. NGOs persistently documented police violence against street children, abusive conditions in detention facilities and
other institutions, and violence against children in homes and schools. Some
individual reports elicited international horror, such as exposés of deadly
levels of neglect in Russian and Chinese orphanages. However, governments
often responded to reports of violence against children as anomalous, isolated
incidents, rather than as global phenomena demanding focused attention.

In many countries, more than 90 percent of children were beaten in their home, most often by their parents.[2] In the classroom, school "discipline" allowed caning, slapping, and whipping that would result in bruising, cuts, humiliation, and in some cases, serious injury or even death. Street children, numbering in the millions worldwide, frequently experienced violence at the hands of police and other law enforcement officials. Seen as vagrants or criminals, street children were subjected to round-ups, extortion, beatings, rape, death threats, and extrajudicial execution. Once in police custody, children were sometimes tortured to extract confessions for crimes. In Nepal, one study found that 85 percent of children interviewed in prisons reported abusive treatment while in the custody of police or security forces, and nearly 60 percent reported torture, including electric shocks.[3] Millions of children in institutions were particularly vulnerable to violence and neglect, often perpetrated by the individuals responsible for their care and safety.[4]

This chapter explores efforts begun by NGOs in the late 1990s to mobilize a stronger United Nations response to the violence that millions of children encountered in nearly every aspect of their lives, including the creation of a high-level post to coordinate a long-term strategy to address the crisis. The strategy entailed a slow, incremental approach utilizing different elements of the United Nations system. Ultimately it took a decade to reach fruition.

Mobilizing for UN Action to End Violence Against Children

To galvanize attention to violence against children, initially international nongovernmental organizations (NGOs) working on children's rights decided to advocate for the creation of a UN special rapporteur devoted to the issue. Other rapporteurs already served as independent experts to monitor government compliance with international standards on violence against women, torture, racism, and other issues.[5] The NGOs believed that a similar special rapporteur devoted to violence against children could raise the international visibility of the issue and, through advocacy and field investigations, mobilize government action to better protect vulnerable children. The World Organization Against Torture (OMCT) conducted an analysis to determine how violence against children was covered by the mandates of existing special rapporteurs. They found that while some cases were taken up by the special rapporteurs on torture, violence against women, and extrajudicial executions, other areas of violence against children simply were not addressed. Roberta Cecchetti, who conducted OMCT's analysis, said, "Violence against children was falling through the cracks, because there was no single entry point in the UN system to deal with violence against children. It could deal with torture, but issues like violence in work settings, and especially violence in the home and family were completely outside the existing system."[6] Backed by OMCT's analysis, NGOs began to lobby government representatives to the UN Commission on Human Rights in Geneva, advocating for the creation for a new special rapporteur on violence against children.

Some governments, particularly that of Mexico and others in Latin America, supported the proposal for a new special rapporteur. However, most governments were unconvinced that a new position was necessary. Some did not believe that violence against children was a significant issue. Despite OMCT's analysis, others believed that the problem could be addressed by existing rapporteurs who covered aspects of violence in their mandate (for example, torture, violence against women, extrajudicial executions) and could be encouraged to give more attention to children. Some cited the fact that there were already two existing mechanisms devoted to children—the special rapporteur on the sale of children, child prostitution, and child pornography (established in 1990) and the special representative to the secretary-general on children and armed conflict (established in 1998). Many expressed the view that there were already simply too many special rapporteurs that were underresourced; they were skeptical about adding yet another mechanism to a system perceived as overloaded and undersupported.

Realizing that governments were unlikely to approve a UN special rapporteur on violence against children, NGOs regrouped and began to develop an alternative strategy, based on the response to children affected by war in the 1990s. A 1996 UN study on the impact of armed conflict on children, conducted by Graça Machel, had become a significant galvanizing force for gaining attention and action on abuses against children in the escalating number of conflicts around the world. The General Assembly requested the study in 1993;[7] the secretary-general then appointed Graça Machel, the secretary of education for Mozambique and wife of slain Mozambican president Samora Moisés Machel, as an independent expert to conduct the study on his behalf. The Machel study brought global attention to issues of child soldiering, the impact of landmines and small arms on children, challenges facing refugee children, and related issues. Expert consultations and specially commissioned case studies informed the study's findings, which were delivered to the UN General Assembly in 1996.[8] The General Assembly responded by creating a new UN entity: a special representative to the secretary-general on children and armed conflict. The position was intended to maintain visibility to the issues highlighted by Ms. Machel's study and to prompt appropriate action. Another of the study's recommendations was the creation of an optional protocol to raise the minimum age for the recruitment and use of child soldiers, ultimately adopted in 2000 (see Chapter 1).

Based on its work on children and armed conflict, Human Rights Watch believed that the Machel study could be used as a model for gaining greater attention to the violence against children in nonconflict settings. It began consulting with others about the idea of advocating for a UN study on violence against children in order to build the basis for a high-level UN mechanism, such as a special representative to the secretary-general, that would be devoted to the issue. Some also believed that securing a special representative would be preferable to a special rapporteur, as such a position typically has much greater staffing and financial support. Cecchetti said, "At OMCT, we were very positive about the study idea, but we were conscious that it would put the proposal for a special rapporteur on hold, because countries would use the argument that they needed to wait for the study to decide. But we were not getting very far with the special rapporteur idea."[9]

NGOs urged the UN Committee on the Rights of the Child to hold a "day of discussion" on violence against children. The committee, established to evaluate states parties' compliance with the Convention on the Rights of the Child, had developed a pattern of holding a "day of discussion" on specific themes each year. For these days, the committee invited written inputs and participation by NGOs and issued a report and recommendations based on the proceedings. Under the chairmanship of Jaap Doek, the committee held two such days on violence against children—one in 2000 and one in 2001. The first focused on violence against children by the state, and the second focused on violence against children in the family and in schools. Dozens of NGOs submitted reports and other information for the discussion days, with many participating in the actual discussions held in Geneva. Human Rights Watch prepared a special publication on violence against children, consolidating the results from its investigations in more than twenty countries and making a UN study on violence against children its primary recommendation.[10] During the days, NGOs continued to promote the idea of special rapporteur, but also rallied together around the idea of an in-depth UN study on violence against children, highlighting the proposal in their oral interventions in Geneva.

The Committee on the Rights of the Child agreed on the need for the study. Chairman Jaap Doek sent a special letter to the UN secretary-general in 2001, recommending an in-depth UN study on violence against children, with the request that the letter be circulated to all UN member states. Advocates then consulted with sympathetic government representatives regarding the most effective way to get the General Assembly to approve the study. The request for the Graça Machel study had been made through a special resolution of the General Assembly drafted primarily for that purpose. However, some government representatives believed that a stand-alone resolution could engender resistance and controversy and advised NGOs to push the request through the omnibus resolution on the rights of the child—an annual resolution by the General Assembly that typically addressed a range of children's rights issues.

Canada took the lead on inserting a brief text into the resolution, requesting the secretary-general to conduct an in-depth study on the question of violence against children and to "put forward recommendations for consideration by Member States for appropriate action, including effective remedies and preventive and rehabilitative measures." NGOs lobbied other governments to support the proposal and found little resistance. The General Assembly adopted the resolution in December 2001.[11]

As governments debated the General Assembly children's resolutions in New York, OMCT convened an international conference on violence against children in Tampere, Finland, bringing together NGOs, governments, and key UN entities including UNICEF and the Office of the High Commissioner for Human Rights. "It was quite a key moment," said Cecchetti. "Key NGOs were around the table, with OHCHR, UNICEF and assistants for some of the special rapporteurs. It was an opportunity to have a discussion about the study and how to move it forward. While we were there, we got the news from New York that the General Assembly had agreed to make the request for the study."[12]

The minimal text from the General Assembly ensured that the proposal for a study generated little controversy among governments, but it also carried the risk that the study would simply be delegated to one of the UN agencies and become little more than a desk review of existing literature. To help ensure that it would become a serious and high-profile undertaking, NGOs began to lobby for the appointment of an independent expert to conduct the study on the secretary-general's behalf, similar to the role played by Graça Machel.

NGOs turned their attention to the UN Commission on Human Rights, which held its annual session in Geneva in April and May of 2002. They lobbied for text in its resolution on the rights of the child that would welcome the UN study and further request the secretary-general to appoint an independent expert to conduct it. NGOs argued that only an independent expert could give the study the attention and profile that it deserved. Working behind the scenes, NGO representatives drafted text for the resolution, providing it to diplomats who were leading the negotiations and sympathetic to the idea of an independent expert. The commission requested an independent expert that year, though it was nearly a year later—in 2003— before the secretary-general appointed his choice—Paulo Sérgio Pinheiro of Brazil. Pinheiro had served as Brazil's secretary of state for human rights, and had served in several previous UN capacities, including as special rapporteur on the human rights situation in Myanmar, special rapporteur on Burundi, and as a member of the Subcommission on the Promotion and Protection of Human Rights.

Until this point, a fairly loose network of interested NGOs had led the advocacy efforts around the study, including Human Rights Watch, OMCT, World Vision, and the Global Initiative to End All Corporal Punishment of Children. Prior to the independent expert's appointment, these NGOs decided that it would be valuable to create a more formal NGO network to provide direct input to Pinheiro and the UN agencies supporting the study and to help coordinate and mobilize the participation of NGOs in the study process. Through the NGO Group for the Convention on the Rights of the Child, a broad network of child-rights organizations, NGOs were invited to submit nominations to form a new NGO advisory panel for the UN Study. Around twenty national, regional, and international NGOs were selected, including Save the Children, Human Rights Watch, OMCT, Defense for Children International, and World Vision.

The advisory panel met regularly in London, Geneva, and New York, developing recommendations regarding the methods, scope, and recommendations of the study. It urged Pinheiro to hold regional consultations with governments, UN agencies, NGOs, and children; advised on ways to engage the participation of children; provided input on research methodology; and mobilized NGOs to submit information on their programs and research that could inform the study. It made recommendations regarding the issues that should be covered by the study, highlighting issues of particular concern such as corporal punishment, and gave input for the study's final recommendations to member states and other actors. To underscore the importance of children's direct input into the study, the NGO advisory panel initiated a parallel children's advisory group, soliciting nominations from NGOs of children who were actively engaged in organizations and efforts to address violence against children. Ten children under age eighteen joined the panel for meetings in Geneva and London, calling themselves "The Geneva 10." They participated in sessions of the advisory panel, held parallel sessions to develop their own recommendations for Pinheiro, and participated in the eventual launch of the study.

A series of thematic and regional consultations were central to the study process. During 2005, UNICEF took responsibility for organizing regional consultations in nine locations around the world. More than three thousand individuals took part, including government ministers, members of Parliament, children, academics, representatives of civil society, and UN agencies. In many cases, regional organizations, such as the African Union and the Arab League helped to organize the events. Regional research reports were prepared for each, and some were widely covered by national and regional media. Participants explored the particular aspects of violence against children that were of concern to their region, highlighted effective and promising programs and responses, and developed recommendations for Pinheiro.

A unique element of the consultations was the participation of children themselves. Many of the child participants were active with child-led organizations that were addressing violence and other child rights issues in their home country. They participated in the consultation plenaries and also held parallel sessions to develop their own recommendations and declarations on violence against children. At the consultation for Southeast Asia, held in Bangkok, children highlighted concerns about corporal punishment. "Nobody has ever talked this openly—it's usually left behind closed doors. Now they're taking this opportunity to give their perspective on corporal punishment in the home," said Margarita Harou, a seventeen-year-old participant from Papua New Guinea.[13]

NGOs and UN agencies also convened thematic consultations to address particular issues, for example, violence against children with disabilities. The NGO advisory panel convened a consultation on violence against children in conflict with the law, drawing together UN and NGO experts in Geneva for discussions on ways to reduce the incidence of violence against children in detention and police custody and to lower the overall numbers of children placed in detention.

As the process progressed, Pinheiro set up an editorial board to assist with drafting the study's final report and reviewing its final chapters. The members were primarily representatives of UN agencies, including UNICEF, the World Health Organization, the Office of the High Commissioner for Human Rights, and the International Labor Organization, but also included two NGO representatives from the NGO advisory panel.[14] This group also ultimately helped shape the final core recommendations of the study, including the recommendation for a special representative to the secretary-general on violence against children.

The study was completed in 2006, and presented that October to the UN General Assembly in New York.[15] The launch of a full book-length version followed on November 20 in Geneva. Among its findings:

·   More than 150 million girls and 73 million boys had been subjected to rape or other sexual violence;

·   More than 3 million girls were subjected to female genital mutilation each year;

·   In some countries, up to 65 percent of children had reported suffering verbal or physical bullying at school during the previous thirty days;

·   More than 50,000 children every year died as a result of homicide;

·   In more than one hundred countries, children could be legally beaten by their teachers or principals in school; and

·   Only sixteen governments, representing 2.6 percent of the world's children, prohibited all forms of violence against children in their national law.[16]

Introducing the study, Secretary-General Kofi Annan identified violence against children as a "major threat" to global development, to gender equality, and to the fight against HIV/AIDS.[17] The study highlighted a dozen core recommendations, including the prohibition in law of all forms of violence against children, including corporal punishment; the creation of national strategies and action plans to end violence against children; and the appointment of ministerial-level coordination mechanisms by each government to ensure an effective government response. Individual chapters focused on violence in specific settings—the home and family, school, care and justice systems, the workplace, and the community—providing specific recommendations on each.

In large part because of continued lobbying by NGOs, the study also rec-ommended the creation of a special representative to the secretary-general (SRSG) on violence against children to serve as a high-level UN advocate in order to maintain attention to the issue and ensure the implementation of the study's recommendations. After the completion of the Machel study, the cre-ation of a special representative post had been essential to keep children and armed conflict high on the international agenda. The special representative had made regular field visits to conflict-affected countries, secured commit-ments from governments and armed groups to end their use of child soldiers and other abuses against children, and had convinced the UN Security Coun-cil to place children and armed conflict on its agenda.[18]

With the study complete, NGOs formed a new advisory council specifically to support implementation of the study's recommendations.[19] Its immediate goal was securing an SRSG post on violence against children. During the 2006 session of the General Assembly, the NGO advisory council lobbied UN mem-ber states in New York supporting Pinheiro's recommendation. They circulated a statement to members of the General Assembly's third committee, stating:

> The independent expert's ground breaking study has brought to light the hor-rific scale of violence suffered by children at the hands of adults around the world. It makes clear that unconscionable violence affects boys and girls of all ages, in all nations, developed and developing alike. We have no choice but to acknowledge that this is a global problem, with devastating effects in all regions of the world. . . . The widespread and devastating impact of violence against children revealed by the Study demands leadership and attention at the highest level of the UN. We need a high-level global advocate who can maintain attention to the epidemic of violence against children and keep it squarely on the international agenda; and who can systematically monitor progress in implementing the Study's recommendations.[20]

Despite the study's recommendation for an SRSG, many states indicated that they needed "more time" to consider the study's recommendations and stated that the creation of any new high-level mandate should be delayed pending the results of an ongoing UN reform process. Some argued that the mandate of other existing mechanisms, such as the special representative on children and armed conflict or the special rapporteur on sale of children, should be expanded to cover other forms of violence against children, or that UNICEF should take on the task. The 2006 lobbying effort for an SRSG failed. "I was completely bewildered," said Peter Newell, coordinator of the Global Initiative to End all Corporal Punishment of Children and a cochair of the NGO advisory council. "How could they not see? Of course the children and armed conflict agenda is important. But there was a complete lack of logic to have an SRSG on children and armed conflict but not on violence against children. I couldn't see any rational reason for it."[21]

Profile: Peter Newell

Peter Newell has worked to end corporal punishment of children for more than three decades.[1] He says, "What's most irritating is the absurd ways that adults find to justify what is clearly unjustifiable and the endless excuses for not taking action to prohibit corporal punishment. No one would openly justify violence against women."

Raised in the UK, Newell began his professional career in the late 1960s as a journalist, initially working for the *Oxford Mail* and then the *Times Educational Supplement*. He wrote increasingly about the education system and concluded that schools were a "deadening" part of children's lives. He became part of the "free schools" movement and helped found and work in a school where children had an active role in decision-making about how the school was run. Soon, he became part of a campaign to prohibit the use of corporal punishment in schools. "Working on education, it was such a completely obvious issue," he said. "It was such a denial of what teachers said they were doing. It had no educational value. The only way it's educational is to teach violence."

Newell also felt that corporal punishment had a much deeper significance. "It's not simply about child protection," he says. "It's a highly symbolic issue in society. The fact that it's legal to hit children reflects a concept of ownership of children. Once issues like that are apparent, you can't leave them until you have won them."

In 1979, Newell helped start the Children's Legal Centre, a UK legal advocacy center that lobbied Parliament to adopt and amend laws to protect children's rights and made applications to the European Court of Human Rights. The same year, he attended a meeting in Geneva about Sweden's pioneering new law that prohibited corporal punishment by parents in the home. Sweden's law made him realize that prohibiting corporal punishment in the schools was not enough. "It was illogical to stop at banning it in schools."

In 1986, the UK campaign to ban corporal punishment in schools reached its goal with the passage of a new law. The same year, Newell left the Children's

NGOs tried again in 2007. The advisory council developed an advocacy document that addressed in detail why the alternatives put forward by various member states were either impractical or inadequate to address the agenda established by the study, and why the appointment was too important to defer because of the UN reform process. Members of the NGO advisory council lobbied their individual governments and in New York organized briefings for

Legal Centre to write a book about banning all corporal punishment of children and to start a new organization, EPOCH, End Physical Punishment of Children. In 1994, he took a landmark case, *A v. UK*, to the European Court of Human Rights, charging the government of the UK with violating the rights of a boy who had been beaten repeatedly by his stepfather. It was the first case before the European Court that dealt with parental corporal punishment, and Newell hoped that it would prompt a change in UK law. However, because the circumstances of the case were severe, the judgment allowed the UK to only prohibit "severe" cases of corporal punishment. "So the campaign continues," says Newell.

Children's rights advocates in other countries expressed interest in the EPOCH campaign in the UK, so in 2001, Newell teamed up with Thomas Hammarberg, a former member of the Committee on the Rights of the Child and former general secretary of Amnesty International, to form the Global Initiative to End All Corporal Punishment of Children. Now sixty-five, he works with NGOs around the globe, traveling a significant portion of the year as he works for legislative reform in dozens of countries to ban all corporal punishment of children. He was also a central figure in the UN study on violence against children, attending all nine consultations and serving on the NGO advisory panel and the study's editorial board.

"Corporal punishment is a difficult issue because it is so personal, for both children and parents," he says. "Most people were hit as children. Most parents have hit their own growing children. We don't like to think badly of our parents, or of our own parenting, and that makes it much more difficult to see the issue clearly as one of human rights and equality."

1. Author interview with Peter Newell, April 19, 2011.

the regional groups of UN member states. These were often held together with Paulo Pinheiro, the study's independent expert, and were attended by more than sixty governments. The NGOs sent letters to all governments and, with the support of the Children's Rights Information Network, initiated a petition campaign that ultimately garnered support from a thousand NGOs from 134 countries.

Members of the advisory council pooled funds to hire Cristina Barbaglia as a part-time staff person. Barbaglia, who also worked for Save the Children, met individually with more than eighty UN missions in New York to discuss the study's recommendations and the need for a special representative. Barbaglia said:

> I think we were very persuasive in explaining how important this mandate would be for children and how the study highlighted how widespread violence against children was around the world. We were organized, prepared, and persistent. We didn't just meet with the missions to say we wanted an SRSG. We gave all the facts, all the reasons. We had all the lobbying material ready. We were all united and gave the same messages in both Geneva and in New York. Member states were impressed by the NGOs all being together with one purpose.[22]

The effort finally succeeded. In December 2007, the General Assembly requested the secretary-general to appoint a special representative "at the highest level possible" for an initial three-year term to "act as a high-profile and independent global advocate to promote the prevention and elimination of all forms of violence against children in all regions."[23] NGOs celebrated their victory. They formulated criteria to submit to the secretary-general for the selection of the SRSG, as well as an informal list of candidates that they encouraged the secretary-general to consider. They urged an appointment as soon as possible to ensure that the momentum that had been created by the study process, including its extensive consultative process, would not be lost.

NGO excitement soon gave way to frustration as the appointment was repeatedly delayed. In early 2008, the Human Rights Council reiterated the General Assembly's request for the SRSG, urging "urgent action" by the secretary-general to appoint a special representative.[24] Later that year, the General Assembly expressed its deep concern about the delay and requested that the secretary-general take urgent action to appoint the SRSG.[25] In March of 2009, the Human Rights Council followed up its 2008 resolution with yet another request for the secretary-general to "proceed urgently" with the appointment.[26] Cecchetti remarked, "This is the first SRSG that has required four separate resolutions by UN bodies to be established." In May 2009, Secretary-General Ban Ki-Moon finally appointed Marta Santos Pais of Portugal as his special representative on violence against children.

By 2012, impact from the study and related advocacy was apparent. When the study was released in 2006, only sixteen governments prohibited all corporal punishment against children in their national law. Five years later, thirty-one states had prohibited all corporal punishment of children in all settings. At least twenty-three more states had either committed to full prohibition or were actively debating prohibition bills in parliament, and the Council of Europe had adopted an explicit campaign to prohibit all corporal punishment in all its forty-seven states.[27] Spurred by the new special representative, governments held high-level regional meetings to develop strategies to more effectively combat violence against children.

Lessons Learned

NGOs worked for a decade to place violence against children on the international agenda and to establish a high-level UN post to address the issue. Through persistent organizing, and being flexible and coordinated in their approach, they ultimately achieved significant progress. Some of the key lessons from their experience included the following.

First, documentation was critical. Initially, NGOs found little recognition of violence against children as a serious problem and little willingness by governments to establish new mechanisms to confront it. Their initial proposal—for a special rapporteur on violence against children—gained little support from either UN staff or member states.[28] NGOs decided to change their strategy and advocate first for a UN study to clearly document the scope and severity of violence against children, and then to use this study as the basis to argue for a high-level follow-up mechanism. The study provided strong and credible evidence of the serious and global nature of violence against children. NGOs were able to use this information to make a compelling case for a high-level UN post to work with governments to follow-up the study's recommendations. The four-year study process itself, including the regional consultations that accompanied it and ongoing submissions by NGOs, helped build greater awareness of the problem and mobilize key actors—NGOs, UN agencies, and governments—on the issue.

After the completion of the study, when NGOs still found resistance to the recommendation for an SRSG, they prepared detailed documentation to address each of the counterarguments raised by member states. Their careful rebuttal won converts and quieted critics. For example, Norway had always been a strong supporter of children's rights, but initially resisted an SRSG. It held a leadership role in UN reform and believed that one of the objectives of the reform process was to streamline the UN and consolidate positions, rather than creating new ones. However, it was eventually persuaded by NGO arguments that only a new high-level post within the UN would create the attention and focus that was needed to adequately address violence against children.

A second important element in the NGO strategy was an incremental approach. The NGOs were successfully able to leverage different parts of the UN system as building blocks to achieve their goals. They began by securing a recommendation for a study from the Committee on the Rights of the Child, which they then used to secure support from the UN General Assembly. Once the General Assembly had requested the study, NGOs then used the Commission on Human Rights to secure an independent expert to conduct it on the secretary-general's behalf. The study, once completed, provided the principle advocacy tool to secure the establishment of the SRSG. Gaining support from both the General Assembly and the Commission on Human Rights/Human Rights Council demanded close coordination between New York and Geneva-based NGOs. According to Roberta Cecchetti, who worked first for OMCT and later for Save the Children in Geneva, "The fact that we could coordinate so well between New York and Geneva was a great advantage. There was substantive trust that we could work on each other's behalf. There was a shared ownership of the process and a lot of respect amongst the groups."[29]

Third, the decision of NGOs to organize themselves as a formal and representative advisory panel/council gave them particular weight with the independent expert, participating UN agencies, and UN member states and ensured that their recommendations would be taken more seriously. "We made ourselves an obligatory interlocutor for the whole process," said Cecchetti.[30] The NGO advisory panel provided a recognized point of contact with the NGO community for both the independent expert and supporting UN agencies. Members of the panel were able to forge a close and collaborative relationship with Pinheiro, which ensured NGOs a "seat at the table" in the editorial board, which made crucial final decisions regarding the recommendations of the study. In at least two instances (the study's recommendations against all corporal punishment of children and the recommendation for the establishment of an SRSG), strong NGO recommendations were decisive. At several stages, NGO advocates played behind-the-scenes roles, drafting the text of the Commission on Human Rights resolution that requested the appointment of the independent expert to conduct the study, producing drafts of portions of the study and suggesting texts for key speeches by individuals connected to the study. According to Peter Newell, "One of the skills is being entirely invisible and getting the most powerful figures to take one's words and put them forward."[31]

The coordination of NGOs through the NGO advisory council was also helpful in approaching UN member states. Barbaglia, who later became a diplomat for the United Kingdom, said, "The Advisory Council was key. It brought together all of the well-respected and powerful NGOs. If you have Save the Children, Human Rights Watch, World Vision, Plan International and the others gathered with one purpose, members pay attention."[32] The involvement of national and regional NGOs from all continents also helped address concerns from some member states that the push for a study and an SRSG reflected a Western agenda that intended to target developing countries. A cross-regional engagement of NGOs helped to demonstrate that violence against children was a global problem and that actors in all parts of the world sought strong action in response.

Finally, individual advocacy meetings with a large number of UN missions in New York were decisive in gaining support for the SRSG post. According to Barbaglia, "The fact that we went mission by mission, one by one, made a huge difference."[33] Peter Newell, cochair of the NGO advisory council, said, "I suspect that the more you talk to missions, the more success you have, because they are not used to being talked to by the children's lobby. Of course it's a decision made at capital, but if you can convince the relevant ambassador, it can be highly important to get the good will of the people in New York."[34]

Summarizing the campaign, Barbaglia concluded, "We were prepared, professional, and united. We achieved the objective because of that. There wouldn't be an SRSG without the NGO campaign."[35] Reflecting on the NGOs' original goal a decade earlier, Newell said, "In retrospect, a study followed by a SRSG on violence against children was a much better outcome than our original goal of a UN special rapporteur. ... Special rapporteurs are notoriously under-resourced and work on a voluntary, part-time basis, while SRSGs have much more status within the UN system and can solicit resources from member states to hire staff that can provide them with proper support."[36]

The NGOs involved in the campaign recognized that while new laws, policies, and the establishment of the SRSG on violence against children represented important steps, their impact on children's lives remained limited and that ongoing advocacy was required. In late 2011, the NGO advisory council released a report showing that five years after the UN Study, levels of violence against children remained "shockingly and unacceptably high."[37] Reviewing more than one hundred separate studies, the council found that on average, two-thirds of children worldwide were subjected to violent punishment on a regular basis and that some forms of violence against children had even become worse. For example, the number of juvenile offenders who were executed for crimes committed before age eighteen increased by more than 50 percent during the five years following the study.[38] The council called on governments to take stronger action to end violence against children. While a decade of advocacy had succeeded in raising the international profile of violence against children and begun to change some laws and policies, real progress for children would take even longer.

PART III

Seeking Accountability

Chapter 6

Bringing Charles Taylor to Justice

No matter how powerful a leader is, no matter how important a leader is, if you
commit crimes in any part of the world, you can be held accountable. The law is
always mightier than power.
—Sulaiman Jabati, Sierra Leonean activist
with the Campaign Against Impunity[1]

THE 1991–2002 WAR IN SIERRA LEONE was marked by some of the most
horrific abuses of the twentieth century. A rebellion against the government
by the rebel Revolutionary United Front (RUF) unleashed a campaign of terror, as RUF forces burned people alive in their homes, abducted
women and girls for rape and sexual slavery, and used axes, machetes, and
knives to kill and mutilate thousands of civilians, often by amputating their
hands, arms, legs, and other body parts. Both rebel and government forces
recruited thousands of children to serve as soldiers in their ranks. Government and civilian defense forces also carried out killings and torture.

In 1997, a group of army officers calling itself the Armed Forces Revolutionary Council (AFRC) overthrew the elected government in a coup and
then invited the RUF to join its rule. The AFRC/RUF alliance ruled the country for nine months before being ousted in February 1998 by a Nigerian-led
peacekeeping force, the Economic Community of West African States Monitoring Group (ECOMOG), which reinstated former president Ahmad Tejan
Kabbah. Kabbah had been elected president in March 1996 in the country's
first multiparty elections in almost three decades.

After being removed from power, the RUF and AFRC resumed a campaign
of widespread atrocities against unarmed civilians in an attempt to regain
control over the country. Despite a 1999 peace accord that gave the RUF a
power-sharing arrangement with the government, the conflict continued. By
the time the war was finally declared over in January 2002, more than half of

the country's population—approximately 2.6 million people— had been displaced and tens of thousands had been killed.

Beginning in the mid-1980s, state and nonstate actors in Liberia, Sierra Leone, Guinea, Cote d'Ivoire, and Burkina Faso have supported rebel insurgencies aimed at destabilizing their neighbors. Both as rebel leader of the Liberian National Patriotic Front of Liberia (NPFL) which sought to unseat then-president Samuel Doe, and later as president of Liberia from 1997 to 2003, Charles Taylor allegedly supported the RUF, the AFRC, and Liberian forces fighting in support of the Sierra Leonean rebels in order to both punish ECOMOG peacekeepers who used Sierra Leone as a staging ground from which to launch military operations against the NPFL and to gain access to its diamond mines. The RUF controlled Sierra Leone's richest diamond-mining areas and used diamonds to fund its military operations. Estimated RUF revenue from the diamonds was between \$25 and \$125 million per year, with the majority of the diamonds smuggled out through Liberia.[2]

In 2000, the UN Security Council established a panel of experts to examine the role of arms and diamond trading in fueling the Sierra Leone conflict.[3] They delivered their first report in December 2000, finding "unequivocal and overwhelming" evidence that Liberia was actively supporting the RUF at all levels, by providing training, weapons, logistical support, and a staging ground for attacks. They found that helicopters from Liberia regularly flew to RUF areas carrying weapons, in violation of an arms embargo, and that a constant flow of weapons and supplies from Liberia to the RUF included mortars, rifles, RPGs, satellite phones, computers, vehicles, batteries, food, and drugs. Most damningly, they found that Charles Taylor was personally and actively involved in fueling the violence in Sierra Leone through strategy meetings with senior leaders of the RUF and by facilitating the RUF's diamond smuggling through Liberia.[4]

In January 2002, the government of Sierra Leone and the United Nations reached an agreement to establish the Special Court for Sierra Leone to prosecute persons "bearing the greatest responsibility" for the grave violations committed from November 30, 1996 of the conflict. The Special Court eventually indicted thirteen individuals for war crimes, crimes against humanity, and other violations of international humanitarian law. The indictees included members of the rebel Revolutionary United Front, the Armed Forces Revolutionary Council, and the government-backed Civil Defense Forces and Taylor.

The Special Court indicted Taylor, then still serving as president of Liberia, in March 2003. His indictment included seventeen counts of war crimes and crimes against humanity against the people of Sierra Leone, including killings, mutilations, rape and other sexual violence, sexual slavery, the recruitment and use of child soldiers, abduction, and the use of forced labor.[5] The indictment was unsealed on June 4, 2003, while Taylor was in Ghana, engaged in negotiations regarding Liberia's war. Unable or unwilling to arrest Taylor, the Ghanaian government gave Taylor safe passage back to Liberia. Two months later, amidst a rebel siege of Liberia's capital, Monrovia, Nigeria offered Taylor asylum in order to induce him to step down as president. Soon after Taylor fled to Nigeria, non-governmental organizations and others began to mount calls for Taylor to be transferred to the Special Court for Sierra Leone to stand trial for his crimes.

The Campaign

Advocates believed that bringing Taylor to justice was essential to address a culture of impunity in the region, to bring stability to West Africa, to illustrate that even a sitting head of state was not above the law, and according to one advocate, to "ensure that justice is done for countless victims of rape, child soldiers, amputees, refugees and others whose lives have been wasted."[6] Getting Taylor transferred to the Special Court to stand trial would not be an easy task, however. Eric Witte, a former special assistant to the prosecutor for the Special Court, reflected, "Very few people thought it could be done, especially in the diplomatic community. We often heard it couldn't be done, that 'the people you're up against are too powerful.' The UN Secretary-General, the US, the UK, and the African Union were all on board with Taylor's exile arrangement, so to chip away at that was a daunting task."[7]

An emerging coalition of organizations adopted a number of strategies to keep Taylor on the international agenda and press for his transfer to the Special Court. They worked on multiple fronts: challenging Taylor's asylum in Nigeria; seeking a formal request from the Liberian government for Taylor's surrender; urging Nigerian president Olusegun Obasanjo to hand Taylor over for trial; and building pressure from key outside actors, such as the United States and the UN Security Council.

From Abuja, Nigeria's capital, the Open Society Justice Initiative worked with local human rights lawyers and advocates to examine the legal basis for Taylor's asylum in Nigeria. They concluded that Taylor's asylum violated both Nigerian and international law. They argued that international law required that persons accused of war crimes and crimes against humanity be brought to justice and that Nigeria had a duty to deny refuge to Taylor because there was clear and credible evidence that he had committed serious crimes. The Justice Initiative approached Nigerian authorities, requesting a formal review of Taylor's status, but received no response. Attempts to discuss the issue with government officials were unsuccessful.[8]

In May 2004, two Nigerians—with the assistance of the Justice Initiative—filed judicial proceedings before Nigeria's Federal High Court to try to force Nigeria to nullify Taylor's asylum and hand him over for trial. The two men, David Anyaele and Emmanuel Egbuna, provided compelling evidence of Taylor's alleged crimes. In 1999 they had been working as traders in Freetown, Sierra Leone, when they were targeted by the Sierra Leonean rebels because of their Nigerian citizenship. Because Nigerian officers were commanding ECOMOG forces in Sierra Leone, the RUF/AFRC considered Nigerians to be enemies. RUF/AFRC soldiers hacked off both Anyaele's hands and mutilated Egbuna. The soldiers told Anyaele to return to Nigeria to "show everyone there what Liberia could do."[9]

Egbuna and Anyaele's application asserted that as a person indicted for war crimes and crimes against humanity before an international court, Taylor was not entitled to asylum status. The Justice Initiative filed an amicus curiae in support of Anyaele and Egbuna's application, asserting the government's obligation to surrender or prosecute individuals accused of serious international crimes and to deny them refugee status. Although Taylor did not respond to the suit, Nigeria's government filed a formal objection, stating that Anyaele and Egbuna did not have standing to initiate the case. Eighteen months later, the Federal High Court ruled in November 2005 that Anyaele and Egbuna had alleged injury by Taylor, and so long as the government's grant of asylum presented an obstacle to their claim, they had the right to challenge his asylum status. The government appealed the ruling.[10]

The case forced Nigeria's government to admit that it had offered Taylor asylum and helped win the attention of Nigerian government officials who had previously refused to discuss Taylor. The Justice Initiative and other NGOs also used the case to build public support and awareness, underlining the courage of individual victims who were willing to speak publicly about rebel abuses and Taylor's responsibility.

In 2005, Amnesty International and the Justice Initiative took the lead in forming the Campaign Against Impunity, uniting more than three hundred

NGOs from seventeen African countries as well as international groups in order to press for Taylor's transfer to the Special Court.[11] Ayodele Ameen, who coordinated the campaign for Amnesty International, reflected, "We realized that this campaign should not just be the international NGOs, but it was important to get local people involved. We wanted to make this not just a Nigerian case, but a regional case. That's why we went for a regional campaign to get as many organizations in West Africa to sign up, and ensure that all partners were on board."[12] The campaign was launched in early July 2005 with press conferences in fifteen African cities calling for Taylor's surrender. The campaign simultaneously issued a declaration calling on the African Union to take action on the issue during its summit, which was taking place in Libya. According to Ameen, "The campaign was biting, and biting hard."[13]

The campaign issued numerous statements, letters, and press releases calling for Taylor's surrender to the court. It called on African entities such as the African Union, ECOWAS, the Nigerian government, and the African Commission on Human and People's Rights, to back Taylor's surrender. Coalition statements emphasized the strong involvement of indigenous NGOs from the countries most affected by Taylor's crimes and quoted representatives from groups based in Sierra Leone, Liberia, and Nigeria. Corinne Dufka, a researcher for Human Rights Watch who had documented abuses during Sierra Leone's war, said, "The Campaign diversified the voices, but the messages always stayed the same: that Charles Taylor had to be turned over."[14] The campaign focused on two key points: turning Taylor over to the Special Court was essential to both bring stability to the region and ensure justice for the war's victims.

The campaign pressed for support from key international figures. For example, just before the UN High Commissioner for Human Rights, Louise Arbour, traveled to West Africa in July 2005, the campaign issued a press release urging her to press for Taylor's surrender to the court.[15] The campaign argued that by calling for Taylor to be turned over to the Special Court, Arbour would be standing up on behalf of justice for the victims of war crimes in Sierra Leone, and that without Taylor's surrender, building effective systems for human rights in West Africa could not be achieved.[16] At the end of her visit to Liberia, Arbour addressed the issue, saying publicly, "I have always been of the view that Charles Taylor should be in Freetown to answer the charges against him. We cannot make justice be subservient to peace; that is a grave mistake. Peace is not sustainable without justice."[17]

Profile: Aloysius Toe

Aloysius Toe became a human rights activist while still a teenager in war-torn Liberia. Once, he and fellow students witnessed soldiers execute a sixteen-year-old girl due to her ethnic status, despite their protests. The event affected him profoundly. "It was like my soul was boiling within me. I could not stand by and simply watch what was happening."[1]

Toe started more than one hundred human rights clubs, promoted human rights education in Liberian schools, and organized a network of 245 volunteers in rural communities to monitor and report human rights abuses. By his early twenties, he was the executive director of the Movement for the Defence of Human Rights, a central figure in national human rights networks, and recognized as one of Liberia's leading human rights activists. He said, "In my work I try to speak for the voiceless; seek justice and liberty for the oppressed; and freedom for the captives."

Under Charles Taylor's presidency, human rights advocates were frequent targets of arbitrary arrest and detention. Toe spoke out publicly to protest such cases, at great personal cost. He said, "I soon realized that the call to speak and advocate for others' rights is often a vocation of agonies, pains and sufferings."[2] In 2002, Toe was repeatedly forced into hiding because of his advocacy and legal campaigns, and he was jailed twice. The first time, he was arrested and detained after protesting the abduction and demanding the release of two sisters of an opposition politician. He was tortured in police custody before being released after four days.

The second time, nineteen armed state police raided his home in the middle of the night. They abducted his wife, taking her to jail wearing only her nightgown, leaving their small children alone at home. The police released her later that day, but authorities announced days later that documents found at his home allegedly linked Toe with the Liberians United for Reconciliation and Democracy (LURD), an armed group fighting the Liberian government. Rather than flee the country and put his family at risk, Toe turned himself in and was charged with treason. He was imprisoned for eight months without trial before he escaped from prison during a rebel attack just before Taylor left office and fled the country.

After Taylor's departure from power, Toe remained devoted to building human rights in postwar Liberia. Toe believed that social inequalities and economic exploitation (including corruption) led to the civil wars in Liberia and abuses of civil liberties and freedoms. In late 2003, he founded the Foundation for Human Rights and Democracy (FOHRD), a research, training, and advocacy organization devoted to spreading democratic values and principles and promoting social and economic rights.

As director of FOHRD, Toe coordinated the Campaign Against Impunity in Liberia and led national efforts to bring Charles Taylor to justice. He said, "Our country needs to enjoy reconciliation. But reconciliation cannot be achieved by turning a blind eye to issues of justice. Can we provide justice for victims of human rights abuses while at the same time creating conditions that will not lead to renewed conflict? That is our hope."[3]

In 2005, at age twenty-seven, Toe received the Reebok Human Rights Award in recognition of his work and courage. He says that he was inspired to become an activist by the writings of Martin Luther King Jr., Mahatma Gandhi, and Henry David Thoreau, but also by the examples of religious and student activists in Liberia, including Samuel Kofi Woods and the human rights lawyer Tiawan Gongloe. "[They] gave me the inner confidence to stand against repression and for the indiscriminate promotion of peoples' well-being."[4]

Asked why he continued he continued his work, despite threats, arrests, and the ordeals experienced by his family, Toe replied, "This is principally because I came into it not for personal gains, but out of conviction that it is a chosen mission by which through my efforts and that of others, tens of thousands of hopeless people regain hope in life."[5]

1. Reebok Human Rights Award website, *Reebok Human Rights Awardees, 2005*. Available at http://www.reebok.com/Static/global/initiatives/rights/text-only/awards/2005.html (accessed May 15, 2011).

2. Frontline, *Testimonies of Human Rights Defenders*. Available at http://www.frontlinedefenders.org/node/133 (accessed May 15, 2011).

3. Reebok Human Rights Award website, *Reebok Human Rights Awardees, 2005*.

4. Cate Malek, *Peacebuilder Profiles: Aloysius Toe (Interview)*, Beyond Intractability, December 2005. Available at http://www.beyondintractability.org/reflections/personal_reflections/Aloysius_Toe_interview.jsp (accessed May 15, 2011).

5. Ibid.

NGOs in Liberia, Sierra Leone, Guinea, and Nigeria each coordinated national-level actions to pressure their individual governments. The NGOs in each country also had a particular and distinctive voice and message. For example, Nigerian NGOs challenged Taylor's asylum, highlighting national laws that prohibited the state from providing refugee status if individuals had been linked to war crimes. In Liberia, NGOs highlighted the destabilizing force that Taylor represented. Amnesty's Ayodele Ameen explained the importance of local involvement to the campaign: "Because of the grassroots campaign, it wasn't just CNN, but it was also in the local newspapers. This made it very difficult for policymakers to run away from the issue."[18]

In Liberia, a group of about ten NGOs were particularly active in the campaign. The groups sent numerous letters to government officials and used radio talk shows across the country to raise the issue. They organized marches in Monrovia, the capital, mobilizing up to five hundred people to walk from one end of the city to the other, as well as assemblies with speeches and testimonies. Aloysius Toe, a leader of the campaign, had been imprisoned twice during Taylor's regime for protesting the arbitrary arrest and imprisonment of other human rights advocates. He said:

> We worked to continuously keep the issue alive and visible in the public domain. Most of us worked in local communities with the local people. We tapped into the hearts and concerns of the people, and tried to build our messages around their concerns. For example, if someone's house was looted or their wife murdered, we would bring morality into play. Most Liberians believe in God, so we brought in what religions would say. When local politicians went to the community, local people would raise the issue, and tell their stories.[19]

The national-level pressure may have contributed to some early results: in July 2005, the leaders of Liberia, Sierra Leone, and Guinea issued a joint communiqué that accused Taylor of continued support for Liberian armed groups and agreed "to suggest to the government of Nigeria that there may now be need for a review of the terms of the temporary stay granted Charles Taylor."[20]

NGOs placed a priority on raising Charles Taylor's status repeatedly with then-Nigerian president Obasanjo. When Obasanjo traveled, advocates planted questions about Taylor with journalists attending Obasanjo's press conferences. Human Rights Watch executive director Kenneth Roth raised the matter of Charles Taylor during a personal meeting with Obasanjo in

Abuja in June 2004 and then, three months later, raised it again at a meeting of the Council on Foreign Relations in New York where Obasanjo was speaking. Reflecting later on the campaign, Roth said, "We spent about two years harassing Obasanjo every place he went. . . . The guy couldn't go anywhere without Charles Taylor staring him in the face."[21]

With Nigerian and Western officials, staff from the Special Court stressed that Taylor had repeatedly broken the conditions for his exile. In accepting exile in Nigeria, he had agreed to stay out of politics and refrain from engaging with the media. Eric Witte, special assistant to the prosecutor, said, "He kept breaching these conditions. We told officials, 'This was not an unconditional agreement, you have every right to break the deal.' This was a main argument, in addition to the moral argument."[22] Obasanjo's response was that the deal to offer Taylor temporary asylum was agreed upon by all key members of the international community seeking to bring Liberia's armed conflict to a close, that Nigeria's actions played a key role in restoring peace to Liberia, and that sending Taylor to the Special Court would reignite armed conflict by Taylor's supporters and undermine the fragile peace that had been achieved.

The campaign in Nigeria, like the court case filed by Anyaele and Egbuna, raised additional legal arguments for why Taylor should not be given safe haven in Nigeria: first, that an agreement between Obasanjo and Taylor to give Taylor safe haven was not legally valid without action by the national Parliament; second, that Taylor had failed to seek asylum status from Nigeria's refugee council; and third, that under Nigerian and international law, individuals indicted as war criminals were not eligible for asylum. According to Ameen, "The fundamental issue was putting before the public that what Obasanjo was doing was unconstitutional. There was an international warrant for Taylor's arrest. We avoided the issue of whether he was responsible for the war. The point was that he had been indicted by a competent court of law. If there's a warrant, you can't just ignore a court of law. To put it as simple as that, a lot of people bought into it, including the media."[23] The campaign printed ten thousand "Charles Taylor Wanted" posters reprinting the "red notice" that Interpol had issued for Taylor after his indictment in 2003. Shortly afterward, Nigeria's State Security Service (SSS) confiscated the posters and arrested two professional printers who had printed the posters, detaining them for five days. When the brother of one of the men went to visit his brother at the SSS headquarters, he was also arrested. The following day, SSS visited the offices of the Justice Initiative, allegedly to take its director to SSS for questioning.

The coalition mobilized its network and made complaints to federal officials, forcing the government to release the detainees and end its harassment.[24]

In New York, advocates from Human Rights Watch worked to put Charles Taylor's surrender onto the UN Security Council's agenda. They believed that while the Security Council's role would not be decisive, it could serve as "important background noise" to bilateral diplomacy with Nigeria. According to Elise Keppler, senior counsel for Human Rights Watch, it "sent the signal to Nigeria that the Security Council is concerned about the issue and it will need to be dealt with."[25]

In May 2005, the Security Council held a session devoted to the Special Court for Sierra Leone. Justice Emmanuel Ayoola, one of the court's judges, briefed the council about the work of the court. He spoke extensively about the importance of trying Taylor and the court's contribution to combating the culture of impunity. During a closed session that followed, nearly every Security Council member endorsed the need for Charles Taylor to face trial. Advocates used the session to press the United States and the UK to intensify quiet diplomacy with Nigeria. They also continued meeting with Security Council members individually to urge them to keep Taylor on the agenda.

In July 2005, the council adopted a resolution extending the UN mission in Sierra Leone (UNAMSIL), which underlined "the importance of ensuring that all those indicted by the Court appear before it, in order to strengthen the stability of Sierra Leone and the subregion and to bring an end to impunity, and encouraging all States to cooperate fully with the Court."[26] This marked the first time that the council made any reference in a formal resolution to the need for Taylor to be surrendered. Advocates felt it was significant, in part because just weeks earlier, legal advisors for several Security Council members had said that it was highly unlikely that the Security Council would mention indictees in the resolution, believing it was tangential to the renewal of UNMIL's mandate.[27] In November 2005, the UN Security Council went further, adopting a resolution specifically empowering the UN Mission in Liberia to apprehend and detain former president Charles Taylor if he returned to Liberia and to transfer him to Sierra Leone for prosecution before the Special Court.[28]

In late 2005, Liberia held its first democratic elections since Taylor was elected in 1997. The outcome of the election was critical for the campaign, as Obasanjo had stated repeatedly that he would only consider surrendering Taylor in response to a request from a duly elected Liberian president.

Twenty-two candidates, including a former soccer star, declared their candidacy for president. During the months leading up to the elections, Liberian NGOs repeatedly called on the candidates to take a position on Taylor's case and declare that if they were elected, they would request that Nigeria hand Taylor over to the court. They published a weekly newsletter, entitled "Promises to Keep," that gave information on the politicians and their positions. The groups sent the newsletter to all the political parties and to the press, who would then ask the candidates about the issue. Very few of the candidates took a firm position on how they would deal with Taylor. Nonetheless, the issue was raised repeatedly.

Ellen Johnson Sirleaf won the election, becoming the first elected female head of state in Africa. During the campaign, she did not take a position on how she would deal with Taylor and came under fire for allegedly supporting Charles Taylor during the war. According to Toe, "When Madam Sirleaf was elected, we directed our attention to her to try to get the government to define what should be done regarding the problem with Charles Taylor."[29] Ten days after she took office in January 2006, the campaign published an open letter urging her to seek Taylor's transfer to the Special Court. They emphasized that she had a limited window of opportunity, as pressure was building to bring the court's operations to a close, and highlighted statements she had made during her campaign. "President Johnson Sirleaf said her presidency will stand for accountability and the rule of law," said a Liberian representative of the campaign to the media. "Now she has a major opportunity to do just that. We hope she will seize this chance."[30]

At Johnson Sirleaf's first press conference, the campaign urged journalists to question her about Taylor. Her response was that her immediate priority was rebuilding Liberia and that Taylor was a "secondary" issue. She said that her government did not want "the Mr Taylor issue to be the issue that constrains us or the issue that causes us not to be able to do what we have to do here for the Liberian people."[31] She indicated that she had consulted with Obasanjo on the matter and that she would consult with other African leaders, but did not provide any details.

Local activists began looking for other ways to influence Johnson Sirleaf. "Our voices were not heard," said Toe, "so we looked at friends in the government who could build pressure within the government and send a message that failure to act would tarnish the reputation of the new government."[32] The campaign reached out to the minister of labor, a former human rights activist.

The minister drafted a memo articulating a personal policy position that the government should request the surrender of Taylor and sent it to the president and colleagues in the cabinet. According to Toe, "The minister was a person of principle and conviction. Some of the other Cabinet members were sympathizers of Taylor. However, his [the Minister's] argument eventually won out."[33]

Advocates worked to enlist the support of the United States, the UK, and other Western countries that had political and financial influence with both Liberia and Nigeria. According to Toe, "Africans are very fearful of losing support and aid from Western countries. In the case of Liberia and other parts of Africa, when you get collaboration with other NGOs and get the US and other Western countries to take positions, it can be very effective."[34] Sulaiman Jabati, an activist with the campaign in Sierra Leone, said, "Nigeria is a big brother in Africa. There was no country in Africa that could influence Nigeria. So our international partners were very important to lobby the US and the UK. This is the pressure we were using. Anytime Obasanjo traveled to the West, we made sure the issue was raised."[35]

In early 2005, the European Parliament adopted a resolution calling on Nigeria to transfer Taylor to the Special Court, for the UN Security Council to urgently take up the issue, and for the European Union and its member states "to build international pressure in order to bring about Charles Taylor's extradiction." The resolution noted that EU member states had contributed more than US$30 million to support the Special Court for Sierra Leone.[36] Members of the Campaign immediately issued press releases urging EU member states to implement the resolution by pressing Nigeria and the Security Council to take action.[37]

In Washington, staff from the Special Court and NGOs including the Coalition for International Justice worked to engage the US Congress. According to Witte, "In 2005, State Department was not supportive at all of efforts to get Taylor to the Court and there was no strong view in the leadership, so that's where Congress came in. Particularly by getting Republicans on board, we helped to ratchet up attention. We met with Congressional staff and sent them a steady diet of updates."[38] The objects of their pressure, however, were both Nigerian president Obasanjo and Liberia's Johnson Sirleaf (who was being pressured to ask for Taylor's surrender.) Both Democrats and Republicans alike used floor debates, resolutions, and meetings with State Department to push the Bush administration to seek Taylor's transfer to the Special Court. In

May 2005, just prior to a meeting between President Bush and Nigerian President Obasanjo, the House of Representatives passed a resolution calling for Nigeria to transfer Taylor to the Special Court; a week later the Senate passed the same resolution by unanimous consent.[39] In July 2005, when the Special Court was in danger of running out of funds, then-senator Barack Obama cosponsored legislation with Senators Hagel, Leahy, and Gregg to provide US$13 million to keep the Special Court up and running.[40]

Once Johnson Sirleaf was elected, US policymakers continued to raise the issue. Even before she took office, a dozen members of the US Congress, including both Republicans and Democrats, wrote to Secretary of State Condoleezza Rice urging the US administration to call on President Johnson Sirleaf to request Taylor's transfer to the Special Court.[41] State Department officials, including the US ambassador in Monrovia repeatedly raised the issue with the Liberian government, as well as with Nigeria's Obasanjo.[42]

In March 2006, two months after taking office, Johnson Sirleaf submitted a request to Nigeria to transfer Taylor so that he could stand trial before the Special Court. Just after requesting Taylor's transfer, Johnson Sirleaf visited Washington, where the House of Representatives had just approved $50 million in aid to Liberia. In a television interview, she acknowledged the international pressure to act on Taylor:

> We also are facing, you know, pressure—I must use that word—from the UN, from the US, from the European Union, who are all our major partners in development, on the need to do something about the Charles Taylor issue. And for us, you know, we are spending too much time with this matter just hanging over our heads, so to speak, taking too much of our energies, causing some slowdown in the commitments that we need from our partners to support our development agenda. And so we think it's time to bring it to closure.[43]

Despite Johnson Sirleaf's request, Obasanjo did not immediately agree to transfer Taylor. Although he had promised to surrender Taylor in response to a request from a democratically elected Liberian government, Obasanjo stated that ECOWAS and leaders of the African Union also had to agree to the handover, because they had been part of the original deal to exile Taylor. Advocates were frustrated that Obasanjo had changed his conditions. They saw this tactic as an effort to delay Taylor's transfer and to avoid taking responsibility for the decision. Human Rights Watch's Corinne Dufka lamented to the press that Obasanjo was "moving the goalposts."[44]

Although the African leaders did not object to Johnson Sirleaf's request, neither the AU nor ECOWAS acknowledged consultations with Obasanjo or made statements supporting Taylor's transfer. Dukfa said, "We were very disappointed with ECOWAS and the AU. After Johnson Sirleaf asked Nigeria to turn Taylor over, a very courageous thing to do, they hung her out to dry. They interpreted African solidarity as an intransigent loyalty to another African head of state."[45]

In late March 2006, Obasanjo was scheduled to make another trip to Washington, DC, and meet with then-president George Bush. Advocates in Washington used this as a point of leverage and contacted allies in Congress and officials at the State Department and National Security Council, arguing that Bush should not agree to meet Obasanjo personally until Obasanjo had agreed to turn Taylor over.

Days before the meeting, the Nigerian government issued a statement saying, "President Olusegun Obasanjo has today, 25 March, informed President Ellen Johnson Sirleaf that the government of Liberia is free to take former president Charles Taylor into custody."[46] Campaign members told the press, "This is a great day for justice, not only for the victims of Sierra Leone's brutal war, but also for the fight against impunity which as devastated so many lives in West Africa."[47]

Despite Nigeria's agreement to hand over Taylor, however, it took no action to take him into custody. In fact, interviews with local witnesses later revealed that any security Taylor had at his villa in Calabar had been withdrawn, paving the way for his escape.[48] Two days later, on the eve of Obasanjo's visit to Washington, it became known that Taylor had disappeared. Members of Congress publicly called for the White House to cancel the meeting with Obasanjo.[49] State Department spokespersons told the press that the United States had made clear to Nigeria both publicly and privately that it was their responsibility that Taylor be apprehended and face justice.[50] This appeared to force Obasanjo to take action. On March 28, Nigerian security forces captured Taylor in northeastern Nigeria as he was trying to cross into Cameroon.[51]

The following day, Taylor was transferred to the Special Court for Sierra Leone. At a press conference, UN secretary-general Kofi Annan said:

> It strikes an important blow to impunity. It sends a message, not only to the people of Liberia, but all around the sub-region and around the continent that impunity will not be allowed to stand and the brutal leaders who brutalize their people, who get engaged in organizing wars, recruiting boys and girls

and turning them into child soldiers, will pay a price. . . . I think it's a warning to all would-be warlords that they will be held to account.[52]

Due to security concerns, the Special Court president requested that Taylor's trial be relocated to the Hague. Taylor's trial began on January 6, 2008, on eleven counts of war crimes, crimes against humanity, and other serious violations of international humanitarian law, including terrorizing civilians, murder, outrages on personal dignity, cruel treatment, looting, recruiting and using child soldiers, rape, sexual slavery, mutilating and beating, and enslavement. On April 26, 2012, the court convicted Taylor on all eleven counts.

Lessons Learned

In securing Taylor's surrender to the Special Court, the campaign was able to overcome a number of obstacles, including threats against local activists and fears among local NGOs that if they pushed too hard for justice, remnants of the forces in the region could rearm themselves and mount new attacks against those who spoke out against the abuses. In both Liberia and Nigeria, local activists were harassed and threatened. Advocates in Liberia received anonymous phone calls telling them to stop their activities, while Nigeria's government used police pressure to try to intimidate members of the Coalition Against Impunity. According to Ameen, "Ensuring that our partners were safe was really challenging, if we weren't present in the area. We tried to make sure that in most of the countries, the top human rights defenders were involved, since that created a level of protection."[53] Communication among far-flung groups located across continents also created challenges. Ameen said, "Sometimes we would need to phone groups in the region to ask them to check their email and respond. You can't assume you can send an email and get a response in thirty minutes. Local people may need to go to an Internet café to get the message."[54]

Political obstacles included Obasanjo's reluctance to reverse his agreement to offer Taylor asylum, and Johnson Sirleaf's resistance to deal with the issue, in part because Taylor remained very popular in parts of Liberia, and the armed men he had supported in both Sierra Leone and Liberia continued to threaten the fragile peace that had taken root in both countries. Some Western countries, such as the UK and the United States, were also reluctant to push for Taylor's transfer because they had helped facilitate Nigeria's offer of exile for Taylor in 2003. Some sources also indicated that officials with State Department were divided over how hard to push Obasanjo, since Nigeria was an increasingly important ally to the United States as a major oil producer and partner in dealing with terrorism and key African concerns, including the war in Sudan.[55] Johnson Sirleaf and Sierra Leonean president Kabbah were also reluctant to pressure Obasanjo because of the role that Nigerian peacekeepers had played in bringing Sierra Leone's and Liberia's conflicts to an end.

The campaign ultimately succeeded for several reasons. The first was the commitment of its members to sustain pressure over the long-term in order to achieve their goal. According to Toe, the most effective aspect of the campaign was simply "continuously keeping the issue alive and visible in the public domain."[56] As Elise Keppler of Human Rights Watch put it, "We knew it wasn't going to be a quick fix."[57]

A second factor was the diverse nature of the campaign and the distinct roles played by its members. African NGOs mobilized domestic pressure on key governments and brought strength and credibility to the campaign; the Open Society Justice Initiative provided legal analysis and spearheaded the challenge to Taylor's asylum bid in Nigeria; Human Rights Watch drafted many of the campaign's public statements and coordinated strategic media outreach; Amnesty International mobilized its broad-based membership and helped build alliances among African NGOs. Staff for the Special Court provided information to members of Congress and conducted public outreach in Liberia, Sierra Leone, and Nigeria about the court. "By bringing together different sets of skills and expertise," said Elise Keppler of Human Rights Watch, "the campaign was able to be a more multi-faceted, credible, and effective effort."[58]

A particularly powerful characteristic of the campaign was the alliance between international NGOs and NGOs based in Africa. According to Eric Witte, "It was important to undercut the notion that this was a Western justice that was at odds with what Africans wanted. It was absolutely vital to have the active engagement of Liberian, Nigerian, and Sierra Leoneon civil society to make clear that the exile agreement didn't meet with their views."[59] Amnesty's Ayodele Ameen pointed out that the campaign sought to involve all of its active members on an equal footing. "It wasn't North/South, big NGOs, small NGOs. We tried to treat everyone equally. Documents were sent to everyone to comment. That created a sense of belonging and buy-in. Organizations saw themselves as part and parcel of the campaign."[60]

A third factor that influenced a positive outcome was the campaign's use of strategic opportunities, in particular Obasanjo's March 2006 scheduled meeting with President Bush in Washington. According to Ayodele Ameen, the threat of a cancelled Bush-Obasanjo meeting was a "decisive" moment for the campaign. It was also the product of sustained advocacy by the campaign with Congress and other officials in Washington. Eric Witte reflected, "In these advocacy campaigns, you have to build these crisis moments and use them to best advantage. You have to get rhetorical commitments from the people who have leverage to make things happen. . . . The pressure from Congress got the administration making quite strong statements that Taylor should be handed over to the court. It didn't give the administration room to back down."[61] He agreed that ultimately, it was the US threat to cancel Obasanjo's meeting with President Bush that prompted Obasanjo to apprehend Taylor and hand him over for trial.

A final element behind the campaign's success was its use of multiple points of leverage. The diverse membership of the campaign and its activity in various locations—African capitals, New York, Washington, Europe-enabled it to target various advocacy targets to strategic advantage, mobilizing individual governments (notably the United States), the international press, the UN Security Council, and the European Parliament. In fact, Johnson Sirleaf's public comments to the press made it clear that international pressure from various quarters was key to her decision to ask Nigeria to return Taylor. The high visibility and constant attention to the issue persuaded her that Taylor's case needed to be resolved to allow her to move forward with her agenda for Liberia.

Eric Witte reflected, "You never know with these advocacy campaigns with so many actors in so many different countries what is going to work, so you have to push on as many fronts as possible."[62] For example, Ayodele Ameen believed that even if the United States had not threatened to cancel Bush's meeting with Obasanjo, other advocacy strategies, including the court case filed by Anyaele and Egbuna, might have brought success. Ameen said, "We strongly felt that we were already very close to getting Obasanjo to hand Charles Taylor over. We could see signs. The court case [in Nigeria] over jurisdiction was ongoing, so even if he wasn't handed over, the court could have forced the Nigerian government to produce Charles Taylor. That would have been extremely embarrassing."[63]

Ultimately, the campaign achieved a result that many initially thought was impossible. Sulaiman Jabati, a campaign activist from Sierra Leone, said that when he traveled to the Hague to see Charles Taylor go on trial, "it was the happiest moment of my life." Reflecting on the impact of the campaign, he said, "No matter how powerful a leader is, no matter how important a leader is, if you commit crimes in any part of the world, you can be held accountable. The law is always mightier than power."[64]

Chapter 7

Seeking Justice for the Abu Salim Prison Massacre

Every time I went to a demonstration I was preparing myself for arrest, my family
were afraid for me. Internal Security called me once after a demonstration and
threatened me with imprisonment. But I have nothing to fear, four of my brothers
were imprisoned in Abu Salim and two of them died there. I am not afraid anymore.
I need to talk about it.
—*Mohamed Hamil Ferjany, who lost two brothers
in the Abu Salim prison massacre*[1]

PRIOR TO THE "ARAB SPRING" that swept the Middle East region beginning in late 2010 and the 2011 uprising that toppled Colonel Mu'ammar
Gaddafi, Libyans had lived under a repressive regime for more than forty
years. Freedom of expression and human rights activity was virtually prohibited. People could be sentenced to life in prison for disseminating information
deemed to "tarnish the country's reputation" or executed for group activity
considered contrary to the al-Fateh Revolution, which brought Colonel Gaddafi to power in 1969. Authorities referred to critics as "stray dogs," and in the
1970s and 1980s, police and security forces rounded up hundreds of academics, students, lawyers, journalists, and others considered "enemies of the revolution." Many were imprisoned or disappeared.

Attempts to form independent human rights organizations were quashed,
and hundreds of individuals had been imprisoned for allegedly belonging
to banned political groups, including the Libyan Islamic Group (or Muslim
Brotherhood Libya) and the Harakat al-Tajammu' al-Islami (the Islamic Alliance Movement). Many had not been charged with any violent act and were
detained for years without charge or trial, often incommunicado. In many
cases, family members of those detained were never given any information
about the whereabouts of the prisoner, nor allowed any contact.

Many of Libya's political prisoners were imprisoned at Abu Salim, a Trip-oli prison run by the International Security Agency and notorious for torture. Prisoners were beaten, hung by their wrists, subject to electrical shocks, and threatened with death. Detainees endured poor and overcrowded conditions, and some reportedly died from lack of medical care.[2]

In 1996, prisoners at Abu Salim rioted over their conditions. Security forces responded with force, gunning down twelve hundred prisoners in a brutal massacre. This chapter describes the courageous efforts of the families of the victims—working in the extremely limited space of an authoritative regime—to seek the truth about the massacre and justice for their loved ones. It also explores the link between the little-known organizing of these families and the 2011 Libyan uprising against the government that ultimately over-turned Gaddafi's rule.

The Abu Salim riot began on June 28, 1996, when some Abu Salim pris-oners reportedly seized a guard who was delivering food and used his keys to release hundreds of other prisoners. According to various accounts, guards on the roof of the prison began shooting at prisoners, and several of the prisoners took two guards hostage. Several guards reportedly were killed by prisoners.[3] Senior security officers came to the prison and began to negotiate with a small group of prisoners who demanded adequate health care, visits by their fami-lies, and fair trials. After lengthy negotiations, and promises of medical care for sick and wounded prisoners, the prisoners returned to their cells.

The following morning, hundreds of prisoners were forced into differ-ent courtyards. According to one former prisoner, a grenade was thrown into one of the courtyards, followed by heavy shooting that continued for more than two hours, leaving large numbers of prisoners dead. The wit-ness said, "I could not see the dead prisoners who were shot, but I could see those who were shooting. They were a special unit and wearing khaki military hats."[4] Other detainees also reported hearing sustained shooting, and later observed evidence of shooting inside individual cells. Another for-mer prisoner reported that the sick prisoners were the first victims. "The security officers asked for the list of sick people to take them to the hospital. Then they blindfolded them and took them to the corner of the prison. They started with them. They were the first ones killed."[5] The following day, secu-rity forces reportedly removed the bodies with wheelbarrows and placed them in trenches that had been dug for a new wall. Guards forced the survi-vors to clean the blood from their cells.

For years, the government refused to acknowledge that any deaths had taken place. A Libyan human rights activist said, "We heard about it, that something had happened to the prisoners, but had no idea that it was as terrible as later came out."[6] Eight years after the massacre, Colonel Gaddafi addressed the issue publicly for the first time, saying in an April 2004 speech to the Supreme Council of Judicial Bodies and to other high-ranking officials that families had a right to know what happened to their relatives during the incidents in Abu Salim in 1996, when large numbers of prisoners were reportedly killed. In 2009, the government finally confirmed that nearly twelve hundred prisoners had been killed in the massacre.

The government's admissions took place in the context of a political opening that began in the late 1990s. For years, the international community regarded Libya as a pariah state because of its repressive regime, its pursuit of weapons of mass destruction, and its backing of attacks against two civilian aircraft in the late 1980s that killed hundreds of civilians. In December 1988, Pan Am flight 103 blew up over Lockerbie, Scotland, killing all 270 passengers, and in 1989, UTA flight 772 was bombed over Niger, killing 170. In response, the UN Security Council imposed air and arms embargoes on Libya, a limited asset freeze, and ordered Libya to end all support for terrorism, to surrender suspects in the plane bombings, and to pay compensation to the victims' families.[7]

Libya began a concerted effort in 1999 to reform its image and improve its international relationships. That year, it surrendered two Libyan nationals suspected of the Pan Am bombing; one was convicted in 2001 by a Scottish court and sentenced to life imprisonment. In 2003, Libya announced that it would give up its weapons of mass destruction programs, limit its long-range missiles, and comply with a number of weapons control treaties. That year it also accepted responsibility for the Pan Am and UTA bombings and agreed to pay compensation to the victims' families. It agreed to pay $10 million to each victim's family—$4 million after UN sanctions were lifted, another $4 million after US sanctions were lifted, and a final $2 million after the US State Department took Libya off its list of states supporting terrorism.[8] The United States restored full diplomatic relations with Libya in 2006, and by November 2008, Libya had fully paid all compensation to the families of the Pan Am and UTA victims. By 2009, Libya's international standing had changed so dramatically that during that year alone, it held the presidency of the UN Security Council, the chair of the African Union, and the presidency of the UN General Assembly.

Reforms inside Libya did not match the significant changes in Libya's international relations, although limited progress was made in several respects between 2000 and 2010. The number of cases of arbitrary arrests and disappearances dropped. The regime began to show greater tolerance for dissent and freedom of expression. New newspapers and Internet sites were allowed to operate and write more critically of the government than previously.[9] One journalist told a human rights organization in 2009, "Overall, it's true, we have more freedom of expression. Before, we wouldn't even try to express ourselves. Now, we're taking risks."[10]

In 2001–2002, the Libyan government released more than five hundred political detainees from its prisons. Families of other detainees approached those released for news of their detained relatives. Many were confronted with a horrible reality: no one had seen their missing loved ones. As families sought information and began to realize that something terrible had happened, bonds were formed between the families. These connections, and the limited political space that was opening inside Libya, set the stage for unprecedented activism by family members of the massacred Abu Salim prisoners even while Colonel Gaddafi retained a firm grip on power.

During the next few years, family members combined complaints to the UN Human Rights Committee, civil claims to Libyan courts, public demonstrations, Internet communications, and dialogue with government officials to seek a full account of the massacre and bring those responsible to justice. The steps taken by the Gaddafi leadership—including acknowledgment of the massacre, notification of the families of the deceased, offers of financial compensation, and tolerance of the country's first independent public demonstrations in more than forty years—went far beyond what many expected was possible under Gaddafi's regime. In February 2011, as antigovernment uprisings swept the Middle East region, the families helped change the course of Libya's history even more profoundly as the catalyst for the Libyan uprising. When their primary representative, a young human rights lawyer, was arrested on February 15, the families took to the streets to demand his release. Thousands joined their protest, which spread across the country and sparked the uprising that ultimately, in August 2011, brought down the Gaddafi regime.

Seeking Truth and Accountability

In May 2004, the first relative of one of the missing prisoners filed a formal complaint with the UN Committee on Human Rights, alleging that Libya was responsible for multiple violations of the International Covenant on Civil and Political Rights in respect to the arrest, incommunicado detention, and death of his brother at Abu Salim.[11] The complaint was filed by Farag Mohammed El Alwani on behalf of his brother, Ibrahim Mohammed El Alwani, who was arrested in July 1995 by members of Libyan internal security forces. When Farag protested that the security officers did not produce an arrest warrant and gave no reason for Ibrahim's arrest, he was also arrested and detained for three days.[12]

Ibrahim was taken to the Benghazi Internal Security Compound and later transferred to Abu Salim. Members of his family went to the prison on several occasions to seek information about Ibrahim and any charges against him. Prison officials denied them access and refused to confirm or deny whether Ibrahim was being held at the facility. The family never received any information regarding his whereabouts, the charges against him, or any legal proceedings. Later, they were told by a former detainee that Ibrahim was being detained on charges of membership in a banned Islamic group.[13]

In June 1996, the family heard rumors that a mutiny at Abu Salim had been violently repressed, resulting in the deaths of hundreds of prisoners, but received no information regarding Ibrahim's fate. In July 2002, the police informed the family that Ibrahim was dead, and in 2003, the family received a death certificate confirming that Ibrahim had died in a Tripoli prison. Authorities did not provide a cause of death or inform the family what had happened to Ibrahim's body.[14]

In response to Farag Mohammed El Alwani's complaint, the Human Rights Committee made four separate requests for information regarding the case from the Libyan government, but received no response. In 2007, the committee issued its findings in the case, determining that Libya had violated prohibitions on arbitrary arrest and detention, incommunicado detention, and deprivation of life, and it had failed to adequately investigate these violations. The committee ruled that Libya was under an obligation to conduct a thorough and effective investigation into the disappearance and death of Ibrahim, provide information on the investigation to Farag, provide adequate compensation to the family, and prosecute, try, and punish those responsible for the violations. It also ruled that Libya was under an obligation to take measures to prevent similar violations in the future.

A second case was filed with the committee in July 2005 by Edriss El Hassy, on behalf of himself and his brother, Abu Bakar El Hassy. As in the

Profile: Edriss El Hassy

Edriss El Hassy was born just a year before Mu'ammar Gaddafi came to power in Libya.[1] His family was prominent in Al Bayda, a major city in the east, where his father was the mayor. After Gaddafi's military coup, however, Edriss's father was forced to resign, and the family came under scrutiny by the security police. During the 1990s, Edriss's older brother, Abu Bakar, was repeatedly detained and questioned by the police about his activities.

In 1995, a police unit came to the El Hassy's home. They arrested Abu Bakar in front of his mother and siblings, placing a black bag over his head. The same day, the police came to the university where Edriss was studying archaeology and arrested him while he was attending a lecture. Edriss was told he would be questioned for five minutes, but ultimately he was imprisoned for more than five years. Both brothers were taken to Abu Salim prison.

Edriss only saw his brother two times at the prison. Once they were briefly placed in adjacent cells, which allowed them to speak. Another time Abu Bakar was brought to Edriss's cell by mistake. Edriss could see that his brother was in extremely poor health. Other detainees told him that Abu Bakar had been interrogated and systematically beaten. When the Abu Salim massacre occurred in June 1996, Edriss said he could hear the gunfire and the screams of detainees being killed. Afterward, survivors described to him what had happened. He was detained at Abu Salim for another four years but never saw or heard of his brother again.

After his release from Abu Salim, Edriss was required to report regularly to the police and threatened against filing any formal complaints regarding his brother. Attempts by other members of his family to gather information about Abu Bakar were unsuccessful. When another brother went to Abu Salim to ask about Abu Bakar, prison officials warned him never to make inquiries again. Edriss finally left Libya in 2005, seeking refuge in the United Kingdom. Before he left, Edriss went to visit two of his sisters in Benghazi. He said, "One of them gave me a photo of my brother, Abu Bakar. She said, 'Don't forget about your brother. Try to do something for him. Try to find out what happened to him and who was responsible.'"

Soon after he arrived in the UK, the World Organization Against Torture approached Edriss, asking him if he would be willing to file a formal complaint with the UN Human Rights Committee. Edriss was worried about the possible repercussions for his family. "I was thinking especially about my brothers," he said, "and whether they will put them in the prison, especially for something they didn't do. But when I talked with them, they said, 'Go ahead, don't worry about us.'"

Edriss agreed to file the complaint. "I stayed 5 ½ years in prison," he said. "My brother died there. This is our right. We want to know what happened exactly. We want our brother's body and to know who killed him. We want to know the truth." Two years after Edriss filed his complaint, the Human Rights Committee issued its findings. It found that Libya had committed numerous violations of the ICCPR by subjecting Abu Bakar El Hassy to enforced disappearance, incommunicado detention, and torture and by failing to investigate the case. The committee requested the Libyan government to investigate the fate of El Hassy, compensate his family, and prosecute, try, and punish those responsible for the violations.[2]

In early 2009, the Libyan government sent a representative to the El Hassy family with a death certificate for Abu Bakar. The official told the family that Abu Bakar died in prison, but offered no reason. A few weeks later, officials came back to offer the family financial compensation. The family refused. Edriss said, "For our family, we are not rich, but we agreed that we will not take any money. We just want to know what happened."

Edriss speaks at public events about the Abu Salim massacre and, every year on the anniversary of the massacre, helps to organize a demonstration at the Libyan embassy in London. He and a small group of others also demonstrate every Saturday in Manchester, UK, where he currently lives, in solidarity with the families of Abu Salim who hold weekly demonstrations in Banghazi.

Just days before the Libyan uprising brought the end of the Gaddafi regime, Edriss said, "I can't describe what I'm feeling. What's happening now should have happened a long time ago." Explaining the impact of Gaddafi's fall on the families of Abu Salim, he said, "No one can return the victims but they can feel justice can take place."

1. Author interviews with Edriss El Hassy, July 8, 2010, and August 17, 2011.
2. Communication no. 1422/2005, *Edriss El Hassy v. Libyan Arab Jamahiriya*, para. 3.2.

case of El Alwani, the Human Rights Committee requested information on the case from the Libyan government on several occasions. The government did not respond. In November 2007, three months after giving its views in the El Alwani case, the Human Rights Committee issued its findings regarding Abu Bakar El Hassy, finding again that Libya had committed numerous violations of the ICCPR. The committee also stated that Libya had "attempted to avoid all accountability for the massacre by blocking all international and domestic scrutiny into what happened," suggesting "a government cover-up."[15]

Other families of Abu Salim prisoners, like the El Alwani and El Hassy families, also tried to make inquiries about their loved ones with Libyan authorities. In some cases, they were simply turned away; in others, they were told their family members were fine, but were denied access. The first inquiries were made on an individual basis, but in 2007 the families of the detainees began to act collectively. Their actions were significant because unlike the complaints to the Human Rights Committee, which were submitted by family members who had left Libya, these families were still inside the country. According to one Libya expert, "These were very, very sensitive issues that had been taboo for years. Lawyers themselves were scared to represent families and take cases forward. The shift came with lawyers being willing to represent them and the relative opening up that has happened over the past few years."[16]

A prominent lawyer named Abdul Hafid Ghogha agreed to represent thirty families, and in March 2007, he lodged a civil claim before the North Benghazi Court, demanding information about the fate of their loved ones. The case was unprecedented. In June 2007 the court declared itself not competent to review the case, but after a court of appeals ruled in favor of the plaintiffs in April 2008, the case was reopened. In June 2008, the North Benghazi Court ruled in favor of the families and ordered the prime minister, the secretary of public security, and the secretary of justice to reveal both the fate of the Abu Salim detainees and the reason for their detention and to provide the families with official information about the missing prisoners.[17] The head of security responded to the judge, claiming that the government had the right to detain people that pose a danger to the security of the country, and that by law they were not obliged to give any information about the prisoners or their whereabouts. Although the court order to reveal the fate of the victims was not implemented, the favorable ruling was a significant milestone.

The court case encouraged the families to organize further. In April 2008, they formed the Coordination Committee of the Families of the

Victims, and that June, they began to hold public demonstrations in Benghazi. The families' actions were extraordinary. According to one Libyan activist, it was the first demonstration since 1976 that was not organized by the government.[18] Independent demonstrations were prohibited by law, and those who formed, joined, or supported group activity that "opposes the ideology of the 1969 revolution" could be sentenced to death. The families demonstrated for about an hour, holding posters with photos of their loved ones and messages demanding to know the truth, such as, "Where is my father? Where is his grave? Where is his corpse?" "We want to see them. We want to see them after death, since we were deprived of seeing them during their lives." "The unjust has denied us of our right to grieve. They took years of our youth away."

Many were aware of the potential risks, but were determined to speak out. One said, "Every time I went to a demonstration I was preparing myself for arrest, my family were afraid for me. Internal Security called me once after a demonstration and threatened me with imprisonment. But I have nothing to fear, four of my brothers were imprisoned in Abu Salim and two of them died there. I am not afraid anymore. I need to talk about it."[19] Security forces observed the demonstrations and filmed family members who participated. Some members were harassed and told to go home. Several of the more active members were summoned for interrogation. However, the absence of more severe consequences emboldened the families to continue their actions. A core group of twenty to thirty families continued to demonstrate every Saturday. Initially, the families were careful to limit participation in their demonstrations to family members who lost a member in Abu Salim. According to one advocate, "They do not want to be accused of recruiting others to demonstrate; it helps keep them safer."[20]

In March 2009, four members of the committee were arrested in Benghazi, including Fathi Terbil, a young lawyer in his thirties who was also the group's spokesperson. The four activists were detained incommunicado for four days. During interrogation, security forces reportedly provided phone records that showed the activists had been in contact with activists outside Libya, including a Switzerland-based group called Human Rights Solidarity. According to a member of Human Rights Solidarity, "Even though they [the activists] had used mobile phones, and changed sim cards bought with cash, security forces had still been able to monitor their conversations, and knew they were in contact with people on the outside."[21]

The four activists were released after four days, following media attention and the personal intervention of Saif al-Islam al-Gaddafi, a son of Mu'ammar Gaddafi and the head of the Gaddafi International Foundation, a quasi-governmental charitable organization. Following the incident, outside groups began limiting their contact with the families, out of concern for their safety. An activist outside the country emphasized the importance of protecting the families' ability to continue organizing within Libya: "Their effectiveness is inside, pursuing cases, not outside. There are already groups outside, human rights NGOs, others to do the job. Our challenge is to keep them inside [the country]. If you leave, you are finished."[22]

In June 2009, on the thirteenth anniversary of the massacre, more than two hundred women, men, and children marched through Benghazi.[23] In 2010, as the demonstrations continued, security forces began organizing counterdemonstrations. In April, a counterdemonstration by a families association for the prison guards and police killed in 1996, known as "the Family of the Martyrs of Duty," prompted a violent attack against members of the coordination committee. A member of the "martyrs" group slashed the head of Fathi Terbil, the lead spokesperson for the Coordinating Committee, requiring emergency medical treatment. When Terbil went to file a complaint with the police, he discovered that the martyrs' group had already filed a complaint against the Coordinating Committee. Advocates believed that top security forces organized the violent protest specifically to prompt the secretary of justice to issue an order prohibiting demonstrations under the pretext of maintaining public security and safety.[24]

The cases that the families filed in civil court, their demonstrations, and the rulings from the Human Rights Committee began to yield noticeable results, including concerted efforts by the government to notify families of the deaths of detainees and to offer monetary compensation. Between 2001 and 2006, Libyan authorities had notified about 112 families that a relative detained at Abu Salim had died, but did not provide any details regarding the death. In early 2009, the government stepped up the notification process significantly. From January to March, the government contacted an additional 351 families to inform them that family members at Abu Salim had died. In April 2009, the Libyan secretary of justice told Human Rights Watch that 800 to 820 families had been notified and received death certificates.[25] By 2010, advocates believed that almost all of the families had been notified.[26]

Some families learned that more than one member of their family had died, including a family in Misurata that discovered in one day that five members of the family were dead, including one who was only fourteen when he was arrested.[27] The death certificates given to the families provided little information. They typically listed the place of death as "Tripoli" and the date as June, July, or September of 1996, rather than June 28 or 29, the dates the massacre is believed to have occurred. They also did not provide a cause of death. One man, who was notified of his brother's death in March 2009, was asked to sign the death certificate. He refused, saying, "Even dogs get a reason for their death."[28]

In 2008, the government began to offer monetary compensation to the victims' families. Initially, the government offered 120,000 dinars (US$98,590) if a victim was single, and 130,000 dinars (US$106,800) if he was married. By June 2009, the government increased the offer to 200,000 dinars (US$164,300). Families who accepted the compensation were required to sign a statement declaring that they would not seek criminal charges or pursue any further legal claims against any Libyan authority, agency, or Libyan officials. Many of the families, particularly those in Benghazi who had participated in the court cases, refused the compensation. Some believed that the amount offered was not enough, while others refused the money on principle, believing that they had a right to know the full details of the prisoners' deaths and that those responsible must be held accountable. One woman who had lost her son said, "I want to sit with the ruler of the country, the guy who is governing us, and I need to know why did they kill my son, on what basis, where, when? Did he do anything wrong? Then, if they refuse this truth, we need to go to the courts. No one can compensate me for my son. To the government, I say, we have lived as poor people, we will live as poor people, but with our dignity."[29] In April 2009, the Libyan secretary of justice stated that the "offers of compensation were made in the context of reconciliation." He said that approximately 30 percent of families had accepted the offer, 60 percent had refused because they believed the amount was not sufficient, and 10 percent had refused the compensation on principle.[30] In August 2009, the Gaddafi Foundation reported that 598 of 1,167 families had accepted compensation.[31]

In March 2009, the Coordination Committee of the Families of the Victims published a list of their demands on Libyan websites abroad. They called on the Libyan government to:

- Reveal the truth about the fate of their relatives;
- Prosecute those responsible;
- Hand over remains of the deceased to the families or reveal their burial sites;
- Issue proper death certificates with the correct dates and place of death;
- Make an official apology in the media;
- Release all other family members of Abu Salim victims who were arbitrarily detained; and
- Increase the compensation offered to equal that provided to families of the Lockerbie incident.

The families also used websites to publicize their activities outside Libya, for example, by taping their weekly demonstrations and posting photos and videos online.[32]

The actions by families were initially centered in Benghazi, but over time the families began to reach out, contacting more than one hundred other families of Abu Salim prisoners. Families in other towns became active and began making inquiries to local authorities regarding family members in Abu Salim. Many of these families also refused compensation offered by the government. Even families that had accepted compensation began joining the weekly demonstrations. A Libyan activist outside the country said, "We tried to send the message that even if they took the compensation, they could still take action. The right compensation has a different meaning: investigations, going to court, etc."[33]

Members of the Coordination Committee met with government officials in both 2008 and 2009. In 2008, several members met with Benghazi officials, where they explained their refusal to accept financial compensation without being given the truth about the massacre. They also made a written request to register the Coordination Committee legally, which was denied.[34] In early 2009, members of the committee were invited to Tripoli to meet with senior officials. One participant later told Amnesty International that he believed that the purpose of the meeting was to convince the family members that the government would offer nothing more than financial compensation and that they should accept the government's approach to "reconciliation."[35]

In November 2009, the Human Rights Society of the Gaddafi Foundation rented a hall in Benghazi for three days and invited family members of Abu

Salim prisoners to come and speak about their loved ones and the problems they faced. Many families did so. According to one activist, "This gave the families, including those that were most active, the feeling that they were being listened to. They had never had that from the state before."[36] The local radio station in Benghazi covered the meetings on its primetime program, "Good Evening Benghazi." It broadcast live ninety-minute segments on three consecutive days, interviewing three of the lawyers representing the families; the general director of the Human Rights Society, Mohamed al-Allagi; and the society's executive director, Mohamed Tarneesh. The program gave the families an unprecedented platform to present the massacre and their case to a wider audience within Libya. However, the staff for the radio program paid a heavy price: in February 2010, seven or eight members were fired.[37]

The three-day session was covered by Libyan websites, and several days later the Human Rights Society issued a press release urging relevant authorities to address the events at Abu Salim in 1996 and to ensure a fair and transparent investigation.[38] The Human Rights Society reiterated its recommendations in its annual report in December 2009, urged authorities to report to families regarding the fate of Abu Salim prisoners, and noted that the prison "caused a state of deep grief in the Libyan citizen's psyche."[39]

Twice the Libyan government announced that it would conduct an investigation into the events at Abu Salim. In April 2005, authorities announced that a committee had been established to investigate the "incident." In July 2006 authorities confirmed the investigation was ongoing, but no details or conclusions were ever made available. In July 2008, Saif al-Islam al-Gaddafi stated in a speech that he had asked for an investigation of Abu Salim several years earlier, but that it had been delayed because of the "sensitivity" of the issue. He stated, "The reality of this topic should be clarified, especially to the families of the people who died. You should be told how your children died. What happened on that day and that night exactly? . . . You have to reveal the truth . . . reveal the lists and reveal the investigation results."[40]

In September 2009, authorities announced that Mohamed al-Khadar, a judge on the High Court and the former public prosecutor of the Military Court, would head a seven-member "independent" committee to investigate, but gave no details regarding the committee's mandate. Shortly after his appointment, Mohamed al-Khadar gave an interview to an official Libyan newspaper, where he stated that up to two hundred guards had been killed in Abu Salim in June 1996.[41] The claim did not correspond to any publicly available information or witness accounts from Abu Salim, prompting concerns among human rights groups and victims' families regarding the credibility and impartiality of the investigation. According to a family member, "Because he is working with the government, we and all the families do not trust him. If there is an investigation, it should not be from us, and not from the government, but from another place." He believed that there was no entity within Libya that could conduct a credible investigation.[42] Although Mohamed al-Khadar stated that a final report would be published six months' after the committee began its work, no information regarding the investigation was ever made available.

Organizations based outside of Libya also worked to bring attention to the Abu Salim massacre. The World Organization Against Torture and Libya Human Rights Solidarity assisted family members of Abu Salim victims to bring formal complaints to the UN Human Rights Committee. In 2009, Human Rights Solidarity submitted forty cases from families with the UN Working Group on Enforced and Involuntary Disappearances, which has a mandate to assist the relatives of disappeared persons to determine the fate and whereabouts of their disappeared family members.[43] The Working Group formally accepted the cases in March 2009.[44] Human Rights Solidarity also published an account of the Abu Salim killings, organized public events in Europe, and helped publicize the actions of family members within Libya.[45]

Amnesty International published reports dealing with Abu Salim in 2004 and 2010, and Human Rights Watch published a report in 2009; each urged the Libyan government to investigate the Abu Salim killings, make a full account of what happened, and bring those responsible to justice. A delegation from Amnesty International met with Mu'ammar Gaddafi in February 2004, after issuing an urgent appeal and writing to Gaddafi to urge a prompt, thorough, and impartial investigation of the Abu Salim killings. During the meeting, Gaddafi referred to the events as a "tragedy." In 2009, an Amnesty delegation visited Libya again, meeting with a range of government officials, including the head of the Internal Security Agency and the secretaries of the General People's Committees for Justice and for Public Security, and calling on authorities to address past and ongoing human rights violations. They visited Abu Salim prison, but their interviews with several prisoners were interrupted by guards and requests to interview several other detainees were denied. Authorities also prevented members of the Amnesty International delegation from boarding a flight to Benghazi where they had planned to meet with family members of Abu Salim victims.[46]

In December 2009, Human Rights Watch held a press conference in Tripoli to release a report on Libya that addressed the Abu Salim massacre. It was the first time that an independent organization had been allowed to criticize Libya's human rights record publicly in Tripoli. Families of Abu Salim victims attempted to attend the press conference, but internal security agents prevented three members of the Coordinating Committee in Benghazi from boarding a plane to Tripoli, and two other committee members were stopped 350 km from Benghazi and told not to go to Tripoli.[47] Nevertheless, several families of Abu Salim victims succeeded in attending the event.

According to Heba Morayef, Human Rights Watch's Libya researcher, "We knew the room would be full of security and that those attending might be too intimidated to ask questions." But after some initial questions from journalists, family members began to speak. One man showed a picture of his brother who had been killed at Abu Salim, saying, "Money is not enough. I want to know what happened to my brother."[48] Others who spoke included family members who had been arrested in March and held for four days before being released. Other individuals attending the conference criticized the demands of the Coordinating Committee. Organizers heard later that some families were paid by authorities to attend and disrupt the press conference. These families had accepted government compensation and were reportedly told by the Gaddafi Foundation to state publicly that the state had offered compensation and that they didn't need anything further.[49]

The conference lasted nearly three hours and was covered by several television outlets, including two from Al Jazeera, as well as the Associated Press, Reuters, Agence France Press, BBC, and several Libyan websites. According to Morayef, "A journalist from London called me on my cell phone and asked me to keep the line open throughout the press conference, and then broadcast it live over his website. Families in Benghazi heard it. It was an incredible experience. At the end, for an hour or hour and a half, only family members were left in the room, just wanting to talk."[50]

In June 2010, activities both inside and outside Libya marked the fourteenth anniversary of the Abu Salim massacre. Family members of victims demonstrated in Benghazi on June 26 as one of their regular Saturday demonstrations, and then again on June 29, the actual anniversary of the massacre. This time, the families were joined by ten to twelve lawyers.

They reiterated their demands and also distributed pamphlets urging others to join them. According to one advocate, "This is very significant, though to outsiders it may seem like nothing."[51] Outside of Libya, advocates held demonstrations at the prime minister's residence in London, at the Libyan embassy in Stockholm, and at a park in Washington, DC. They also organized conferences and lectures in Geneva, Switzerland; Washington, DC; and Manchester, UK.

In early 2011, the relatively unknown struggle of the Abu Salim families sparked a profound change in the course of Libyan history. Throughout the Middle East, antigovernment uprisings began in what became known as the "Arab Spring," toppling regimes in Egypt and Tunisia and challenging others from Syria to Yemen to Bahrain. In Libya, protests began when Fathi Terbil, the spokesperson for the Abu Salim families and two other members of the group, were arrested and detained on February 15, 2011, in Benghazi. Government officials had discovered that Terbil and the Abu Salim families were calling for public actions on February 17; by arresting Terbil, they hoped to quash the plans.[52] In response to the arrests, members of the Abu Salim families immediately went to the police station to demand the release of Terbil and the other activists. Twenty or thirty members, mostly women, protested for two or three hours. As they chanted, they called on the people of Benghazi to join them, saying "Stand up, this is your day."[53] Officials finally agreed to release Terbil and the others. Empowered, the families marched two to three kilometers into the city's central square that evening. As they passed through different neighborhoods, they encouraged youth and other residents to join them and announced further demonstrations the next day. More than two thousand Benghazi residents joined them in protests that grew and spread to other cities in Libya. Government security forces responded with violence, killing at least two hundred civilians in Benghazi.

Terbil set up a live online video broadcast from the roof of the Benghazi courthouse, called "Free Libya Radio." Within a week, tens of thousands of protesters had taken control of Benghazi's streets and declared the city "liberated." Like protesters in Egypt and Tunisia, they chanted the slogan, "The people want to bring down the regime." Terbil told a British journalist, "We, the Abu Salim families, ignited the revolution. The Libyan people were ready to rise up because of the injustice they experienced in their lives, but they needed a cause. So calling for the release of people, including me, who had been arrested became the justification for their protest."[54]

In other parts of Libya, protests continued amid brutal government reprisals. Thousands of civilians were killed as government security forces attacked protesters, used heavy weaponry against funeral processions, and set up snipers to shoot at worshippers leaving mosques. Saif al-Islam Gaddafi, the son of Gaddafi who had previously pressed for investigations into the Abu Salim massacre, appeared on state television to defend his father's regime, stating, "We will fight to the last minute, to the last bullet."[55] Senior government and military officials defected from Gaddafi's government in protest. The opposition created a Transitional National Council as the "political face of the revolution" with Fathi Terbil as one of its members. In late February, the UN Security Council referred the Libyan conflict to the International Criminal Court for investigation, and in March, it imposed a no-fly zone over Libya and authorized measures to protect civilians under threat of attack.

For six months, opposition forces struggled against the Gaddafi regime for control of the country as NATO forces carried out air strikes to protect the civilian population. On June 26, the International Criminal Court announced that it was issuing arrest warrants for Mu'ammar Gaddafi, his son Saif al-Islam Gaddafi, and military intelligence chief Abdullah al-Sanussi on the grounds of murder as a crime against humanity. In late August, opposition forces entered Tripoli and took over Gaddafi's compound. The forty-two years of the Gaddafi regime had finally come to an end. On October 20, militia forces captured Gaddafi near Sirte and executed him in an apparent act of vengeance.

As opposition forces took control of Tripoli in August, detainees inside the Abu Salim prison were largely unaware of the uprising or resulting conflict that had taken place over the previous six months. They heard gunfire and explosions as the rebels struggled with Gaddafi loyalists. One said, "We expected another massacre." Instead, the guards deserted the prison, leaving the prisoners on their own. They broke open each other's cells, and on August 24, an estimated twenty-five hundred prisoners left the Abu Salim prison. One, Saad al-Eshouli, who had spent fourteen years inside the prison, said, "There is no way to describe how great it felt to be free." Another, who survived the 1996 massacre, told a journalist after the prison had been liberated, "I can't believe I am here, in this place, speaking my mind. I am no longer afraid."[56]

As Libya entered a new era, the families of the Abu Salim massacre and their allies continued their campaign for truth and justice. During the uprising, they established a tent in Benghazi with photos of victims of the massacre, with an ongoing presence to allow family members and others to learn about the massacre and share information. In June 2011, the fifteenth anniversary of the massacre, they organized five days of lectures, films, and other activities. After the liberation of the Abu Salim prison, they took steps to preserve evidence that could be used for future trials. Switzerland-based Human Rights Solidarity worked with the Transitional National Council to ensure the prison site was secure, to arrange excavations, and to work with forensic experts who could help identify mass graves and conduct DNA testing on the remains of victims of the massacre.[57] According to a spokesperson, the search for the bodies "is the most important event in the new Libya. It buries the ghosts of the past."[58] As the country entered a period of transition, advocates continued to maintain files on those implicated in the massacre and witnesses that could testify in criminal trials or in truth and reconciliation proceedings, hopeful that under a new government, truth and justice could finally be achieved.

Lessons Learned

Years before the Libyan uprising, the families of the Abu Salim prison massacre took advantage of modest political openings to seek the truth about Abu Salim and justice for their loved ones. In doing so, they took considerable risks and faced significant obstacles, including severe constraints on human rights activity inside Libya, the vested interests of Libya's security apparatus and senior leadership in avoiding accountability, and insufficient outside pressure by allies. However, not only were they able to garner some remarkable concessions from the Gaddafi regime, but also they provided the impetus for the uprising that toppled the Gaddafi regime.

When the families began organizing, domestic reforms lagged far behind Libya's steps to regain international acceptance, and the space for advocacy within Libya remained extremely limited. The families of the victims, the lawyers representing them, and their sympathizers faced significant risk of reprisals and intimidation, as evidenced by the detention of several key members in March 2009, surveillance of the group, the dismissal of radio station employees involved in the November 2009 broadcasts of programs related to the massacre, and the violent counterattack against demonstrators in April 2010. A Libyan who left the country said, "The security apparatus is very effective. They are the ones that really run the country. They had the right to do anything if they think you are against their rule. They can come to your house, take those they want, and no one will say a word, even mothers and brothers. If families lose one, they don't want to lose another. There's a state of fear."[59]

Many Abu Salim families believed that the massacre implicated the highest levels of Libya's leadership, and that Abdallah al-Sanussi, Gaddafi's brother-in-law and the senior security official that negotiated with Abu Salim prisoners the night before the killings, was directly involved in the massacre, acting on direct orders from Gaddafi. They believed that the involvement of such senior officials and this family relationship made any admission of responsibility by the government very unlikely. In addition, the centralized nature of the government also meant that no remedies could be taken regarding the massacre without the approval of the government's most senior leadership. Said one advocate, "Nothing happens in Libya without Gaddafi's order. Nothing."[60]

Although the government tolerated organizing by the families, it also actively instigated opposition and counterorganizing. For example, when the families began demonstrating in Benghazi, the government encouraged family members of security forces who were killed during the prison uprising to demonstrate as well. They did so at the same time and place in Benghazi as the prisoners' families. They claimed that the prisoners killed were not political prisoners and urged an inquiry into the deaths of their loved ones. On at least one occasion, the counterdemonstrators provoked a violent attack on the Abu Salim families. Despite the violence, advocates for the families affirmed justice for all. One Libyan human rights activist said, "The families of both have the right to know what happened. The government should investigate everything, all cases, whether prisoners or security."[61]

Another impediment to justice was the failure of outside governments to exert significant pressure on Libya to resolve the Abu Salim case, in part because Libya had emerged as a strategic ally for many Western states, cooperating with the United States on counterterrorism efforts and with Italy and other European countries to control irregular migration into Europe. According to one Abu Salim family member, "No one makes pressure to make changes inside Libya. Everything changed outside, but not inside. [The Western powers] said, 'you give up nuclear weapons, okay, you're good now,' but they don't care about the people inside."[62] In June 2010, Amnesty International suggested that instead of encouraging domestic reforms, the European

Union and the United States might be "turning a blind eye" to the human rights situation in Libya in order to further their national interests.[63]

In the face of these obstacles, the developments around Abu Salim and the activity by family members and other advocates under Gaddafi's rule were extraordinary. Libya's top leadership acknowledged the massacres, took steps to notify families that their loved ones were deceased, offered financial compensation, engaged in dialogue with representatives of the families, pledged investigations, and tolerated independent public demonstrations for the first time in forty years.

Outside activists agreed that the most important factor in prompting the government to respond was the role of the Abu Salim families themselves. Guimma El Omami of the Switzerland-based Libya Human Rights Solidarity said, "What really triggered the action by the government were the actions by the families. The government felt there must be a solution."[64] Human Rights Watch's Heba Morayef agreed, saying, "It really is incredible. It's a significant change and it's happened purely because of the families' activism."[65]

Because of the constraints of the Libyan regime, the family members of Abu Salim victims pressed their cause strategically. They were careful to limit their demands to the cases of their loved ones and avoided activity that could be perceived as political. Fathi Terbil said in a video statement in early 2010, "Our demands are human rights demands, not political demands. We have no political ambitions. . . . All we want is to live a secure life, a stable life, a life with some dignity . . . let's open a new page [with the authorities], a page based on what is right, on justice, on truth, on the establishment of truth."[66]

Another factor in winning concessions from the government was the strategic alliances and support from both international NGOs and quasi-governmental groups within Libya. The World Organization Against Torture and Libya Human Rights Solidarity helped families bring formal complaints to UN bodies, while Amnesty International and Human Rights Watch published reports on the massacre and Amnesty representatives raised the issue with Gaddafi directly. The Gaddafi International Foundation's Human Rights Society's active engagement with Abu Salim family members and public calls for the truth about Abu Salim also influenced the government to take some modest steps and also encouraged the families to continue to speak out. Because the foundation was run by Mu'ammar Gaddafi's son, Saif al-Islam al-Gaddafi, it was the only organization in the country that could raise human rights issues. Perversely, it was Saif al-Islam Gaddafi who vigorously denounced the protests once the Libyan uprising began, pledging to "destroy seditious elements" and threatening a bloody civil war where his father's forces would "fight until the last man."[67] In June 2011, the prosecutor for the International Criminal Court issued a warrant for his arrest for his alleged involvement in the murder and persecution of civilians during the crackdown against the protests. In November, Libya's new transitional government took him into custody, but vowed to try him in Libya.

Like other successful campaigns, the families effectively used multiple points of leverage—domestic courts, UN complaints mechanisms, public demonstrations, direct negotiations with the government, and outreach through the Internet—to keep the issue alive and to force the government to confront their demands. In particular, the Benghazi court case provided an early win that empowered the families and bolstered additional organizing.

Finally, a critical factor for the families' campaign was timing. The limited political opening in Libya in the 1990s as the Libyan government sought greater international acceptance made the families' initial organizing possible. They sustained their efforts over the course of several years, continuously looking for new avenues of advocacy and political developments that could benefit their cause. At the time that they began, the families likely had no idea that the end of Gaddafi rule was just a few years away or the role that they would play in sparking a national uprising. When the Arab Spring swept the Middle East, the families were ready to take advantage of that singular moment and poised to take the lead. Their tenacious efforts had proven they were able to mobilize, stand up against authority, demonstrate publicly, and take risks. According to one Libyan human rights advocate, "Others were meeting on the street, asking 'who is going to lead this?' They were not organized, they didn't know each other. But the families were prepared."[68] The families took the initiative to plan broader protests, and when their leaders were arrested, they seized that catalytic opportunity to engage the broader population in large-scale protests. The result changed the course of Libya's history.

Chapter 8

Demanding Accountability for War Crimes in Sri Lanka

Many people have died. Whenever they heard there were bodies, they would collect for burial. Two months ago, my father went missing. I went to the hospital to look for my father. I found his body. The entire back of his head was missing. Only his face was there. We asked the doctor to do something to his head so we could bury him, but they said we should just be grateful that we had a body to bury.

—Jagdeshwaran, whose father was killed by a shell while riding his bicycle in a so-called no-fire zone in Sri Lanka in 2009[1]

FOR TWENTY-FIVE YEARS, a brutal civil war raged in Sri Lanka between the government and the separatist Liberation Tigers of Tamil Eelam (LTTE, or Tamil Tigers). The war was marked by gross human rights abuses by both sides, cost more than one hundred thousand lives, and prompted more than six hundred thousand Tamils to flee the country. The war finally culminated in May 2009 with the military defeat of the Tamil Tigers. The cost of peace, however, was horrific. Tens of thousands of civilians were killed during the final military offensive, and the final months of the conflict were described as an "unimaginable humanitarian catastrophe."[2]

The Tamil Tigers' goal had been to establish an independent state for Sri Lanka's ethnic Tamil minority in the north and east of Sri Lanka, in response to decades of systematic discrimination by the Sinhalese majority. Led by Vellupillai Prabhakaran, the Tamil Tigers recruited thousands of children into its armed struggle, often by force, and bombed both military and civilian targets, including buses, commuter trains, hotels, and office buildings, often killing large numbers of civilians. It engaged in massacres, retaliatory killings, and carried out more than two hundred suicide bombings, using suicide bombers to assassinate former Indian prime minister Rajiv Gandhi in 1991, and Sri Lankan president Ranasinghe Premadasa in 1993. The Tamil Tigers presented itself as the sole representative of the Tamil people and assassinated leaders of rival Tamil parties, journalists, and other individuals who spoke out against their tactics.

The government, in turn, carried out massacres of Tamil civilians and engaged in indiscriminate aerial and artillery bombardment of civilian areas, including medical facilities and places of worship where civilians had taken refuge. Tens of thousands of people "disappeared" while in the custody of Sri Lankan security forces during the course of the conflict. Suspected Tamil Tigers sympathizers were subject to mass arrests, extrajudicial executions, and prolonged detention without trial.

A ceasefire was brokered by Norway in 2002, but was marred by continued violations, particularly ongoing child recruitment and killings of Tamil opponents by the Tamil Tigers. Peace negotiations made no headway. War resumed in 2006, with the government and the Tamil Tigers renewing military operations. In October 2008, the government launched a major military offensive, after issuing an order prohibiting international aid agencies and journalists from the Vanni, the northern territory held by the Tamil Tigers. The order prevented civilians in the area from receiving adequate relief assistance and, by barring both human rights monitors and journalists, severely limited any independent assessments of violations of human rights or international humanitarian law, as well as their impact on the civilian population.

The government steadily captured LTTE-held territory, and by early 2009, the rebels were trapped within a shrinking strip of land along the northeast coast, along with hundreds of thousands of civilians that had been forced to retreat alongside them. The Tamil Tigers used these civilians as human shields, refusing to allow them to leave the conflict zone, and in numerous instances, shooting and killing those who tried to flee to safety. The government urged civilians to congregate in unilaterally declared "no-fire" zones, but then carried out aerial bombardment and fired artillery indiscriminately into these densely populated areas. The government claimed that it was engaged in a "humanitarian rescue operation" with a policy of "zero civilian casualties." A UN panel of experts, however, found that government forces deliberately shelled the "no-fire" zone from all directions, including land, air, and sea, subjecting an estimated 300,000 to 330,000 civilians to repeated bombardment.[3] Government armed forces not only deliberately shelled the no-fire zones, but also systematically and repeatedly hit makeshift hospitals in the conflict area in dozens of artillery and aerial attacks, killing hundreds of civilians, despite the fact that the locations of the hospitals were well-known to the government.[4]

Casualties skyrocketed. Thousands of civilians died and many more were wounded, but they had little access to medical care. Both the government and the LTTE resisted international calls for a "humanitarian pause" in the fighting or a humanitarian evacuation to allow civilians to leave the conflict zone. As fighting continued, UN officials began to warn of a "bloodbath."[5] By mid-March, 35,000 people had managed to flee, only to be detained in government camps under strict military control. Humanitarian agencies were given only tenuous access to the camps. By the end of the war, approximately 280,000 displaced persons were crowded into the camps, lacking adequate food, water, sanitation, and medical care.

On May 19, 2009, the Sri Lankan government declared victory over the LTTE, announcing that in a final attack, it had killed eighteen of the remaining top LTTE leaders, including Vellupillai Prabhakaran. The war was finally over, but at a terrible price. Ultimately as many as forty thousand civilians died in the final months of fighting, most due to government shelling, according to a UN Panel of Experts report in 2011. The report described the final devastation: "The dead were strewn everywhere; the wounded lay along the roadsides, begging for help from those still able to walk, but often not receiving it. Some had to be torn away from the bodies of their loved ones left behind. The smell of the dead and dying was overwhelming."[6] In the aftermath of the conflict, more evidence emerged of war crimes. British television broadcast cell-phone video depicting Sri Lankan soldiers executing bound and blindfolded Tamil prisoners at point-blank range. Allegations surfaced that the Sri Lankan defense secretary had ordered the execution of LTTE political leaders who had attempted to surrender and instructed his field commander to "finish the job by whatever means necessary."[7] The government, however, continued to deny any violations of international humanitarian law. In a speech in June 2010, President Mahinda Rajapaksa stated that "we left no room for even one bullet to be fired against ordinary civilians."[8]

This chapter explores the concerted efforts by a trio of international organizations—Amnesty International, Human Rights Watch, and the International Crisis Group—to respond to the Sri Lankan crisis. As the war escalated, they tried to mobilize the international community to halt massive civilian casualties and gain access for humanitarian agencies and independent monitors to those affected by the conflict. After the war's end, they pressed for an international investigation to ensure accountability for the massive violations that had occurred during the final months of the conflict.

The Advocacy Response

Amnesty International, Human Rights Watch, and the International Crisis Group had long documented abuses and conducted advocacy related to Sri Lanka's conflict.[9] They scaled up their activity beginning in late 2008. According to Alan Keenan, Sri Lanka project director and senior analyst for the International Crisis Group, "it was a disaster waiting to happen. ... We sent a private letter to Bank Ki-moon after the eviction of the UN and humanitarian groups from the Vanni. From that point on, it was clear why they were being thrown out, it was to keep eyes off of what was going to happen. I don't think we and others were ready for the scale of what was going to happen but we were alert for something catastrophic."[10] The organizations stepped up their research to spotlight escalating violations and focused their advocacy on several targets: the media, influential capitals, the UN Security Council, the UN Human Rights Council, and the International Monetary Fund (IMF).

During the first half of 2009, Amnesty International and Human Rights Watch each published more than twenty press releases on the worsening conflict, drawn from testimonies from displaced persons, aid workers, local officials, and local doctors treating the wounded. Human Rights Watch deployed members of its emergencies team on several missions to Sri Lanka to document the growing crisis and worked with the American Association for the Advancement of Science (AAAS) to obtain satellite images of the attacks to corroborate testimonies from the ground. Both Human Rights Watch and Amnesty were in regular telephone contact with doctors in the no-fire zones to receive accounts of civilian casualties. According to Human Rights Watch's Asia Director, Brad Adams, "We were getting lots of real-time reports from civilians indicative of what was going on on the ground which was a scorched-earth policy. We made a strategic decision to do as much daily reporting as we could, rather than do big reports that would become out of date quickly."[11] During the final days of the war, both Human Rights Watch and Amnesty International were issuing up to three releases a week regarding continued shelling, escalating casualties, and the urgent need for international action, receiving extensive international media coverage. All three organizations provided a constant flow of information about the crisis to policymakers in key capitals, including Washington, Brussels, London, Paris, and Berlin, to UN ambassadors in New York and Geneva, and to foreign embassies in Colombo. The groups worked to influence policymakers by placing commentaries in major international publications. Op-eds by the International Crisis Group appeared in the *New York Times, Le Temps, European Voice, The Guardian, Foreign Policy, and the International Herald Tribune,* while Human Rights Watch published commentaries in US, British, and Japanese newspapers.

The Sri Lankan government reacted to the criticism with attacks of its own. The Sri Lankan Defense Department posted regular statements on its website assailing rights groups and portraying them as LTTE sympathizers. One government official referred to Amnesty International representatives as "liars and apologists for terror."[12] Another statement accused Human Rights Watch of showing "clear hostility" toward the Sri Lankan government and "citing mountains of allegations based on questionable evidence."[13] Sri Lankan government officials repeatedly denied any shelling of populated areas in the no-fire zones and grossly misrepresented the actions of security forces, despite ample testimony from witnesses and satellite imagery that proved otherwise.

The NGOs began pushing the UN Security Council to take a more active role in addressing the crisis in Sri Lanka. A core issue was whether members of the Security Council would be willing to place Sri Lanka on the council's formal agenda—a prerequisite to stronger Security Council action, including resolutions or sanctions. Placing an issue on the Security Council's agenda is highly political and requires support from nine of the Security Council's fifteen members. Governments often argue that situations of internal armed conflict, like Sri Lanka's, are not a "threat to international peace and security" and therefore not an appropriate concern for the Security Council. Underlying these arguments are issues of national self-interest for countries like China and Russia. Both countries are widely believed to resist placing internal armed conflicts on the council's agenda for fear that such action would open the door to consideration of the conflicts in Chechnya or Tibet.

Advocates and researchers just back from the field met with members of the Security Council and representatives of the secretary-general's office, providing up-to-date information on the situation. They urged the Security Council to actively press both the Sri Lankan government and the Tamil

Tigers to protect civilian lives and stop abuses of international humanitarian law. Between late February and mid-May, the Security Council held four informal briefings on Sri Lanka, including presentations from UN officials regarding their visits to Sri Lanka.[14]

In late April and early May, both advocates and individual Security Council members began to take the temperature of the Security Council to determine whether it would be possible to muster the nine votes needed to place Sri Lanka on the Security Council's agenda. Perceived allies included the United States, the UK, France, Austria, Costa Rica, Mexico, and Croatia. Russia, China, Libya, and Vietnam were believed to almost certainly oppose such an initiative, while Japan, Uganda, Turkey, and Burkino Faso were considered swing votes. Japan was considered particularly important, not only because of its membership on the Security Council, but because of its influence as a key Asian power and Sri Lanka's largest bilateral donor.[15] To influence Japan, Amnesty International, Human Rights Watch, the International Crisis Group, and the Global Center for the Right to Protect issued a letter to the Japanese prime minister, Taro Aso, urging Japan to engage more actively with Sri Lanka on both humanitarian and human rights issues and to support formal consideration of Sri Lanka by the Security Council.[16]

A sharp increase in Sri Lankan casualties over the weekend of May 9-10 intensified pressure on the Security Council. During a twenty-four-hour period, heavy shelling in the north reportedly killed 378 people and injured at least 1,122.[17] Human Rights Watch's Brad Adams reflected, "It was one of the most traumatic things I've watched from a distance. That couple of weeks, every day I was sick to my stomach."[18] Secretary-general Ban Ki-moon issued a statement that he was "appalled" at the killing of hundreds of civilians and warned the warring parties that "the world is watching events in Sri Lanka closely, and will not accept further violations of international law."[19]

On May 11, humanitarian and advocacy NGOs briefed Security Council members as part of an informal session hosted by UK foreign secretary David Miliband and French foreign minister Bernard Kouchner, who had just returned from Sri Lanka in a failed attempt to secure a truce between the government and Tamil Tigers. Kouchner pushed other members to put Sri Lanka on the Security Council's agenda, but key members—Russia, China, Libya, Vietnam, and Burkino Faso—did not attend the briefing. Two days later, the Security Council held closed consultations to discuss the situation in

Sri Lanka and issued its first—and only—press statement on Sri Lanka, calling for urgent action by all parties to ensure the safety of civilians.[20] However, the council did not have sufficient support to move Sri Lanka onto its formal agenda.

When the war ended a week later, active consideration of formal Security Council action immediately died. Even members previously supportive of placing it on the council's agenda concluded that the situation no longer posed a threat to international peace and security. Members also believed that since the Human Rights Council had agreed to hold a special session to consider Sri Lanka, it was now an issue for Geneva to consider, rather than New York.

Human rights groups had begun in March to press members of the UN Human Rights Council to hold a special session devoted to the crisis in Sri Lanka. Mounting casualty figures also prompted rights groups to begin seeking an international commission of inquiry to investigate possible war crimes by both the Sri Lankan government and the Tamil Tigers. Rights groups lobbied various governments, particularly the European Union, to press for a special session and began to raise the idea of an international investigation. The EU finally proposed a special session, which was scheduled for May 26-27, 2009. With input from NGOs, the Swiss took the lead in drafting a resolution bringing attention to abuses on both sides and calling for the establishment of a commission of inquiry.

The special session backfired. Just a week before it took place, the Sri Lankan government declared its military victory over the LTTE. In numerous contacts with other government missions in Geneva, Sri Lankan government representatives stressed their success in defeating a ruthless terrorist organization and argued that their victory was to be celebrated, not censured. The government drafted its own resolution for the council, trumpeting its success. Despite active lobbying by advocates, the European resolution referencing violations and accountability was roundly rejected. Instead, by a vote of 29 to 12, the council adopted the resolution initiated by the Sri Lankan government, which welcomed "efforts by the Government to ensure safety and security for all Sri Lankans and bringing permanent peace to the country."[21] Absent was any criticism of the government for human rights abuses, any reference to independent access to the camps or conflict areas, or mechanisms to address accountability or impunity. Countries supporting the measure included China, Russia, Pakistan, Saudi Arabia, Indonesia, and India, while those opposed were primarily European states, joined by Canada, Chile, and Mexico. Six abstained.

The head of Sri Lanka's delegation to the Human Rights Council, Mahinda Samarasinghe, claimed the result "was a strong endorsement of President Mahinda Rajapaksa's government's efforts at routing terrorism and the successful handling of the world's biggest hostage crisis."[22] UN personnel in Sri Lanka spoke privately regarding the damage the resolution did to their work on the ground. One said, "They've won a double victory—first with the war, and now, they are using the resolution as evidence that the international community is behind them."[23]

In early March 2009, the government of Sri Lanka was facing bankruptcy because of a balance of payments deficit and approached the International Monetary Fund (IMF) for an emergency $1.9 billion loan. Although the IMF insists that human rights are outside its mandate,[24] NGOs saw Sri Lanka's request as a significant point of leverage, in part because Sri Lanka's Central Bank had stated that some of the requested funds were to develop war-affected areas and help "bring a sustainable solution to the conflict."[25] Both Human Rights Watch and ICG contacted government representatives to the IMF in Washington and finance ministers in other capitals, including London, Paris, Berlin, and Tokyo, arguing that Sri Lanka's conduct in the war was counterproductive to the intended goals of the IMF loan. They urged IMF members to insist on concrete human rights improvements by the Sri Lankan government before approving the loan. Members of the US Congress also raised concerns that approving the loan would send the wrong message.[26] IMF directors reported that they received hundreds of emails from the Tamil diaspora, urging them to refuse the loan.

Although some governments insisted that human rights considerations should not influence IMF lending, political pressure and international attention to the escalating crisis in Sri Lanka convinced others that approving a loan to a government engaged in war crimes would not be wise. Both US secretary of state Hillary Clinton and British foreign secretary David Miliband made public statements expressing concerns about the proposed loan.[27] By mid-May, IMF officials stated that the loan was still being negotiated, but admitted privately to human rights advocates that the political controversy was delaying the loan, and that the IMF managing director did not want to submit the loan for a vote unless support from the board was assured.[28] The Sri Lankan government tried to downplay its need for the loan in public, while simultaneously seeking other sources of income, including a US$500 million loan from Libya. NGOs continued to raise concerns about the loan with key governments, arguing that to approve a multibillion dollar loan without any human rights improvements by the Sri Lankan government was "a reward for bad behavior, not an incentive for improvement."[29]

After lengthy delays, the executive board finally voted to approve the loan on July 24, although the United States, the UK, France, Germany, and Argentina each took the highly unusual position of abstaining from the vote. Germany had never before abstained from a loan on human rights grounds, and it was the first time that the UK had abstained on an IMF vote since it did so for technical reasons on a 2004 loan to Argentina. Both the United States and the UK issued public statements regarding their reservations.[30] Together, the abstaining governments held 33 percent of the IMF's votes.[31] While the abstentions were not enough to defeat the loan, such a large number of abstentions were nearly unprecedented and sent a strong signal of disapproval.

Immediately following the end of the war, UN secretary-general Ban Ki-moon traveled to Sri Lanka where he and President Mahinda Rajapaksa signed a joint communiqué stating that "the government will take measures to address allegations related to violations of international humanitarian and human rights law." However, the Sri Lankan government never made an effort to carry out this pledge.

NGOs continued to work to keep Sri Lanka on the international agenda and to push for a credible international investigation, believing that the Sri Lankan government was both unable and unwilling to identify those responsible for abuses and bring them to justice. They pressed their point through the media and raised concerns with individual governments, the secretary-general's office, and other parts of the United Nations, including the Human Rights Council. Urged by Human Rights Watch and with key support from Senator Patrick Leahy, the US Congress requested a report on possible war crimes committed during the conflict.[32] The resulting report, produced by the State Department Office of War Crimes, detailing more than three hundred alleged incidents, including attacks on civilians by both LTTE and government forces, LTTE child recruitment, government killing of captives and combatants attempting to surrender, disappearances of civilians by government forces or government-supported paramilitaries, and limits on the provision of humanitarian assistance.[33] Just a few days later, President Rajapaksa announced that he would appoint a committee, a "group of eminent persons," to "examine carefully" the allegations in the State Department report and to prepare recommendations for him. The group's report was never submitted.

May 2010 marked the one-year anniversary of the end of the war. Amnesty International, the International Crisis Group, and Human Rights Watch all used the date to accelerate pressure for an international investigation. Amnesty International launched a global action among its members to focus worldwide attention on continuing impunity in Sri Lanka. More than thirteen thousand individuals participated in an online petition to Secretary-General Ban Ki-moon, urging him to establish an independent international investigation.[34]

The International Crisis Group published an extensive report on war crimes in Sri Lanka, based on numerous eyewitness statements and hundreds of photographs, video, satellite images, documents, and electronic communications. The group concluded that tens of thousands of Tamil civilians were killed during the final months of the war, countless more wounded, and hundreds of thousands deprived of adequate food and medical care. In assessing the probable number of casualties, the Crisis Group stated that it was "difficult to arrive at a figure for the killed and missing that is lower than 30,000."[35] The Crisis Group concluded that the large-scale civilian casualties were likely the result of a "deliberate policy, formulated at the highest levels of the government, to violate the most basic laws of war,"[36] and it called on the United Nations and its member states to authorize an independent international inquiry into alleged war crimes during the final year of the conflict, as well as inquiries into the conduct of the United Nations.[37]

"We did a full court press with that report," said Alan Keenan of the ICG.[38] The Crisis Group gave advance copies of the report to the *New York Times, The Guardian,* and *Le Monde.* They lined up interviews for Louise Arbour, the president of the Crisis Group and former UN High Commissioner for Human Rights, and held a launch event in the UK at the Royal Institute of International Affairs, together with Arbour and speakers from Human Rights Watch and Amnesty International. ICG staff held several days of meetings with EU officials in Brussels and traveled to Paris, Berlin, Oslo, London, New York, and Washington to meet with policymakers. "The reaction from northern European countries was generally quite positive," said Keenan. "The US and UK were respectful but less enthusiastic."[39]

Writing in the *Global Post,* Louise Arbour compared the Human Rights Council's "speedy dispatch" of a fact-finding mission to Gaza to investigate allegations of violations during the military operations in Israel and the Occupied Palestinian Territory in December 2008 and January 2009 to "the deafening silence" of the world to the plight of Sri Lankan civilians trapped in the Vanni. She noted that while the UN mission headed by South African Justice Richard Goldstone reported Palestinian casualty figures ranging between 1,166 and 1,444, the number of dead in Sri Lanka probably reached the tens of thousands.[40]

The Crisis Group cautioned that the Sri Lankan government's use of unrestrained military action, refusal to negotiate, and disregard for humanitarian concerns set a dangerous precedent, and that the "Sri Lankan option" was already being discussed as a possible response to insurgencies in various countries, including Israel, Myanmar, Thailand, Nepal, Pakistan, India, Colombia, and the Philippines.[41] The Crisis Group argued that without accountability, governments could find it increasingly expedient to disregard international law and sacrifice civilian lives to defeat so-called extremist groups. "I found when speaking to other governments, the 'Sri Lanka option' was the strongest argument for accountability, the idea that other countries are learning that this kind of approach is acceptable," said Keenan. "If we limit the argument to Sri Lanka, we lose, because Rajapaksa is so strong and other governments think that if we push too strongly on accountability, we only strengthen his hand domestically. But if we broaden the argument to other countries, we get more traction."[42]

In response to growing international pressure, in May 2010, President Mahinda Rajapaksa announced that he would establish a "Lessons Learned and Reconciliation Commission" to report on the lessons learned from the failure of the ceasefire and the events between February 2002 and May 2009 and to recommend measures to "ensure that there will be no recurrence of such a situation." The commission had no mandate, however, to take any action or make recommendations regarding accountability for violations that occurred during the conflict apart from reporting on possible methods of restitution to victims.[43] Human Rights Watch immediately criticized the initiative, saying "Every time the international community raises the issue of accountability, Sri Lanka establishes a commission that takes a long time to achieve nothing."[44] The organization pointed out that Sri Lanka had a long history of creating ad hoc commissions to deflect international criticism of its human rights record. During a sixty-year period, Sri Lanka had established at least nine such commissions, none of which had led to any meaningful results.

Amnesty International documented Sri Lanka's history of failed and politicized commissions of inquiry in a June 2009 report, *Twenty Years of Make-Believe: Sri Lanka's Commissions of Inquiry*, finding repeated failures by successive governments to provide accountability for enforced disappearances, unlawful killings, torture, and other violations. The report concluded that the commissions of inquiry functioned as "window dressing" and "proved to be little more than tools to launch partisan attacks against opponents or to deflect criticism when the state has been faced with overwhelming evidence of its complicity in human rights violations."[45]

When invited to appear before the Lessons Learned Commission, Amnesty International, the Crisis Group, and Human Rights Watch issued a joint public letter declining the invitation accompanied by simultaneous press releases that were covered by the BBC, international wire services, and the Indian and Sri Lankan press. The organizations outlined the deep flaws in the structure and practice of the commission, including the failure of its mandate to require it to investigate violations by both parties to the armed conflict, the lack of witness protection, and the government's continuing failure to address impunity.[46] The letter emphasized the lack of independence of the commission, pointing out that members of the commission were senior government officials during the final months of the war and had publicly defended the conduct of the military against allegations of war crimes.[47]

The Sri Lankan government remained hostile to any moves toward accountability or an international investigation. In February 2010 President Rajapaksa stated he would not allow "any investigations in this country. There is no reason. Nothing wrong happened."[48] After former army commander Sareth Fonseka stated that he would be willing to testify before an international commission about the conduct of the army and that the defense secretary had ordered the execution of LTTE leaders attempting to surrender, he was arrested and courts martialed. According to press accounts, Defense Secretary Gotabhaya Rajapaksa threatened to hang Fonseka for treason if he testified before an international commission.[49] The human rights situation within Sri Lanka did not improve with the end of the war, with local human rights advocates and journalists subject to threats, intimidation, and arbitrary arrest. According to Amnesty's Yolanda Foster, "When we see some traction internationally on accountability, the reaction domestically is to put a boot down on any local human rights voices. There's a climate of fear, and very little space at the domestic level to bring human rights violations to public attention."[50]

Feeling pressure to take action on Sri Lanka, secretary-general Ban Ki-moon announced in March 2010 that he intended to appoint a panel of experts to advise him on options for accountability for possible violations of humanitarian and human rights law during the final stages of the conflict in Sri Lanka, as a follow-up to the commitment President Rajapaksa made to Ban in May 2009. The Sri Lankan government immediately denounced the panel as "uncalled for and unwarranted" and stated that "the allegations about Sri Lanka were motivated misrepresentations by apologists of the LTTE" and

Profile: Yolanda Foster

Yolanda Foster remembers the moment in 2008 when the government of Sri Lanka ordered international NGOs to leave the northern, LTTE-controlled region of Sri Lanka.[1] "Massive alarm bells were ringing," she said. "I remember thinking that there was likely to be a bloodbath. It was quite clear that the government was preparing a war without witnesses."

Yolanda was a Sri Lanka expert and researcher for Amnesty International. She routinely documented human rights violations, wrote reports, spoke to the media, and conducted advocacy with government and UN officials. But when the war in Sri Lanka began to really escalate, the nature of her work changed.

"We operated in crisis mode from January on," she said. "We had a small team working in the office, with me, a campaign assistant, and a volunteer. We were trying to pull together the documentation as best we could, but we had such limited information. At the same time, we had to serve quite a large number of victims' families. We literally had hundreds of petitions coming in on a daily basis from the Tamil diaspora, and had desperate individuals calling in with family members stuck in the Vanni. That's what it's like to work for a human rights organization in the midst of a crisis."

As civilian casualties mounted, Yolanda and her colleagues continued to document violations. Through press releases, statements, and meetings, they pressed officials for action. But despite their efforts, the death toll continued to rise. Yolanda remembered a poignant moment on May 1, 2009. "Confronting the horror that was going on on the ground, all we could do was issue an urgent action on behalf of the remaining civilians still trapped in the zone." Typically such actions are usually issued on behalf of individuals. She admitted, "It was an act of desperation."

"misguided" NGOs that were working on an agenda that was directed against Sri Lanka.[51] On June 22, Ban appointed three persons to the panel and issued a statement that "accountability is an essential foundation for durable peace and reconciliation in Sri Lanka."[52]

The Panel of Experts report, released by the secretary-general in April 2011, was damning. It estimated that up to forty thousand civilians had been killed during the final months of the war and found credible reports of war crimes and crimes against humanity by both the government and the LTTE.

As hundreds of thousands of civilians were subjected to repeated attacks, Yolanda began reading biographies of other war survivors to try to understand how they sustained themselves. She says she found inspiration in *The Diary of Anne Frank.* "I did something I haven't done since I was a teenager—wrote out a passage from her book and stuck it on my bedroom mirror." The passage was from July 8, 1944: "It's really a wonder that I haven't dropped my ideals because they seem so absurd and impossible to carry out. Yet, I keep them, because in spite of everything I still believe that people are really good at heart. I simply can't build up my hopes on a foundation consisting of confusion, misery and death." Yolanda said that nearly two years after the end of the conflict, she met a teenage Sri Lankan who had survived the war. The young woman had also sought comfort in *The Diary of Anne Frank.* She showed Yolanda the passage she had highlighted, from July 6, 1944: "It doesn't matter (what) keeps people on the right path. It isn't the fear of God but the upholding of one's own honour and conscience."

"She appealed to me and Amnesty International to stand by our principles and continue our call for an international investigation into what happened in those final months of the war," said Yolanda. "There are no quick cures, but I remain hopeful for the very long term. Hopefully one day, when there is more of an appetite, we may get some action."

1. Author interview with Yolanda Foster, August 1, 2011; Yolanda Foster, "Sri Lanka: Survivors Appeal for Justice Two Years On," May 17, 2011. Available at Amnesty International blog, http://livewire.amnesty.org/2011/05/17/sri-lanka-survivors-appeal-for-justice-two-years-on/ (accessed July 24, 2011).

It concluded that the government had carried out large-scale shelling on three consecutive no-fire zones, causing the majority of civilian casualties in the final phases of the war; intentionally and repeatedly shelled hospitals on the frontlines; and systematically deprived persons in the conflict zones of humanitarian assistance, including food and basic medical supplies. It found that the LTTE used civilians as a human buffer, killed civilians attempting to leave LTTE-controlled areas, and forcibly recruited children. "Indeed," the panel concluded, "the conduct of the war represented a grave assault on the entire regime of international law designed to protect individual dignity during both war and peace."[53] The panel found that the Lessons Learned and Reconciliation Commission established by the Sri Lankan government was "deeply flawed" and did not meet international standards for an effective accountability mechanism. It recommended that the secretary-general establish an independent international mechanism to independently investigate the allegations.[54] The Sri Lankan government immediately denounced the report, calling it "illegal," "biased, baseless, and unilateral,"[55] while NGOs called on the secretary-general to act on the panel's recommendations and establish an international investigation that could lead to prosecutions.[56]

Both the media and NGOs used video taken during the final weeks of the war to expose the serious nature of abuses and the need for accountability. In June 2011, British Channel 4 broadcast a full hour program, *Sri Lanka's Killing Fields*, examining the final weeks of the war. The program included footage captured on mobile phones from within the no-fire zone depicting the aftermath of government shelling, including video of Sri Lankan soldiers executing Tamil prisoners, footage depicting the bodies of female Tamil fighters who appeared to have been sexually assaulted and killed, as well as interviews with Tamils who had been present in the no-fire zone at the end of the conflict. Amnesty, Human Rights Watch, and ICG had all worked with the film's producer, providing extensive background information, directing them to sources of footage and contacts to interview. Once the documentary was completed, the NGOs organized screenings of the film and panel discussions for members of Parliament in Britain's House of Commons, members of the US Congress in Washington, and government representatives to the United Nations in both Geneva and New York. The film was viewed extensively online, both inside of Sri Lanka and around the world, generating thousands of online comments from viewers. Amnesty's Yolanda Foster described the screening for diplomats in Geneva: "Sitting through the reality of violations for 60 minutes was just chilling. There were ambassadors and senior diplomats there who were literally silent. The film was transformative at that level and led to renewed discussion about the need to do something."[57]

Throughout the conflict and its aftermath, the substantial Tamil diaspora was very vocal in criticizing the Sri Lankan government and calling for international action. More than one-quarter of Sri Lanka's Tamils fled Sri Lanka during the war, creating a diaspora of six to eight hundred thousand that settled primarily in Canada, India, the UK, the United States, Germany, France, and Australia. Many members fled because of government abuses and maintained loyalties to the Tamil Tigers. Tamil groups in the West organized political support for the Tamil Tigers and raised millions of dollars to support their war effort.[58] During the final months of the war, diaspora groups actively protested the government's military offensive in the north. For example, in the United States, Tamils Against Genocide organized rallies outside the White House, lobbied members of Congress, and hired lawyers to file human rights violations charges against Sri Lankan officials. In Toronto and London—home to some of the largest concentrations of Sri Lankan Tamils—Tamils staged massive demonstrations. In London, two hundred thousand Tamils marched in mid-April to protest the humanitarian crisis. Following the march, UK Parliamentarians (many with large Tamil constituencies) intensely questioned UK foreign secretary David Miliband regarding the UK's policy toward Sri Lanka.

Although most of the Tamil diaspora groups were partisan and supported the Tamil Tigers, some took a balanced human rights perspective and criticized both sides. The Sri Lanka Democracy Forum (which included both Sinhalese and Tamil members), for example, issued statements, published op-eds, gave media interviews, and organized events in both London and New York calling on both the Tamil Tigers and the Sri Lankan government to address the humanitarian crisis. Members of the group also held regular meetings with UN, UK, and US government officials.[59]

After the conclusion of the war, the diaspora continued organizing. Members of the diaspora set up the Centre for War Victims and Human Rights to invite members of the diaspora to submit documentation about violations committed during the war from relatives and friends in Sri Lanka.[60] The center solicited submissions to the panel of experts to the secretary-general and set up contact points in a dozen countries to receive information.[61] Members of Tamil diaspora groups actively lobbied members of Congress and Parliament in several countries. In the United States, their pressure in part led to a series of letters from members of Congress to Secretary of State Hillary Clinton and a Senate resolution calling for an international investigation into war crimes in Sri Lanka.[62] Parliamentarians in the UK and Australia made similar calls.

The release of the UN panel of experts' report in April 2011 and Channel 4's documentary in June 2011 bolstered calls for an independent international investigation and accountability mechanism. Despite the mounting evidence of war crimes, however, governments and the UN leadership were still reluctant to act. Two years after the end of the war, a credible accountability process for the massive violations that took place during the war had still not begun.

Lessons Learned

Taken on face value, several factors should have created an environment that would allow human rights advocates to influence Sri Lankan government action. First, Sri Lanka has relatively little geopolitical influence, making it easier for outside governments to openly criticize human rights abuses and use financial and other leverage to push for changes in policy without putting their own national interests and critical geopolitical alliances at risk. Secondly, as a functioning democracy, Sri Lanka and its leadership would presumably be sensitive to international opinion, risks to its international reputation, and possible backlash from its own citizens as criticism of its abuses mounted. Previous experience had shown, for example, that Sri Lanka was highly sensitive to scrutiny from the UN Security Council. Third, the timing and size of the emergency loan Sri Lanka's Central Bank sought from the IMF created a unique point of leverage to seek human rights improvements, since Sri Lanka's precarious financial position gave it few alternatives to avert bankruptcy. However, none of these factors were sufficient to allow human rights advocates to successfully secure human rights improvements by the Sri Lankan government or the Tamil Tigers while the war was still taking place, or to win meaningful steps toward accountability by Sri Lanka's government following the war's conclusion.

A major impediment was the context of the global "war on terror" and the Sri Lankan leadership's single-minded focus on destroying the Tamil Tigers. According to Human Rights Watch's Adams, "We realized our leverage was minimal. The regime was determined to do what it was going to do no matter what."[63] Sri Lanka's leaders calculated correctly that a decisive defeat over an internationally recognized terrorist organization would mitigate criticism over its actions. In an interview two months after the war ended, President Mahinda Rajapaksa invoked George W. Bush's antiterror policies in justifying Sri Lanka's campaign. "They're [the US and Europe] the people who encouraged us to defeat terrorism. We followed what [George W.] Bush said. We accomplished what he wanted: eliminate terrorism. They must give credit to us. We fought their war. We showed that you can defeat terrorism."[64] Some observers believe that the Sri Lanka government had at least tacit support from outside governments.

According to Alan Keenan, "In general, the problem was that there was a decision that all governments took that Sri Lanka should be allowed to defeat the Tigers. The more clear the cost would be so severe, the closer they were to succeeding. Governments were reluctant to snatch that prize out of the government's hands."[65] The governments where advocacy was strongest and who were most outspoken—the United States and the UK —also held the least influence with Sri Lanka. The Rajapakse government, first elected in 2005 and reelected in January 2010, deliberately distanced itself from Western countries while actively seeking stronger relations with Asian and other powers, including China, India, Pakistan, Libya, and Iran. The shift was also apparent in donor trends: funding from Western countries to Sri Lanka was declining while financial support and investment from China and Iran grew.[66] During the last year of the war, China reportedly supplied Sri Lanka with a billion dollars of military aid, while Russia and Pakistan provided artillery shells and small arms, and Iran supplied fuel.[67] At the Human Rights Council, Sri Lanka successfully cultivated political support from governments such as Brazil and South Africa.

Adams believed that governments that could have influenced Sri Lanka deliberately chose to take a soft line:

> Japan decided to engage only in quiet diplomacy, and we were unable to move them. India was the most decisive third power, but a lot of people misread how important the Tamil vote was inside India. There was an overly confident view that India would intervene to protect Tamil lives. What we learned was that there were no domestic consequences to stand on the sidelines. They urged Sri Lanka not to pursue a scorched earth policy, but they proved themselves to be a paper tiger. Sri Lanka knew that they would not intervene.[68]

The Rajapakse government became increasingly hostile to Western countries that raised human rights concerns, denouncing "bullying," "aggression,"

"interference," and "persecution" by Western countries.[69] These attacks rein-
forced beliefs that the West was somehow trying to rescue the Tamil Tigers.
Amnesty's Yolanda Foster believes that the Sri Lankan government's aggressive stance helped silence critics. "What we see is Western donors bruised
because they have to deal with a truculent client. The Sri Lankan government
is successfully bullying these states that have a commitment to international
humanitarian law. At some level, it seems as if these governments feel they've
played all their cards and lost all their leverage."[70]

With a 74 percent Sinhalese majority in Sri Lanka, the government was
able to pursue its military campaign against the Tamil Tigers with little
dissent from a population that had long tired of the war, while solidifying
support from the country's Sinhala nationalists. After the end of the war,
Rajapakse was, according to various news reports, hailed as the nation's "sav-
ior" and repeatedly compared to King Dutugemunu, a legendary Sinhalese
king who routed a rival Tamil monarch and unified much of the country two
thousand years ago.[71]

The sudden end of the war immediately changed the advocacy landscape.
During the period when war-time abuses were intensifying and the humanitarian situation deteriorating, human rights advocates were able to maintain a sense of emergency and keep international policymakers engaged on
the issue. During April and early May 2009, for example, they were able to
build some momentum among key allies for action by the Security Council and Human Rights Council and successfully delay the IMF loan. However, the momentum dissipated as soon as the war ended, as evidenced by
the counterproductive outcome of the Human Rights Council special session and the immediate abandonment of the issue at the Security Council.
Although abuses continued, particularly in relation to the Sri Lankan government's detention of some 280,000 internally displaced persons, the fact
that civilians were no longer being killed in active hostilities meant that the
situation lost its urgency.

Mustering support for effective accountability measures was also difficult,
as many governments believed that in the postwar era, it was a higher national
priority to cultivate a good relationship with the Sri Lankan government, particularly given the strength and domestic popularity of the Rajapaksa regime.
Despite growing evidence of war crimes brought forward by the UN Panel
of Experts, key governments were still reluctant to initiate an international
investigation. Even governments like the United States and UK, who had

spoken out against abuses, wanted to judge the final outcome of Sri Lanka's Lessons Learned and Reconciliation Commission before establishing an international accountability mechanism.

Many of these external political factors were outside the advocates' control. Reflecting on their strategy, however, they identified several things they wish they had done differently. ICG's Keenan, for example, believed that advocates should have invested more energy in advocacy with non-Western governments. "We focused lots of attention in Brussels, New York and Washington, but what we're learning is that that's not enough. Sri Lanka is a very skillful government that cultivates support from other governments like Mexico, Argentina, Brazil and South Africa. We need to get better at that."[72] In retrospect, Adams felt that the organizations should have tried harder to get visual images from the war out to the public much earlier. "Sometimes we are not focused enough on the visual side of things and how much it moves people." He also believed that the organizations should have been more publicly critical of the UN's response while the conflict was going on, and its efforts to downplay the civilian cost of the war. "We had a belief that anger from UN officials on the ground would lead to policy change at the leadership level. But we might have spent less time doing quiet diplomacy and more going after them publicly to embarrass them."[73]

Despite advocates' failure to change substantially the behavior of the warring parties, they succeeded in several respects: gaining significant international attention to human rights and laws of war violations by both sides; securing the personal engagement of senior UN and government officials, including Hillary Clinton, Bernard Kouchner, David Miliband, and Ban Ki-moon; and having some impact on the Sri Lankan government's treatment of people displaced by the war. Amnesty's Yolanda Foster said, "We have to be honest that our successes were very limited because of the global context." She and others, however, believe that NGO pressure at the end of the war influenced the Sri Lankan government to improve conditions in government-run camps and to allow the 280,000 Sri Lankans who had fled the war zone to leave the camps fairly quickly after the war and return home.[74] ICG's Alan Keenan also believes, "If we weren't screaming those last few months, perhaps there would have been more people killed. We probably saved some people's lives."[75]

The advocates were able to keep Sri Lanka on the agenda through several means. One of the most important was simply the organization's persistence.

According to Adams, "The relentlessness of our advocacy has been the most effective. We've been told that the Panel of Experts report was the result of the three organizations [Human Rights Watch, Amnesty International, and ICG] constantly putting pressure on Ban. It wasn't because of state pressure. Even the Channel 4 documentary is because we kept at it. We directed them to the footage, gave them huge amounts of information, and contacts to make the program."

A second factor was the credible research and documentation that the organizations produced. Through on-the-ground investigations, interviews with Tamils in the war zone, and satellite imagery, they brought crucial information regarding abuses to light that policymakers were unable to ignore and worked with the media to bring searing images and testimony to widespread public attention.

A third element was utilizing multiple points of leverage for advocacy. The advocates worked with individual governments, the UN Human Rights Council, the UN Security Council, the IMF, the UN panel of experts, and the media. These efforts resulted in statements from individual governments, the report from the US State Department, and recommendations from the UN panel of experts established by the UN secretary general that helped to build and maintain pressure for accountability.

Finally, coordination among the three organizations was essential. The organizations shared information constantly, organized joint events, and coordinated their advocacy strategy. Brad Adams called it "one of the most positive collaborations I've been part of. We were all singing from the same sheet. We had shared outrage." He believed that having all three organizations deeply involved was decisive in influencing Ban to set up the Panel of Experts. "It mattered that it was all three organizations. We couldn't have done it ourselves."[76]

More than two years after the end of the war, the NGOs had not yet met their goals. Accountability for Sri Lanka was an unfinished agenda. Advocates continued to look for opportunities to highlight the scale of crimes that had been committed, to expose the Sri Lankan government's continued failure to pursue accountability, and to convince governments and UN officials that only an international investigation could provide the victims of the war with any hope of justice. The advocates remained hopeful that their efforts for accountability would eventually bear fruit. ICG's Alan Keenan, interviewed before the release of the UN Panel of Experts' report, said, "In terms of accountability, the ball game's not over. If we ever get over the hurdle and get to an investigation, there is a wealth of evidence. There could still be some victories down the line."[77] Human Rights Watch's Brad Adams was optimistic that the UN would eventually launch an international investigation into Sri Lankan war crimes: "I think it's inevitable, I do. . . . There's too much information to be ignored."[78]

PART IV

New Media and New Alliances

Chapter 9

Using New Technologies in the Campaign to Free Tibet

The 2008 Beijing Olympics

The Olympics and the uprising showed us and showed Tibet and the world that not only are we alive and kicking, but we can do things. We are sure of our own power and sense of unity from the uprising. Tibetans are more united now than ever in our history. We have a new-found unity, sense of purpose, pride, and anger.
—*Lhadon Thethong, Students for a Free Tibet*[1]

I N 1950, soon after the establishment of the People's Republic of China, Chinese military forces entered Tibet, beginning more than sixty years of human rights violations by the Chinese government against the Tibetan people. The Chinese government imposed strict prohibitions on Tibetans' freedom of speech, religion, and assembly; destroyed almost all of Tibet's six thousand monasteries; and brutally suppressed protests. Chinese troops crushed a 1959 Tibetan uprising, driving the Tibetans' political and spiritual leader, the Dalai Lama, into exile. According to Tibetan groups, an estimated eighty-six thousand Tibetans were killed.[2]

The government subjected thousands of Tibetans to arbitrary arrest and detention.[3] UN sources cite torture, beatings, shackling, and other abusive treatment of Tibetans, in particular Tibetan monks and nuns, by public officials and security forces.[4] The Chinese government forced monks and nuns to undergo compulsory political indoctrination and enacted policies to suppress Tibet's language and culture. Under a policy of "segregation and assimilation," it encouraged millions of Han Chinese to migrate to Tibet, offering them higher wages and other inducements. By the 1980s, an estimated 7.5 million Han Chinese had settled in Tibet, outnumbering the 6 million resident ethnic Tibetans, and enjoyed higher life expectancy, literacy rates, and per capita incomes than ethnic Tibetans.[5]

The Dalai Lama characterized China's economic and social policies in Tibet as "Chinese apartheid," stating, "Tibet is being colonized by waves of Chinese immigrants. We are becoming a minority in our own country. The new Chinese settlers have created an alternate society: a Chinese apartheid which, denying Tibetans equal social and economic status in our own land, threatens to finally overwhelm and absorb us."[6] The Chinese government invested millions of dollars building infrastructure in Tibet, including roads, buildings, power plants, and the China-Tibet railway. As part of a "Western Development" campaign, it confiscated land and forcibly resettled large numbers of Tibetan herders to make way for mining, infrastructure projects, and urban development. According to Chinese government authorities, seven hundred thousand people were resettled in Western China between 2000 and 2005.[7]

In 2000, China announced its bid to hold the 2008 Summer Olympics in Beijing. In seeking to host the games, the Chinese government claimed that its human rights record had improved and that it would provide journalists with unrestricted access to cover the games. Just before Beijing was awarded the Olympics in July 2001, the vice president of the Beijing Olympic Games Bid Committee stated, "The human rights conditions in China have improved during the last 50 years, especially in the 1990s with the reform and opening policies. We are confident that with the Games coming to China we are going to not only promote the economy, but also enhance all social sectors including education, medical care, and human rights. . . . Certainly we will give the media complete freedom to report on anything when they come to China. . . . We will welcome the media of the world."[8] International Olympic Committee (IOC) officials also stressed that the games would be beneficial for human rights. A year ahead of the games, IOC president Jacques Rogge said, "We believe the Games are going to move ahead the agenda of the social and human rights as far as possible; the Games are going to be a force for good."[9]

The promises of the Chinese government and IOC proved false. Although the government announced new regulations on media freedom, which would allow foreign reporters to talk to any consenting interviewee and travel anywhere they wanted in China, journalists continued to be routinely harassed, intimidated, detained, and denied access to well-known dissidents.

A few months before the Olympics were to begin, on March 10, 2008 (the anniversary of the failed 1959 uprising against Chinese rule), nonviolent protests began in Lhasa and spread throughout the Tibetan plateau. During the course of four days, hundreds of monks peacefully protested in different locations. On March 14, the demonstrations turned violent, as protesters burned police cars, Chinese shops, and government buildings. As the protests spread throughout Tibetan areas, the government expelled foreign media and deployed military, armed police, and public security forces throughout the region. Witnesses described security forces kicking and hitting protesters with batons and rifle butts, and in several cases, opening fire on demonstrators.[10] The Tibetan government-in-exile claimed that more than two hundred Tibetans were killed.[11] Thousands of demonstrators were arrested. The government said it subsequently released most of them, but two years after the uprising, hundreds remained unaccounted for.[12] China's premier, Wen Jiabao, publicly accused the Dalai Lama of conspiring to "incite sabotage" of the upcoming Olympic Games.[13]

The link between the Tibet uprising and the Olympics was debatable. But for Tibetan organizations and Tibetan support groups that had been organizing for years to bring attention to the occupation of Tibet and human rights abuses against Tibetans, the Beijing Olympics provided a clear and galvanizing focus. An estimated twenty-five thousand foreign journalists were expected to travel to Beijing to cover the 2008 Olympics, while an estimated 4.7 billion people worldwide watched at least a portion of the games. This chapter examines Students for a Free Tibet's campaign use of the games to shine a spotlight on Tibet through innovative and strategic use of direct action and new technologies.

The Campaign

Students for a Free Tibet (SFT) began in New York City in 1994 when a group of Tibetans and students decided to campaign in solidarity with the Tibetan struggle for independence. When China announced its Olympic bid, members of SFT saw it as a unique opportunity. "A campaign against the Beijing bid was the obvious thing," said Lhadon Tethong, SFT's executive director. "The minute they were awarded the games, it immediately became the short-term focus. Our guiding principle had been to make the occupation of Tibet too costly to maintain—financially, politically, or socially. The campaign against the Olympics fit all three categories. What became clear was that our job was to take the Olympic spotlight and turn it to Tibet."[14]

The campaign asserted that China was trying to use the Olympic Games to whitewash its human rights record and legitimize its occupation of Tibet.

Profile: Lhadon Tethong

According to her colleagues, Lhadon Tethong was an outspoken Tibetan independence activist "from the moment she learned to talk." She was born and raised on Vancouver Island in Western Canada. Although there were only a few hundred Tibetan-Canadians in British Colombia, her ties with Tibet were intensely personal: her father had fled Tibet in 1949 and served as a personal interpreter to the Dalai Lama and a minister in the Tibetan government in exile.

Lhadon attended university in Halifax, Nova Scotia, where she founded the first chapter of Students for a Free Tibet at the University of King's College. After she graduated, she moved to New York City in 1999 to begin working for Students for a Free Tibet headquarters, eventually becoming the organization's executive director and a leading figure in the Tibet movement.

One of her earliest organizing successes, in 2000, was working with a coalition of activists to convince the World Bank to cancel plans for a project that would have underwritten the resettlement of tens of thousands of Chinese settlers in Tibet. A compelling and dynamic speaker, she has addressed diverse audiences all over North America, from student and community groups, to shareholders for BP Amoco and ExxonMobile, to a crowd of sixty-six thousand at the 1998 Tibetan Freedom Concert in Washington, DC. She has given hundreds of television, radio, and print interviews, appearing not only in mainstream international news media, but also in publications like France's *Elle* magazine.

Lhadon's approach to organizing was shaped by the examples of nonviolent leaders like Martin Luther King Jr. and Gandhi but also by activists from environmental direct-action groups such as Greenpeace, the Rainforest Action Network, and the Ruckus Society. In the late 1990s, she attended a Ruckus Society camp. "I met all these people at the right moment," she said. "These activists helped to raise us and opened our minds and eyes to all the possibilities. Up until then, the Tibet support network was pretty tame. For example, we would have a demonstration but never step off the sidewalk or do anything outside the constraints of the law. We had talked about nonviolent direct action, Martin Luther King and Gandhi, but we weren't really emulating them. With direct action, we took advocacy in the Tibet movement to another level."[1]

Lhadon relied on a close-knit group of colleagues at Students for a Free Tibet as a "brain trust" to generate collective ideas for moving their strategy forward. "When we were hanging out at bars or having fun together, we'd have great ideas."[2] The idea for the 2007 "Beijing Wide Open" blog emerged from such a gathering, leading Lhadon to spend a week in Beijing a year before the Olympics reporting daily on preparations for the Olympics and China's use of the Olympics to legitimize its role in Tibet. She was ultimately detained and deported, but felt the project was one of the most powerful aspects of the Olympics campaign. "Watching that drama unfold really captured people's attention," she reflected. "People told us that they went through emotions of being scared, nervous, excited, happy. . . . It drew them into a sense that everyone had to be involved."[3]

Lhadon worked for Students for a Free Tibet for ten years. She said, "SFT provided me with endless opportunities to work for Tibetan freedom and advance my strategic campaigning and media skills."[4] In turn, the organization benefited from Lhadon's leadership, growing exponentially and becoming a recognized leader in the Tibetan movement, particularly through its Beijing Olympics campaign.

In 2009, Lhadon resigned as executive director of SFT to start the Tibet Action Institute, a new initiative sponsored by SFT. Lhadon envisioned the institute as expanding SFT's leadership training program, with a focus on building the capacity of the Tibetan movement and enhancing its use of technology. Launching the institute in March 2011, Lhadon said, "It's all about taking advantage of the latest and greatest technologies, fusing them with good strategic nonviolent organizing principles and methodologies, and then training people to use these powerful tools within good strategies so that ultimately we can win, Tibetans can win the nonviolent struggle for rights and freedom inside Tibet."[5]

1. Author interview with Lhadon Tethong, February 3, 2010.

2. Ibid.

3. Ibid.

4. Students for a Free Tibet, "A Message from Lhadon Tethong About Transition at SFT," September 10, 2009. Available at http://blog.studentsforafreetibet.org/2009/09/a-message-from-lhadon-tethong-about-transition-at-sft/ (accessed May 14, 2011).

5. Tibet Action Institute, Tibet Action Institute launch video, March 9, 2011. Available at https://tibetaction.net/ (accessed May 14, 2011).

"China was trying to use this moment to kill the Tibet issue forever," said Tethong. "We knew that if the Olympics went quietly and Tibetans didn't fight, Tibetans would lose serious ground."[15] Another SFT activist described a key objective of the campaign: "We were going to show the real face of China. We were able to publicize not only what happens in Tibet, but also what happens to protesters in China. We were able to show that China is an authoritarian state, and shine a light on its underbelly."[16]

Although SFT began protesting China's bid for the Olympics in 2000, it launched an intensive campaign around the games in early 2007. Two key elements made the campaign distinctive. The first was a series of dramatic, strategically timed nonviolent direct actions staged on Mt. Everest, the Great Wall of China, the iconic Olympic Bird's Nest Stadium in Beijing, and at international landmarks along the Olympic torch relay route, including Westminster Bridge in London and the Golden Gate Bridge in San Francisco. The second was the innovative and savvy use of cutting-edge technology that enabled the campaign to broadcast its actions to a global audience despite China's notorious "Great Firewall" of Internet censorship and engage thousands of people around the world in actions related to Tibet.

On April 26, 2007, the International Olympic Committee announced the route for the Olympic torch relay that would begin the following year. China had indicated it planned to take the torch relay through Lhasa, Tibet, and up Mount Everest. Many Tibetan activists believed that this was an attempt by China to solidify and legitimize its claim to Tibet. The day before the IOC announcement, SFT staged a dramatic action at Everest base camp, where four activists unfurled banners reading "One World, One Dream: Free Tibet 2008" in English and "Free Tibet" in Tibetan and Chinese. The banner played off the Beijing Olympics official slogan, "One World, One Dream." Tenzin Dorjee (known as Tendor), a Tibetan-American, was part of the team, and SFT believed, the first exiled Tibetan to return to take direct action inside Tibet.

For many activists involved in the Olympics campaign, the Mt. Everest action was not only one of the most visible and dramatic moments of the campaign but also the most significant. According to Tethong: "From a Tibetan perspective, that was one of the most exhilarating and empowering moments of the campaign. You have to be Tibetan to understand what it means to have a Tibetan on Tibetan soil on Everest, singing the Tibetan national anthem. It was an overwhelmingly successful action. It really did inspire people on the inside and outside and raised some kind of hope that we could do things."[17] The action demanded considerable planning. Three different teams of activists climbed to the camp, elevation 17,600 feet, from three different routes. One team posed as a wedding party; two members were to be "married" at the base camp, with another member filming the event. Seventy Chinese climbers were also at the base camp, preparing a trial climb to see if it was possible to take a torch to the top of the 29,028-foot Mount Everest.

The most significant technological challenge was capturing visual images of the action and making sure they were disseminated quickly. Because the group expected that the demonstrators would be immediately arrested and their equipment confiscated, SFT utilized satellite technology to transmit images directly from the base camp. Nathan Freitas, who coordinated the technical side of the action, said that the technology they used was inspired by Everest climbers who had done live broadcasts during their ascents and by embedded reporters in the Iraq war. He arranged for a satellite phone, a portable, battery-operated satellite modem, and wireless HD video camera, and he set up a satellite account with a commercial satellite company to broadcast their images at a rate of about US$7 per minute of video. During the action, a former TV producer filmed the demonstration with the wireless video recorder and mic, which was then transmitted to the modem and laptop set up in a tent a short distance away. The tech member of the team operating the equipment in the tent then transmitted the video via satellite to Freitas in Brooklyn. Freitas recorded it and posted it on the Internet.

The team on Everest was arrested, detained, interrogated, and deported. However, within two hours of the action, the footage was on YouTube, where it was viewed more than three hundred thousand times and linked to numerous blogs and other Internet sites. The demonstration also received significant coverage by the mainstream media, including the BBC, Fox, NBC, CBS television, Australian radio, the Associated Press, Agence France Press, and other print media.

In August 2007, the Chinese government planned a one-year countdown celebration, a year before the games were to start. Just before the countdown, Lhadon Tethong, SFT's executive director, went to Beijing with another SFT activist, Paul Golding, and launched a video blog, "Beijing Wide Open," to "expose the truth about China's occupation of Tibet." For a week, she posted and recorded blogs from various locations in and around Beijing, including Tiananmen Square and the Olympic Village. The activists came under surveillance nearly immediately. They were followed by plainclothes security officers on foot and in several vehicles. According to Tethong, "We were under surveillance from at least day 2, but they let us continue, because they didn't want the backlash from shutting us down. Our whole strategy was to use this against them." Despite the scrutiny, Tethong recorded one or two video blogs every day, which were uploaded onto the SFT website.

Freitas provided technological support for Tethong and set up shifts to monitor her twenty-four hours a day. "She was a good test. She was someone who was tech savvy, but not a geek."[18] Freitas set up Skype on Tethong's laptop computer so that all she needed to do was to hit "call" to record a blog. He received and recorded the transmissions and posted them on the Internet. Tethong's computer was also set up in her hotel room so that if security officers came to arrest her, she could activate Skype before opening the door and record what happened.

On August 7, seven days after the blog began and the day before the official one-year countdown ceremony, another SFT team carried out an action on the Great Wall of China. A team of six SFT members from the United States, the UK, and Canada unfurled a 450-square-foot banner on the Great Wall, reading "One World, One Dream: Free Tibet 2008." Members of the team filmed the event and uploaded video footage via satellite before being arrested. The video was posted on YouTube almost immediately, and viewed more than one hundred thousand times. The BBC and other major media outlets included the action as part of their coverage of the one-year countdown. The activists were detained for thirty-six hours, interrogated, and deported to Hong Kong.

The Great Wall action increased the scrutiny from Chinese security on Tethong and her partner, who had continued to record and upload video blogs. The day after the Great Wall action, thirty plainclothes officers kept them under surveillance and finally detained and deported them just hours before the one-year countdown ceremony began in Tiananmen Square. Tethong reflected later on the blog that "watching that drama unfold really captured people's attention. People told us that they went through emotions of being scared, nervous, excited, happy. . . . It drew them into a sense that everyone had to be involved."[19] According to Freitas, "We built up momentum with the blog. Every day, there was more surveillance, more police. We were weaving a story and building it up."[20]

In March 2008, the Olympic torch relay began in Greece, host to the 2004 summer Olympics. During the course of 129 days, the torch relay traveled through twenty-one countries and six continents. Protests were organized by various organizations at many locations along the route, highlighting not only China's occupation of Tibet but also human rights abuses related to Darfur, China's relationships to Myanmar and Zimbabwe, repression against Falun Gong members, and other issues. Students for a Free Tibet saw the Olympic Torch relay as an important opportunity to stage high-profile protests that would bring attention to Tibet. "The torch relay seemed designed for a bunch of direct action junkies," said Tethong. "It was a no-brainer. If we weren't ready, I would have been ashamed."[21]

SFT organized dramatic "banner hangs" in London, Paris, and San Francisco. In London on April 5, activists abseiled from the Westminster Bridge to hang a 74-square-meter banner reading, "One World, One Dream: Free Tibet 2008." Four activists were detained and released. On April 7 in Paris, two activists abseiled off the Pont Au Change, a bridge over the Seine river, and unfurled a banner reading "Pas de Flamme au Tibet" [No torch in Tibet] before being detained by police. During the action, more than sixty pro-Tibet marchers gathered spontaneously on surrounding bridges and streets, chanting "Free Tibet" slogans. Numerous protests by other groups disrupted the torch relay in London and Paris, and at several points demonstrators extinguished the torch flame. The Chinese government described the attacks on the torch in London and Paris as "despicable" and condemned them as "deliberate disruptions . . . who gave no thought to the Olympic spirit or the laws of Britain and France" and who "tarnish the lofty Olympic spirit."[22]

The same day as the torch relay in Paris, SFT mounted an action in San Francisco, which was to receive the torch relay two days later. Three SFT activists scaled the Golden Gate Bridge to hang another massive "Free Tibet" banner. The action was covered live by CNN and other major television networks and was pictured on the front page of international and national newspapers including the New York Times. The activists remained on the bridge for two hours before descending voluntarily and being arrested by California police. One team member, San Francisco resident Laurel Sutherlin, spoke to a local TV stations live from his cell phone while suspended from the bridge, urging the International Olympic Committee to ask China not to allow the torch to go through Tibet.

The campaign mobilized thousands of people to demonstrate and disrupt the torch relay route in San Francisco. Technology experts within SFT set up a text-messaging system, which allowed individuals to sign up for text updates by simply texting "SFTorch" to 4141. Two thousand people signed up for the updates. The campaign then set up a communications center that gathered information on the torch's location from police scanners and people on the street with cell phones. The campaign set up a Google map on its website with markers to show the location of the torch in real time. Organizers deployed three live video cameras to track the torch, including one on a man's bike helmet. SFT activists said that among those relying on SFT to identify the location of the torch were CNN producers working with Wolf Blitzer.

The effort was successful. Activists turned out into the streets, forcing the organizers of the relay to repeatedly reroute the torch and ultimately cancel a closing ceremony at Justin Herman Plaza due to large numbers of protesters at the site. The torch was ultimately moved by bus to San Francisco International Airport for a makeshift closing ceremony that was closed to much of the media. "We shut it down. We let them know they weren't welcome," said Freitas.[23] The massive protests of the relay in London, Paris, and San Francisco, including assaults on torchbearers, led the president of the International Olympic Committee, Jacques Rogge, to describe the situation as a "crisis" for the organization.[24] The IOC later announced that it would not support international torch relays for future Olympic Games.

The torch relay took place just weeks after the March uprising in Tibet. SFT mobilized actions protesting China's plan to take the Olympic torch through Tibet and urging the IOC to cancel the Tibet leg of the relay. SFT launched a dedicated website, www.NoTorchInTibet.org, which featured an animated version of the official Beijing logo, depicting a protestor being beaten, with text stating, "Do you share this dream? We don't. No torch in Tibet." The animation received more than 870,000 views and was uploaded to more than twenty-five hundred online locations. The website provided sample letters and urged individuals to contact their national Olympic committees and IOC members in advance of its June 2008 executive committee meeting in Athens. Thousands of SFT members faxed and called the IOC demanding that Tibet be removed from the torch relay route. At the Athens meeting, SFT organized a press conference, a protest outside the hotel where the IOC was meeting, and a "die-in" by Tibetan activists. During other actions, SFT press statements highlighted the continuing crackdown in Tibet and called for cancellation of the Tibetan leg of the relay.[25]

After the extensive protests and controversy generated in Paris, London, and San Francisco, campaign organizers had some hope that the IOC would respond and cancel plans for Tibet leg of the relay. Although protests continued in Argentina and other countries across Asia, the intensity dropped considerably. The torch arrived in Lhasa, Tibet, on June 20, although the leg was cut from three days to one and carried out under a heavy military and security presence.

As part of its campaign, SFT launched a dedicated website—www.Athelete Wanted.org—to suggest ways that Olympic athletes could show support for Tibet during the games. Activists handed out hundreds of leaflets and packets to athletes at the US track-and-field trials in Eugene, Oregon, in June. Shortly before the games began, the group paid for a full-page ad in the *New York Times*, with text reading, "At every Olympics there is one athlete who ends up inspiring the world with their courage and character. We hope that athlete is reading this." As US athletes began congregating at the US Olympic processing center at San Jose State University, members of the San Francisco-area "Team Tibet" handed out packets to athletes arriving at the San Francisco airport and the San Jose campus. The packets contained a copy of the *New York Times* ad, flyers with information about Tibet and the ongoing crackdown, a "Team Tibet" patch, small Tibetan flag, and ideas of nonviolent actions that athletes could take for Tibet during the games. In other countries, Tibetan groups also approached their national athletes as part of the Athlete Wanted campaign.

Olympic officials repeatedly warned athletes during their orientations not to bring politics into the Olympic Games. The British Olympic Association received a firestorm of criticism when British press revealed that British athletes were asked to sign a clause stating that they would not comment on any "politically sensitive issues."[26] While IOC president Jacques Rogge stated that competitors were "free to express their political views," he also stressed that the Olympic Charter prohibited any kind of demonstration or propaganda in any Olympic venue.[27] The IOC did not issue an interpretation of whether the display of a Tibetan flag or other Tibetan symbols would constitute propaganda, leaving many athletes confused about what they could do or say during the games without being sent home or stripped of their medal.[28] Athletes were also aware that foreigners living and working in China were being expelled and subject to visa restrictions, which may have created a chilling effect on any symbolic action.[29]

One athlete to take action was Szymon Kolecki, a Polish weightlifter who shaved his head in a gesture of solidarity with Tibetan monks before his competition, where he won a silver medal. In the months leading up to the Olympics, he was outspoken about China's abuses in Tibet. After the March uprising, he told Polish media, "I am outraged by what's going on in Tibet. When I read about it, I can hardly believe I'll compete in a country that bloodily suppresses street protests and persecutes people who don't agree with the party. I can't believe the Chinese have launched an immense operation to block Lhasa." Kolecki pledged that unless the Chinese government became more moderate, he would compete with his head shaved "in a gesture of solidarity with the Tibetan monks."[30] Head-shaving was one of the suggestions the Athlete Wanted campaign made to Olympic competitors. After winning his medal in Beijing, Kolecki's comments to the press were carefully calibrated, presumably in response to the warnings athletes had received. He told a Polish news outlet, "This haircut is from this morning. I can't directly say why I did it. It's connected with certain things that the Olympic Charter forbids. But I will say that it's symbolic."[31] No other athlete made any visible protest related to Tibet during the games.

During the lead-up to the torch relay and the games, the campaign organized twenty trainings for volunteers involved in campaign activities. The trainings were held in Mexico City, London, Paris, and cities across North America, and they focused on direct-action tactics, media, and the use of communications technology. In San Francisco, for example, five or six trainings preceded the San Francisco torch relay. Two international trainings—held in Oakland and near Dusseldorf—prepared the seventy activists involved in actions in Beijing during the games, as well as coordinators of actions at Chinese consulates and embassies. Approximately fifty individuals participated as trainers, many drawing on experiences with other nonviolent direct action groups, including Greenpeace, EarthFirst, and the Ruckus Society.

Members of SFT participated in nonviolent direct action camps organized by the Ruckus Society in 1998 and 1999, providing the group with key connections with veteran direct-action activists. Many of the activists who participated in SFT's more dramatic actions, including the banner hangs from the Great Wall and Golden Gate bridge, had climbing skills and been active with Greenpeace or other nonviolent direct-action groups. The Ruckus Society also introduced SFT to some of the technological experts, such as Nathan Freitas, who became central to the Beijing campaign.

Leading up to the games, "Team Tibet" groups organized city by city, often through Facebook. On August 6, two days before the games began, SFT and the city "teams" organized simultaneous nonviolent actions at Chinese embassies and consulates around the world, including Brussels, San Francisco, New York, London, Paris, Toronto, Ottawa, and Vancouver.

Seven teams of SFT activists were able to enter Beijing to stage a series of actions that began two days before the Olympics opening ceremony and continued throughout the two weeks of the games. Organizers put a significant technological infrastructure in place to support the teams and publicize the actions. Each team had one tech/media person with a cell phone or iPhone, digital camera, and laptop in order to capture and broadcast images of the teams' actions. Media hubs were organized in different locations in North America, Europe, and Asia, accessible through a central phone number that was programmed to "roll" from one hub to another, depending on the time zone. As a result, the media team was available around the clock to both journalists and the teams in Beijing.

All of the teams had twitter capabilities in order to communicate with each other and organizers outside China. A virtual phone system was set up so that every team member could call a central number and use preassigned numbers in order to be redirected to the media team, tech support, or the San Francisco support hub that maintained contact with the activists' families. For security reasons, the system was set up so that outsiders who dialed into the number but did not know the preassigned numbers would access an innocuous message. Each member of the team was required to call in every twelve hours; if they failed to do so, it was assumed that they had been arrested and detained. According to Freitas, the elaborate infrastructure and support system was essential. "The big issue is how to keep your people safe and informed and to stay on top of the situation. People were literally risking their lives; they could have been shot or beaten up. You want people to feel supported and confident that what they do matters and that it is going to be seen."[32]

The first action was a dramatic banner hang from two 120–foot light poles just outside the iconic Bird's Nest Stadium. Two days before the games' opening ceremony, two climbers scaled the poles and unfurled banners reading "One World One Dream Free Tibet" and "Tibet will be Free" in both English and Chinese. The climbers stayed on the poles for nearly an hour before being detained and even conducted telephone interviews with journalists while still hanging from the poles. Because the Chinese government had repeatedly asserted that they would maintain strict security throughout the games, many journalists were impressed at SFT's success in staging the action. Kate

Woznow, SFT's campaign director, said "There had been lots of build up around Chinese security, and people were told that no one would be able to penetrate it. Journalists didn't think that anything was going to happen, so after the action, they called us and said, 'That was brilliant.'"[33]

As the games continued, other actions included a display of Tibetan flags near the Bird's Nest just before the opening ceremony began; a symbolic die-in at Tiananmen Square; a protest by a Tibetan woman with flags outside Tiananmen Square; and a blockade of the Chinese Ethnic Culture Park. On August 15, two SFT activists rappelled from the top of a large billboard outside of the Chinese state television's Beijing headquarters. The billboard was promoting the Olympics and read "Beijing 2008." The activists dropped a banner reading "Free Tibet" in English and Chinese, partially obscuring the billboard. The climbers and three support people were all detained after about thirty minutes.

The final action took place close to midnight on August 19 outside the Bird's Nest Stadium, where a team of five US activists unfurled a banner spelling out "Free Tibet" in bright blue LED lights. The 10 mm light-emitting diodes (known as "throwies") were powered by small batteries. SFT believed that the action was the first time the lights were ever used on a banner. The team was able to display the banner for only twenty seconds before being detained by security personnel. Nevertheless, the tech members of the team were able to take photos and video images that were immediately uploaded and picked up by numerous media sources.

The SFT actions were the largest coordinated protest effort during the games. Many of the other groups that had organized protests on other human rights issue during the lead-up to the games, including the torch relay, had dropped out. "We knew we were it," said Freitas. In all, seventy campaign activists traveled to Beijing for the games; fifty-five were detained and then deported. Several were held for six days before being forced to leave the country.

SFT organized several major press conferences during the campaign. In conjunction with the torch relay in May, it held its first-ever press conference via live webcast. International journalists were able to log on to the webcast, which featured spokespersons located in New York, Toronto, and London, and were able to pose questions via email or the conference moderator. A second in-person conference was held in June in Athens at the International Olympic Committee's final executive board meeting before the Olympics began.

Another webcast press conference was held just before the games began, featuring campaign organizers based in Asia, New York, and Toronto. Again, journalists could go online to view the conference and ask questions via webchat or by phone through the conference moderator.

SFT developed close relationships with many journalists, issued dozens of press releases, and did extensive outreach to the traditional press corps throughout the campaign. However, many of its actions demanded a different approach. Alerting journalists to the actions on Mt. Everest and the Great Wall was impractical, and because of security concerns, many of the group's direct actions could not be shared with the mainstream media in advance. During the Beijing games in particular, Freitas said, "journalists were a liability for us. We couldn't tell them about our actions ahead of time because they were monitored and followed. So we had to have our own media teams."[34]

Organizers improved their ability to get images to the media as the campaign progressed. At the time of the Everest action in 2007, media companies weren't able to immediately access the video footage that SFT had posted on the Internet for their own broadcasts. It took twelve hours after the action for organizers to burn a DVD with the footage and get the Associated Press to put it into the media pool. By the following year, campaign organizers had built up a good relationship with media outlets, who shared the mechanisms that their own journalists used to post high-quality images and footage to ftp servers. When actions took place during the Olympics, journalists had access to SFT's broadcast-quality footage within an hour of the events.

For the two weeks of the games, the campaign operated a twenty-four-hour online TV channel, Free Tibet 2008 Television, or FT08.TV. The channel went live on August 28 and broadcast through the end of the games on August 24. The channel broadcast breaking reports about the campaign's actions in Beijing, analysis and background on the situation in Tibet, reporting on protests by Tibet supporters in other parts of the world, interviews, and Skype/chat/call-in talk shows. The channel posted videos submitted by SFT grassroots membership and also provided the media with high-resolution photos and videos of the campaign's protests and other events. FT08.TV was coproduced from several different cities, with a central production hub in London. According to organizers, during the two-week period of the Olympic Games, it was the most-watched online TV site.[35]

Lessons Learned

The 2008 Beijing Olympics allowed SFT to take advantage of unprecedented media attention on China and the games to spotlight ongoing human rights abuses accompanying China's fifty-year occupation of Tibet and to challenge China's public claims that it had improved its human rights record. At the same time, China's intransigence and powerful national interests limited the scope of what the campaign could achieve. The campaign was also hampered by limited resources and a lack of organizing capacity within Tibet itself.

Activists knew that using the Olympics to achieve their ultimate goal—an end to the Chinese occupation of Tibet—was simply impossible. The political importance of Tibet to the Chinese government and China's relative imperviousness to international criticism of its human rights practices were simply too strong. As a result, the campaign was forced to select a more achievable objective of simply raising the international profile of human rights in Tibet. Organizers admitted, "We didn't free Tibet or resolve the issue, but that was not the goal."[36]

The campaign faced perceptions that Tibetans were no longer seeking independence, and that decades of Chinese occupation had diluted their aspirations. The last popular uprising to happen inside Tibet had taken place in 1988 and 1989, and many China and Tibet experts believed that another such uprising was unlikely. However, the uprising of March 2008 made clear that Tibetans were still unhappy under Chinese rule, and for many Tibetan activists, the events transformed the political landscape. According to Woznow, "The uprising showed that the Tibetan people want their freedom, they want the Dalai Lama back, they want to determine their own lives. Perceptions have dramatically changed since the uprising. Now there is a sense of inevitability that things will change."[37]

While the March uprising demonstrated Tibetans' desire to end Chinese rule and energized the Tibetan movement, it also revealed the lack of strategic and operational capacity of the Tibetan movement inside Tibet. When the uprising started in Lhasa and quickly spread to other Tibetan areas, Tibetans were able to call people on the outside to report on mass arrests and violence by security forces. However, Tibetans on the inside didn't have the technological capacity to get images out of either the Tibetan protests or the subsequent Chinese crackdown. Said Woznow, "We had assumed that people inside would figure out a strategy, but then realized that on the technological side, there wasn't much there. That was a big mistake. Even the basic mechanisms that were present in Burma that allowed images to come out [during the Saffron revolution] in 2007 were not present in Tibet. It was great on the one hand, but also showed the weakness of the movement. We had no way to get images out. If you don't have a photo, it didn't happen."[38] Organizers reported that Tibetans inside Tibet were calling Tibetans on the outside and asking what they should do. The lack of technological and strategic capacity has prompted some members of SFT to refocus their efforts on strengthening communications networks and providing more support and training for Tibetans inside Tibet.

The Olympics campaign was also extraordinarily ambitious given SFT's small size. Before the campaign began, SFT operated on a US$300-400,000 annual budget with a small core staff. The campaign demanded both an influx of money and organizing capacity. The group stepped up its fundraising, including through the marketing of "Team Tibet" jackets and other merchandise related to the campaign. It doubled the number of donors giving money through its online Action Network and participated in a Facebook "Causes" Giving Challenge, raising more than US$220,000 through online donations, seven times the amount raised online in the previous year.[39] In total, the group was able to raise US$1 million to fund the Olympics campaign. This also enabled the group to hire additional staff, including an Olympics coordinator who was brought on five months before the Olympics began. During the most intensive phase of the campaign, twenty-five people were working full time at various locations around the world, some on full salary and some on stipends, with more than one hundred others intensively involved on a volunteer basis.

Despite the increase in staff, the complexity of the campaign, the number of individuals involved, and the detailed logistics involved in planning multiple actions around the globe all put an enormous strain on the key organizers. Campaign director Kate Woznow said, "It was really stressful, like low-level warfare. I can't imagine ever doing anything like that again. From Everest to the end, it never really stopped. Actions, trainings, preparation for more actions. We worked around the clock, but felt it was such an important moment."[40] Despite the intense efforts of the campaign's leadership and volunteers, some opportunities were missed due to lack of resources. For example, organizers felt that they weren't able to fully capitalize on the enormous expression of interest from individuals who learned about the campaign; with more resources, they might have mounted more intensive engagements with the International Olympic Committee.

Despite the inherent limitations it faced, a core accomplishment of the campaign was to bring much greater visibility to Tibet and the ongoing Chinese occupation. The campaign generated extensive media, particularly outside the United States, making Tibet an ongoing theme of Olympic coverage. "People are now clear that Tibet matters," said Tethong. "The Olympics and the campaign helped make it a legitimate issue that demands global attention in relation to this rising power."[41]

A particular strength of the campaign was SFT's ability to seize key moments and maximize their advocacy potential. The structure of the Olympics—including clear benchmarks such as the one-year countdown, the torch relay, and the games themselves—provided opportunities for creative and high-profile actions that could be planned in advance. SFT spent considerable time analyzing the potential opportunities that the Olympics and its lead-up offered and the kind of actions that would best enable the group to gain attention for Tibet. Organizers also made extensive contingency plans to anticipate the possible scenarios that they might encounter, particularly for their major direct actions.

Campaign organizers strategically planned their actions in order to take advantage of major news cycles, for example, organizing events in advance of major Olympic events such as the official one-year countdown and the Olympic opening ceremony. Such timing helped ensure that the campaign's images and messages became part of the media's coverage of "official" Olympic developments. When the BBC did a story about the one-year countdown, for example, it featured SFT's Great Wall action.

A second strength of the campaign was its use of new technologies. Campaign director Kate Woznow described it as "our secret weapon." She said, "We had good spokespeople and messaging, but it was the tech that really gave us the edge."[42] Use of new technology allowed SFT not only to publicize its actions in dramatic and unprecedented ways—for example, broadcasting video images via satellite from Mt. Everest—but also to circumvent the notorious "Great Firewall," China's sophisticated system of Internet censorship and surveillance. In the face of Chinese attempts to limit protests and information, SFT believed that its strategic advantage was to get information out of China and disseminate it broadly. Systems set up by SFT's technological experts—including twitter communications and a virtual phone system for teams doing actions in Beijing, and the use of Skype—allowed secure communication and coordination among SFT's international network, while the use of digital satellite broadcasts, ftp servers, YouTube, online press conferences, and Internet blogging allowed the campaign to reach a global audience in unprecedented ways.

The campaign put particular emphasis on visual images. "There's no denying the power of TV and moving images," said Tethong. "When you give people images in real time that people can be inspired by, organize around, be entertained, it changes everything."[43] Although SFT developed effective systems for making its images available to the mainstream press, it put particular emphasis on online dissemination, including posting videos on YouTube that would be accessible over time and creating videos that had the potential to "go viral." According to Freitas, "The number of viewers is what matters. If you only focus on coverage of a live event, people miss it. It's more important to get a clip on YouTube that can be shared, rather than have live coverage for an hour."[44]

A third important element was outreach to the mainstream media. Although the campaign utilized new technologies to excellent effect, it also build strong relationships with many of the traditional journalists covering the games, garnering coverage from CNN, the BBC, the *New York Times*, the *Washington Post*, and other major print and broadcast outlets. Journalists learned to rely on SFT for solid information about Tibet, as well as for dramatic visual images to accompany their stories. Woznow said that during the Tibetan uprising in March 2008, "People already knew us as the action people, but when we started putting information out about the uprising, people started to learn that we also had hard information and that we could speak to what was actually happening."[45] She recalled that while the organization had difficulty accessing the media at the beginning of the campaign, by the end, "It was incredibly easy. Journalists saw that we were the only ones challenging the Chinese authorities. They were taken with the idea that these kids got through and pierced the security apparatus."[46]

A fourth crucial component was extensive training and contingency planning, particularly with the volunteers involved in direct actions. "We did twenty major actions in a two-year period," said Woznow. "Without eight years of preparation, we wouldn't have had the relationships, skills or confidence to carry it out strategically."[47] Particularly for the activists involved in actions in Beijing, or other events that held the risk of arrest, it was essential to conduct thorough security, legal, and contingency planning. For both ideas and expertise, organizers identified collaboration with activists from other movements, including environmental groups with a history of direct action, as particularly valuable. "I felt like we were the poster child for collaboration and cross-movement training," said Tethong. "These activists helped to raise us and opened our minds and eyes to all the possibilities."[48]

Finally, the campaign used extensive outreach to engage thousands of new people in information and action networks around Tibet. It effectively used its website, Facebook, and other online venues; trainings; and creative ideas such as the mobilization of "Team Tibet" groups to engage in local activities. During the Olympics campaign, 170 new local chapters of Students for a Free Tibet formed, expanding the organization's chapters to 700 across forty countries, with significant growth in France, Japan, Germany, Poland, and Mexico. SFT's online Action Network grew to more than fifty thousand members with more than fourteen thousand new members joining during the months leading up to the Olympics. The number of people subscribed to SFT's Facebook groups increased from twelve thousand to thirty-eight thousand.[49] National branches of SFT expanded or were established, particularly in Japan, Hong Kong, Taiwan, India, and the UK.[50]

Although Tibetan independence remained an elusive goal, organizers believe that the campaign, together with the March uprising, energized the Tibetan movement in significant ways. Prior to the Olympic campaign, many Tibetan activists felt frustrated by a lack of results on Tibet issues. According to Tethong, "The Olympics and the uprising showed us and showed Tibet and the world that not only are we alive and kicking, but we can do things. We are sure of our own power and sense of unity from the uprising. Tibetans are more united now than ever in our history. We have a newfound unity, sense of purpose, pride, and anger."[51]

Chapter 10

Organizing for LGBTI Rights in Jamaica and Nepal

To be gay in Jamaica is to be dead.
—*letter in the* Jamaica Observer, *2004*

Knowing the problems other LGBTs face in Nepal, like blackmail, rape, exclusion,
abuse, and more, I thought we can't continue living like this.
—*Sunil Pant, founder of Nepal's Blue Diamond Society*[1]

L IKE MANY OTHER COUNTRIES around the world, both Jamaica and Nepal
have a history of violence against their lesbian, gay, bisexual, transgender,
and intersex (LGBTI) citizens.[2] In each country, police have committed
grave abuses against the LGBTI community, including arbitrary arrests and
violent physical attacks. Laws in both countries allowed criminal prosecution
and prison terms for consensual homosexual activity.[3] Members of the LGBTI
community have faced severe homophobia and discrimination.

Beginning in 2006, these similarities began to end. In just a few years,
Nepal became known as a "gaytopia," while Jamaica remained labeled "one
of the most homophobic places on earth."[4] Despite persistent and creative
organizing, antigay violence continued in Jamaica, accompanied by government denials of homophobia and fierce resistance to changing the country's
sodomy laws. By contrast in Nepal, the Supreme Court granted full rights
to gays, lesbians, bisexuals, and transgender people and nullified laws used
to prosecute sexual minorities for homosexual conduct. The Nepal Tourism
Board announced plans to make Nepal one of the world's leading gay tourism
destinations, and the country was poised to become one of the first nations to
legalize same-sex marriage.

In both countries, efforts were led by a single LGBTI organization that pursued a broad range of strategies, including direct support and services for members of the LGBTI community, HIV/AIDS education, outreach to the media, engagement with political leaders and other opinion leaders, and advocacy for constitutional and legislative reform. However, differing political environments and other factors led to starkly different outcomes.

Jamaica

Jamaica has one of the highest rates of antigay violence in the world. Gays and persons perceived to be gay have been harassed, subjected to mob violence, and murdered. At least thirty-five gay men were murdered in Jamaica between 1997 and 2010, including Brian Williamson, the cofounder of the country's only gay rights organization, the Jamaica Forum for Lesbians, All-Sexuals and Gays (J-FLAG). Williamson was found dead in his home in 2004, his body covered with dozens of knife wounds. Afterward, a crowd gathered outside the crime scene, laughing and calling "Battyman [Jamaican slang for homosexual; "batty" means "buttocks"] he get killed!" "Let's get them one at a time," "That's what you get for sin," and "Let's kill all of them." Another prominent activist who advocated for HIV prevention and treatment, Steve Harvey, was abducted from his home and shot dead in November 2005.

During an eighteen-month period in 2008 and 2009, more than thirty cases of mob violence targeted gays or those perceived to be gay.[5] In one attack, a group of fifteen to twenty men broke down the door of a house where four men lived, demanded that they leave the area, and began beating and slashing the inhabitants with stones, knifes, sticks, and machetes. Police did not arrive until ninety minutes after the men called for help. Two of the victims were hospitalized; one fled and was pursued by the mob. He was never found and presumed dead.[6] In a 2007 incident, a mob pursued three gay men into a pharmacy, where they were trapped for nearly an hour as a crowd of approximately two hundred people shouted insults and threatened to kill the men. When the police arrived, the officers called the victims "nasty battymen" and struck one in the face, head, and stomach. As the police finally escorted the men outside the pharmacy, members of the crowd threw stones, hitting one of the men in the head. The police refused to accept complaints from the men and told them never to return to the police station.[7]

LGBTI activists in Jamaica used pseudonyms to protect their identity. Hundreds of gays, lesbians, bisexual, or transgendered persons fled Jamaica and sought asylum in other countries.[8] Gareth Henry, a prominent member of J-FLAG and one of the three men targeted in the pharmacy attack, sought refugee status in Canada in 2008. He said thirteen of his friends had been killed in the previous four years. "When you find police officers who are leading mob attacks," he said, "turning up at people's home like myself, pointing guns at my window, with civilians with them, and saying that I need to leave or they're going to kill me, it reinforces homophobia."[9]

In 2011, Jamaica was one of seventy-six countries worldwide that criminalized homosexual activity.[10] Under Jamaican law, "the abominable crime of buggery" (anal sex) was punishable by up to ten years' imprisonment with hard labor.[11] "Acts of gross indecency" (usually interpreted as any kind of physical intimacy) between men, either in public or private, was punishable by up to two years' imprisonment, with or without hard labor.[12] In 1994, the UN Human Rights Committee ruled that laws punishing consensual adult homosexual conduct violated the rights to privacy and nondiscrimination protected by the International Covenant on Civil and Political Rights, which Jamaica ratified in 1975.[13]

Prime Minister Bruce Golding pledged publicly in 2009 that he would not change the law and stated in a BBC interview that he would not include gays in his cabinet. He described gay advocates as "perhaps the most organized lobby in the world," but said, "we are not going to yield to the pressure, whether that pressure comes from individual organizations, individuals, whether that pressure comes from foreign governments or groups of countries, to liberalize the laws as it relates to buggery."[14] During a Parliamentary debate in February 2009, MP Ernest Smith called homosexuals "abusive and violent" and called for increased penalties of up to life in prison for homosexual activity. Soon after, he called for gay and lesbian organizations to be outlawed.[15] Jamaican authorities denied that members of the LGBTI community were targeted with violence. The Senior Superintendent of Police in Jamaica stated in 2008, "We haven't had any reports about violence against homosexuals. . . . We never have any cases of gay men being beaten up. I know that there is a sort of revulsion against homosexuals and lesbians, but evidence does not substantiate that there is any level of violence perpetrated against them."[16]

Jamaican police not only turned a blind eye to homophobic violence, but often perpetrated it. Members of the Jamaican police carried out beatings and other physical violence against members of the LGBTI community and subjected them to harassment, arrest, and detention on suspicion of being gay. In some instances, police officers participated actively in mob attacks. Victims of homophobic violence reported that the police frequently refused to investigate or take reports on the crimes and harassed or even tortured those seeking assistance from the police.[17]

Because of homophobic laws and social stigma, gay men were reluctant to seek health care or take precautions against sexually transmitted diseases, fueling Jamaica's HIV/AIDS epidemic. In 2008, a survey commissioned by the Ministry of Health found that 31.8 percent of gay men in Jamaica were living with HIV.[18] In 2009, UNAIDS reported that the Caribbean had the second-highest rate of HIV prevalence among adults in the world, after sub-Saharan Africa.[19] Overall, an estimated 1.6 percent of Jamaican adults were living with HIV/AIDS in 2007; in the Caribbean, only Haiti and the Bahamas had higher rates of adults living with HIV/AIDS.[20] Human rights groups asserted that Jamaica's discriminatory laws and violence against the LGBTI community undermined government measures to combat HIV. In some cases, Jamaica's sodomy laws were used to arrest "peer educators" who provide HIV/AIDS information and condoms to other gay men. "Until Jamaica addresses the epidemic of homophobic violence, it will have no hope against the epidemic of HIV/AIDS," said the author of a 2004 Human Rights Watch report on homophobia and HIV in Jamaica.[21]

J-FLAG, Jamaica's first organization to advocate for the rights of the LGBT community, formed in 1998 by a group of twelve human rights activists, businesspeople, educators, lawyers, and other professionals. It provided support for members of the LGBTI community and advocated for constitutional protections for sexual minorities and repeal of Jamaica's sodomy laws. Thomas Glave, who cofounded J-FLAG with Brian Williamson, said, "When we came out to the public, we were facing an enormous amount of opposition. There was a ferocity we encountered, scathing is not enough to describe it—more like horror. Yet, we had a powerful and growing micro-community. From that core we did an enormous amount of work."[22]

For its first couple of years, J-FLAG organized monthly social events ("lymes") for the lesbian, all-sexual, and gay community, regularly drawing up to 350 people. The events were intended to provide a "safe space" for lesbian, all-sexual, and gay people to meet and socialize. However, a series of violent incidents forced organizers to suspend the events. The hostile environment experienced by gays in Jamaica forced J-FLAG leaders to remain anonymous and use pseudonyms when engaging with the media and the public.

However, the group issued press releases and conducted media interviews, produced educational literature, and conducted workshops and trainings for government officials, health care workers, media, and students. It set up a telephone helpline and assistance programs for LAG people who were subject to harassment and attacks, including documentation for individuals who decided to leave the country and pursue asylum claims in the United States, Canada, or the UK.

One of J-FLAG's first major initiatives was to submit a proposal for the inclusion of sexual orientation as a protected category under Jamaica's constitution. The 1962 Jamaican constitution specifically prohibits discrimination based on race, place of origin, political opinions, color, or creed, but made no reference to sexual orientation or gender identity.[23] In 2000, the Parliament began discussions on possible amendments to the constitution's bill of rights and particularly proposals to add a new provision that would prohibit discrimination based on gender. J-FLAG submitted a proposal to the Joint Select Committee on the Charter of Rights Bill, arguing that the inclusion of sexual orientation would provide members of the LGBTI community the same rights and protections that all other sectors of Jamaican society already enjoyed and would strengthen the rights of self-determination and self-expression for all Jamaican citizens.[24]

J-FLAG enlisted the support of other organizations, such as the UK Black Gay and Lesbian Community Online (Asante) and the International Gay and Lesbian Human Rights Commission to support J-FLAG's submission through petitions and letters to Jamaican authorities. In June 2001, the Joint Select Committee rejected the proposal, reportedly because the committee feared that the provision would force reform of marriage, taxation, and other laws. However, later that year, it recommended that the House of Parliament consider repealing laws criminalizing consensual gay sex. Parliament rejected the proposal in January 2002. In 2009, a proposed Charter of Fundamental Rights and Freedoms to amend the constitution was presented to Parliament for discussion. Again, J-FLAG again worked to advocate in favor of an antidiscrimination provision on the basis of sexual orientation.

J-FLAG made repeated attempts to establish dialogue with senior government officials, with limited results. When J-FLAG requested meetings with the prime minister and minister of tourism regarding the concerns of the LGBTI community, the requests were denied. Most senior government officials consistently rejected any moves to protect sexual minorities under the law or to decriminalize homosexual activity, bolstered by public opinion polls that showed that 96 percent of Jamaicans opposed legalizing homosexual relations.[25] Maurice Tomlinson, legal counsel to J-FLAG, said, "What we've been told is, 'Look, we're not willing to expend any political capital on this [LGBTI issues]. You need to make the Jamaican public ready for LGBTI rights, then we'll be able to address it.'"[26] J-FLAG's program manager, Jason McFarlane, concurred: "The MPs want to keep their jobs. We have support from some; but they take their cues from society."[27]

In 2004, J-FLAG joined with UK-based OutRage! and the Black Gay Men's Advisory Group to campaign against homophobia in Jamaican reggae and dancehall music. Popular artists, including Buju Banton, Beenie Man, Sizzla, and Bounty Killer, often performed songs featuring violence against gays. For example, Buju Banton's 1992 hit, "Boom Bye Bye" boasts of shooting gays with submachine guns and burning them with acid. A song by Elephant Man included the lyrics, "Battyman fi dead! Please mark we word, Gimme tha tecnine, Shoot dem like bird" [Queers must be killed! Please mark my words. Give me the Tec-9 (semiautomatic weapon). Shoot them like birds]. In 2001, a Jamaica Labor Party candidate adopted T.O.K.'s "Chi Chi Man" as a campaign anthem during his run for prime minister. The song's lyrics included: "From dem a par inna chi chi man car, Blaze di fire mek we bun dem! (Bun dem!)" [Those who get together in a queer's car, Blaze the fire, let's burn them! (Burn them!)][28]

J-FLAG staff reported that many Jamaicans who came to the organization for help after being assaulted said that their attackers sang the lyrics to homophobic dancehall songs during the attack. For example, members of the crowd that gathered outside the scene of Brian Williamson's 2004 murder reportedly sang lines from "Boom Bye Bye." J-FLAG director Jason MacFarlane said, "'Boom Bye Bye' is an anthem to some people. The music exacerbates public homophobia."[29]

J-FLAG, OutRage!, and other groups began to refer to the songs as "murder music." In 2003, OutRage! called on the British police to arrest Bounty Killer for incitement and conspiracy to commit murder during his UK tour. When the groups launched the Stop Murder Music Campaign the following year, they called for boycotts of concerts and albums by artists that performed homophobic songs and for corporate sponsors to withdraw their support. The campaign organized letter-writing, picketing of events, and published a

"Dancehall Dossier" of lyrics and factsheets on eight dancehall artists.[30] The campaign generated significant media attention, particularly in Europe and North America. More than sixty organizations in more than a dozen countries participated in the campaign.

In Canada, the Stop Murder Music campaign brought together a broad range of groups to hold press conferences in Toronto and Montreal, calling on government officials to deny entry to performers who advocated antigay violence in their lyrics. The campaign argued that the performance of such music violated both the Canadian Criminal Code and the Canadian Human Rights Act by inciting violence and murder against the lesbian, gay, bisexual, and trans-identified communities. When Elephant Man and Sizzla were allowed entry into Canada for concert tours, the Canadian Jewish Congress wrote to the Minister of Citizenship and Immigration to urge him to revoke their visas and deport them.[31] Member organizations wrote to Pepsi to protest its sponsorship of Elephant Man and publicly urged the Canadian music and entertainment industry not to promote, sponsor, or do business with the artists. Three companies cancelled their agreements to lease venues to organizers of Elephant Man concerts.[32]

The campaign forced the artists to cancel hundreds of concerts. In 2004, Beenie Man cancelled thirty US concerts and Capleton canceled seven. Buju Banton cancelled a Scandinavian tour and four other dates in Europe, while Sizzla canceled two UK tours and a San Francisco show.[33] Award nominations for some of the artists targeted by the campaign and numerous sponsorship deals were withdrawn.[34] Outrage!'s Peter Tatchell estimated that the campaign cost performers in excess of five million US dollars.[35]

In 2007, three of the top dancehall performers, Beenie Man, Sizzla, and Capleton signed the Reggae Compassionate Act, renouncing violence and homophobia and pledging not to make statements or perform songs that would incite hatred or violence against any community. Stop Murder Music Campaign activists and the artists had negotiated the text of the statement with a UK reggae promoter acting as a go-between. Campaign activists hailed the agreement as a significant milestone. "This commitment is a major blow against homophobia in the Caribbean and in popular music," said Peter Tatchell of OutRage! "Having these major reggae stars renounce homophobia will influence their fans and the wider public to rethink bigoted attitudes. The beneficial effect on young black straight men will be immense."[36]

The campaign simultaneously called for continued pressure and boycotts of five other "murder music" artists who had not signed the pledge: Elephant Man, TOK, Bounty Killa, Vybz Kartel, and Buju Banton. Banton signed the pledge a month later. While welcoming the signed agreements, activists also warned that the performers who signed the Reggae Compassionate Act may have done so only for financial and professional gain. Organizers urged journalists to test the performers' sincerity by publicizing the pledges and asking the performers about the pledge in interviews. They also said they would review the agreement in six months' time.[37]

The organizers' skepticism was well-placed. Just days after Buju Banton signed the pledge, Banton's manager denied to a Jamaican radio station that Banton had signed the agreement. Similarly, Beenie Man reportedly told the *Jamaica Observer* that he had not signed the act and would not promise to abide by it.[38] The Stop Murder Music Campaign posted copies of the statements online showing the performers' signatures and denounced the performers' comments. Brett Lock of Outrage! told a journalist, "We have never accepted any agreement whereby an artist agrees to not perform homophobic lyrics at concerts in Europe and the US, but continues performing them in the Caribbean. The idea that these singers can incite the murder of gay people in Jamaica and then come to Europe and be accepted as legitimate artists is morally sick and indefensible."[39]

By 2009, the campaign had brought tangible results in Jamaica. In February, the Jamaican Broadcasting Commission banned radio and television stations from airing songs with content considered explicitly sexual and violence. During a high-level reception during Reggae Month, a prominent Jamaican poet, Mutabaruka, called on the government to respond to concerns about Jamaica's dancehall music. Prime Minister Golding ordered the country's minister of information, culture, youth, and sports, Olivia Grange, to form a task force and hold a forum to address the issue. He said, "We are going to have to find a way to deal with what is going on out there with the music. If we have to change the law, let us prepare the legislation and go to Parliament and change it. . . . [W]e can't allow this assault on our music, on our psyche and identity as a people to continue."[40] Advocates reported in 2010 that the artists who had signed the Reggae Compassionate Act pledge were by and large sticking to their commitment.[41]

In 2008 and 2009, international groups concerned about continuing anti-gay violence in Jamaica initiated controversial boycotts, calling for tourists to avoid Jamaica as a holiday destination and to boycott Jamaican rum and Red Stripe beer. In early 2008, the Stop Murder Music (Canada) campaign called for a tourist boycott of Jamaica if the Jamaican government did not take action by May 12, 2008, to denounce homophobic violence and begin repealing laws that criminalize homosexual behavior. The call for the boycott gained momentum following Gareth Henry's request for asylum in Canada. Henry was a prominent member of J-FLAG and fled Jamaica after being subject to harassment and a mob attack. His arrival in Canada in 2008 generated significant media attention to the high incidence of homophobic violence in Jamaica.

J-FLAG criticized the proposed boycott. In a statement, the organization said, "Because of the possible repercussions of increased homophobic violence against our already besieged community, we feel that a tourist boycott is not the most appropriate response at this time. In our battle to win hearts and minds, we do not wish to be perceived as taking food off the plate of those who are already impoverished."[42] In an interview with a Canadian journalist, J-FLAG's coordinator, Jason MacFarlane, said, "I personally understand where they're coming from, but . . . they can't see what's happening day to day. . . . If JFLAG had one case [of violence against gay people] a week, since the boycott we have three. They're not seeing the reality. It is essentially bringing more violence on the community."[43]

Stop Murder Music (Canada) called off the boycott on May 15, 2008, three days after the deadline they had set, after receiving a letter from Anne-Marie Bonner, the Jamaican consul general. Bonner's response did not mention homosexuality or repealing laws prohibiting homosexual activity, and stated that the government had no intention to add protections for specific groups into the constitution. Nonetheless, campaign organizers stated that the response was sufficient to call off the boycott and welcomed its references to government commitments to reduce the incidence of crime in Jamaica.[44]

In March 2009, a prominent San Francisco blogger, Michael Petrelis, instigated another boycott targeting Jamaican tourism, as well as Jamaican rum and Red Stripe beer. Petrelis said that the catalyst for the boycott was a new human rights report issued by the US State Department that cited "arbitrary detention, mob attacks, stabbings, harassment of homosexual patients by hospital and prison staff, and targeted shootings of homosexuals."[45] At a kick-off event in the Castro in San Francisco, advocates organized a "rum dump" where they publicly poured Myer's rum and Red Stripe beer into the street. Activists at The Stonewall Inn in New York, the Greenwich Village bar where the Stonewall riots began in 1969, also poured Jamaican alcohol into the sewer. Shortly after the launch of the boycott, Petrelis told the *Jamaica Gleaner* that at least twelve gay bars and restaurants had agreed to stop serving Jamaican alcohol.[46]

Again, J-FLAG opposed the boycott. The organization issued a public letter to its international friends and supporters, thanking them for their support and saying that their allies had "strengthened our voice and made it possible for us to make progress where we hardly thought it possible." However, the letter called the boycott of Jamaican products "unfortunate" and stated that the targeting of Red Stripe in particular was "extremely damaging to the cause of LGBT activists in Jamaica."[47] In April 2008, Red Stripe had ended its sponsorship of music festivals that featured performers known for advocating antigay violence and issued a public statement saying that it "would not be party" to live performances where artists propagated violence and antisocial lyrics.[48] J-FLAG criticized outside groups for failing to do sufficient research to ensure that their actions did not harm the credibility or the cause of the communities they intended to defend and said that "the misguided targeting" of Red Stripe did tremendous damage to more than a decade of efforts by Jamaican activists. Its letter said:

> Jamaica's deeply ingrained antipathy toward homosexuality and homosexuals is a social phenomenon that will not be undone by boycott campaigns or government dictate. It requires the painstaking effort of confronting the society and talking to social actors who can bring change in the way society sees LGBT people. . . . It is important that our international allies understand the nature of our struggle and engage us in a respectful way about it. Unless they are willing and able to lead the struggle in the trenches as we have done, it is important that they be guided by us. To do otherwise would be to act in a manner that destroys the space for dialogue that we have managed to create over the past decade and set back our struggle.[49]

Petrelis declared that the boycott would continue, stating that Red Stripe's explanation for withdrawing its sponsorship of live concerts was too vague and did not specifically refer to antigay violence linked to Jamaican dancehall music.[50] In private, some J-FLAG members expressed support for the boycott. "The Jamaican government will not take the LGBT community seriously until they realize we have strong allies with purchasing power who are going to press their point home," said one. "We need to push the economic imperative."[51]

In an indication that the boycott had some influence, a representative of the Jamaican Tourist Board, requested a meeting with J-FLAG. Representatives of the board were concerned that negative publicity in Canada regarding homophobia in Jamaica was hurting its efforts to build the tourism market in that country. J-FLAG's program manager agreed to the meeting, but it never took place. Members of J-FLAG believe that plans for the meeting may have been halted by more senior members of the tourist board, or the Ministry of Tourism. [52]

In predominantly Christian Jamaica, religious leaders helped fuel anti-gay sentiments. In 2001, for example, while the government considered the recommendation from a joint select committee of Parliament that it repeal Jamaica's buggery law, the Caribbean Catholic bishops publicly opposed the recommendation. Senior government officials, including the prime minister and leader of the opposition, belonged to religious communities known for their intolerance of homosexuality. According to Tomlinson, "The difficulty is that the right wing, the Pentecostals, thrive on this kind of [antigay] rhetoric because it brings in parishioners."[53]

J-FLAG worked to cultivate support among religious leaders, but made limited in-roads. As part of a long-term strategy to foster more sympathetic clergy, J-FLAG began a dialogue with a theological college in Jamaica that trains clergy from seven or eight denominations throughout the Caribbean, seeking changes in the curriculum to encourage a more positive response to the LGBTI community from the churches.[54] In 2010, the group created a public service announcement that was shown on television, featuring an Anglican priest (who was also a former army chaplain) urging the need for tolerance. The group identified some religious leaders who were willing to speak with their peers regarding LGBTI rights, but felt it was an uphill battle.

In 2010, J-FLAG adopted a more public, vocal advocacy strategy. It organized the first public events in Jamaica to challenge homophobia and protest Jamaica's sodomy laws, and for the first time since the well-publicized murders of Brian Williamson and Steve Harvey, had leadership that was willing to step forward and be publicly identified. Early that year, Maurice Tomlinson (his real name) became legal advisor to J-FLAG and took on the coordination of J-FLAG's advocacy. He said that previously, J-FLAG's advocacy "was piecemeal, with lots of discouraging moments."[55] His willingness to take a public leadership role made it much easier for J-FLAG to push forward a sustained advocacy agenda. Tomlinson worked to make J-FLAG and LGBTI issues more visible, appearing on local call-in radio shows, organizing regular letters to the editor in Jamaica's major newspapers, and mobilizing public demonstrations. "We need to raise the profile, confront the rhetoric and put a face to this thing," he said.[56]

During the year, J-FLAG and other groups organized several public demonstrations, beginning with a "Walk for Tolerance," bringing together more than a hundred members of the LGBTI community, sex workers, and people with AIDS. Despite initial fears about security, an organizer said that "once the walk started, even the timid were caught up in the event. When we were greeted with the very few derogatory comments, we answered boldly and proudly. And the people quickly backed down."[57] A few weeks later, a broad coalition of more than a dozen groups organized "Stand Against Silence" to observe the International Day Against Homophobia and Transphobia. Outside Emancipation Park in Kingston, thirty people gathered, some with their mouths covered and with placards reading "Break the Silence! End the Fear" and "Stop the Hate Before Too Late." A joint press release issued by sponsoring organizations included statements from J-FLAG, AIDS organizations, Amnesty International, and the president of the European Union missions in Jamaica. In July 2010, another J-FLAG-organized demonstration targeted the Caribbean Community (CARICOM), outside the Montego Bay resort where the heads of all CARICOM countries were holding their annual meeting. The demonstration called for the repeal of the sodomy laws still on the books in eleven of the fifteen CARICOM member countries and an end to discrimination against gays throughout the Caribbean.[58] For Tomlinson, the demonstrations—and the fact that they were public, focused directly on LGBTI rights, and took place without incident—represented the movement's greatest accomplishment to date. "They give a sense of hope to the community."[59]

J-FLAG worked for years with the Jamaican police to address both the need for better protection for members of the LGBTI community and the participation of police officers in direct attacks against LGBTI persons. With the support of high-ranking police officers, the group was able to hold numerous meetings with the police commissioner to raise their concerns. Organizers felt that securing police protection for the 2010 public demonstrations was a real milestone and helped send an important message to the public. "We've moved from a position where police were instigating attacks [against LGBTI persons] to providing us with public protection," said Tomlinson.[60] J-FLAG secured police protection for its 2010 demonstrations only after sustained negotiations. After the first event took place without incident, organizers found that it became easier to engage the police for subsequent events.[61]

A police reform program supported by the British government helped foster change within the police force. Beginning around 2005, the UK police sent several midlevel British police officers to serve in Jamaica's police force. Advocates believe that these officers helped to influence the attitudes and behavior of Jamaican police toward sexual minorities. By 2010, incidents of direct police attacks against members of the LGBT community had nearly ended, although securing investigations of antigay harassment and violence remained difficult. "People avoid reporting [antigay crimes] for a variety of reasons," said McFarlane. "One of our challenges is to get clients to have confidence in the police that they will respond, because history has shown that they do not respond."[62]

In 2010 and 2011, J-FLAG stepped up its advocacy further, both at a national level and through international mechanisms. It continued holding public demonstrations and began organizing regular trainings for members of the LGBTI community on human rights issues and security issues. According to McFarlane, "As the community becomes more visible, it is also more at risk."[63] To influence public opinion, the group helped produce a public service announcement featuring the former Miss Jamaica Universe, speaking of her love for her brother, who is gay, and calling on all Jamaicans for tolerance.[64]

As Parliament geared up to again debate constitutional amendments through a Charter of Fundamental Rights and Freedoms, J-FLAG launched a petition campaign and publicly called for provisions prohibiting discrimination on the basis of gender and sexual orientation. The charter was adopted in April 2011 without any such protections. On the basis of a submission from J-FLAG and other groups, the UN Committee on Human Rights criticized Jamaica for failing to prohibit antigay discrimination in the charter and urged Jamaica to amend its laws to prohibit discrimination on the basis of sexual orientation or sexual identity and to decriminalize same-sex sexual behavior. It also urged the government to send a clear message that harassment, discrimination, and violence on the basis of sexual orientation would not be tolerated.[65]

During 2011, J-FLAG received more than sixty reports of murder, mob attacks, extortion, home evictions, and verbal and physical violence against individuals for their sexual orientation or gender identity. As J-Flag marked its thirteenth anniversary in December 2011, it noted that "much more needs to be done to make Jamaica a cohesive and just society where everyone can live, work and raise their family." However, it also noted that Jamaica had "come a long way":

> Thirteen years ago there were more dancehall and reggae artistes singing homophobic songs, more persons right to life was being violated because of their sexual orientation, the Commissioner of Police would never instruct police officers to respect the rights of all civilians, regardless of their sexual preference, political representatives would never meet with us and publicly support LGBT rights, the media would never openly advocate the repeal of the buggery law, and HIV programmes were not catering to the needs of gay, bisexual and other men who have sex with men (MSM).[66]

Nepal

As in Jamaica, members of the LGBTI community in Nepal faced harassment, discrimination, violence, and police abuse. *Metis* (transgender people; biological males who dress and identify as women) were particularly vulnerable to police abuse, including arbitrary arrest and detention, beatings, verbal abuse, intimidation, extortion, and rape. During a three-month period in 2003, the Blue Diamond Society, Nepal's leading LGBTI organization, documented six incidents of police brutality against *metis* and HIV/AIDS outreach workers in Kathmandu. In one 2003 incident, police attacked a group of nine men who were cross-dressing for a disco party, kicking them, beating them with batons and guns, and whipping them with belts. Several were taken into custody and beaten further. In April 2005, police attacked a group of eighteen *metis* walking to a New Year's festival, severely beating nine of them with batons, gun butts, and sticks. When the group attempted to make a police report on the incident, they were refused entry to the police station.[67]

In July 2004, the Blue Diamond Society organized a peaceful rally to protest a violent rape and assault of two *metis* by two men that had occurred the previous month. Participants were marching to the Parliament building to deliver a petition for the prime minister when police attacked several protesters and forced the crowd to disperse. A few weeks later, police conducted a series of raids on restaurants, bars, and streets frequented by *metis* and arrested and detained thirty-nine members of the Blue Diamond Society. They were charged with "spreading perversion" under the Public Offenses Act,[68] held for eleven days, and released only after international protests by UNAIDS, human rights, and gay rights organizations.[69] In August 2004, a Nepali police officer forced a *meti* to perform oral sex on him and then slit her throat, prompting public outrage. The same year, a Nepali lawyer petitioned the Supreme Court to outlaw the Blue Diamond Society, stating that the group was "polluting the culture of Nepal," and that by allowing the group to function, the government was abetting immoral activities.[70]

In a 2004 statement directed to the government, members of the LGBT community described their experiences of persistent violence and discrimination:

> Nepalese lesbians, gays, bisexuals, and transgender people confront harassment from police; abuse by our neighbors and our families; and violence and brutality—sometimes punitive rape—on the public places. We are discriminated against in the workplace. Many of our families force us into marriages against our will, in the hope of changing our inmost selves. Some of us, among them the very young, are evicted from our homes because of prejudice and fear.[71]

From 1996 to 2006, Nepali government forces and Maoist rebels engaged in a civil war that cost approximately sixteen thousand lives. Maoist leaders called homosexuals "unnatural" and denounced them for "polluting" society. Maoists used intimidation and violence against members of the LGBTI community. In one campaign, Maoist cadres reportedly went from house to house in Kathmandu telling owners not to rent rooms to gays.[72] Nepal's law did not specifically criminalize homosexual activity, but prohibited "unnatural sexual acts," which were punishable by up to one year in prison or a fine of Rs 5000. The law included no definition of what constituted an unnatural act, and police used the law to harass and arrest members of the LGBTI community.

In 2001, Sunil Pant and several friends organized Nepal's first organization to address issues faced by Nepal's sexual minorities. The prior year, Pant had returned to Nepal after studying computer science in Belarus. He said, "I didn't plan in 2000 to start the Blue Diamond Society. I just wanted to meet other LGBT people and know more about the culture and problems. After meeting many LGBTs in Kathmandu and knowing the problems other LGBTs face in Nepal, like blackmail, rape, exclusion, abuse, and more, I thought we can't continue living like this."[73] Pant chose the name Blue Diamond Society for the group, explaining that in Buddhism, people who are compassionate and enlightened are known as "diamond beings," while in Russia, he had found that people would ask "are you blue?" to ascertain if they were gay.[74]

Profile: Sunil Pant

Sunil Pant may be South Asia's first openly gay member of Parliament and the most visible member of Nepal's LGBT movement, but he never planned to become an activist.[1] When Pant started Nepal's first LGBT organization in 2001, he was a shy person who didn't think he could speak publicly. "I didn't even know the word 'strategy' until 2005," he says. But he was troubled by the police violence and harassment that he saw against gays and transgendered people. "It was seeing it with my own eyes that convinced me that we must get organized."

Pant is a computer scientist by background. He had no human rights training, but simply responded intuitively to incidents of police violence and arrests of gays and transgendered people. "When I heard of an arrest, I would go to the police station," he said. "I would tell the police I was there and would document it, write things down. The next day, I would go back with a journalist to get the word out. I wasn't strategizing, I didn't have a plan. For the first four or five years, it was mostly responding to incidents."

Initially, Pant found it difficult to organize other members of the LGBT community. A lot of individuals were being thrown out of homes, schools, and jobs for being sexual minorities, and didn't want to be blacklisted for being involved with the Blue Diamond Society. He said, "I couldn't find anyone to sit on the board of BDS so I went to my parents and sisters and brothers and got them to sit on the board without telling them what I was doing. No one wanted to come to the office. We met in temples and shops."

His decision to come out publicly was made spontaneously. In 2002, Pant decided it was important to make LGBT issues more visible in the media. He contacted a sympathetic journalist and found twenty members of the LGBT community who agreed to speak to her. When the journalist arrived, however, the members of the group he had assembled had all disappeared from the room. "It was really embarrassing," said Pant, "so I decided I would come out. It wasn't planned. My family read about it in the newspaper the next day." It would be another three years before other members of the LGBT community in Nepal came out publicly.

The group focused initially on HIV education and sexual health. When Pant attempted to register his organization, an official refused to accept the application until Pant removed a reference to "homosexuality." However, Pant soon concluded that it was impossible to work effectively on HIV without also addressing discrimination and violence against the LGBTI community.

Pant was inspired by HIV and AIDS activists from South Africa that he met at an international AIDS conference in 2002, including members of the South African Treatment Action Group. "They were very visible, very effective, standing up, challenging, and absolutely clear giving their messages." He learned from their example, but believes that advocates shouldn't try to copy each other's techniques. "Our culture, our setting, our mentality is different. Something that worked in Kathmandu may not work in the Terai." He also believes that advocates should not be afraid to experiment. "If we are overly worried about the reaction, we don't do justice to our efforts."

For the first few years after founding the Blue Diamond Society, Pant struggled to get LGBT issues recognized, but he assumed a much higher profile and gained unprecedented visibility following the Supreme Court ruling in favor of LGBT rights in 2007, and his election to the new Constituent Assembly in 2008. In part because of his public role, he is very conscious of the link between his personal life and his advocacy. "I think it's important to practice what you preach," he says. "Your behavior, how you live your life, your practice tells a lot. You send messages every moment. You advocate all the time, whether you socialize, whether you go out. Some members of Parliament never met me, but they heard that I was disciplined and they could trust me. So they were willing to work with me. Making an image helps."

As the drafting of Nepal's new constitution met continuing delays, Pant was approached by young Nepalis who were frustrated by the existing political leadership, and said he was giving serious consideration to forming a new political party. "Initially, I was not so keen to get involved in politics, but now I see that it is an effective forum that can change things a lot. Once the constitution guarantees LGBT rights, we don't need to worry so much. Then we can focus on creating jobs, protecting the environment, supported by energetic young people. That may be the next step I will take on."

1. Author interview, April 11, 2011.

Pant began to document cases of violence against sexual minorities and HIV activists. He submitted the information to the inspector general of police in Kathmandu, requested protection for sexual minorities, and held meetings with police and other officials to discuss human rights violations against the LGBTI community. However, the group wasn't satisfied with the results. "They continually ignored us," Pant said.[75] Pant approached the press and the legal community to highlight cases of police violence. For example, after an early morning police raid on a disco in 2003 resulted in the arrest of several gays and *metis*, Pant called both a reporter and a lawyer before the men were released. The story made front-page news the next day, and the police chief later apologized.[76]

The Blue Diamond Society established a hotline and drop-in center for sexual minorities; set up a clinic for prevention and treatment of sexually transmitted diseases; expanded its outreach programs, including health and HIV education; and provided psycho-social counseling. To respond to the challenges the LGBTI community faced in getting employment, the group initiated vocational programs to train individuals as drivers, beauticians, and security guards.[77] The organization created forums for the LGBTI community to meet to discuss their concerns. For example, in February 2004, it brought together more than fifty lesbian, gay, bisexual, and transgender people from fifteen cities across the country. The gathering issued a public statement that articulated their challenges and called on the government to support a resolution at the UN Commission on Human Rights on sexual orientation, gender identity, and human rights.[78] By 2007, the Blue Diamond Society was receiving international awards for its work. The International Gay and Lesbian Human Rights Commission called it "one of the most effective human rights groups in the world."[79]

Despite its sustained efforts, the group was frustrated with continuing discrimination and violence and little response from police and government officials. In 2007 the Blue Diamond Society turned to the judicial system. Together with three other Nepali LGBT groups, the group filed a suit with Nepal's Supreme Court, demanding that the government recognize the civil rights of transgender and "third gender" people without requiring them to affirm one gender identity or another;[80] create a new law forbidding discrimination and violence against LGBT communities; and make reparations to sexual minorities for state violence and discrimination.

The Supreme Court ruled in the petitioners' favor in December 2007 and issued a full judgment in November 2008. The Supreme Court nullified the law against "unnatural sexual conduct" and directed the government "to formulate appropriate legislation or amend existing legislation to end discrimination against the LGBT community," to establish a "third gender" category for government documents, and to establish a committee to study the possibility of gay marriage.[81] In its ruling, the Supreme Court said, "The fundamental rights set forth in the constitution and the human rights enshrined in the international human rights treaties to which Nepal is a party, cannot be interpreted in a way that only heterosexual men and women can enjoy it. . . . The State has the obligation to create such environment and formulate laws in that line."[82] The court specified that the committee to study gay marriage should be composed of seven members, including representatives of the Ministries of Law, Population and Environment, the National Commission on Human Rights, and the national police. According to the court directive, the committee was to consider how other countries had extended full rights—including the right to marry—to their LGBTI citizens, and to make recommendations to the government to form the basis of new legislation legalizing same-sex marriage.[83] The ruling was unprecedented. A statement by the Blue Diamond Society said, "This is the first time ever any Supreme Court has spoke such a positive manner on gender identity issues ever on [sic] the world."[84]

The Blue Diamond Society found that the ruling created an almost immediate change in attitudes and behavior toward the LGBTI community. Within months, the group reported that incidence of violence and police abuse against gays, lesbians, and *metis* had already dropped.[85] Sunil Pant told journalists, "The ruling was remarkable and gave us a strong foundation to build our lives and to stand to advance our rights, ensuring freedom, dignity and love. It's a matter of great justice."[86] Following the Supreme Court ruling, authorities issued the first citizenship certificate identifying a Nepali as "third gender" to Bishnu Adhikari. The Central Bureau of Statistics began consultations regarding including the "third gender" in the 2011 census, and Nepal's Election Commission began work to ensure that voters in subsequent general elections could be registered as male, female, or third gender.[87] In 2009, government leaders invited the International Gay and Lesbian Human Rights Commission and Lambda Legal to advise the study and drafting committee established by the Supreme Court order regarding new antidiscrimination legislation.[88]

In November 2006, the government and the Maoists signed a comprehensive peace agreement that brought an end to the country's ten-year-long civil war and established a formal role for the Maoists in government. National elections were scheduled for April 2008 in order to elect a new "constituent assembly," responsible for drafting a new constitution. Members of the LGBTI community had participated actively in the popular movement that helped end Nepal's monarchy, and the Blue Diamond Society saw the dramatic political transformation of the country as an opportunity to engage in the political process and advance the rights of the LGBTI community. In January 2007, the group organized a conference, "Nepal's New Constitution and the Fundamental Rights of Minorities." One of the speakers was Justice Edwin Cameron, South Africa's first openly gay judicial leader, who spoke about the implementation of South Africa's constitution, the first in the world to outlaw discrimination based on sexual orientation.

In 2008, ten gay and *meti* members of the Blue Diamond Society, including Sunil Pant, ran for election to the new constituent assembly. In declaring their candidacy, Pant said, "It is a prejudiced society. We are standing in the elections to fight the discrimination against our community. This is a very symbolic approach to tell all Nepalis that we have equal rights."[89] Pant and the Blue Diamond Society continued to hold meetings and dialogues with members of various political parties, including the Maoists. As a result, the Communist Party of Nepal (Maoist), the Nepali Congress Party (the second-largest party) and the Communist Party (United) all included LGBT rights in their election manifestos.[90]

Backed by the LGBTI community, Pant garnered 15,500 votes. He said that the result made "a statement that LGBTI people are interested in matters of politics and governance and not just sex. The campaign not only gave LGBTI issues visibility but a platform to negotiate for rights."[91] The Communist Party of Nepal, United, named Pant as one of its five representatives to the constituent assembly, making him Nepal's first openly gay lawmaker.

The Blue Diamond Society continued to build a foundation for inclusive legislation and the new constitution. In 2008, it organized a two-day "national consultation of sexual minorities" to discuss the proposed constitution and identify key demands. In 2009, it brought together two hundred members of the LGBTI community to draft sample legislation to protect the rights of sexual minorities.[92] It also organized "interaction" programs with members of the constituent assembly to educate them regarding LGBT issues, particularly with regard to inclusion in the new constitution, and a meeting with the prime minister to discuss implementation of the 2007 Supreme Court decision.[93] In 2008, for the first time, Nepal's budget included a provision for sexual and gender minorities. The minister of finance delivered a budget speech to the legislature in which he stated, "The State will accord special priority to solve the core problems of Nepali people relating to sexual and gender minorities," and that it would allocate funds for a "common house" for fifty people from the LGBTI community.[94]

In 2009, the Nepal Tourism Board began promoting Nepal as a tourism destination for LGBTI travelers, as part of its goal to increase foreign tourists to the country from four hundred thousand to one million. Although tourism revenue in 2008 totaled US$352 million, making it Nepal's largest industry and its largest source of foreign exchange, international tourism had suffered during Nepal's civil war.[95] The Ministry of Tourism held a series of meetings with international tour agencies and operators to promote Nepal as a destination for LGBTI travelers, including the possibility of gay marriage ceremonies at the base of Mt. Everest and wedding processions on elephant-back. In late 2009, the minister of tourism, Sharat Sing Bhandari, wrote to the International Conference on Gay and Lesbian Tourism, saying "We are honored to uphold the rights of all LGBTI people in our country. . . . I, therefore, would like to take this opportunity to invite and welcome all the sexual and gender minorities from around the world."[96] In February 2010, Nepal hosted the 1st Asian Symposium on Gay and Lesbian Tourism in Kathmandu for top tour operators to explore opportunities for gay tourism in Nepal. Pant actively pushed the effort and helped to establish a travel agency called Pink Mountain, specifically to cater to LGBTI travelers.[97] In 2011, couples from the UK and the United States held high-profile wedding ceremonies in Nepal.

By early 2012, the Constituent Assembly still had not finalized a new permanent constitution and a committee responsible for drafting a law to legalize same-sex marriage had yet to submit its report to the government. According to Pant, however, the provisions of the draft constitution to protect LGBT rights had universal support from the political parties. "There's no disagreement," he said. "All the parties agree."[98]

The Blue Diamond Society continued to build the visibility of the LGBT community. In 2009 and 2010, it trained four hundred members in strategic leadership and advocacy. By mid-2011, three hundred thousand members of the LGBT community were in contact with forty offices across the country, and the Blue Diamond Society was building a new five-story LGBTI center in Kathmandu to provide space not only for local members of the community to meet and organize but also as a regional LGBTI rights hub.[99] Pant received invitations from all over the world to speak about the transformation that had happened in Nepal, and LGBT leaders from other South Asian countries came to Nepal to learn more about Blue Diamond Society's work. "The gains in Nepal for the LGBTI community reverberate across the region," says Rosanna Flamer-Calder, an LGBT activist from Sri Lanka. "No longer can the naysayers point and say this [LGBTI rights] is a Western phenomenon."[100]

Lessons Learned

The changes in Nepal were extraordinary. In just a few years, the country affirmed equal rights for all LGBTI citizens, decriminalized homosexual conduct, allowed transgender and intersex persons to be officially identified as "third gender," began a process to become one of the first countries in the world to allow same-sex marriage, and began promoting itself internationally as a gay-friendly tourist destination. Acts of violence and harassment against members of the LGBTI community, through never comprehensively documented, appeared to decline significantly.

Although Nepal's transformation followed years of strategic and committed organizing, Pant identified two important catalysts. One was the attention garnered by events of a single week in August 2004, when a police officer sexually assaulted and slit the throat of a transgender person and police rounded up thirty-nine members of the Blue Diamond Society and jailed them for eleven days. The incidents sparked international protest and generated both horror and sympathy among Nepalis. The second was the Supreme Court's 2007 ruling affirming full rights for LGBT persons in Nepal, prompting significant shifts in both government policy and public opinion. The *Hindustan Times* declared that the Supreme Court's ruling made Nepal "the most progressive country in South Asia."[101] According to Pant, "The extraordinary thing is that Nepal is in many ways still a very conservative, traditional country. The movement for LGBT rights is just beginning, but the court and the governments have thus far outpaced many Western countries with long-established civil rights movements. We still face many problems, but we've made an enormous amount of progress in a short time."[102]

In Jamaica, progress was tangible, but more modest. Jamaica's leading LGBTI organization, J-FLAG, was able to build a broad coalition of support for LGBTI rights, bringing together religious groups, mainstream human rights groups, HIV/AIDS organizations, UNAIDS, and European government leaders. Maurice Tomlinson of J-FLAG said, "We've raised the profile. UNAIDS is saying the same thing about changing the [buggery] law to prevent HIV, the Ministry of Health is saying the same thing. The US ambassador, some of the churches, and the Spanish ambassador as president of the EU. So there has been tremendous pressure."[103] According to Jason McFarlane, "We have been able to generate a conversation around this issue and the fact that LGBT persons have a right to be part of this plural society."[104]

The international Stop Murder Music Campaign was hugely successful in bringing global attention to violent, antigay lyrics in Jamaican dancehall music, forcing the cancellation of hundreds of concerts, and prompting several leading performers to sign pledges promising to stop performing homophobic songs. It helped prompt the prime minister to order the formation of a task force to examine violent lyrics in Jamaican reggae. Sustained engagement with the police helped bring an end to police participation in antigay violence, and by 2010, police provided protection at public demonstrations challenging homophobia and affirming the rights of Jamaica's LGBTI community—the first ever held in Jamaica. Despite these signs of progress, Jamaican advocates had little success overturning Jamaica's buggery laws or securing legal protection from discrimination, and political leaders remained largely resistant to addressing LGBTI issues.

A number of external factors may help explain the differing results in the two countries. One was the differing political dynamics in the two countries. As a country emerging from a ten-year-long civil war and going through a dramatic political transformation from a monarchy to a fledgling democracy, Nepal offered LGBTI advocates unprecedented opportunities to insert themselves in the political process and to advocate for greater rights for LGBTI persons as the country reconstituted its government, rewrote many of its laws, and prepared a new constitution. In contrast, Jamaica's political environment was more static. Senior officials continually expressed antigay sentiments, bolstered by strong public opinion polls that opposed changing Jamaica's laws banning homosexual conduct. An editorial in the *Jamaica Observer* stated that "few legislators, on either side of the political divide, would be willing to risk their political capital among the Jamaican populace, which is severely intolerant of homosexuality."[105]

The comparative rates of violent crime in the two countries may have influenced public perceptions toward homophobic violence and the LGBTI community. Jamaica had one of the highest murder rates in the world, while Nepal had one of the lowest.[106] In Jamaica, where the homicide rate was nearly thirty times the rate in Nepal, police had been implicated in hundreds of killings, and murder cases of gays failed to shock a public that was used to the number of homicides topping fifteen hundred each year. Media outlets often portrayed violence against the LGBTI community as "gay-on-gay" violence. In contrast, the 2004 case of a Nepali police officer slitting the throat of a *meti* in Kathmandu created a national scandal in a country with a very low rate of violent crime. Sunil Pant identified the case, along with the arrest of thirty-nine Blue Diamond Society members, as a "turning point" in the LGBT struggle. "We became much stronger in responding to violence against us," he said.[107] Media coverage of the events roused both horror and sympathy among the Nepali public and government officials.

Differing religious and cultural traditions in Jamaica and Nepal also had an impact. In predominantly Christian Jamaica, prominent religious leaders routinely condemned homosexuality and fanned antigay rhetoric. In Nepal, by contrast, Hindu temples depict the god Shiva as half-man, half-woman, and the Blue Diamond Society used Hindu texts celebrating same-sex love to illustrate that homosexuality was part of the country's tradition.

Despite differing contexts, the two movements used many of the same strategies to pursue their goals, including continual efforts to engage with government officials, to utilize the media, and to build the capacity of the LGBTI community through trainings and direct services. Advocates in both Nepal and Jamaica collaborated with international allies, for example, by seeking legal assistance from international NGOs when proposing legal reforms. Both movements successfully leveraged the financial interests of key stakeholders to further their goals. In Jamaica, reggae music was regarded as a centerpiece of the country's cultural identity, and generated $14.5 billion in revenues each year.[108] By targeting dancehall artists that performed homophobic music, the Stop Murder Music campaign raised worldwide attention to antigay violence in Jamaica and changed the practices of prominent performers in the music industry. In the case of Nepal, government tourism officials were eager to recover lost revenues resulting from the civil war between the government and Maoists. Gay activists encouraged the Nepal government and tourism industry to promote a "gay-friendly" Nepal as a way to increase the number of international tourists and tap into the US$670 million spent annually by international gay and lesbian travelers.[109]

Perhaps the biggest strategic difference between the two movements was the use of the judiciary. The Blue Diamond Society's decision to file suit with the Supreme Court paid enormous dividends when the court affirmed full rights for LGBT persons in its landmark 2007 decision. The Blue Diamond Society's research was instrumental in winning the court's favorable judgment. Pant said, "I did not realize that the documentation I did over the years, the piles of photographs, medical reports, and incidents, could be so useful to the courts. The judges studying those could not believe the level of inhumane treatment that had happened from the security forces."[110] In Jamaica, J-FLAG began in 2010 to pursue a strategy for challenging Jamaican law through the courts, but the outcome was far from clear and would take time.

A second significant difference in strategy—the role of public figures in the two movements—was dictated by external factors. For example, in Jamaica, high rates of homophobic violence in Jamaica drove LGBTI advocates underground. Maurice Tomlinson of J-FLAG said, "After Brian Williamson and Steve Harvey were killed, everyone shied away from being publicly identified." Until Tomlinson went public in 2010 as legal counsel for J-FLAG, advocates with J-FLAG routinely used pseudonyms. Tomlinson was the first J-FLAG advocate in years to use his real name and help give a public face to the issue. In Nepal, by contrast, Sunil Pant's highly visible role helped gain attention to LGBTI rights and mobilize the LGBTI community. His election to the Constituent Assembly was a key turning point, giving him (and the LGBTI community) a strong platform for urging legislative, policy, and other reforms.[111]

In both countries, advocates saw societal transformation as an ongoing process. Organizers acknowledged that their struggle for lasting equality and justice would take time and require continual organizing, but they also believed that the gains they had achieved were irreversible. After Jamaica's first public demonstration for LGBTI rights, organizers said, "Today marked a change in Jamaica and the country will never be the same."[112] Sunil Pant reflected, "We have moved from being a marginalized and persecuted lot who were thrown out of homes, schools, and jobs to people who have human rights and are now protected by the police, the same people who once harassed us."[113]

Chapter 11

Abolishing Sentences of Life Without Parole for Juvenile Offenders

I often felt it would have been better to be executed. Because that's what they
are doing now. It's just a much slower way of doing it. It took me a very long
time to figure out that I would never be getting out . . . before my brain actually
understood that it meant "forever."
*—prisoner in California serving a life sentence with no possibility of parole for a
crime committed before age eighteen*

My family members still ask me when my son is getting out of prison, and I say,
"What part of 'life without parole' don't you understand? Never."
*—Debi Hodge, whose son was sentenced to life in prison
for a crime committed at age seventeen[1]*

I
N 2012, more than twenty-five hundred individuals in the United States
were serving a sentence that did not exist in any other part of the world:
spending the rest of their lives in prison for crimes committed before they
were eighteen years old. Forty-three states allowed the sentence, although only
thirty-eight states have actually imposed the sentence on juvenile offenders.
In some states, children were sentenced to die in prison for crimes committed
when they were only thirteen years old.[2]

The Convention on the Rights of the Child and the International Covenant on
Civil and Political Rights (ICCPR) both strictly prohibit the sentencing of juvenile
offenders to life without the possibility of parole. In other parts of the world, ten
countries have laws on the books that allow juvenile offenders to be sentenced to
life without parole, but only the United States imposes the sentence.[3]

Before 1980, children in the United States were only rarely sentenced to
life without parole. However, increases in crime rates and concerns about

an escalation in juvenile crime prompted widespread changes in US criminal justice policies during the 1980s. Nearly every state modified its laws to allow children to be tried as adults—and face harsher sentences. Legislators expanded the range of offenses subject to prison sentences and increased the length of such sentences. Getting "tough on crime" became a reliable way for many policymakers to increase their chances of reelection.

The number of child offenders sentenced to life without parole increased through the late 1980s and peaked in 1996, when 152 individuals received the sentence. By 2009, the states with the largest number of juveniles sentenced to life without parole included Pennsylvania (444), Michigan (346), Louisiana (335), Florida (266), and California (250).[4]

Although life without parole sentences were intended for the worst criminal offenders—murderers beyond any hope of rehabilitation—the profile of juvenile offenders receiving the sentence was often far different. A 2005 study by Amnesty International and Human Rights Watch found that nationwide, 59 percent of juvenile offenders serving life without parole had received the sentence for their first-ever conviction—either in juvenile or adult court.[5] Sixteen percent were between thirteen and fifteen years old when they committed their crimes. And while the majority was convicted of murder, approximately 26 percent were convicted of felony murder. In such cases, the youth participated in a crime, such as a robbery or burglary, which resulted in a murder committed by a codefendant, but played no physical part in the killing, and may not even have known that their partner was armed.[6]

In many states, judges and prosecutors' hands were tied: once an individual—whether a child or adult—was convicted of a particular crime, they were required by law to impose life without parole as a mandatory sentence. In some cases, judges made public their reluctance to impose the sentence and stated in open court that if they had the option, they would impose an alternative sentence. For example, one judge referred to a life without parole sentence for a fifteen-year-old look-out in a murder case as "blatantly unfair and highly unconscionable."[7] While sentencing a fifteen-year-old accomplice to a murder in 2002, a Chicago judge stated for the record, "If I had my discretion, I would impose another sentence, but this is mandated by law."[8]

Because the vast majority of child offenders sentenced to life without parole were sentenced under state rather than federal laws, eliminating the use of the sentence meant laborious state-by-state legislative efforts. In Michigan, Colorado, Illinois, Texas, and other states, activists undertook legislative efforts to amend their state laws. One of the most impressive mobilization efforts took place in California, where 250 child offenders were serving life without parole sentences in 2010. Although most had committed their crimes at age sixteen or seventeen, some had been sentenced to die in prison for offenses committed when they were only fourteen.[9] The California campaign mobilized a broad-based and unlikely alliance of actors, bringing together family members of youth serving life without parole sentences, families of murder victims, youth offenders who had previously been in prison, law professors, students, religious leaders, and former prosecutors and law enforcement officers. Together they undertook an unprecedented and intensive legislative effort to change California's laws.

The Campaign

In California, several groups were already working on juvenile justice issues. For example, in 2002, young people in Los Angeles who had been personally affected by the justice system came together to form the Youth Justice Coalition. Each one had either been arrested, detained, or incarcerated, or had an immediate family member similarly affected by the system. Profoundly affected by their experience, members of the coalition wanted to challenge the overuse of incarceration to respond to violence and crime in their communities. Their research found that close to fifty thousand youth were arrested in Los Angeles each year and that the county had the highest incarceration rate in the world. The coalition campaigned for better conditions of confinement, community-based alternatives to detention, and persuaded the city of Los Angeles to change its gang-reduction tactics.

The first organization to focus specifically on juveniles sentenced to life without parole was Human Rights Watch. It began by conducting research on juveniles sentenced to life without parole (JLWOP) in California, and made a public records act request to the California Department of Corrections requesting information in 2006. The Department of Corrections responded nearly a year later with data on 227 individuals, providing names, birth dates, and information regarding the time and type of offense for which they were convicted. All but one had been convicted since 1990. The information allowed pro bono attorneys and numerous volunteers to use online legal and press resources to compile additional information about individual cases. In 2007, Human Rights Watch sent a survey to all the individuals who had been identified by the Department of Corrections, requesting information about their case, their personal background, their experience of trial and sentencing, their feelings, and conditions in prison. More than 50 percent responded; many provided lengthy addendums. Human Rights Watch researchers and volunteers then conducted in-person interviews with twenty-seven individuals in eight different prisons.[10]

The research, published in January 2008, revealed some shocking findings, including profound racial disparities: African American youth in California were sentenced to life without parole at a rate that was 18.3 times the rate for white youth. Hispanic youth were sentenced at five times the rate of white youth. Eighty-five percent of the California youth sentenced to life without parole were persons of color.[11] The research also found that in more than half of the cases involving an adult codefendant, the adult offender received a *lower* sentence than the child offender. Forty-five percent said that they were not convicted of physically committing the murder for which they were serving life without parole; it was a codefendant who was the "trigger person."[12] Many of the youth offenders told Human Rights Watch that they didn't really understand the legal proceedings of their case, and many apparently had poor representation. The majority said that their lawyer called no witnesses on their behalf and nearly half said their lawyer failed to ask the court for a lower sentence.[13]

Two of the core organizers for the campaign were Elizabeth Calvin, a lawyer and California advocate on children's rights for Human Rights Watch, and Javier Stauring, a Catholic lay chaplain who worked extensively with juvenile offenders and their families and the director of Faith Communities for Families and Children. Calvin and Stauring initially formed a small working group of about fifteen individuals to analyze the issue and what might be possible. Over time, the working group decided that the issue of juveniles sentenced to life without parole was a good place to begin, in terms of state legislative reform and in changing public opinion on broader juvenile justice issues. More than fifty organizations joined the effort—known as Fair Sentencing for Youth—including religious, labor, mental health, civil rights, legal, and children's organizations.

The campaign approached state senators in order to identify a champion who would be willing to introduce a bill to eliminate the sentence of life without parole for child offenders in California. Eventually, they identified Senator Leland Yee, a Democrat representing San Francisco and San Mateo. His background was ideal for taking on the issue. With a doctorate in child psychology, he was familiar with developments in neuroscience that showed that adolescents were less able to control their impulses or comprehend the risk and consequences of their actions than adults, and that their stage of development made them particularly amendable to change and rehabilitation.

Yee first introduced the California Juvenile Life Without Parole Reform Act in February 2007. The bill would have amended the California penal code,[14] eliminating sentences of life without parole for juvenile offenders,

Profile: Javier Stauring

When his mother asked Javier Stauring to join her church's volunteer program at a Los Angeles juvenile hall, his reaction was, "Why should I give up my Sundays to go to jail?" But from his first visit, he was hooked.[1]

Growing up, Javier felt like an outsider. He was born in Los Angeles, but moved to Mexico when he was nine, not knowing any Spanish. Shortly after the move, his father died. "In the jails, I heard a lot of stories from kids, stories of loss and being an outsider from society. I could connect with their emotions."

For four years, Javier volunteered at juvenile hall, going to visit on Wednesdays and Sundays. Professionally, he was a gemologist in the jewelry business, but eventually he found it too hard to balance his career and his volunteer work. "I couldn't keep going to jewelry shows and then hear about some fourteen-year-old kid getting a sentence of seventy-five years to life," he said. He began looking for another job. He became a gang intervention counselor and then was hired by the Archdiocese of Los Angeles to direct their detention ministries. He has been there for more than seventeen years.

Javier said that one of the things that opened his eyes to the need for systemic reform was accompanying kids to court. "Knowing the individual kids and their stories and the cards that life had dealt them, and then seeing them getting sentences of seventy-five years to life in prison, it was shocking. I had sat down with these kids and heard the realities and the difficulties they faced, and saw how the unfairness and injustice perpetuates throughout their lives. I needed to get involved, I owed it to them."

Javier felt that part of his ministry was to speak out on behalf of the rights of those who were incarcerated. In 2003, he started meeting with reporters to draw attention to the terrible conditions for juveniles who were locked up in Los Angeles' Men's Central Jail. They were confined to their cells for 23 ½ hours a day, slept on thin foam mats, and received no education. After two boys and replacing them with sentences of twenty-five years to life. The bill passed the Senate Public Safety Committee by a vote of 3 to 2, but could not muster the votes to pass the full Senate. Because the original law had been created through a statewide referendum, any change in the law would need to be adopted through a two-thirds majority of votes in the state legislature, rather than a simple majority. The threshold was simply too high given the political make-up of the legislature, and Yee withdrew the bill.

attempted suicide, Javier organized a press conference outside the Jail. When he said publicly that it was sinful what was being done to the children in the jail, the *Los Angeles Times* led a high-profile article with his quote. He said, "That day, I got a call from the jail telling me not to come back." Officially, the jail said that they were revoking his clearance because he had disclosed confidential information about inmates and was not allowed to speak to the press. Javier sued the department, arguing that its policies violated his rights to free speech. After two years, the LA Country Sheriff's Department finally reinstated him and changed their policies.

Javier has been part of several campaigns around juvenile justice issues, often mobilizing other members of the religious community. As policy director for Faith Communities for Families and Children, an interfaith coalition, he has arranged for dozens of religious leaders to visit juvenile hall to meet with youth sentenced to life in prison. He has also been a core organizer for Juvenile Justice Sabbath, which has raised awareness about juvenile justice issues within hundreds of faith communities in California.

Javier says, "We lose more battles than we win in California. For twenty-five years there hasn't been a bill that has brought sentencing relief. Legislation has only made sentences tougher. But what keeps me going is just the commitment to the individual kids and the personal relationships with them and their families. For them to know that there are people outside that are trying to make things better and that they haven't been forgotten, that in and of itself is very powerful. It creates hope and even keeps people alive. We can meet with legislators and talk about statistics and strategies, but it really just comes down to the people. I'm very fortunate because I have the opportunity to be in these relationships. That fuels everything else that I do."

1. Author interview with Javier Stauring, August 15, 2011.

The campaign partners took stock and decided to continue their efforts. Calvin consulted with legal advisors for the state legislature to explore whether there were ways to eliminate JLWOP through legislation that did not require a two-thirds majority vote. After a series of meetings, she was able to come up with a formulation that satisfied the attorneys. Instead of abolishing life without parole sentences for juveniles, the new proposal would provide an opportunity for review and resentencing after ten years or more of incarceration.[15] Under the proposal, youth offenders serving life without parole would have to submit a petition to the sentencing court showing that they met certain criteria.[16] Those that met the criteria would have the opportunity for a resentencing hearing. For those that could demonstrate that they had matured and changed, the court could impose a new, lesser sentence.

Senator Yee introduced the new bill, the Fair Sentences for Youth Act, SB 399, in February 2009. "Life without parole means absolutely no opportunity for release," he said in a statement. "It also means minors are often left without access to programs and rehabilitative services while in prison. This sentence was created for the worst of criminals that have no possibility of reform and it is not a humane way to handle children. While the crimes they committed caused undeniable suffering, these youth offenders are not the worst of the worst."[17]

The campaign's core message was that all youth offenders, no matter how horrible their crime, deserved the opportunity to show that they could rehabilitate themselves and that no youth offender should be denied a second chance to rejoin society if he or she could prove that they had grown and changed. The message that "no one is beyond redemption" resonated particularly with the religious community. The campaign backed its arguments regarding young people's capacity for rehabilitation with recent findings from neuroscience on adolescent brain development. The background of Senator Yee, the bill's main sponsor, as a child psychologist, helped reinforce these messages. The campaign repeatedly stressed the modest nature of the bill, emphasizing that it was not a "get out of jail free" card. There would be no guarantee of parole, only the opportunity to earn it. Youth offenders would have to meet set criteria to be eligible for a new sentencing hearing. Even those that qualified for a new hearing had no guarantee of getting a lesser sentence, and those that did would not be released until serving a minimum of twenty-five years. Those who were deemed to pose a continuing threat to society would stay in prison.

The coalition asked economists at two leading universities to research the potential financial savings to the state for reforming JLWOP laws and how it could alleviate California's severe financial crisis. The campaign found that since 1990, the state had spent more than $66 million incarcerating youth offenders sentenced to life without parole. It estimated that if the 250 juvenile offenders already serving life without parole sentences remained in prison until their deaths, it would cost the state an additional $500 million, and that each new youth offender given the sentence would cost the state approximately $2.5 million.[18]

Organizers made special efforts to reach out to family members of juvenile offenders serving life without parole. They contacted offenders who had responded to the Human Rights Watch questionnaire to invite them to provide contact information for family members that might be interested in being involved. From the information provided, organizers were able to contact more than five hundred family members to inform them of the legislative campaign and invite their participation in a "Family and Friends" group. The coalition organized a Family Members and Youth Summit, held at a Catholic retreat house near Sacramento, the state capitol, in April 2009. Thirty-five family members of juveniles sentenced to life without parole, as well as ten youth who had served time in the juvenile or criminal justice system, participated.[19]

In a meeting facilitated by Stauring and James Tramel, an Episcopal priest who had served over twenty years for a murder committed at age seventeen, family members talked about their experiences. "It was transformational," said Calvin. Debi Hodge, whose son has spent sixteen years in prison for a murder committed when he was seventeen, was one of those who participated. She said, "For the first time in sixteen years, I felt like someone understood. That was very important to me, because this situation is very isolating. You don't know what other people's opinion is going to be when they find out about your son. Sitting in the room with fifty others, it soothed my soul."[20] Another participant, whose brother is serving a sentence of life without parole, agreed. "So many of us feel like we have been carrying this around by ourselves for so long," she said. "It's our dirty little secret."[21]

The family members and youth participated in a day-long training on the legislation, how to educate legislators, and how to talk to the media. The following day, they joined dozens of other advocates, including law professors, law students, and religious leaders in a lobbying day. They participated in a press conference and testified at a hearing before the Public Safety Committee. Debi Hodge was one of those who testified. "I talked about my son and who he was," she said. "How he's not at all like the person you would think he would be or how he was portrayed."[22] The hearing concluded with members of the audience being invited to express their views on the bill. More than one hundred people stood in line to speak, including many family members.

The Family and Friends group established an email list and began having regular conference calls. One set up a Facebook page. They approached friends, family members, and colleagues and asked them to sign letters on behalf of SB399. Some set up tables at churches to collect signatures. Debi Hodge said, "If I go to the prison to visit my son, I'll take the letter with me and talk with people in the waiting area."[23] Members of the group participated in lobbying in Sacramento and also helped reach out to other family members to invite them to be involved. Brandy Novak, whose brother was serving life without parole, said, "I'd call them [other family members] and say, 'You don't know me, but I'm in the same situation as you. Someone you love is serving life without parole; someone I love is too.'"[24]

California has the largest prison population in the United States, with thirty-three prisons housing 165,000 inmates.[25] Its prison guards union, the California Correctional Peace Officers Association (CCPOA), was widely recognized as one of the most powerful political forces in the state. The union represented thirty thousand parole and correctional officers and claimed that its members "walk the toughest beat in the state." With an annual budget of more than $20 million, CCPOA spent heavily on political campaigns and lobbied consistently for tough crime legislation, including a notorious "three strikes" ballot measure adopted in 1994. With its strength directly related to its membership, the union had an interest in maintaining a large prison population, which provided more jobs for its members.

Supporters of Fair Sentencing for Youth approached the union several times during a three-year period beginning in 2006. "I spent a lot of time thinking about how to frame the issue from their perspective," said Calvin.[26] When she met with CCPOA's political director and president, she emphasized that when inmates have no hope of release, they may experience increasing despair and become dangerous to other inmates and to prison guards. She argued that the possibility of parole would provide incentives for better behavior and consequently enhance safety for CCPOA's members.

The argument carried weight. Calvin also found that "we had a lucky convergence with the people involved." The union's political director previously had worked with the state's Department of Juvenile Justice, which can keep youth until age twenty-five. The political director told Calvin that from his experience, "I know how much they change between age seventeen and twenty-five. I've watched them mature and make different decisions." The president of CCPOA also had perspectives shaped by personal experience: after his son got into trouble with the law, he spoke out publicly about the overincarceration of youth. "If we don't give those kids hope of a future, of a life, of an ability to make something of themselves, they don't care about life," he said in a magazine interview. "Nobody's willing to forgive anymore. And we are willing to lock people up for unreasonable periods of time."[27] Aware of the comments, Calvin raised them in her meeting.

During their meeting to discuss the bill, Calvin said "I almost fell out of my chair when they said they thought they could get their executive council to support the bill." The council voted to support the bill and subsequently wrote a letter of support that was submitted as part of the official record for the bill. Campaign members considered the endorsement of the CCPOA a major coup, since it gave the initiative significant backing from the law enforcement community. Seven other organizations had come out in opposition to the bill, all representing either law enforcement or victims' organizations. Coalition members raised the union's support in all of their lobbying meetings with state legislators and listed the union as a supporter on its website. In January 2009, before the bill was to be considered by the Assembly Public Safety Committee, coalition members delivered packages of fifty organizational letters of support for SB399 to each member of the committee, ensuring that the CCPOA letter was on top.[28]

The campaign approached the California District Attorneys Association, another powerful lobbying force, but received a chilly reception. The association saw the possibility of life without parole sentences as an essential tool in negotiating plea deals with charged offenders and actively opposed the bill. In the absence of other support from law enforcement groups, the campaign reached out to individuals that were sympathetic to the goals of the bill, including former district and US attorneys. In June 2010, three of these—a former police officer, a former prosecutor, and the former director of the California Department of Corrections and Rehabilitation—published a joint op-ed in the *Los Angeles Times* supporting SB399. "Collectively, we have put or kept a lot of people in prison," the authors said, but went on to explain that it was precisely their experience in law enforcement that led them to support the bill and that they had seen dramatic transformations among young people in the correctional system. "Our laws should recognize that they are capable of redemption and reform."[29]

Coalition members believed that the support of law enforcement would be particularly important if the bill reached the governor's desk. Five years previously, then-governor Arnold Schwarzenegger had vetoed another criminal justice bill whose only opposition was the DA's Association. "When we get to the governor's desk, we want him to be aware that there is law enforcement in support of the bill," said a coalition member. "We also want to get past the attitude of 'us vs. them' that pits those in favor of criminal justice reforms against law enforcement and victims' groups."[30]

A key strategy for the group was to facilitate direct contact between religious leaders and juveniles sentenced to life without parole. According to Stauring, "What gets religious leaders involved is the first-hand experience of going in, sitting down, and getting to know some of the kids. That's always been transformational for the religious leaders." Beginning in 2006, Faith Communities for Families and Children began arranging for delegations of religious leaders to visit LA's juvenile hall to meet with youth sentenced to life without parole. During a three-year period, more than fifty religious leaders made such visits. Faith Communities tried in particular to arrange visits by religious leaders in positions of authority, who had many congregations under their umbrella. For example, after the presiding imam of the Islamic Shura Council visited juvenile hall, he began inviting Stauring to speak about juvenile justice issues at meetings where sixty mosques were represented. Other faith groups got involved, not only through advocacy on Bill 399 but also through direct programs and services. Members of one congregation began teaching a theater class in one of the units, and a professor from another began teaching a leadership-skills class for incarcerated youth.

Stauring said:

> I was a little surprised that the visits were so profound with some of the religious leaders. . . A presiding elder of the AME churches in Los Angeles

told me, "I marched with Martin Luther King, I've been around the world, I've shaken hands with many presidents. I've never been as touched as I was sitting down with these kids. I knew this existed, but I didn't really know."[31]

In 2008, Faith Communities for Families and Children began sponsoring a "Juvenile Justice Sabbath," inviting faith communities to unite with others to raise awareness of the issues surrounding children and families affected by violent crime, including incarcerated youth. Many of the religious leaders who had visited juvenile hall became involved, and by 2009, more than two hundred faith-based organizations, including Jewish, Christian, and Muslim communities, participated in the Sabbath by focusing prayers, sermons, services, and meditations on juvenile justice issues. Faith Communities for Families and Children provided flyers, fact sheets, sample prayers, and lists of actions that could be used by participants, including contacting state legislators on behalf of SB399, and linked congregations with former juvenile detainees or family members of youth serving life without parole who were willing to speak about their experiences.[32]

Faith Communities for Families and Children approached a Catholic church with a video production program and proposed making a short documentary video. The church agreed and produced a five-minute film featuring several religious leaders, including a priest, rabbi, and imam, discussing sentencing practices from the perspective of their religious faiths. A rabbi described sentences of life without parole as "one of the greatest tragedies that our society is inflicting on other human beings," while a Jesuit priest was featured saying, "Not only do I think God forgives, I know God forgives. I've seen it in their faces and the subsequent actions of these young people. . . . Jesus wouldn't throw away these kids. He wouldn't say that they're worthless."[33] The video was posted on YouTube and several websites, and it was sent to every organization participating in the Juvenile Justice Sabbath, as well as chaplains working on juvenile justice in each of California's twelve Catholic archdiocese. Some congregations showed it after every service during the Sabbath.[34]

Over a number of years, Stauring and others raised juvenile justice issues with the California Catholic Conference, which represents eleven million Catholics and more than a thousand parishes, encompassing 29 percent of the state's population. In 2009, the conference chose passage of SB399 as one of three legislative priorities for its annual lobby day in Sacramento. In late April more than seven hundred Catholics from around the state met with legislators and urged support for the bill. "Young people—even those serving life sentences—have the capacity to change for the better," said the conference. "The Catholic approach leads us to encourage models of restorative justice that address crime in terms of the harm done to the victims and communities—not simply as a violation of the law."[35]

In 2010, organizers expanded the Juvenile Justice Sabbath to a full week, called Juvenile Justice Week of Faith. They described the week as "a call for faith communities to reach our most marginalized youth and to help them know that they are all children of God."[36] More than three hundred congregations of all faiths participated. In many places of worship, family members of incarcerated youth shared their stories. A delegation of religious leaders from the LA Council of Religious Leaders visited juveniles facing life sentences at a juvenile hall in Sylmar and then shared their experiences with their congregations. One of the delegates said he asked one of the youths, "What would you want people to know about you?" The youth replied, "That some of us have made mistakes, but that doesn't mean that we are all bad or that we can't change. . . . I just wish they would give us a second chance."[37]

Eleven high schools in Los Angeles participated in the Juvenile Justice Week of Faith. At Palisades High School, students built an actual-size replica of a prison cell on campus to show students the "living space" of a person serving life in prison. Other students wore nametags with the name of a juvenile offender and shared that individual's story with other students. At another school, students created art installations using balloons to signify the number of youth serving life without parole sentences in California. Throughout their events, students gathered signatures to letters urging their Assemblymembers to support the Fair Sentences for Youth Act. Later, they held individual meetings with several members of the state legislature to lobby for the bill and to deliver the letters they had collected.[38]

The coalition identified several cases of juvenile offenders serving life without parole where the circumstances of their crime evoked public sympathy or where the youth had clearly demonstrated efforts at rehabilitation while incarcerated. One example was Sara Kruzan, who was sixteen when she killed the man who had raped her at age twelve and lured her into prostitution at age thirteen. Kruzan was tried as an adult and sentenced to life without parole, even though the California Youth Authority determined that she was amenable to rehabilitation and motivated to make positive changes in her life.

The coalition made a video featuring Kruzan. Then twenty-nine, Kruzan expressed remorse for her crime, saying "I'm very sorry to have taken his life like that. I definitely deserve punishment. You don't just take somebody's life like that and think it's okay." She also spoke about her commitment to educate herself and desire to play a constructive role in society: "Every day is a challenge, but I realize that I've found the ability to believe in myself, and that I have a lot of good to offer. Now, the person I am today at twenty-nine, I believe that I can set a positive example. I'm very determined to show that no matter what you've done or where you've come from or your experiences in life, it's up to you to change."[39] The video was posted on YouTube and, by mid-2010, had been viewed 280,000 times. Her case was repeatedly cited by the media and by SB399's sponsor, Senator Yee. Individuals interested in her case started a petition on her behalf and set up a Facebook page devoted to gaining her a new trial, gaining more than sixty-six hundred members.[40] In January 2011, just before leaving office, outgoing governor Arnold Schwarzenegger granted clemency to Kruzan, reducing her sentence to twenty-five years to life and providing her with the opportunity of parole after serving nine additional years in prison. Although disappointed that Kruzan was not released, advocates hailed the decision as the first time a juvenile offender serving life without parole had received clemency.

Throughout the campaign, the coalition cultivated media coverage with regular press releases, press conferences, and contacts with editorial boards of key newspapers in the state. Of particular importance was a series of favorable editorials from state and national papers before key votes in Sacramento. In May 2009, the *Sacramento Bee* called life without parole sentences for juvenile offenders "costly and cruel," and endorsed the SB399, saying it "makes sense on financial as well as humanitarian grounds."[41] In June 2009, the *Ventura County Star* urged members of the Assembly Public Safety Committee to approve the bill, citing its modest scope and that juvenile offenders should be treated differently than adults.[42] The *San Francisco Chronicle* and *Los Angeles Times* each ran several editorials on the bill. In one, the *Chronicle* stated, "One of California's most senseless practices, in its waste of tax dollars and human capability, is a law that allows juvenile offenders to be sentenced to life in prison without the possibility of parole." It called passing the bill "the right thing to do for a society that respects medical science and the value of redemption and rehabilitation—and for a state that cannot afford to squander money and waste lives."[43] The week before the critical August 2010 vote, four California newspapers—*the Los Angeles Times, the San Francisco Chronicle, the Ventura County Star, and the San Diego Tribune*—all published editorials supporting the bill.

On May 17, 2010, the US Supreme Court issued a ground-breaking decision that it was cruel and unusual punishment to sentence someone to life without parole for crimes committed before the age of eighteen that did not involve homicide. Advocates had been uneasy about the case. They worried that the Supreme Court justices would rule that the punishment was not "cruel and unusual" since the vast majority of US states still imposed the sentence. In addition, the case was only applicable to a small fraction of those serving life without parole sentences for crimes before age eighteen; of the more than twenty-five hundred serving the sentence, only one hundred twenty-nine of them had been convicted for nonhomicide crimes.

The eventual 6–3 Supreme Court ruling was very favorable.[44] The justices embraced the same rationale behind their 2005 decision rendering capital punishment for juvenile offenders unconstitutional: that juvenile offenders have "limited culpability" due to their youth and immaturity, making such extreme sentences cruel and unusual.[45] Justice Kennedy wrote in the majority opinion that "The juvenile should not be deprived of the opportunity to achieve maturity of judgment and self-recognition of human worth and potential." Justice John Paul Stevens, in a concurring opinion, cited evolving standards of decency: "Society changes. Knowledge accumulates. We learn, sometimes, from our mistakes. Punishments that did not seem cruel and unusual at one time may, in the light of reason and experience, be found cruel and unusual at a later time."[46]

In California, only four of the two hundred fifty-five juvenile offenders serving life without parole had been convicted of a nonhomicide offense. Nevertheless, the campaign used the decision to bolster their arguments that all juvenile offenders deserved the chance to redeem themselves and to highlight the importance of SB 399, including with the media. Following the decision, the *Sacramento Bee* for the first time called on the state legislature to pass SB 399.[47] The *Los Angeles Times* wrote, "If the state may not execute juveniles or imprison them for life for crimes other than murder, why is it constitutional to sentence juvenile convicted of murder to life in prison without parole? That practice may not be as unusual as the one struck down on Monday, but it's just as cruel."[48]

The coalition mobilized key constituents and spokespeople to participate in lobby days and hearings around key votes in Sacramento. Organizers tried in particular to involve individuals who had direct contact with
the juvenile justice system and could speak compellingly of the capacity
of juvenile offenders for rehabilitation. For example, at one early hearing
before the Senate Public Safety Committee, Rev. James Tramel testified
about becoming an ordained Episcopal priest while serving a prison term
for killing a homeless man as a teenager in 1985. Tramel did not receive a
life without parole sentence for his crime, and he told committee members
that the possibility of parole had enabled him to turn his life around. He
testified, "The dim light of hope at the end of a long tunnel of incarceration
was sufficient to help me navigate the treacherous shoals of our penal system
while building the character that would make me suitable for a return to the
community."[49]

The Youth Justice Coalition was particularly active in lobbying legislators. For one advocacy day, two hundred young people from the coalition—all who had personal experience with the justice system or family
members—traveled to Sacramento to meet with legislators. The coalition
also mobilized hundreds of members to do phone banking, letter writing
and petition campaigns, place op-eds, hold rallies, and meet with legislators. Hundreds of other advocates, including law professors, law students,
religious leaders, and families of juveniles serving life sentences travelled
to Sacramento before key votes on the bill, or they met with their representatives in their district. In Sacramento, advocates participated in press
conferences, testified at hearings before the committee, and split into teams
to meet with individual legislators and their staffs. During one round of
meetings, the campaign enlisted two former federal prosecutors together
with a father whose son had been murdered by a seventeen year old to visit
more than twenty Assembly offices and demonstrate the wide base of support for the bill. At the same time, organizers worked to identify influential supporters in key legislative districts. They approached political donors
and religious and civic leaders, asking them to contact their senators and
urge support for the bill. They established a website with testimonials from
victims, youth, and family members, sample letters, and sample scripts for
phone calls to Assemblymembers' offices.

To get the bill adopted, the campaign needed to surmount several
hurdles. The bill needed to be passed by both the Public Safety and the

Appropriations Committee in both the Senate and the Assembly before a full vote in each body. If approved, the bill also had to be signed by the governor. In addition, due to the state's economic crisis, the leadership in each house also set limits for bills to be passed out of appropriations, requiring that in the Senate, the financial impact of a bill be no more than $50,000, and in the Assembly, no more than $150,000.

The bill was first introduced into the Senate in February 2009. The bill passed both committees, and in May 2009, it went to a floor vote before the full State Senate. It passed, 23 to 15. Calvin said, "I was in shock. Up until the last minute it looked like we didn't have enough votes. But we had more than enough." After the Senate vote, the bill went to the State Assembly. For a hearing scheduled in late June before the committee, the campaign organized what they believed was their strongest yet line-up of witnesses, including a former federal prosecutor, a family member of a murder victim, a priest who worked with young people in prison, the California Psychiatric Association, and Calvin. Two former legislators also attended to show their support: one known for his conservative approach to sex offenders, the other a former speaker of the Assembly.

Aqeela Sherrills testified about the murder of his nineteen-year-old son while home on a college break in 2004. The perpetrator was seventeen. Sherrills had been active in antigang work for many years and told the committee, "I am all too familiar with the conditions that create despair in the hearts and imagination of many of our young people. I want my son's killer to be punished, yes, but I also want him to have the chance to turn around. I support this bill's giving him four chances to do so."[50] During the hearing, other family members of murder victims testified in opposition to the bill. One woman spoke about the anguish she and her family experienced when two teenagers killed her husband. She objected to a lighter sentence for the perpetrator and raised concerns about the trauma that any review process would create for her family.

The committee rejected the bill by a vote of 4 to 3. Those voting against the bill cited the concerns of victims' family members as the decisive factor behind their vote. Senator Yee moved for reconsideration of the bill, which allowed it to be taken up again in 2010. The campaign redoubled its efforts to build support for the bill, mobilizing letters, phone calls, and visits. At the same time, the speaker of the Assembly decided to change the composition of the Public Safety Committee. The new membership, fortunately for the campaign, was weighted in favor of the bill. In January 2010, the bill again came before the Public Safety Committee. This time it passed, 4 to 2. Five months later, the bill passed out of the Assembly Appropriations Committee.

The campaign mounted a final push before an August 2010 vote before the full Assembly. They worked to identify sympathetic individuals and groups in districts where they were not represented, urging contacts in favor of the bill with Assemblymembers. They organized a final "Summit" in Sacramento, bringing together the Family and Friends group together with other advocates, holding a rally at the Capital, and a final round of meetings with legislators' offices.

During the weeks before the final vote, thousands of individuals called and wrote letters in support of the bill. Hundreds of people met with their representatives. Calvin was told repeatedly by legislators and staff, "We've never seen anything like this."[51] Ultimately, the bill failed. Over the course of a week, the bill came up for vote three times, each time without the majority of votes needed. During the final vote, on August 30, 2010, the bill was defeated, only two votes shy of the 41 needed for passage.

In 2011, the campaign tried again, mobilizing again through hearings, meetings with legislators, calls, letters, demonstrations, and vigils. They worked even harder to engage members of murder victims. Again, they were able to get the bill through all committees of the Senate and Assembly. But again, in a final Assembly vote in October 2011, the bill failed. This time, they were short by only one vote.

Lessons Learned

The campaign faced an uphill battle to win passage of the Fair Sentences for Youth Act. For decades, the trend in California (as in most US states) was toward stiffer sentencing. In the previous twenty years, all bills adopted by the legislature related to sentencing had increased criminal penalties. SB 399 was the first bill in decades to make strides toward reducing sentences for criminal offenders. Despite the bill's failures in the State Assembly, coordinator Elizabeth Calvin felt that the movement that had built around the bill had created significant change. In a message to supporters after the 2010 vote, she said:

There's no question: our goal was to pass that bill. And it did not pass. However, while we worked on SB399, something else happened. Perspectives changed. People were educated. We helped build a foundation for broader change in California. . . . We saw the concrete results during the floor debate: Assembly members who spoke in support of the bill understood the issue and were thoughtful, passionate advocates. Their voices are solid evidence of the change that is happening. I believe that power and change don't only come from wins. I watched the struggle for this bill build a movement. I saw people transformed by their work on this campaign. I've been honored to have my own views and life transformed by those who became committed to this effort: family members of incarcerated youth, victim family members, youth, people of many faiths, university students, advocates, those sentenced to juvenile life without parole, and plan old lovers of justice.[52]

Calvin attributed the bill's failure in 2010 to several factors. One was a full-court press by the California District Attorneys Association, the California Police Chiefs Association, and Crime Victims United to oppose the bill. During the weeks before the final vote, these organizations had three professional, fulltime lobbyists working against the bill in Sacramento. Another factor was that the vote took place just a couple of months before elections where many incumbent Assemblymembers were fearful of losing their seats. In particular, those in close races may have voted against the bill to avoid controversy and opposition from powerful law enforcement groups. Finally, Calvin said, "In its understanding of effective juvenile justice policy, the State Assembly is just not there yet. The legislature is still focused on an outdated way of thinking—that increased incarceration is the only way to deal with crime."[53]

Brandy Novak, whose brother was serving life without parole, agreed. She said that one of the toughest challenges during the campaign was "breaking through this old method of thinking that if you do something wrong, you go to jail and you don't come out. . . Also, people make an assumption that we want to let everyone out, that we want to release everyone. We don't want the worst released from prison, but we want to give fifteen and sixteen year olds the idea that if you do something different, there can be light at the end of the tunnel."[54]

A powerful obstacle to eliminating sentences of life without parole was the direct testimony of families whose loved ones had been murdered by juvenile offenders. Many of these family members did not believe that their family member's killer deserved any opportunity to leave prison and said that a parole hearing would force the family to relive the trauma of the crime. Some victims' families organized against the bill, and several times, individual family members testified at hearings before the legislature. After the bill passed the Assembly Public Safety Committee in January 2010, the Heritage Foundation posted a statement claiming that the committee had voted to "revictimize victims."[55] According to Stauring, "The victim's piece is uniquely important. You can do so much, put so much work into this and lobby, but then a victim stands up with autopsy pictures of their loved one who was murdered and that's all that's needed to swing legislators and the media."[56]

As a result, the campaign worked even harder in 2011 to engage family members of victims who had been killed by juvenile offenders to show that not all victims' families supported extreme sentences. "It's important to recognize that the perspective of victims is not monolithic," said Calvin. "The fact is that they have a wide variety of perspectives, ranging from a belief that the death penalty is appropriate for juveniles to the belief that juveniles should never go to adult prison, regardless of the crime."[57] Stauring, who works with victims as the codirector of the Office of Restorative Justice agreed, noting, "I think the opposition to this bill presented victim perspectives as if there is only one right way for victims to feel."[58]

Other members of the campaign also emphasized the importance of humanizing and highlighting the offenders' diverse stories and circumstances. One said, "Legislators are more open to relating to the victims. If they don't know anyone who's committed a crime or has a family member who has committed a crime, they don't have empathy for them. They think they are defective human beings, that these people can't be saved."[59]

Although by the end of 2011, the campaign had still not been able to change California's law, they had built a powerful movement on behalf of juvenile justice. When asked about the most effective aspect of the campaign, two family members of juvenile offenders serving life terms both had a similar response. "Cold hard facts," said Brandy Novak. She said when she met with legislators' offices in Sacramento, "you could throw out a stat and see their eyebrows raise and know that something had gotten through to them."[60] Organizers' research on the application of life without parole to juvenile offenders in California enabled the campaign to show how the sentence was imposed disproportionately against youth of color and often used against first-time offenders and those that were not directly involved in committing murder. The advocates' statistics helped to dispel the myth that the sentence was reserved for only the worst offenders and to demonstrate that the sentence was both excessive and unfair.

The father of another juvenile offender serving a life term agreed: "Educating people and giving them the information is the most important. Most people are stunned. They can't even believe it. . . . The senators were pretty unaware, which surprised the heck out of me. You'd think that being in the legislature, they'd know."[61]

A second strength of the campaign was its broad base, uniting very diverse constituencies. Calvin said, "It is very exciting and very effective to be working hand in hand with people who are directly affected by this human rights violation, and with a very diverse coalition, including people of faith, youth, law professors, family members of the incarcerated and victim family members. It's been a very dynamic process."[62] For many of the family members involved, the campaign was a life-changing and extremely empowering experience. A school administrator whose daughter is serving a life sentence said, "There's a lot of guilt and shame and everything else associated with having a child who has this sentence. I felt very, very isolated and really didn't talk to anyone about it. I didn't know how to address it. . . . Once I got involved, I started talking to people. I felt like I had people behind me; I felt empowered. I found a voice to be able to speak on this."[63] Building a broad coalition took persistence. Several key allies only agreed to support the bill after repeated approaches and, in some cases, years of cultivation. Stauring reflected, "You have to educate, build a relationship, and keep pushing."[64] It also required the willingness to approach nontraditional or even unlikely allies, such as the powerful state prison guards' union, and to carefully consider the arguments that might appeal to their interests. The campaign's success in winning their support effectively showed that law enforcement did not have a monolithic stance on the issue and won influence with many legislators.

A third element that was critical to the campaign was direct advocacy with state lawmakers. Kim McGill, a core organizer for the Youth Justice Coalition, said, "I think the most effective thing has been the meetings with legislators. While they don't always agree with us 100 percent, we have started to turn their heads and their hearts on this issue. A critical piece is the voice of young people and their families."[65] Making the meetings effective required training and preparation. Campaign organizers held multiple trainings, particularly for family members and others who had not previously been involved with advocacy campaigns, to discuss how to conduct effective meetings and to hold practice role plays. Advocacy days in Sacramento required substantial planning, from the logistics of transporting hundreds of volunteers to Sacramento, to putting together strategic advocacy teams in order to ensure that important perspectives, such as those from former law enforcement and victims' families, were included. In seeking the support of crucial members of the Assembly, the campaign also identified influential individuals—including the legislators' priest or personal friends—who could help persuade them to support the bill.

In addition to the one-on-one meetings with legislators, the campaign generated thousands of letters and phone calls to state Senators and Assemblymembers. This was important to show legislators that the bill—which many lawmakers considered controversial and potentially damaging to their political careers—had broad grassroots support. Active backing from their constituents would make them more likely to vote in favor of the bill and less fearful of negative political consequences.

Finally, the campaign's cultivation of the media was important and strategic. Organizers reached out individually to editorial writers from the states' key newspapers—often multiple times—to educate them about sentences of life without parole for juvenile offenders, what the bill would do, and to seek favorable editorials. They also wrote op-eds about the issue. While the editorials were useful for public education, their primary purpose was to influence legislators. Similar to the rationale behind generating strong constituent support, active endorsement from the mainstream media for the bill could influence legislators' votes.

At this writing, the campaign was seeking another vote in 2012. After one of the bill's defeats, Calvin reflected, "So much has happened, it's hard to be completely depressed about the vote. It's really amazing the way people from all walks of life rallied around this issue. I feel we made important gains, but more importantly, the response to this issue gives me hope that people are committed to changing how young people are treated. That fact, and the incredible group of people I work with, make this feel more like a bump in the road than a dead end."[66] Among those transformed by the campaign were some of the individuals serving life without parole sentences for crimes committed as juveniles. One wrote to the organizers from prison after the 2010 vote: "I felt like I had a light at the end of the tunnel for the first time in fifteen years. Before [the campaign] contacted me, I didn't care about anything. Now I care about everything. It's like I was a crumpled piece of paper in the trash can and someone plucked me up and smoothed me over. . . . We did not lose! It will just take us a little longer to win."[67]

THE CASE STUDIES IN THIS BOOK encompass a diverse range of issues and contexts. Some of the advocacy campaigns presented are national in scope, while others are global. Some advocates are organizing in highly restrictive environments, while others organize freely and openly. Some are working for very specific, narrow objectives, while others have broad, far-reaching goals. Despite the differences, a number of key themes emerge. These include the importance of diverse and broad-based alliances, the involvement by those most affected by abuses, strategic timing and the value of "opportunistic advocacy," credible research and documentation, and the use of multiple points of leverage.

Broad-based Alliances

Broad-based and strategic alliances have been at the heart of the most success-ful human rights advocacy efforts in recent years. These alliances magnify the voices of individual members, bring strength and credibility to their efforts, and allow advocates to bring a unified message to critical issues. They enable advocates to dispel stereotypes about their issues and engage new partners to create fundamental changes in societal attitudes.

Advocates involved in the Coalition to Stop the Use of Child Soldiers identified the alliance between human rights, child rights, and humanitar-ian groups as one of the key factors behind the coalition's success in winning the adoption of the optional protocol to the Convention on the Rights of the Child. The members' respective expertise in research, advocacy, and provid-ing rehabilitation and reintegration services for former child soldiers helped establish the credibility of the coalition and made it an effective lobbying force during the negotiation of the protocol. Similarly, the support of nearly every major child rights NGO for the creation of a special representative to the secretary-general on violence against children was decisive in winning the support of the General Assembly for the post. According to one advocate who later became a diplomat for the United Kingdom, "If you have Save the Children, Human Rights Watch, World Vision, Plan International and the others gathered with one purpose, [UN member states] pay attention."[1]

In key instances, alliances—particularly between NGOs in the North and the South—allowed members to fight stereotypes about their objectives and demonstrate that their objectives were broadly held. The Campaign Against Impunity engaged both international NGOs and NGOs from across Africa, making clear that Africans affected by the war were deeply committed to bringing Charles Taylor to justice and that the effort to put him on trial was not a "Western" agenda. Similarly, the campaign to defeat human rights abusers from election to the Human Rights Council brought the firsthand credibility and experience of national NGOs in the candidate countries together with the strength of international advocacy NGOs to make an effective case that countries targeted by the campaign did not meet the standards required for membership in the council.

At the local level, alliances with diverse local stakeholders are often key to changing attitudes and building a climate for national-level change. Domestic worker advocates in Tanzania and the Philippines found that creating partnerships with local churches, educators, and leaders were particularly effective in helping them reach domestic workers and their employers to conduct rights education programs, develop domestic workers' networks, and in some cases, establish child labor committees or implement local by-laws or ordinances. In the Philippines, advocates abandoned an approach that focused on rallies and demonstrations in favor of engagement with churches and schools, finding it a more effective approach for creating positive dialogue about domestic worker issues. Filipino advocates identified one of their biggest successes as shifting societal attitudes, as evidenced by a widespread change in the term used to refer to domestic workers.

The broad campaign built in California to fight sentences of life imprisonment without the possibility of parole for juvenile offenders brought together religious leaders, family members of the incarcerated, youth, law professors, and other human rights advocates for an impressive grassroots lobbying effort. The broad involvement enabled the campaign to make hundreds of visits to lawmakers' offices and generate thousands of letters and phone calls, demonstrating that the issue was of broad concern to Californians. It also engaged nontraditional allies—including the state's powerful prison guards' union, former federal prosecutors, and family members of murder victims— to dispel assumptions that law enforcement and crime victims were uniformly opposed to changing the law.

In several cases, national NGOs relied on alliances with international groups for particular expertise, for example, when Jamaican and Nepali NGOs asked international groups to help draft proposals for legislative reform to ensure rights for LGBTI persons, when families of the Abu Salim massacre in Libya worked with the World Organization Against Torture and Libya Human Rights Solidarity to file formal complaints with UN bodies, or when local activists in Brazil and Jordan linked with international NGOs to coordinate the country visits of UN special rapporteurs.

Working in broad-based alliances or coalitions demands time, sensitivity, good communication, and coordination. Consultation processes require adequate time to ensure that all members of the alliances are on board with key decisions and have time to respond. In the case of the campaign against Sri Lanka's election to the Human Rights Council, for example, international groups held off on action until Sri Lankan NGOs had decided that they would back the campaign. Northern-based advocates who are online constantly through computers and smart phones need to remember that colleagues in the South with less computer access may not be able to respond to messages immediately and be sensitive to the power dynamics that can arise when smaller and underresourced groups from the South ally with well-funded and highly visible groups from the North. In several of the campaigns featured here, for example, organizers ensured that public statements featured a range of spokespeople, with well-established, larger groups sometimes taking a back seat.

Despite the availability and ease of virtual communication, face-to-face meetings—such as the pivotal 2006 Dutch conference of domestic workers that launched the campaign for an international domestic worker convention—still play a vital role in solidifying relationships and shaping campaign strategies. Diverse alliances also work best with designated leadership to ensure communication and coordination, and delegation of responsibilities to utilize each member's strengths to advantage. The campaign to bring Charles

Taylor to justice is a good illustration, where national NGOs focused on country-specific advocacy, while international NGOs took on different tasks, including legal analysis, media work, drafting statements, or coordinating NGO outreach.

Organizing by Those Most Affected

Individuals and family members most directly affected by human rights abuses have emerged as dynamic leaders for many recent human rights movements. By speaking directly to their own experiences they are often the most effective and compelling advocates for human rights. Their circumstances, however, often require them to overcome threats, repression, isolation, and marginalization in order to mobilize and speak out.

In Jamaica and Nepal, members of the LGBT community were the driving force in addressing homophobia and antigay violence, even when under direct threat. In Nepal, where LGBT activists were able to be more public and put a face to their demands, progress came more quickly. In Jamaica, where gay activists had been killed and members of the LGBT community were reluctant to be identified, progress was slower. Campaigns organized by international NGOs, such as the Stop Murder Music campaign, were very effective in shining a spotlight on homophobia in Jamaica, but others, primarily a boycott of Red Stripe beer instigated by US and Canadian activists, were strongly criticized by Jamaican LGBT activists who felt they were poorly conceived in large part because they failed to consult adequately with Jamaican LGBT activists who were most familiar with the local situation.

Although the International Labor Organization had recognized as early as 1965 the need for global standards for domestic workers, it was only after domestic workers themselves began mobilizing, first at national level and then internationally, for a minimum wage, rest days, overtime pay, and other rights enjoyed by other workers that an international labor rights convention on decent work for domestic workers was finally achieved. The campaign to defeat human rights abusers to the UN Human Rights Council included active participation by dissidents and NGOs from Azerbaijan, Belarus, Sri Lanka, and other countries running for election to the council, who enhanced the credibility of the campaign by bringing firsthand perspectives about the abuses perpetrated by their governments.

In Libya, international NGOs had publicized the Abu Salim prison massacre, but human rights advocates agreed that it was the mobilization by family members of detainees killed at the prison that was decisive in prompting action by Gaddafi's regime. In California, family members of juvenile offenders serving life without parole were actively involved in the campaign to change state law. Many not only became effective spokespeople but also found that getting involved in the campaign was a life-changing experience that enabled them to overcome feelings of shame, isolation, and powerlessness. One said, "Once I got involved . . . I felt that I had people behind me. I felt empowered. I found a voice to be able to speak on this."[2]

In some of these instances, the affected individuals had little or no prior advocacy experience. In order to mount an effective campaign, they organized trainings to empower their members and build the capacity of their movement. In Nepal, for example, the leading LGBT group trained four hundred of its members in strategic leadership and advocacy. Domestic worker groups in various countries routinely organized training and awareness-raising sessions for their members. As the leader of a domestic worker network in Latin America said, "It is not easy. We are not trained as professionals. . . . [W]e do not necessarily have the basic organizing skills. However, we are convinced that we have to win back our rights and it is through our activists that we grow and learn how to organize and defend the rights of our members and friends."[3]

Timing and "Opportunistic Advocacy"

For many of the advocacy efforts documented here, specific events or developments created unique advocacy opportunities or allowed progress that might not have been possible under other circumstances. Advocates seized these opportunities to move their issues forward, to launch significant new campaigns, and to take advantage of the leverage they provided.

The most dramatic example was the organizing by Libyan families of prisoners who were massacred at the Abu Salim prison in 1996. Modest political reforms that began in 1999 created a greater tolerance for dissent and freedom of expression and allowed the families to speak out about the massacre and press for the truth about what had happened to their loved ones in a way that would not have been possible just a few years earlier. In 2011, when antigovernment uprisings swept the entire Middle East region and the families' spokesperson, Fathi Terbil, was arrested, a singular moment of opportunity arrived. Bolstered by years of organizing and public demonstrations, the families protested Terbil's arrest and sparked large-scale demonstrations across Libya, leading to a six-month armed uprising that brought down the Gaddafi regime. In Nepal, the unprecedented political transformation following a decade-long civil war allowed the LGBT movement to participate in the political process as Nepal transitioned from a monarchy to a fledgling democracy. LGBT advocates ran for seats in the constituent assembly and provided input for the country's new constitution, using the political moment to bring visibility to their concerns, establish a face for their movement, and place their issues squarely onto the political agenda.

For advocates working to bring Charles Taylor to justice, the confluence of a visit by Nigerian President Obasanjo to the United States with the unexpected disappearance of Taylor from his Nigerian villa created an exceptional opportunity that proved decisive for the campaign. Advocates seized on a planned face-to-face meeting between Obasanjo and US President George Bush as leverage, pushing US administration officials to refuse the meeting unless Obasanjo agreed to find Taylor and hand him over for trial by the Special Court for Sierra Leone. The strategy worked, and Liberian authorities quickly produced Taylor.

Members of the Coalition to Stop the Use of Child Soldiers found that their efforts to achieve an international ban on the use of child soldiers were bolstered by the recently concluded negotiations on the Mine Ban Treaty and the Rome Statute for the International Criminal Court. The United States, initially a key opponent of the optional protocol, had also opposed both the landmine treaty and the ICC and was keenly aware of its "outlier" status. Its desire to avoid being on the outside of a high-profile human rights treaty for the third consecutive time motivated it to compromise in order to be part of a final agreement on the optional protocol.

Shifts in government also helped certain campaigns. The United States emerged as a powerful ally during the negotiations on the ILO domestic worker convention despite poor national law, in large part because of strong positions taken by the Department of Labor under the new Obama administration. During the final phase of the negotiations of the child soldiers optional protocol, the Greens were briefly in power in Germany, which influenced a strong German government position opposing the use of under-eighteens in armed conflict.

For Students for a Free Tibet, the decision by the International Olympic Committee to allow Beijing to host the 2008 summer Olympic Games provided the impetus for a focused two-year campaign to take advantage of the massive international attention the games would bring to China. According to the organization's director, "Our job was to take the Olympic spotlight and turn it to Tibet."[4] Campaign organizers strategically planned their actions in advance of major Olympic events, such as the torch relay passing through London, Paris, and San Francisco, in order to take advantage of major news cycles. Such timing helped ensure that the campaign's images and messages became part of the media's coverage of official Olympic developments.

Human rights advocates may not be able to predict when these decisive moments of opportunity might arrive, but they can take steps to make sure that they are prepared to maximize their potential when they do. For example, Eric Witte recalled how members of the campaign to bring Charles Taylor to justice had conducted advocacy for several years to get key US policy members to go on the record calling for Taylor to stand trial. When critical events converged—specifically, Charles Taylor's disappearance on the eve of Nigerian President Obasanjo's meeting with US President George Bush—the US administration had little choice but to act. "In these advocacy campaigns, you have to build these crisis moments and use them to best advantage," said Witte. "You have to get rhetorical commitments from the people who have leverage to make things happen."[5] In this and other cases, including the campaigns for accountability in Libya and Sri Lanka, a key strategy was to simply keep an issue on the international agenda until political developments or other circumstances made a breakthrough possible.

Credible Research and Documentation

Research, investigation, and documentation are among the most powerful tools of human rights advocacy. By spotlighting patterns of abuse, advocates can often let the facts speak for themselves. Careful and timely documentation can enhance the credibility of advocates, make it more difficult for policymakers to ignore violations, and may be essential to access valuable avenues of advocacy, for example, claims through the courts or UN human rights procedures.

Advocates working for the establishment of the special representative to the secretary-general on violence against children found that much of the resistance from UN member states to creating such a high-level post dissolved after the publication of the UN study on violence against children, which documented the severe and widespread nature of violence against children in many aspects of their lives. Similarly, during the campaign to defeat human rights abusers from the UN Human Rights Council, advocates found that many UN diplomats were simply unaware of the poor human rights records of some of the candidates and that highlighting evidence of abuses by a candidate's government helped influence the votes of some UN member states.

Advocates working in California to end sentencing of juveniles to life without parole reflected that one of their most valuable advocacy tools was information, and that many legislators were persuaded by the facts that the campaign was able to present, including the racial disparities in the application of the sentence and data showing that juvenile offenders were more likely to be sentenced to life without parole than their adult codefendants. The Coalition to Stop the Use of Child Soldiers also used research as a central component of its campaign, publishing several regional reports to document the extent of child soldier use. A cofounder of the coalition wished that even more research had been available before negotiations on the optional protocol began. "That's one of the things I would do differently if I were doing it again. I would do a major study before the negotiations started so that the real issues were clear. When we started most people didn't have an idea about the issue, including foreign ministries."[6]

In seeking accountability for war crimes in Sri Lanka, NGOs including Tamil groups provided evidence that helped produce a damning report by the UN secretary-general's panel of experts regarding abuses that occurred during the final months of the war. They also documented the Sri Lankan government's inability and lack of political will to address impunity on its own. Amnesty International's report "Twenty Years of Make-Believe" detailed repeated failures by the government to investigate human rights abuses in the country, bolstering the organization's argument that only an independent, international investigation would effectively bring justice to the war's victims and countering diplomats who were too quick to believe the government's promises that it could respond to the allegations of abuses on its own.

In Nepal, research was fundamental to the watershed 2007 Supreme Court ruling that prohibited discrimination on the basis of sexual orientation and represented a turning point for Nepal's LGBT movement. Sunil Pant, the head of Nepal's leading LGBT organization, said, "I did not realize that the documentation I did over the years, the piles of photographs, medical reports, and incidents, could be so useful to the courts. The judges studying those could not believe the level of inhumane treatment that had happened from the security forces."[7] UN special rapporteurs assigned to investigate thematic human rights violations also stressed the importance of documentation from human rights groups to their field missions and reporting.

Advocates have many ways to make their documentation available to their advocacy targets: through the publication of reports, briefing papers, press releases, press conferences, web postings, submissions to UN rapporteurs, formal complaints to UN bodies and the courts, informal contacts with the media, one-on-one advocacy meetings, and email communications. Ensuring that research is accurate, timely, and responds to the particular concerns of policymakers can provide the backbone of a campaign and position advocates to win allies and advocacy successes.

Multiple Points of Leverage

Nearly all the campaigns relied on a multifaceted approach and multiple points of leverage to create and maintain pressure for change, often not know-ing what might create the "tipping point" that would ultimately achieve their goal. In many cases, advocates combined advocacy with UN entities (such as the Security Council, the Human Rights Council, or UN special procedures), with court challenges, media work, engagement with influential third-party governments, prominent figures, and other forms of pressure.

In the Philippines, local and international NGOs had advocated for years to expose rising numbers of extrajudicial executions and worked to engage third-party governments, who also raised their concerns directly with the Philippines government. In the case explored here, a country mission and public statements by the UN special rapporteur on extrajudicial executions, Philip Alston, effectively added to existing pressures to finally prompt gov-ernment action to curtail the killings. Similarly, the UN special rapporteur on torture, Manfred Nowak, was able to build on numerous investigations, reports, and calls from national and international NGOs for the closure of Al-Jafr prison in Lebanon, to persuade the government to shut the facility down.

The campaign to bring Charles Taylor to justice worked to engage a wide range of actors, including the Security Council, the OHCHR, the African Union, the European Union, individual governments, such as the United States, and to maintain domestic pressure in the key countries of Liberia and Nigeria. Liberian President Johnson Sirleaf admitted in a media interview that pressure from the United States and other Western governments had been decisive in her decision to formally request Charles Taylor's handover from

Nigeria for prosecution for war crimes. These governments had been engaged systematically by the campaign and were perceived as critical to Liberia's economic development after the war. One advocate reflected, "You never know with these advocacy campaigns with so many actors in so many different countries what is going to work, so you have to push on as many fronts as possible."[8] For example, although US government pressure just prior to Nigerian President Obasanjo's scheduled meeting with US President Bush was decisive in getting Taylor handed over for trial, some advocates believed that the judicial challenge to Taylor's asylum status in Nigeria might have eventually forced Nigeria to transfer Taylor.

Two of the other campaigns explored here—in Nepal and Libya—also successfully used court challenges as one part of their strategy, and another—in Jamaica—was beginning to develop such a strategy to challenge homophobic national laws. According to LGBT advocates in Nepal, the Supreme Court ruling in 2007 that nullified Nepal's laws against "unnatural sexual conduct" and directed the government to formulate laws to end discrimination against the LGBT community was a breakthrough for their movement and a major catalyst in shifting attitudes toward the LGBT community. In Libya, families who lost loved ones in the Abu Salim massacre won a civil claim filed in a Libyan court, which ordered the government to reveal the fate of the detainees. Although the government challenged the validity of the judge's order, the favorable ruling gave momentum to the families' efforts and added pressure to the government to respond to their demands for justice.

In some cases, different points of leverage were used incrementally as stepping stones toward a larger goal. To create a high-level post in the UN system devoted to violence against children, for example, advocates first secured the support of the UN Committee on the Rights of the Child before lobbying the Commission on Human Rights and the General Assembly to obtain a UN study on violence against children conducted by an independent expert. The advocates then used the results of the study to lobby successfully for the establishment of a special representative to the secretary-general on violence against children. Advocates reflected that while the incremental approach was slow and painstaking, it ultimately allowed them to gain stronger government support and a higher-level post than they had originally sought—and governments had rejected initially—at the beginning of their campaign.

In the Philippines, when domestic worker advocates initially failed to win passage of national legislation to ensure rights of domestic workers, they adopted an alternative approach, seeking the adoption of local ordinances at the city level, containing many of the same components as the draft national legislation. Several cities adopted the ordinances, providing a stronger basis for the ongoing campaign for the federal-level legislation. Similarly, the movement for an international labor convention for domestic workers was strengthened by national-level legislative reforms that had been won by domestic worker unions and associations in a number of countries. These victories positioned the governments involved to take leadership at the ILO on behalf of stronger international standards.

Some campaigns successfully engaged nontraditional advocacy targets to highlight their issue and gain some successes. Examples include LGBT activists' focus on the "dancehall" music business in Jamaica and the tourism industry in Nepal, advocacy with the International Monetary Fund regarding abuses in the Sri Lankan war, and NGOs efforts to gain support from employers' organizations during negotiations for the Domestic Workers Convention. In other instances, advocates felt that they did not engage a wide enough or strategic enough array of actors. For example, an advocate addressing wartime abuses in Sri Lanka criticized an overreliance on traditional Western governments as human rights allies. "What we're learning is that that's not enough," he said. He believed advocates needed to get better at cultivating allies such as Mexico, Argentina, Brazil, and South Africa.[9]

Other Lessons

In addition to the central strategies above, the case studies offer some additional insights for effective advocacy. Many of the campaigns, for example, utilized the media effectively to build pressure and raise visibility for their cause. Well-timed op-eds in major newspapers by influential world leaders such as Desmond Tutu, Václav Havel, and Adolfo Pérez Esquival were instrumental in defeating several abusive candidates to the Human Rights Council. The California Campaign for Fair Sentencing of Youth secured several favorable editorials from state newspapers just before key votes in the state legislature. The campaign to bring Charles Taylor to justice persuaded journalists to raise the issue repeatedly with Liberian President Johnson Sirleaf and Nigerian President Obasanjo. Students for a Free Tibet masterfully timed dramatic actions to take advantage of key reporting periods around the Beijing Olympics and made extensive use of new media and alternative technologies to spotlight Tibet. In other cases where the mainstream media was not accessible, such as the Abu Salim massacre, advocates also utilized websites, YouTube, and alternative media to put out their message.

Not every issue is conducive to media coverage, particularly those that are ongoing and endemic. Activists working for the adoption of a Domestic Workers Convention found journalists uninterested in the negotiations. NGOs advocating for greater attention to violence against children also had difficulty securing media attention. In both cases, advocates were able to secure their goals without the high profile that the international media provided.

In conducting advocacy with governments, several cases illustrated the value of systematic and painstaking one-on-one meetings with individual representatives. Campaign representatives working on Human Rights Council elections and violence against children met individually with more than half of the member states that make up the UN General Assembly. NGOs working for the Domestic Workers Convention met with dozens of the governments taking part in the ILO negotiations, while in California, members of the Campaign for Fair Sentencing of Youth met with virtually every member of the California state legislature, often multiple times. Such meetings allow advocates to present their information and arguments on their issue, respond to individual concerns, cultivate allies based on personal relationships, and most importantly, present their requests for action.

Advocates interviewed for this volume also reflected on the importance of crafting their message. Advocates for child soldiers felt that their campaign for an optional protocol as effective in part because of its simple and clear message that no child under eighteen should be recruited or participate in war. Hundreds of groups were involved in the Campaign Against Impunity to bring Charles Taylor to justice, but advocates remarked that the message was always the same: that to achieve justice for the victims of the war, Taylor had to be turned over to the Special Court. The California advocates working to change sentencing laws for juvenile offenders carefully tailored their message to specific audiences, for example, stressing to the prison guards' union that the incentive of possible release could influence better behavior by inmates and emphasizing with faith communities the principle of redemption and giving juvenile offenders a chance for rehabilitation. In addressing the election of candidates for the Human Rights Council, campaign allies such as Adolfo Pérez Esquivel drew effective parallels between his own experience with an abusive regime and the practices of the candidate countries.

Another lesson is the importance of persistence and long-term commitment. All of the campaigns depicted in this volume were multiyear efforts, and many are ongoing. Students for a Free Tibet's campaign around the 2008 Beijing Olympics, for example, was most public during the year leading up to the Olympics and during the games themselves, but took years' of preparation. Advocates for children worked for nearly a decade to establish a high-level post at the UN to address violence against children. Domestic workers organized over decades to gain recognition for their rights. When the Domestic Workers Convention was finally adopted, the chair of the International Domestic Workers Network, Myrtle Witbooi, said, "If someone had told me forty-five years ago that we would be here today, I would not have believed it." In the cases that could be considered failures—efforts to achieve accountability for war crimes in Sri Lanka and to change laws sentencing juvenile offenders to life without parole in California—advocates remain committed to the cause and believe that with more time and effort, they may yet achieve success. As a juvenile offender serving a life sentence stated, "We did not lose! It will just take us a little longer to win.[10]

External Factors

In some cases, the most persistent efforts and creative campaigning simply aren't enough to overcome powerful or entrenched national interests. Governments are willing to withstand even intense international criticism in order to continue practices they consider vital to their military or other strategic interests, or are unwilling to expose individual leaders who may be implicated in abuses.

The Coalition to Stop the Use of Child Soldiers found that there were simply too many governments that allowed seventeen year olds to volunteer for military service to make it possible to reach a consensus on a "straight-18" protocol that would prohibit all military recruitment of children under age eighteen. Ultimately, they were forced to accept a compromise that allowed governments to accept under-eighteens as volunteers in their military forces. Students for a Free Tibet recognized that China had long-standing political and economic interests in maintaining its occupation of Tibet and that few outside countries were willing to exert political capital on the issue or had much influence on China's human rights practices. As a result, the organization was modest in its ambitions around its Beijing Olympics campaign, seeking primarily to keep the ongoing occupation of Tibet on the international agenda.

In some cases, the most senior leadership of governments may be implicated in abuses, making governments even more resistant to pressure to address human rights concerns. In Libya, for example, the Gaddafi regime took a number of steps to acknowledge the Abu Salim massacre and make information about the deceased prisoners available to their families, but resisted attempts to establish accountability for the killings. Advocates believed that true accountability in this case would implicate senior government officials and was therefore extremely unlikely so long as Gaddafi was in power. By comparison, offering financial compensation, issuing death certificates, and admitting to the massacre was much less costly for the regime. Advocates seeking accountability for violations during Sri Lanka's war found fierce resistance from Sri Lanka's government, which was also anxious to shield its political leadership from being implicated in possible crimes.

The timing of external events can also have a negative impact on advocacy efforts. In California, the 2010 vote on legislation to end sentencing of juvenile offenders to life without parole occurred just weeks before an election. Advocates believed that the timing may have cost them votes from legislators who were running for reelection and were fearful of losing support from powerful law enforcement groups. Similarly, advocates working for accountability in Sri Lanka found that the sudden end of the war just prior to the UN Human Rights Council's special session on Sri Lanka helped the Sri Lankan government defeat a resolution calling for an investigation of war-time abuses and, instead, muster support for a resolution congratulating the government for its victory over the Tamil Tigers.

Other external factors may also be outside advocates' control and thwart their best efforts. For example, advocates involved in the elections to the Human Rights Council were able to mount successful campaigns to defeat abusive candidates in competitive elections, but found that in many cases, governments refused to compete, mounting "clean slates" where the number of candidates from each region was the same as the number of seats available. In such instances, the only option that advocates had was to criticize the practice and draw attention to candidates' abusive records, knowing that they would still be elected.

Conclusion

Human rights advocacy is an art, not a science. There is no one formula that will work for every situation, nor a guarantee of success. Each advocacy effort must be based on an individual assessment of the opportunities for change and the tools and strategies that are available, and adapted as situations unfold. Some of the best campaigns are essentially opportunistic in nature, taking advantage of new developments as they arise and seizing a particular moment for its maximum advocacy potential. In other cases, advocates must simply work to keep their issue alive until that moment of opportunity arrives when change becomes possible.

Despite the many variables at play, the case studies presented here suggest that successful results are more likely when human rights advocacy is based on broad-based alliances, organizing by those most affected by human rights abuses, strategic timing and "opportunistic advocacy," credible research and documentation, and multiple points of leverage. Within these fundamental principles are myriad tools and tactics for human rights advocates to employ.

Both seasoned advocates and individuals who are just entering the field of human rights can learn from the experiences of others. We can apply their innovative ideas and successful strategies to our own work, learn from their failures, and be inspired by their victories as we build an even stronger human rights movement.

Notes

Chapter 1

1. Amnesty International, *No End to War on Women and Children: North Kivu, Democratic Republic of Congo* (London: Amnesty International, 2008), 21.

2. Coalition to Stop the Use of Child Soldiers, *Africa Report on the Use of Child Soldiers* (Geneva: Coalition to Stop the Use of Child Soldiers, 1999).

3. Convention on the Rights of the Child, G.A. res. 44/25, U.N. Doc. A/RES/44/25 (adopted November 20, 1989; entered into force September 2, 1990).

4. Article 38 of the Convention on the Rights of the Child is based on the 1977 Additional Protocols to the Geneva Conventions, which state that "children who have not attained the age of fifteen years shall neither be recruited in the armed forces or groups nor allowed to take part in hostilities."

5. Author interview with Martin MacPherson, chairperson, Coalition to Stop the Use of Child Soldiers, April 16, 2010.

6. US Code Title 10, Section 505 (a).

7. United States demarche on the involvement of children in armed conflict, March 1998. Author's files.

8. Author interview with Rachel Brett, Quaker United Nations Office, Geneva, December 15, 2010.

9. Author interview with Stuart Maslen, former coordinator, Coalition to Stop the Use of Child Soldiers, July 13, 2011.

10. Brazil, Canada, Denmark, Finland, Germany, Norway, Switzerland, and Uruguay.

11. Statement delivered by Jo Becker, chairperson, Coalition to Stop the Use of Child Soldiers, Berlin, October 20, 1999. Author's files.

12. Coalition to Stop the Use of Child Soldiers, "Europe Accused of Double Standards on Child Soldiers," press release, October 20, 1999. Author's files.

13. Author interview with Rachel Brett, December 15, 2010.

14. Author interview with Andreas Rister, Terres des Hommes, Germany, December 20, 2010.

15. Author interview with Stuart Maslen, July 13, 2011.

16. Author interview with Rachel Stohl, former representative of the Center for Defense Information to the US Campaign to Stop the Use of Child Soldiers, January 7, 2011.

17. Statement attributable to the Spokesman for the Secretary-General on the Minimum Age of Peacekeepers, New York, October 29, 1998. Author's files.

18. Jimmy Carter, "Kid Soldiers a War's Most Tragic Victims," *USA Today,* June 30, 1998. Available at http://www.cartercenter.org/news/documents/doc1300.html (accessed on January 23, 2011).

19. Organization of African Unity, CM/DEC.482 (LXX) Decision on the "African Conference on the Use of Children as Soldiers," endorsed by the OAU Assembly of Heads of State and Government without amendment, July 1999.

20. European Parliament resolution on the tenth anniversary of the UN Convention on the Rights of the Child, B5–0256, 0257, 0258, 0264, 0265 and 0266/1999, para. 8. See also European Parliament resolution B4–1078, passed December 17, 1999.

21. See, for example, Statement on Child Soldiers, adopted by the 8th Assembly of the World Council of Churches in Harare, Zimbabwe, December 3–14, 1998.

22. S/1999/957, Report of the Secretary-General to the Security Council on the Protection of Civilians in Armed Conflict, September 8, 1999.

23. Countries included in the survey were Afghanistan, Bosnia-Herzegovina, Cambodia, Colombia, El Salvador, France, Georgia/Abkhazia, Israel/OPT, Lebanon, Nigeria, Philippines, Russian Federation, Somalia, South Africa, Switzerland, United Kingdom, and the United States.

24. ICRC, *The People on War Report: ICRC Worldwide Consultation on the Rules of War* (Geneva: International Committee of the Red Cross, 1999).

25. For example, in January 1998, sixty-three members of Congress wrote to President Clinton, expressing dismay that the United States was obstructing progress on the optional protocol and urging the United States to either change its position or not stand in the way of negotiations. Resolutions introduced into Congress (for example, H.Con Res 209, introduced October 26, 1999) urged the United States not to block efforts to establish eighteen as the minimum age of participation in armed conflict.

26. December 1997 letter to President William J. Clinton. Author's files.

27. Author interview with Martin MacPherson, April 16, 2010.

28. Author interview with Rachel Brett, December 15, 2010.

29. Ibid.

30. Elizabeth Olsen, "US Fights Tide on a Move to Raise the Military Service Age," *New York Times,* January 15, 2000, A5.

31. Statement by Ambassador E. Michael Southwick, to the UN working group on child soldiers, Geneva, January 13, 2000.

32. Afghanistan (2003), Bosnia-Herzegovina (2003), Chile (2005), Colombia (1999), Denmark (2001), Democratic Republic of Congo (2003), Finland (2000), Iraq (2003), Kazakhstan (2001), Republic of Korea (2004), Norway (2002), Portugal (1999), Rwanda (2001), Sierra Leone (2007), Slovakia (2002), South Africa (1999), Sudan (2008), Switzerland (2002), Timor Leste (2004), and Yemen (2002). In addition, Belgium, Greece, and Paraguay made binding declarations in accordance with the optional protocol raising their minimum age of voluntary recruitment to eighteen, though without changing their national legislation.

33. Author interview with Stuart Maslen, July 13, 2011.

34. Author interview with Rachel Brett, December 15, 2010.

35. Ibid.

36. Author interview with Stuart Maslen, July 13, 2011.

37. Ibid.

38. Author interview with Martin MacPherson, April 16, 2010.

39. Author interview with Stuart Maslen, July 13, 2011.

40. Author interview with Martin MacPherson, April 16, 2010.

41. Author interview with Rachel Stohl, January 7, 2011.

42. Ibid.

43. Ibid.

44. Ibid.

45. The coalition government of the Social Democrats and the Green Party. The Green Party was known for its pacifist ideals.

46. Author interview with Andreas Rister, December 20, 2010.

47. Author interview with Martin MacPherson, April 16, 2010.

48. Author interview with Rachel Brett, December 15, 2010.

49. Ibid.

Chapter 2

1. Jonathan Blagbrough, *They Respect Their Animals More: Voices of Child Domestic Workers* (London: Anti-Slavery International, 2008), 2. Diwata is a pseudonym.

2. Migueline Colque, cited in Celia Mather, *Respect and Rights: Protection for Domestic/Household Workers!* (Tilberg and Geneva: IRENE and IUF, 2008), 43.

3. In 2011, the International Labour Organization (ILO) used official statistics (mainly labor force and household sample surveys) from 117 countries to estimate a minimum of 52.6 million domestic workers worldwide. The organization stated that because official data undercount domestic workers, the true number of domestic workers could be closer to 100 million. See ILO, *Global and Regional Estimates on Domestic Workers, Domestic Work Policy Brief 4* (Geneva: International Labour Office, 2011), 6.

4. Some workers, particularly in Latin America, prefer the term "household workers." However, the term domestic workers is more common and used throughout this chapter.

5. ILO-IPEC, *Bunga-bunga di Atas Padas: Fenomena Pekerja Rumah Tangga Anak Di Indonesia* [Flowers on the rock: Phenomenon of child domestic workers in Indonesia] (Jakarta: International Labour Organization, 2004).

6. Human Rights Watch, *As If I Am Not Human: Abuses Against Asian Domestic Workers in Saudi Arabia* (New York: Human Rights Watch, 2008).

7. International Labour Organization, *Helping Hands or Shackled Lives?: Understanding Child Domestic Labour and Responses to It* (Geneva: International Labour Office, 2004), 58–59.

8. Human Rights Watch, *Always on Call: Abuse and Exploitation of Child Domestic Workers in Indonesia* (New York: Human Rights Watch, 2005).

9. Human Rights Watch, *Walls at Every Turn: Abuse of Migrant Domestic Workers Through Kuwait's Sponsorship System* (New York: Human Rights Watch, 2010), 3.

10. Human Rights Watch, *Swept Under the Rug: Abuses Against Domestic Workers Around the World* (New York: Human Rights Watch, 2006), 18.

11. Oscar Godoy, *El Salvador: Trabajo infantile domestic: Una evaluación rápida* (Geneva: ILO-IPEC, 2002), 24.

12. Nicole J. Sayres, *Analysis of the Situation of Filipino Domestic Workers* (Manila: International Labour Office, 2007), 7.

13. World Bank, *Migration and Remittance Factbook, 2011* (Washington, DC: World Bank, 2010).

14. Statement by the government of the Philippines, International Labour Conference, 99th Session, Geneva, June 3, 2010.

15. Author interview with Cecilia Flores-Oebanda, president, Visayan Forum, June 11, 2010.

16. Ibid.

17. Ibid.

18. Samahan at Ugnayan ng mga Mannggagawang Pantahanan sa Pilipinas Inc.

19. Personal statement by Lilibeth Masamloc, secretary general, SUMAPI, provided to the author, May 3, 2010.

20. Social Weather Survey of August 26–September 5, 2005. Available at http://www.sws.org.ph/pr050916.htm (accessed June 14, 2010).

21. Author interview with Cecilia Flores-Oebanda, June 11, 2010.

22. Author interview with Lilibeth Masamloc, June 5, 2011.

23. Ibid.

24. Ibid.

25. ILO, *Emerging Good Practices on Actions to Combat Child Domestic Labour in Kenya, Tanzania, Uganda and Zambia* (Geneva: International Labour Office, 2006), 3, 8.

26. Florence Rugemalira, cited in IUF, *Respect and Rights*, 104.

27. ILO, *Tanzania: "Not Just our Traditional Things,"* interview by Celia Mather, Lusaka, July 4, 2006. Available at IUF Women Workers News, http://www.iuf.org/women/2007/05/not_just_our_traditional_thing.html (accessed June 14, 2010).

28. Ibid.

29. Author interview with Vicky Kanyoka, director for women and organization, CHODAWU, July 16, 2010.

30. ILO, *Emerging Good Practices*, 31.

31. ILO, *Tanzania.*

32. ITUC, *Spotlight Interview with Titus Mlengeya*, national chairman, CHODAWU, interview by Samuel Grumiau, July 28, 2009. Available at http://www.ituc-csi.org/spotlight-interview-with-titus,4118.html (accessed July 15, 2010).

33. Ruge Florence, cited in Mather, *Respect and Rights*, 104.

34. ITUC, Spotlight Interview with Titus Mlengeya.

35. Author interview with Vicky Kanyoka, July 16, 2010.

36. The international conference followed an April 2005 conference on the role of trade unions in Europe to organize and protect domestic workers, organized by the European Trades Union Confederation (ETUC), International Restructuring Education Network Europe (IRENE), and the Platform for International Cooperation on Undocumented Migrants (PICUM).

37. Alfred Angula, general secretary, Namibia Domestic and Allied Workers' Union, cited in Mather, *Respect and Rights*, 26.

38. See http://www.hrw.org/category/topic/women%E2%80%99s-rights/women -workers (accessed June 14, 2010).

39. See, for example, Report by the Special Rapporteur on Migrant Workers, Ms. Gabriela Rodríguez Pizarro to the Commission on Human Rights, E/CN.4/2004/76, January 12, 2004.

40. The ILO was established in 1919 and became the first UN specialized agency in 1946.

41. ILO: *Record of Proceedings*, International Labour Conference (ILC), 31st Session, 1948, Appendix XVIII: Resolutions adopted by the Conference, 545–46.

42. ILO: Official Bulletin (Geneva), July 1965, Supplement I, 20–21.

43. See ILO: Maritime Labour Convention. Available at http://www.ilo.org/global /What_we_do/InternationalLabourStandards/MaritimeLabourConvention/lang- -en/index.htm (accessed July 1, 2010).

44. ITUC, *Global Trade Union Body Calls for International Convention to Protect Domestic Workers*, press release, October 31, 2007. Available at http://www.ituc-csi .org/global-trade-union-body-calls-for.html?lang=en (accessed July 4, 2010).

45. ILO Governing Body (GB.301/2, paras. 2 and 9).

46. Government members of the Governing Body supporting the proposal included the Group of Latin American and Caribbean (GRULAC) states (including individual statements from Brazil, Peru, Cuba, Barbados, and Venezuela), South Africa, Australia, Sri Lanka, Spain, Romania, Germany, Greece, Ireland, Morocco, Russia, and Italy. The employers group and two governments proposed to simply hold a general discussion of the issue.

47. International Labor Organization, *Decent Work for Domestic Workers, Report IV (1)*, International Labour Conference, 99th Session 2010 (Geneva: International Labour Office, 2009), 50.

48. Ibid., 1.

49. Ibid., 94.

50. Author interview with Myrtle Witbooi, secretary general, South African Service and Allied Workers Union, June 10, 2010.

51. Author interview with Vicky Kanyoka, July 16, 2010.

52. Lauri Garcia Dueñes, "Domestic Workers Demand Latin American Governments to Recognize Their Rights at Work," Confederación Latinoamericana y del Caribe de Trabajadoras del Hogar (CONLACTRAHO), September 29, 2009. Available at http://docs.google.com/fileview?id=0B8fJgUjCgEvlNTQ1Mzc4YmYtNTkwO-C00YTA5LWI1ZWEtMjExNTY4M2JmNjU0&hl=en (accessed July 6, 2010).

53. See http://dwglobalcampaign.mfasia.org/ (accessed July 6, 2010).

54. International Domestic Worker Network, "Platform of Demands," International Labour Conference, 99th Session, Geneva, June 2010. Available at http://www.domesticworkerrights.org/sites/default/files/Platform%20of%20Demands_HR_ENGLISH_26052010.pdf (accessed July 6, 2010).

55. See, for example, Human Rights Watch and Anti-Slavery International, *Decent Work for Domestic Workers: Recommendations to ILO Members Regarding the Law and Practice Report and Questionnaire,* advocacy document, June 2009. Available at http://www.hrw.org/en/news/2009/07/20/decent-work-domestic-workers (accessed January 1, 2011).

56. Email correspondence to the author from Barbro Budin, IUF, July 10, 2010.

57. ILO, *Decent Work for Domestic Workers: Report IV (2).*

58. Ibid.

59. Statement by K. Rahman, employers' spokesperson, International Labour Conference, June 2, 2010.

60. Statement by Halima Yakob, workers' spokesperson, International Labour Conference, June 2, 2010.

61. Statement by Vicky Kanyoka to the ILO Tripartite Committee on Domestic Work, June 2, 2010, Geneva. Statement available at http://idwnilo.wordpress.com/2010/06/11/governments-need-imagination-and-commitment/#more-237 (accessed July 14, 2010).

62. Governments voting in favor of a nonbinding recommendation included Bahrain, Bangladesh, India, Indonesia, Islamic Republic of Iran, Kuwait, Malaysia, New Zealand, Oman, Panama, Qatar, Saudi Arabia, Singapore, and the United Arab Emirates. Those abstaining included Congo, Estonia, Israel, and Japan. ILO, Provisional Record no. 12, "Decent Work for Domestic Workers: Report of the Committee on Domestic Workers," March 2010, 99th Session, Geneva, 2010. Available at http://www.ilo.org/global/What_we_do/Officialmeetings/ilc/ILCSessions/99th-Session/reports/lang--en/docName--WCMS_123731/index.htm (accessed July 14, 2010).

63. International Domestic Workers Network ILO Blog, June 2, 2010. Available at http://idwnilo.wordpress.com/ (accessed July 6, 2010).

64. See proposed conclusions, ILO, Provisional Record no. 12, "Decent Work for Domestic Workers: Report of the Committee on Domestic Workers," March 2010, 99th Session (Geneva: International Labour Office, 2010), 124–32.

65. Human Rights Watch also prepared a detailed response to the International Organization of Employers written submission to the ILO regarding the instrument.

66. Statement by Myrtle Witbooi in the ILO Domestic Workers Committee workers' group, Geneva, June 10, 2011.

67. Author interview with Vicky Kanyoka, June 9, 2011.

68. Conversation between UK diplomat and the author, Geneva, March 18, 2010.

69. Ibid., 8.

70. SUMAPI, "Strategic Planning for the SUMAPI," undated document. Available

at http://www.ilo.org/wcmsp5/groups/public/---asia/---ro-bangkok/---ilo-manila /documents/genericdocument/wcms_126012.pdf (accessed January 3, 2012).

71. Marcelina Bautista, secretary general, CONLACTRAHO, cited in Mather, *Respect and Rights*, 40a.

72. Alfred Angula, general secretary, Namibia Domestic and Allied Workers' Union, cited in Mather, *Respect and Rights*, 64.

73. Early domestic worker groups included Brazil and Chile (1920s), the United States (1979), Bolivia (1980's), India (1985), the United Kingdom (1987), and Namibia (1990).

74. International Domestic Workers' Network, *Platform of Demands*.

75. Author interview with Jill Shenker, coordinator, National Domestic Workers Alliance, June 3, 2010.

76. Author interviews with ILO delegates, Geneva, Switzerland, June 2011.

Chapter 3

1. Author interview with Lawrence Moss, Special Counsel for UN Reform, Human Rights Watch, January 18, 2011.

2. General Assembly resolution A/RES/60/251, April 3, 2006.

3. Burundi, Cambodia, Cote d'Ivoire, North Korea, Haiti, Myanmar, the Palestinian territories, Somalia, Syria, and Sudan. For thematic mandates, see http://www2. ohchr.org/english/bodies/chr/special/themes.htm.

4. General Assembly resolution A/RES/60/251, adopted April 3, 2006.

5. The geographical distribution of the forty-seven seats is as follows: thirteen seats for Africa, thirteen for Asia, six for Eastern Europe, eight for Latin America and the Caribbean, and seven for Western Europe and other countries (which includes the United States, Canada, and Israel). Each member can run for reelection once, but then must rotate off the council for at least one year before running again.

6. Author interview with Dokhi Fassihian, executive director, Democracy Coalition Project, January 14, 2011.

7. Original members included the African Women's Development and Communication Network (FEMNET), Cairo Institute for Human Rights Studies, Centro de Estudios Legales y Sociales (CELS) (Argentina), Democracy Coalition Project, Human Rights Watch, International Helsinki Federation for Human Rights, People in Need (Czech Republic). By 2009, its core membership included fourteen NGOs representing all regions of the world.

8. General Assembly resolution A/RES/61/175, adopted December 19, 2006.

9. Author interview with Dokhi Fassihian, January 14, 2011.

10. NGO Coalition for an Effective Human Rights Council, "Say No to Belarus," May 10, 2007 statement. Available at http://www.hrw.org/legacy/no-on-belarus/ (accessed on January 25, 2011).

11. Václav Havel, "Statement on the Candidacy of Belarus for Membership in the United Nations Human Rights Council," May 7, 2007, issued by Civic Belarus.

Available at http://www.ngo.ee/orb.aw/class=file/action=preview/id=14694/Belarus +and+UN+HRC.pdf (accessed on January 25, 2011).

12. Author interview with Lawrence Moss, January 18, 2011.

13. Ibid.

14. Human Rights Watch, *World Report 2008* (New York: Human Rights Watch, 2009).

15. "Sri Lankan NGOs Oppose Sri Lanka's HRC Candidacy," April 28, 2008. Available at http://www.hrw.org/legacy/effectiveHRC/SriLanka/ (accessed June 19, 2009).

16. Ibid.

17. Asian Human Rights Commission, "Asian NGOS call on UN member states to reject Sri Lanka's Human Rights Council election bid," May 17, 2008. Available at http://www.ahrchk.net/statements/mainfile.php/2008statements/1545/ (accessed January 25, 2011).

18. Desmond Tutu, "No Right to Be There," *The Guardian*, May 15, 2009. Available at http://www.guardian.co.uk/commentisfree/2008/may/15/norighttobethere (accessed January 23, 2011).

19. Adolfo Pérez Esquivel, "Sri Lanka y la ONU," *Página 12*, May 17, 2008. Available at http://www.pagina12.com.ar/diario/elmundo/4–104335–2008–05–17.html (accessed January 23, 2011).

20. NGO Coalition for an Effective Human Rights Council, "UN: Sri Lanka's Defeat a Victory for Human Rights Council," press release, May 21, 2008. Available at http://www.hrw.org/en/news/2008/05/20/un-sri-lanka-s-defeat-victory-human -rights-council (accessed January 25, 2011).

21. Yap Swee Seng, executive director of FORUM-ASIA, in Human Rights Watch, "UN: Elect Rights-Respecting States to Human Rights Council," press release, April 21, 2009. Available at http://www.hrw.org/en/news/2009/04/21/un-elect-rights -respecting-states-human-rights-council (accessed January 25, 2011).

22. NGOs for an Effective Human Rights Council website is available at http:// www.hrw.org/sites/default/files/features/hrc2009/index.html (accessed January 1, 2011).

23. Ibid.

24. "Azerbaijani Civil Society Says Vote No on Azerbaijan," letter to members of the UN General Assembly, April 14, 2009. Available at http://www.hrw.org/sites /default/files/features/hrc2009/azerbaijan/letter.html (accessed January 1, 2011).

25. "Human Rights Groups Around the World Call for Azerbaijan's Defeat," May 5, 2009, letter to members of the UN General Assembly. Available at http://www.hrw .org/sites/default/files/features/hrc2009/azerbaijan/letter2.html (accessed January 25, 2011).

26. Václav Havel, "A Table for Tyrants," *New York Times*, May 11, 2009. Available at http://www.nytimes.com/2009/05/11/opinion/11havel.html (accessed January 25, 2011).

27. Ibid.

28. Lorena Fries, president of Corporación Humanas Centro Regional de

Dereschose Humanos y Justicia de Género, in Human Rights Watch, "UN: Lack of Competition Mars Vote on Human Rights Council," press release, May 12, 2009. Available at http://www.hrw.org/en/news/2009/05/12/un-lack-competition-mars -vote-human-rights-council (accessed January 25, 2011).

29. Author interview with Dokhi Fassihian, January 14, 2011.

30. Ibid.

31. Author interview with Lawrence Moss, January 18, 2011.

32. Ibid.

33. Author interview with Dokhi Fassihian, January 14, 2011.

34. Author interview with Elizabeth Sepper, UN advocacy fellow, Human Rights Watch, June 19, 2009.

35. Author interview with Lawrence Moss, January 18, 2011.

36. Ibid.

37. Ibid.

38. Ibid.

39. Author interview with Dokhi Fassihian, January 14, 2011.

40. Author interview with Elizabeth Sepper, June 19, 2009.

41. Author interview with Dokhi Fassihian, January 14, 2011.

42. Steven Groves, quoted in Howard LaFranchi, "Syria, Under Pressure, Drops Bid for UN Rights Council. Is that Progress?" *The Christian Science Monitor,* May 11, 2011. Available at http://www.csmonitor.com/USA/Foreign-Policy/2011/0511/Syria -under-pressure-drops-bid-for-UN-rights-council.-Is-that-progress (accessed July 25, 2011).

43. Author interview with Yolanda Foster, Sri Lanka and Nepal researcher, Amnesty International, August 1, 2011.

Chapter 4

1. Author interview with Philip Alston, UN special rapporteur on extrajudicial, summary, or arbitrary executions (2004–10), September 20, 2010.

2. As of May 2012, the special procedures included ten country mandates and thirty-six thematic mandates. See http://www2.ohchr.org/english/bodies/chr/special/index.htm.

3. Office of the High Commissioner for Human Rights, "United Nations Special Procedures: Facts and Figures 2010," Geneva, 2011. Available at http://www2.ohchr.org/english/bodies/chr/special/docs/Facts_Figures2010.pdf (accessed July 21, 2011).

4. Office of the High Commissioner for Human Rights, "Special Procedures of the Human Rights Council." Available at http://www.ohchr.org/EN/HRBodies/SP/Pages /Introduction.aspx (accessed May 13, 2012).

5. The mandate for the special rapporteur on Sudan was changed in 2009 to a mandate for an independent expert.

6. For a list of countries that have extended a standing invitation to thematic procedures, see http://www2.ohchr.org/english/bodies/chr/special/invitations.htm.

7. Ted Piccone, *Catalysts for Rights: The Unique Contribution of the UN's*

Independent Experts on Human Rights, Final Report of the Brookings Research Project on Strengthening U.N. Special Procedures (Washington, DC: The Brookings Institution, 2010).

8. Ibid., ix.

9. The Brookings study found that of a total of 8,713 communications issued by seventeen thematic mandate holders between 2004 and 2008, 58.56 percent received either no reply or an immaterial reply. According to the Office of the High Commissioner on Human Rights, a quarter of all communications sent by the special procedures in 2009 were directed to just five countries: Iran, Mexico, China, Sri Lanka, and Colombia. The special rapporteur on human rights defenders—established in 2000 to help protect local advocates for human rights who may be under threat—typically sends the most communications, sending almost five hundred in 2008 alone. Large numbers of urgent actions are also typically sent by the special rapporteurs on freedom of expression (more than four hundred in 2008), torture (more than two hundred), and summary executions (more than one hundred).

10. Author interview with Manfred Nowak, UN special rapporteur on torture, October 29, 2010.

11. Karapatan, *Karapatan Monitor* April–June 2010. Available at http://www.karapatan.org/Karapatan-Monitor-AprJun-2010 (accessed January 29, 2011). Estimates of the number of killings vary substantially. The *Philippines Daily Inquirer* reported 299 killings between October 2001 and April 2007; the Task Force Utig, an investigative body of the Philippines National Police, found 115 cases of "slain party list/militant members" and 26 members of the media killed between 2001 and 2006.

12. Major General Jovito Palparan, quoted in Fe B. Zamora, "In his all-out war against the reds, this General dubbed the butcher claims conscience is the least of his concerns," *Sunday Inquirer Magazine*, July 2, 2006; "Palparan: Leftists Making Me Symbol of Military Abuses," *Philippine Daily Inquirer*, October 28, 2005, A1; "General Palparan: Leftist Rebellion Can Be Solved in 2 Years," *Agence France Presse*, February 2, 2006.

13. Karapatan, *Karapatan Monitor* April–June 2010. Amnesty International estimated that at least fifty extrajudicial executions took place during the first six months of 2006, compared to sixty-six documented by the organization in all of 2005. See Amnesty International, *Philippines: Political Killings, Human Rights, and the Peace Process* (London: Amnesty International, 2006), 3.

14. Independent Commission to Address Media and Activist Killings, *Report*, January 22, 2007, 53. Available at http://www.pinoyhr.net/reports/meloreport.pdf (accessed January 29, 2011).

15. Author interview with Cookie Diokno, secretary-general, Free Legal Assistance Group, October 7, 2010.

16. Philip Alston, Report of the Special Rapporteur on Extrajudicial, Summary or Arbitrary Executions, Addendum, Mission to the Philippines, A/HRC/8/3/Add.2, April 16, 2008.

17. Philip Alston, "Extrajudicial killings have a corrosive effect on civil society and

political discourse in the Philippines, says UN independent expert at the end of visit," press statement, Manila, February 22, 2007. Available at http://www.ohchr.org/EN /NewsEvents/Pages/DisplayNews.aspx?NewsID=8022&LangID=E (accessed on January 29, 2011).

18. Philip Alston, Report of the Special Rapporteur on Extrajudicial, Summary, or Arbitrary Executions, Addendum, Mission to the Philippines, A/HRC/8/3/Add.2, April 16, 2008.

19. Author interview with Cookie Diokno, October 7, 2010.

20. Author interview with Philip Alston, September 20, 2010.

21. Veronica Uy, "UN Exec to RP: Admit Extrajudicial Killings Are Happening: Many Murders 'Convincingly Attributed' to Military," *Inquirer.net*, February 21, 2007. Available at http://newsinfo.inquirer.net/topstories/topstories/view/20070221-50791/ UN_exec_to_RP%3A_Admit_extrajudicial_killings_are_happening (accessed January 29, 2011).

22. Author interview with Cookie Diokno, October 7, 2010.

23. Philip Alston, "Preliminary Note on the Visit of the Special Rapporteur on Extrajudicial, Summary, or Arbitrary Executions, Philip Alston, to the Philippines (February 12–21, 2007), A/HRC/4/20/Add.3, March 22, 2007; Philip Alston, Report of the Special Rapporteur on Extrajudicial, Summary, or Arbitrary Executions, Addendum, Mission to the Philippines, A/HRC/8/3/Add.2, April 16, 2008.

24. Karapatan, *Karapatan Monitor*, April–June 2010; see also Philip Alston, "Report of the Special Rapporteur on Extrajudicial, Summary, or Arbitrary Executions, Philip Alston, Addendum, Follow-up to Country Recommendations, Philippines," A/HRC/11/2/Add.8, April 29, 2009.

25. Ibid.

26. Human Rights Watch, "The Philippines," *World Report 2010* (New York: Human Rights Watch, 2010).

27. Philip Alston, "Report of the Special Rapporteur on Extrajudicial, Summary, or Arbitrary Executions, Philip Alston, Addendum, Follow-up to Country Recommendations, Philippines," A/HRC/11/2/Add.8, April 29, 2009.

28. Human Rights Watch, "The Philippines," *World Report 2010* (New York: Human Rights Watch, 2010).

29. Human Rights Watch, letter to President Aquino regarding extrajudicial killings in the Philippines, July 12, 2010. Available at http://www.hrw.org/en /news/2010/07/12/letter-president-aquino-regarding-extrajudicial-killings-philippines (accessed September 25, 2010).

30. Author interview with Philip Alston, September 20, 2010.

31. Ibid.

32. Ibid.

33. Author interview with Cookie Diokno, October 7, 2010.

34. Author interview with Philip Alston, September 20, 2010.

35. Article 68 of the Temporary Constitutional Provisions Act (1998).

36. Federal Decree no. 4.887 (2003).

37. Data from the National Institute for Colonization and Agrarian Reform (INCRA), available at http://www.incra.gov.br.

38. Active organizations included ACONERUQ (the Association of Rural Negro Quilombos Communities of Maranhao), SMDH (Maranhao Society of Human Rights), Polis Institute, and the Centre on Housing Rights and Evictions (COHRE).

39. COHRE, "The Situation on Human Rights in Traditional Negro Communities in Alcântara," Geneva, 2003.

40. COHRE, Brazil Quilombos Project, COHRE website, available at http://www .cohre.org (accessed September 14, 2010).

41. Report of the Special Rapporteur on Adequate Housing as a Component of the Right to an Adequate Standard of Living, Miloon Kothari, Addendum, Mission to Brazil, February 18, 2005, E/CN.4/2005/48/Add.3.

42. Presidential decree dated August 27, 2004. The Interministerial Working Group included the Presidential Civic Affairs Office; Ministries of Science and Technology; Defense; Agrarian Development; Cities; Health; Education; Tourism; Planning; Culture; Environment; Agriculture; Energy and Mines; External Relations; Labour and Employment; Social Development and Hunger Combat; the Secretariat of Political Coordination; the Special Secretariat for Policies of Promotion of Racial Equality; the Special Secretariat for Water Use Improvement and Fisheries; the Special Secretariat for Human Rights; the Brazilian Space Agency; and the Air Force Command Structure.

43. Report of the Special Rapporteur on Adequate Housing as a Component of the Right to an Adequate Standard of Living, Miloon Kothari, Addendum, Mission to Brazil, February 18, 2005, E/CN.4/2005/48/Add.3., para. 78.

44. Advisory Group of Forced Evictions, UN-Habitat, *Forced Evictions: Towards Solutions? First Report of the Advisory Group on Forced Evictions to the Executive Director of UN-HABITAT* (Nairobi: UN-Habitat, 2005), 80–81.

45. Report of the Special Rapporteur on Contemporary Forms of Racism, Racial Discrimination, Xenophobia and Related Intolerance, Doudou Diène, Addendum, Mission to Brazil, February 28, 2006, E/CN.4/2006/16/Add.3.

46. COHRE, "Forced Evictions and Violations of the Right to Adequate Housing and Land of Quilombo communities of Marambaia Island- Rio de Janeiro and Alcântara, MA/Brazil," Geneva, 2005.

47. Raquel Rolnik, "Brazil: Regression in Quilombo Communities' Rights Could Breach International Laws, Says UN Expert," press release, May 26, 2010. Available at http://www.ohchr.org/en/NewsEvents/Pages/DisplayNews.aspx?NewsID =10065&LangID=E (accessed January 29, 2011).

48. Combate ao Racismo Ambiental: O Estatuto da Igualdade Racial em Entrevista com Damião Braga ("The Statute of Racial Equality in Interview with Damião Braga"), June 22, 2010. Available at http://racismoambiental.net.br/2010/06/o-estatuto-da-igualdade-racial-em-entrevista-com-damiao-braga/ (accessed January 29, 2011).

49. Convention Concerning Indigenous and Tribal Peoples in Independent Countries, ILO Convention 169 (1989).

50. Author interview with Sean T. Mitchell, assistant professor of anthropology, Rutgers University, November 16, 2010.

51. National Centre for Human Rights, *Status Report of Human Rights, Hashimite Kingdom of Jordan 2005* (Amman: NCHR, 2006). Available at www.nchr.org.jo (accessed September 13, 2010).

52. National Centre for Human Rights, *Third and Fourth Periodical Reports on Reform and Rehabilitation Centres in Jordan* (Amman: NCHR, 2005 and 2006). Available at www.nchr.org.jo (accessed September 13, 2010).

53. Cited in Amnesty International, *Jordan: "Your Confessions Are Ready for You to Sign": Detention and Torture of Political Suspects* (London: Amnesty International, 2006), 49.

54. Amnesty International published at least nine reports or other documents on the treatment of detainees in Jordan between 1986 and 2006.

55. Interview with Tania Baldwin-Park, Amnesty International, August 24, 2009.

56. Report of the Special Rapporteur on Torture and Other Cruel, Inhuman, or Degrading Treatment or Punishment, Manfred Nowak, Addendum, Mission to Jordan, January 5, 2007, A/HRC/4/33/Add.3.

57. Ibid., para. 8.

58. Ibid.

59. Ibid., para. 9.

60. Author interview with Manfred Nowak, October 29, 2010.

61. Amnesty International, *Jordan: "Your Confessions Are Ready for You to Sign."*

62. National Centre for Human Rights, *Fourth Periodical Reports on Reform and Rehabilitation Centres in Jordan.*

63. Piccone, *Catalysts for Rights,* ix.

64. Paulo Sérgio Pinheiro, "Musings of a UN Special Rapporteur on Human Rights," *Global Governance* 9 (2003), 7–13.

65. Author interview with Manfred Nowak, October 29, 2010.

66. Author interview with Mara Bustelo, coordinator of human rights and economic and social issues, Office of the High Commissioner for Human Rights, September 22, 2009.

67. Office of the High Commissioner for Human Rights, "United Nations Special Procedures: Facts and Figures 2010."

68. Philip Alston, Report of the Special Rapporteur on Extrajudicial, Summary, or Arbitrary Executions, Philip Alston, A/HRC/14/24, May 20, 2010.

69. Author interview with Manfred Nowak, October 29, 2010.

70. According to Karapatan, under the Philippines' new president, Benigno Aquino III, 55 extrajudicial executions were reported between July 2010 and September 2011, compared to 235 in 2006. *Karapatan Monitor,* July–September 2011. Available at http://www.karapatan.org/Karapatan-Monitor-3rdQuarter-Jul-Sept2011 (accessed January 2, 2012).

71. Human Rights Watch, "Philippines: New Killings as Impunity Reigns," press

release, July 18, 2011. Available at http://www.hrw.org/news/2011/07/18/philippines -new-killings-impunity-reigns (accessed January 2, 2012).

72. Ibid.

73. Interview with Mara Bustelo, September 22, 2009.

Chapter 5

1. United Nations, *Report of the Independent Expert for the United Nations Study on Violence Against Children*. Promotion and Protection of the Rights of Children. United Nations General Assembly, 61st session. A/61/299. 2006.

2. Global Initiative to End All Corporal Punishment of Children. Available at http:// www.endcorporalpunishment.org/pages/frame.html (accessed October 21, 2010).

3. Penal Reform International and Advocacy Forum, *Assessment of Children and Young Persons in Prisons, Correction Home and Police Custody in Nepal, Juvenile Justice in Nepal Series 2, (*Kathmandu: UNICEF, 2006).

4. International Save the Children Alliance, *A Last Resort: The Growing Concern About Children in Residential Care* (London: Save the Children UK, 2003); Barth RP, *Institutions vs. Foster Homes: The Empirical Base for a Century of Action* (Chapel Hill: University of North Carolina School of Social Work, Jordan Institute for Families, 2002); Human Rights Watch, *Abandoned to the State: Cruelty and Neglect in Russian Orphanages* (New York: Human Rights Watch, 1998).

5. See Chapter 4 for a more complete discussion regarding the role of UN special rapporteurs.

6. Author interview with Roberta Cecchetti, NGO Advisory Council for Follow-up to the UN Study on Violence Against Children, October 15, 2010.

7. General Assembly resolution, A/48/157, adopted December 20, 1993.

8. General Assembly resolution A/51/306, adopted August 26, 1996.

9. Author interview with Roberta Cecchetti, October 15, 2010.

10. Human Rights Watch, *Easy Targets: Violence Against Children Worldwide* (New York: Human Rights Watch, 2001).

11. General Assembly resolution A/Res/56/138, adopted December 19, 2001.

12. Author interview with Roberta Cecchetti, October 15, 2010.

13. Karen Emmons, "Thailand: Regional Conference on Violence against Children," press release, UNICEF, June 14, 2005. Available at http://www.unicef.org /infobycountry/Thailand_27408.html (accessed January 28, 2011).

14. Jo Becker of Human Rights Watch and Peter Newell of the Global Initiative to End All Corporal Punishment of Children.

15. *Report of the Independent Expert*, A/61/299.

16. Paulo Sérgio Pinheiro, *World Report on Violence Against Children* (Geneva: UN Secretary-General's Study on Violence Against Children, 2006).

17. Ibid., XI.

18. The first SRSG on children and armed conflict, Olara Otunnu, served from 1998 to 2005; Radhika Coomaraswamy was appointed as SRSG on children and armed conflict in 2006.

19. The new body, named the NGO Advisory Council for follow-up to the UN Study on Violence Against Children, included nine international NGOs and nine regional representatives. The previous NGO Advisory Panel was disbanded, as its mandate—to support the study process—was complete.

20. Statement to the UN General Assembly Third Committee from the NGO Advisory Panel for the UN Secretary-General's Study on Violence Against Children, October 11, 2006. Available at http://www.crin.org/resources/infodetail.asp?id=10654 (accessed January 28, 2011).

21. Author interview with Peter Newell, Global Initiative to End All Corporal Punishment of Children, October 14, 2010.

22. Author interview with Cristina Barbaglia, former consultant, NGO Advisory Council for Follow-up to the UN Study on Violence Against Children, September 16, 2010.

23. General Assembly Resolution A/Res/62/141, adopted December 18, 2007.

24. Human Rights Council resolution 7/29, adopted March 28, 2008.

25. General Assembly Resolution A/63/241, adopted December 24, 2008.

26. Human Rights Council resolution 10/14, adopted March 26, 2009.

27. Global Initiative to End All Corporal Punishment of Children. Available at www.endcorporalpunishment.org (accessed December 31, 2011).

28. Ironically, although many member states argued in 1999 that the UN system already had too many special rapporteurs as a reason not to create one devoted to violence against children, the Commission on Human Rights and its successor, the Human Rights Council, created eighteen more such mandates over the following decade, nearly doubling the number of special rapporteurs between 2000 and 2010.

29. Author interview with Roberta Cecchetti, October 15, 2010.

30. Ibid.

31. Author interview with Peter Newell, October 14, 2010.

32. Author interview with Cristina Barbaglia, September 16, 2010.

33. Ibid.

34. Author interview with Peter Newell, October 14, 2010.

35. Ibid.

36. Ibid.

37. NGO Advisory Council for Follow-up to the UN Study on Violence Against Children, *Five Years On: A global Update on Violence Against Children* (New York: NGO Advisory Council, 2011), 2.

38. Ibid.

Chapter 6

1. Author interview with Sulaiman Jabati, executive secretary, Coalition for Justice and Accountability, Sierra Leone, May 20, 2010.

2. Panel of Experts on Sierra Leone Diamonds and Arms, Report of the Panel of Experts appointed pursuant to Security Council resolution 1306 (2000), para. 19, in relation to Sierra Leone, S/2000/1195, December 20, 2000.

3. Security Council resolution 1306, adopted July 5, 2000.

4. Ibid.

5. In March 2006, the indictment was amended from seventeen to eleven counts of war crimes, crimes against humanity, and other violations of international humanitarian law.

6. David Mafabi, Global Pan African Movement, in Campaign Against Impunity, "Liberian Elections and Charles Taylor," statement, September 1, 2005. Available at http://www.refugee-rights.org/Newsletters/WestAfrica/Taylor090105.htm (accessed January 29, 2011).

7. Author interview with Eric Witte, former political advisor and special assistant to the prosecutor, Special Court for Sierra Leone, January 3, 2012.

8. Open Society Justice Initiative, "Civil Society Pressure: Ending Charles Taylor's Asylum," Annual Report 2007 (New York: Open Society Justice Initiative, 2007). Available at http://www.justiceinitiative.org/db/resource2?res_id=102870, (accessed December 11, 2010).

9. Ibid.

10. Ibid.

11. International members included Amnesty International, Human Rights Watch, the Open Society Justice Initiative, and the Amputees Rehabilitation Foundation.

12. Author interview with Ayodele Ameen, campaign officer, Africa Programme, Amnesty International, May 27, 2010.

13. Ibid.

14. Author interview with Corinne Dufka, senior researcher, Human Rights Watch, August 24, 2009.

15. Campaign Against Impunity, "Sierra Leone: UN rights chief should call for Taylor's surrender," press release, July 13, 2005. Available at http://www.amnesty.org.au/news/comments/899/ (accessed January 29, 2011).

16. Ibid.

17. "UN Rights Chief Favors Taylor Handover to Sierra Leone War Crimes Court," Liberian Observer, July 13, 2005. Available at http://allafrica.com/stories/200507140798.html (accessed January 29, 2011).

18. Author interview with Ayodele Ameen, May 27, 2010.

19. Author interview with Aloysius Toe, director, Foundation for Human Rights and Democracy, May 27, 2010.

20. "Communiqué of the Special Summit of Heads of State and Government of the Mano River Union—28th July 2005," cited in International Crisis Group, Liberia's Elections: Necessary but Not Sufficient (Brussels: ICG, 2005), 9.

21. Kenneth Roth speech at the Global Philanthropy Forum, Redwood City, California, April 10, 2008. Transcript available at http://www.philanthropyforum.org/images/forum/2008Conference/Collateral/GPF_ConferenceTranscript_Book_2008.pdf (accessed January 29, 2011).

22. Author interview with Eric Witte, January 3, 2012.

23. Author interview with Ayodele Ameen, May 27, 2010.

24. Statement by Chidi Anselm Odinkalu, "We Are Not Fugitives, Charles Taylor Is," August 3, 2005, in Open Society Justice Initiative, "Civil Society Pressure."

25. Author interview with Elise Keppler, senior counsel, International Justice Program, Human Rights Watch, December 12, 2009.

26. S/RES/1610 (2005), Security Council resolution 1610, adopted June 30, 2005.

27. Email communication, July 8, 2005. Author's files.

28. Security Council Resolution S/RES/1638, adopted November 11, 2005.

29. Author interview with Alyosius Toe, May 27, 2010.

30. "Taylor 'Not a Priority' for Liberia," BBC, January 27, 2006. Available at http://news.bbc.co.uk/2/hi/africa/4655186.stm (accessed January 29, 2011).

31. Ibid.

32. Author interview with Aloysius Toe, May 27, 2010.

33. Ibid.

34. Ibid.

35. Ibid.

36. European Parliament, "European Parliament Resolution on the Special Court for Sierra Leone: The Case of Charles Taylor," RSP/2005/2516, adopted February 24, 2005.

37. Human Rights Watch, "EU: Press Nigeria to Hand Over Charles Taylor," press release, February 24, 2005. Available at http://www.hrw.org/en/news/2005/02/24/eu-press-nigeria-hand-over-charles-taylor (accessed January 29, 2011).

38. Author interview with Eric Witte, January 3, 2012.

39. H.Con.Res.127, introduced by Rep. Ed Royce (R-CA). The bill was adopted by a vote of 421 to 1 on May 4, 2005, in the House of Representatives, and adopted by unanimous consent in the US Senate on May 11, 2005.

40. Foreign Operations, Export Financing and Related Programs Appropriations Act, 2006, Public Law 109–102–Nov. 14, 2005.

41. Letter to Secretary Condoleeza Rice, December 13, 2005, signed by Rep. Ed Royce (R-CA), Rep. Henry Hyde (R-IL), Sen. Lincoln Chafee (R-RI), Rep. Betty McCollum (D-MN), Sen. Patrick Leahy (D-VT), Rep. Frank Wolf (R-VA), Sen. Barack Obama (D-IL), Sen. Jack Reed (D-RI), Rep. Vic Snyder (D-AR), Rep. Sue Kelly (R-NY), Rep. Dianne Watson (D-CA), Sen. Russ Feingold (D-WI), and Rep. Chris Smith (R-NJ).

42. Author interview with Aloysius Toe, May 27, 2010.

43. PBS Newshour with Jim Lehrer, "Interview Between Johnson Sirleaf and Margaret Warner," March 23, 2006. Available at http://www.pbs.org/newshour/bb/africa/jan-june06/liberia_3-23.html (accessed July 21, 2010).

44. Email communication from Dufka to author, January 6, 2012. Author's files.

45. Author interview with Corinne Dufka, August 24, 2009.

46. "Nigeria to Give Up Charles Taylor," BBC, March 25, 2006. Available at http://news.bbc.co.uk/2/hi/africa/4845088.stm (accessed January 29, 2011).

47. Ibid.

48. Email communication from Dufka to author, January 6, 2012. Author's files.

49. A statement from Barack Obama on Charles Taylor, March 28, 2006, said "The inability of the Government of Nigeria to provide adequate security around the residence of Charles Taylor, one of the world's worst war criminals, is inexcusable. President Bush should cancel tomorrow's meeting with President Obasanjo, in order to send a clear message that the United States stands unequivocally for bringing Charles Taylor to justice." At a Senate Appropriations Subcommittee hearing, Senator Patrick Leahy said to Secretary of State Condoleezza Rice that he believed that Obasanjo bore responsibility for letting Taylor escape and that the United States should cancel Bush's meeting with Obasanjo "until Taylor is in the custody of the court where he belongs." Voice of America, "US 'Deeply Concerned' by Reports of Taylor Disappearance," March 28, 2006. Available at http://www.voanews.com /english/news/a-13-2006-03-28-voa66.html (accessed January 29, 2011).

50. State Department Daily Press Briefing, March 27, 2006. Transcript available at http://2001-2009.state.gov/r/pa/prs/dpb/2006/63728.htm (accessed January 29, 2011).

51. Clarence Roy-Macauley, "Taylor to Be Tried on War Crimes Charges," Associated Press, March 29, 2006. Available at http://www.usatoday.com/news/world/2006 -03-29-liberia-taylor_x.htm (accessed December 30, 2011).

52. UN Secretary-General statement to CNN and UNTV, March 29, 2006. Transcript available at http://www.un.org/apps/sg/offthecuff.asp?nid=857 (accessed January 29, 2011).

53. Author interview with Ayodele Ameen, May 27, 2010.

54. Ibid.

55. "Trial Sought for Ex-Leader of Liberia," Associated Press, April 10, 2005.

56. Author interview with Aloysius Toe, May 27, 2010.

57. Author interview with Elise Keppler, December 12, 2009.

58. Author interview with Elise Keppler, December 22, 2011.

59. Author interview with Eric Witte, January 3, 2012.

60. Author interview with Ayodele Ameen, May 27, 2010.

61. Ibid.

62. Author interview with Eric Witte, January 3, 2012.

63. Author interview with Ayodele Ameen, May 27, 2010.

64. Author interview with Sulaiman Jabati, May 20, 2010.

Chapter 7

1. Statement by Mohamed Hamil Ferjany to Heba Morayef, August 2009. Email communication with the author, May 2010.

2. Report of the Special Rapporteur, Sir. Nigel S. Rodley, to the UN Commission on Human Rights, E/CN.4/1999/61, January 12, 1999.

3. For accounts of the Abu Salim massacre, see Human Rights Solidarity, *Abuslim* (Geneva: Human Rights Solidarity, 2009); Amnesty International, *Libya: Time to Make Human Rights a Reality* (London: Amnesty International, 2004) (AI Index MDE 19/002/2004), 54–56; Amnesty International, *Libya of Tomorrow: What Hope for Human Rights?* (London: Amnesty International, 2010) (AI Index MDE 19/007/2010),

68–83; and *Human Rights Watch, Truth and Justice Can't Wait: Human Rights Developments in Libya Amid Institutional Obstacles* (New York: Human Rights Watch, 2009), 46–48.

4. Al-Shafa'I, cited in Human Rights Watch, *Truth and Justice Can't Wait*, 48.

5. Author interview with Edriss El Hassy, July 8, 2010.

6. Author interview with Giumma El Omami, Libya Human Rights Solidarity, March 19, 2010.

7. See UN Security Council resolutions S/RES/731, adopted January 21, 1992; S/RES/748, adopted March 31, 1992; and S/RES/883, adopted November 11, 1993.

8. UN Security Council Resolution S/RES/1506, adopted September 12, 2003.

9. Some affiliated with the Gaddafi Charitable Foundation.

10. Human Rights Watch interview, cited in *Truth and Justice Can't Wait*, 20.

11. The optional protocol to the International Covenant on Civil and Political Rights allows individuals to file individual complaints to the Human Rights Committee in cases when they have exhausted all domestic remedies, or that such remedies are not available. Libya acceded to the Covenant in 1970 and the optional protocol in 1989.

12. Communication no. 1295/2004, Farag Mohammed El Alwani v. Libyan Arab Jamahiriya, Views adopted by the Human Rights Committee on July 11, 2007, paras. 2–2.4, CCPR/C/90/D/1295/2004, issued August 29, 2007.

13. Ibid.

14. Ibid.

15. Communication no. 1422/2005, Edriss El Hassy v. Libyan Arab Jamahiriya, para. 3.2.

16. Author interview with Heba Morayef, researcher, Middle East and North Africa Division, Human Rights Watch, January 15, 2010.

17. North Benghazi Primary Court Ruling, Case no. 5/2007, June 8, 2008.

18. Author interview with Giumma El Omami, March 19, 2010.

19. Statement by Mohamed Hamil Ferjany to Heba Morayef, August 2009. Email communication with the author, May 2010.

20. Author interview with Heba Morayef, January 15, 2010.

21. Author interview with Giumma El Omami, March 19, 2010.

22. Ibid.

23. Amnesty International, *Libya of Tomorrow*, 82.

24. "Libya: Families of Victims of the Abu Salim Prison Massacre Targeted in Attack," Alkarama, April 19, 2010. Available at http://en.alkarama.org/index.php?option=com_content&view=article&id=501:libya-families-of-victims-of-the-abu-salim-prison-massacre-targeted-in-attack&catid=27:communiqu&Itemid=138 (accessed July 26, 2010).

25. Human Rights Watch, *Truth and Justice Can't Wait*, 52–53.

26. Email communication with Libya Human Rights Solidarity, July 24, 2010.

27. Human Rights Watch, *Truth and Justice Can't Wait*, 54.

28. Ibid., 55.

29. Mother of a deceased prisoner, recorded statement provided by Libya Human Rights Solidarity, March 19, 2010.

30. Human Rights Watch interview with Counselor Mostafa Abdeljalil, Secretary of Justice, Tripoli, April 26, 2009, cited in Human Rights Watch, *Truth and Justice Can't Wait*, 55.

31. Amnesty International, *Libya of Tomorrow: What Hope for Human Rights?*, 77.

32. See www.libya-al-mostakbal.org (Libya Future).

33. Author interview with Giumma El Omami, March 19, 2010.

34. Amnesty International, *Libya of Tomorrow: What Hope for Human Rights?*, 80.

35. Ibid., 81.

36. Author interview with Heba Morayef, January 15, 2010.

37. Email communication from Libya Human Rights Solidarity, July 25, 2010.

38. Human Rights Society, *Statement by the Human Rights Society in Solidarity with the Abu Salim Victims' Families*, November 24, 2009. Available at http://gdf.org.ly/index.php?lang=en&CAT_NO=4&MAIN_CAT_NO=4&Page=105&DATA_NO=591 (accessed July 24, 2010).

39. Human Rights Society, *The Human Rights Society's Annual Report*, December 20, 2009. Available at http://www.gicdf.org/index.php?option=com_content&view=article&id=174:the-human-rights-societys-annual-report&catid=3:the-news&Itemid=55 (accessed July 24, 2010).

40. Speech entitled "Libya: Truth for All," July 24, 2008, cited in Amnesty International, *Libya of Tomorrow: What Hope for Human Rights?*, 78.

41. Amnesty International, *Libya of Tomorrow: What Hope for Human Rights?*, 73.

42. Author interview with Edriss El Hassy, July 8, 2010.

43. The Working Group on Enforced or Involuntary Disappearances accepts cases from any country "on a purely humanitarian basis," regardless of whether the government concerned has ratified the International Convention for the Protection of All Persons from Enforced Disappearance or other legal instruments which allow an individual complaints procedures.

44. Author interview with Giumma El Omami, March 19, 2010.

45. See http://www.lhrs.ch/english/default.asp.

46. Amnesty International, *Libya of Tomorrow*, 14–15.

47. Heba Morayef, "Is Libya Opening Up?" *The Guardian*, January 5, 2010. Available at http://www.guardian.co.uk/commentisfree/libertycentral/2010/jan/04/libya-human-rights-reform (accessed January 29, 2011).

48. Author interview with Heba Morayef, January 15, 2010.

49. Ibid.

50. Ibid.

51. Email communication from Libya Human Rights Solidarity, July 24, 2010.

52. Author interview with Giumma El Omami, September 10, 2011.

53. Ibid.

54. Lindsay Hilsum, "Meeting the Families Left Behind by Gaddafi's Prison Massacre," Channel 4 News, March 1, 2011. Available at http://blogs.channel4.com/

world-news-blog/meeting-the-families-left-behind-by-gaddafis-prison-massacre/15306 (accessed August 26, 2011).

55. Al Jazeera, "Gaddafi's Son in Civil War Warning," February 21, 2011.

56. Thomas Erdbrink, "Libyans Find Freedom at Moammar Gaddafi's Abu Salim Prison in Tripoli," *Washington Post*, August 26, 2011.

57. Author interview with Giumma El Omami, September 10, 2011.

58. Khaled Saleh, Human Rights Solidarity, quoted in Martin Chulov and David Smith, "Search for Tripoli Prison Massacre Victims Seeks to Heal Old Wounds," *The Guardian*, September 9, 2011. Available at http://www.guardian.co.uk/world/2011/sep/09/search-victims-tripoli-prison-massacre (accessed September 10, 2011).

59. Author interview with Giumma El Omami, March 19, 2010.

60. Author interview with Edriss El Hassy, July 8, 2010.

61. Author interview with Giumma El Omami, March 19, 2010.

62. Author interview with Edriss El Hassy, July 8, 2010.

63. Amnesty International, *Libya of Tomorrow*, 9.

64. Author interview with Giumma El Omami, March 19, 2010.

65. Author interview with Heba Morayef, January 15, 2010.

66. Amnesty International, *Libya of Tomorrow*, 81–82.

67. Al Arabiya News, "Gaddafi's Son Warns of 'Rivers of Blood' in Libya," February 21, 2011. Available at http://www.alarabiya.net/articles/2011/02/21/138515.html (accessed August 28, 2011).

68. Author interview with Giumma El Omami, September 10, 2011.

Chapter 8

1. Human Rights Watch, "Sri Lanka: 'Boat People' Recount Horrors of No-Fire Zone," press release, May 5, 2009. Available at http://www.hrw.org/en/features/sri-lanka-boat-people-recount-horrors (accessed January 30, 2011).

2. United Nations, *Report of the Secretary-General's Panel of Experts on Accountability in Sri Lanka* (New York: United Nations, March 2011), 36.

3. Ibid., 28.

4. See Human Rights Watch, "Sri Lanka: Repeated Shelling of Hospitals Evidence of War Crimes," press release, May 8, 2009. Available at http://www.hrw.org/en/news/2009/05/08/sri-lanka-repeated-shelling-hospitals-evidence-war-crimes (accessed January 30, 2011).

5. John Holmes, "Let Them Decide: Civilians Trapped with Tamil Tiger Fighters Must Be Offered an Exit Before a Bloodbath Ensues," *The Guardian*, April 8, 2009. Available at http://www.guardian.co.uk/commentisfree/2009/apr/08/tamil-protests-sri-lanka-john-holmes (accessed January 30, 2011).

6. United Nations, *Report of the Secretary-General's Panel of Experts on Accountability in Sri Lanka* (New York: United Nations, March 2011), 36.

7. Sri Lankan army officer testimony to Channel 4, "Sri Lanka 'War Crimes' Soldiers Ordered to 'Finish the Job,'" broadcast July 27, 2011. Available at http://

www.channel4.com/news/sri-lanka-war-crimes-soldiers-ordered-to-finish-the-job (accessed July 28, 2011).

8. Ibid., 48.

9. Amnesty's research encompassed rape and torture in custody, abductions, politically motivated killings, violations related to emergency regulations, the plight of internationally displaced, and the failure of commissions of inquiry to investigate and bring to justice those responsible for human rights violations. Human Rights Watch's reports documented the involvement of Sri Lankan government forces in forced disappearances and extrajudicial executions, as well as the Tamil Tigers' political killings, recruitment of child soldiers, and its use of extortion in Tamil communities in Canada and the UK to pay for its war effort. ICG published on the failed peace process, the impact of the war on Sri Lanka's Muslims, Sinhala nationalism, and other issues. See www.hrw.org; www.amnesty.org; and www.crisisgroup.org.

10. Author interview with Alan Keenan, Sri Lanka project director and senior analyst, International Crisis Group, December 17, 2010.

11. Author interview with Brad Adams, executive director, Asia Division, Human Rights Watch, July 27, 2011.

12. Statement by Rajiva Wijesinha, secretary-general of the Secretariat for Coordinating the Peace Process (SCOPP), "An Amnesty for the Tigers," April 8, 2009. Available at http://www.peaceinsrilanka.org/press-releases-details/press-releases-details/2199 (accessed January 30, 2011).

13. Chandrani Gunaratna, "Human Rights Watch's War on Sri Lanka," May 11, 2009. Available at http://www.defence.lk/new.asp?fname=20090511_09 (accessed January 30, 2011).

14. The sessions were held on February 27, March 26, April 22, and May 13, 2009.

15. As of September 2007, Japan had signed agreements with Sri Lanka for approximately US$1.7 billion in donor funding, including water and sanitation, transportation, power, health, agriculture, and rural development. World Bank, *Sri Lanka Country Assistance Strategy 2009–2012* (Washington, DC: World Bank, 2008), 102–3.

16. Amnesty International, Human Rights Watch, International Crisis Group, Global Center for the Responsibility to Protect, "Joint Letter to Japanese Prime Minister on Sri Lanka," May 10, 2009. Available at http://www.hrw.org/en/news/2009/05/10/joint-letter-japanese-prime-minister-sri-lanka (accessed January 30, 2011).

17. "'Steep Rise' in Sri Lanka Deaths," BBC, May 10, 2009. Available at http://news.bbc.co.uk/2/hi/south_asia/8042341.stm (accessed January 30, 2011).

18. Author interview with Brad Adams, July 27, 2011.

19. Statement attributable to the spokesperson for the secretary-general on Sri Lanka, New York, May 11, 2009. Available at http://www.un.org/apps/sg/sgstats.asp?nid=3839 (accessed January 30, 2011).

20. Security Council press statement SC/9659, May 13, 2009.

21. Human Rights Council resolution A/HRC/S-11/2, May 27, 2009.

22. "Sri Lanka Praises UN Human Rights Council Resolution," *Earthtimes*, May 28, 2009, citing Sri Lanka's *Daily News*. Available at http://www.earthtimes.org

/articles/news/270698,sri-lanka-praises-un-human-rights-council-resolution.html (accessed January 30, 2011).

23. Telephone conversation between UN official (Colombo) and the author, June 19, 2009. Author's files.

24. The mandate of the IMF is to promote international monetary cooperation and exchange rate stability, facilitate the balanced growth of international trade, and provide resources to help members in balance of payments difficulties or to assist with poverty reduction. See www.imf.org.

25. Central Bank of Sri Lanka, "Sri Lanka Commences Negotiations with IMF for a Stand-by Arrangement for US\$ 1,900 Million," press release, March 4, 2009. Available at http://www.cbsl.gov.lk/htm/english/02_prs/p_1.asp?yr=2009 (accessed January 30, 2011).

26. A June 5, 2009, letter to Secretary of State Hillary Clinton from Senators Patrick Leahy and Robert Casey said that to approve the loan "would suggest that to gain international support, the Sri Lankan government did not need to heed the world community's concerns, it merely needed to win the war."

27. Peter Apps, "Analysis: Sri Lanka IMF War Row Shows Geopolitics Matters," Reuters, May 15, 2009. Available at http://www.reuters.com/article/2009/05/16/us-imf-geopolitics-srilanka-analysis-sb-idUSTRE54E3SA20090516 (accessed January 30, 2011); Louis Charbonneau, "Britain 'Appalled' by Civilian Deaths in Sri Lanka," Reuters, May 11, 2009. Available at http://www.reuters.com/article/2009/05/11/idUSN11531687 (accessed January 30, 2011).

28. Telephone conversation between IMF official and author, May 2009.

29. Human Rights Watch, "Sri Lanka: IMF Should Not Condone Abuses," press release, July 22, 2009. Available at http://www.hrw.org/en/news/2009/07/22/sri-lanka-imf-should-not-condone-abuses (accessed January 30, 2011).

30. The UK issued a statement saying that it remained concerned with the humanitarian situation in the IDP camps, and that its objectives for Sri Lanka included reconciliation and a fully inclusive political settlement. On July 24, 2009, a US Treasury spokesperson said that the US position "was based on an assessment, in the current circumstances, of the ability and commitment of the government to carry out necessary policy adjustments during an IMF program."

31. In 2009, the United States held 16.77 percent, Germany 5.88 percent, France and the UK each held 4.88 percent, and Argentina held 0.97 percent.

32. Joint explanatory statement accompanying the Supplemental Appropriations Act, 2009 (P.L. 111–32).

33. US Department of State, *Report to Congress on Incidents During the Recent Conflict in Sri Lanka* (Washington, DC: US Department of State, 2009).

34. Amnesty International, "Call on UN to Investigate Sri Lanka Rights Violations," Action, May 17, 2010. Available at http://www.amnesty.org/en/appeals-for-action/call-un-investigate-sri-lanka-rights-violations (accessed January 30, 2011).

35. International Crisis Group, *War Crimes in Sri Lanka*, 6.

36. Ibid., 29.

37. Ibid., ii–iii.

38. Author interview with Alan Keenan, December 17, 2010.

39. Ibid.

40. Louis Arbour, "Sri Lanka Still Demands Justice," *Global Post*, June 8, 2010. Available at http://www.globalpost.com/dispatch/worldview/100607/sri-lanka -war-government-tamil-tigers (accessed January 30, 2011).

41. International Crisis Group, *War Crimes in Sri Lanka*, 29.

42. Author interview with Alan Keenan, December 17, 2010.

43. Government of Sri Lanka, "President Appoints Lessons Learnt and Reconciliation Commission," press release, May 17, 2010. Available at http://www.priu.gov .lk/news_update/Current_Affairs/ca201005/20100517president_appoints_lessons_ learnt_reconciliation_commission.htm (accessed January 30, 2011).

44. Human Rights Watch, "Sri Lanka: Government Proposal Won't Address War Crimes," press release, May 7, 2010. Available at http://www.hrw.org/en /news/2010/05/07/sri-lanka-government-proposal-won-t-address-war-crimes (accessed January 30, 2011).

45. Amnesty International, *Twenty Years of Make-Believe: Sri Lanka's Commissions of Inquiry* (London: Amnesty International, 2009), 3.

46. Amnesty International, Human Rights Watch, International Crisis Group, "Letter to S.M. Samarakoon, Secretary, Commission of Inquiry on Lessons Learnt and Reconciliation," October 14, 2010. Available at http://www.amnesty.org/en/library /asset/ASA37/015/2010/en/b8167216–c0aa-48be-99f8–bdcb5cab5d84/asa370152010en .pdf (accessed January 30, 2011).

47. Ibid.

48. Andrew Wander, "Fighting Impunity in Sri Lanka," Al Jazeera, May 18, 2010. Available at http://english.aljazeera.net/focus/2010/05/20105186355957306.html (accessed January 30, 2011).

49. Stephen Sackur and Katy Stoddard, "Sri Lanka Government Threatens to Execute Fonseka," *The Guardian*, June 6, 2010. Available at http://www.guardian.co.uk /world/2010/jun/06/sri-lanka-sarath-fonseka (accessed January 30, 2011).

50. Author interview with Yolanda Foster, August 1, 2011.

51. Government of Sri Lanka, "'Special Panel on Sri Lanka Uncalled for and Unwarranted'- President to Ban Ki-moon," press release, March 6, 2010. Available at http://www.lankamission.org/content/view/2688/9/ (accessed January 30, 2011).

52. UN News Centre, "Ban Appoints Panel to Advise on Human Rights Issues During Sri Lankan Conflict," statement, June 22, 2010. Available at http://www .un.org/apps/news/story.asp?NewsID=35099&Cr=lanka&Crl (accessed January 30, 2011). Ban appointed Marzuki Darusman of Indonesia as chair of the panel, together with Yasmin Sooka of South Africa and Steven Ratner of the United States. The experts were requested to examine "the modalities, applicable international standards and comparative experience with regard to accountability processes, taking into account the nature and scope of any alleged violations in Sri Lanka," and to conclude its work within four months.

53. United Nations, *Report of the Secretary-General's Panel of Experts on Accountability in Sri Lanka* (New York: United Nations, March 2011), ii.

54. Ibid., vii, 96.

55. Government of Sri Lanka, "Government Rejects Illegal Moon's Committee Report," April 19, 2011, statement. Available at http://www.news.lk/home/17911–government-rejects-illegal-moons-committee-report (accessed July 24, 2011).

56. Human Rights Watch, "Sri Lanka: UN Chief Should Establish International Inquiry," press release, April 25, 2011. Available at http://www.hrw.org/en/news/2011/04/25/sri-lanka-un-chief-should-establish-international-inquiry (accessed July 24, 2011).

57. Author interview with Yolanda Foster, August 1, 2011.

58. See Human Rights Watch, *Funding the Final War: LTTE Intimidation and Extortion in the Tamil Diaspora* (New York: Human Rights Watch, 2006).

59. See http://www.srilankademocracy.org/.

60. See www.cwvhr.org.

61. Australia, Belgium, Canada, Denmark, France, Germany, Italy, Netherlands, New Zealand, Norway, Sweden, and Switzerland.

62. "US Lawmakers Urge Sri Lanka Rights Probe," AFP, December 17, 2010. Available at http://www.google.com/hostednews/afp/article/ALeqM5hFPTPiyEm879DFP OQqrB-qOkMFGw?docId=CNG.56ebdf0712e722f2c904a46ee1aa03d3.c31 (accessed January 22, 2011); Senate Resolution 84, adopted March 2, 2011.

63. Author interview with Brad Adams, July 27, 2011.

64. Jyoti Thottam, "The Man Who Tamed the Tamil Tigers," Time.com, July 13, 2009. Available at http://www.time.com/time/world/article/0,8599,1910095,00.html (accessed January 30, 2011).

65. Author interview with Alan Keenan, December 17, 2010.

66. International Crisis Group reported in April 2009 that China and Iran were each funding over one billion US dollars' worth of projects in Sri Lanka. At the same time, most European donors, including the British, Germans, Swedes and Dutch had significantly reduced their bilateral aid. The reduction was in part because of concerns about human rights abuses, and in part because Sri Lanka had become considered a "middle-income" country. International Crisis Group, *Development Assistance and Conflict in Sri Lanka: Lessons from the Eastern Province,* Crisis Group Asia Report no. 165 (Brussels: ICG, 2009).

67. Jon Lee Anderson, "Death of the Tiger: Sri Lanka's Brutal Victory Over its Tamil Insurgents," *The New Yorker,* January 17, 2011, 48.

68. Author interview with Brad Adams, July 27, 2011.

69. See, for example, statements by Rajiva Wijesinha, secretary-general of the Secretariat for Coordinating the Peace Process (SCOPP), May 15, June 4, and July 27, 2009, www.peaceinsrilanka.org.

70. Author interview with Yolanda Foster, August 1, 2011.

71. "Sri Lanka Leader Hailed as King for Beating Rebels," Associated Press, June 3, 2009. Available at http://www.msnbc.msn.com/id/31087854/ns/world_news-south _and_central_asia/ (accessed January 30, 2011).

72. Author interview with Alan Keenan, December 17, 2010.

73. Author interview with Brad Adams, July 27, 2011.

74. Author interview with Yolanda Foster, August 1, 2011; email communication with James Ross, Legal and Policy Advisor, Human Rights Watch, June 5, 2011. Author's files.

75. Author interview with Alan Keenan, December 22, 2010.

76. Author interview with Brad Adams, July 27, 2011.

77. Author interview with Alan Keenan, December 22, 2010.

78. Author interview with Brad Adams, July 27, 2011.

Chapter 9

1. Author interview with Lhadon Thethong, February 3, 2010.

2. Free Tibet, "1959 Tibetan Uprising." Available at http://www.freetibet.org /about/1959–tibetan-uprising; (accessed February 26, 2010).

3. According to the US Congressional-Executive Commission on China's Political Prisoner Database, 527 Tibetan political prisoners were believed to be detained or imprisoned as of September 2011, though the commission noted that their information was far from complete as the status of hundreds of Tibetans arrested during the March 2008 uprising was unknown. Congressional-Executive Commission on China, Annual Report 2011 (Washington, DC: US Government Printing Office, 2011), 219.

4. Committee Against Torture, Concluding Observations on China, November 21, 2008, CAT/C/CHN/CO/4.

5. Martin L. Lasater and Kenneth J. Conboy, "Why the World Is Watching Beijing's Treatment of Tibet," Heritage Foundation, October 9, 1987. Available at http:// thf_media.s3.amazonaws.com/1987/pdf/em177.pdf (accessed January 29, 2011).

6. A. A. Shiromany, ed., The Political Philosophy of His Holiness the XIV Dalai Lama: Selected Speeches and Writings (New Delhi: Tibetan Parliamentary and Policy Research Centre, 1998), 65.

7. "The Ecological Migration Policy in Western China Has Already Resettled 700,000 People" [Wo guo xibu diqu shengtai yimin yi da 70 wan ren], 2005 speech by Du Ping, director, Western Development Office, State Council, People's Republic of China, report by the Xinhua news agency and cited by Human Rights Watch, No One Has the Liberty to Remain: Tibetan Herders Forcibly Relocated in Gansu, Quinghai, Sichuan and the Tibetan Autonomous Region (New York: Human Rights Watch, 2007), 4.

8. Wang Wei, vice president of the Beijing Olympic Games Bid Committee, quoted by AFP, July 12, 2001, and cited by Human Rights Watch, "In the Words of Chinese Officials." Available at http://china.hrw.org/in_the_words_of_chinese_officials (accessed January 29, 2011).

9. Nick Mulvenney, "Games a Force for Good but No Panacea: Rogge," Reuters, August 6, 2007. Available at http://www.reuters.com/article/2007/08/06/us-olympics -beijing-rogge-idUSPEK7117220070806 (accessed January 29, 2011).

10. Human Rights Watch, "I Saw It with My Own Eyes": Abuses by Chinese Security Forces in Tibet, 2008–2010 (New York: Human Rights Watch, 2010).

11. Free Tibet, "2008 Uprising in Tibet." Available at http://www.freetibet.org/node/1350 (accessed January 6, 2012).

12. Free Tibet, "Political Prisoners." Available at http://www.freetibet.org/campaigns/political-prisoners (accessed February 28, 2010); Human Rights Watch, "I Saw It with My Own Eyes," 16.

13. Richard Spencer and James Miles, "China Accuses Dalai Lama of 'Inciting' Tibet Riots to 'Sabotage' Olympics," *The Telegraph*, March 18, 2008. Available at http://www.telegraph.co.uk/news/worldnews/1582114/China-accuses-Dalai-Lama-of-inciting-Tibet-riots-to-sabotage-Olympics.html (accessed January 29, 2011).

14. Author interview with Lhadon Tethong, executive director, Students for a Free Tibet, February 3, 2010.

15. Ibid.

16. Author interview with Jonathan Hulland, member of the board of directors, Students for a Free Tibet, October 28, 2009.

17. Author interview with Lhadon Tethong, February 3, 2010.

18. Author interview with Nathan Freitas, technology advisor and member of the board of directors, Students for a Free Tibet, February 11, 2010.

19. Author interview with Lhadon Tethong, February 3, 2010.

20. Author interview with Nathan Freitas, February 11, 2010.

21. Author interview with Lhadon Tethong, February 3, 2010.

22. "China Condemns 'Despicable' Torch Disruptions," *Reuters*, April 7, 2008. Available at http://www.reuters.com/article/2008/04/08/us-olympics-torch-idUSPEK13147120080408 (accessed January 29, 2011).

23. Author interview with Nathan Freitas, February 11, 2010.

24. Andrew Jacobs, "Olympic Official Calls Protests a 'Crisis,'" *New York Times*, April 11, 2008. Available at http://www.nytimes.com/2008/04/11/world/asia/11china.html?pagewanted=all (accessed January 29, 2011).

25. Students for a Free Tibet, "Tibet Activists Scale Golden Gate Bridge to Protest China's Torch Relay," press release, April 7, 2009. Available at http://www.studentsforafreetibet.org/article.php?id=1456 (accessed January 29, 2011).

26. Philip Hersh, "Juggling Free Speech for Beijing Olympics," *Los Angeles Times*, February 12, 2008. Available at http://articles.latimes.com/2008/feb/12/sports/sp-oly12 (accessed January 29, 2011).

27. Rule 51.3 of the Olympic Charter provides that "no kind of demonstration or political, religious or racial propaganda is permitted in any Olympic sites, venues or other areas."

28. "IOC Flags Athlete Free Speech Dilemma," *The Australian*, April 12, 2008. Available at http://www.theaustralian.com.au/news/ioc-flags-athlete-free-speech-dilemma/story-e6frg6t6-1111116039064 (accessed January 29, 2011).

29. Author interview with Lhadon Tethong, February 3, 2010.

30. Tenzin Sangmu, "Polish Silver Medalist Kolecki's Tibet Protest," Phayul.com, August 19, 2008. Available at http://www.phayul.com/news/article.aspx?article=Polish+Silver+Medalist+Kolecki's+Tibet+protest&id=22543 (accessed January 29, 2011).

31. Ibid.

32. Author interview with Nathan Freitas, February 11, 2010.

33. Author interview with Kate Woznow, campaigns director, Students for a Free Tibet, February 19, 2010.

34. Author interview with Nathan Freitas, February 11, 2010.

35. Author interview with Jonathan Hulland, October 28, 2009.

36. Author interview with Lhadon Tethong, February 3, 2010.

37. Author interview with Kate Woznow, February 19, 2010.

38. Ibid.

39. Students for a Free Tibet, Report for August 1, 2007, to August 2, 2008. Author's files.

40. Author interview with Kate Woznow, February 19, 2010.

41. Author interview with Lhadon Tethong, February 3, 2010.

42. Author interview with Kate Woznow, February 19, 2010.

43. Author interview with Lhadon Tethong, February 3, 2010.

44. Author interview with Nathan Freitas, February 11, 2010.

45. Author interview with Kate Woznow, February 19, 2010.

46. Author interview with Lhadon Tethong, February 3, 2010.

47. Author interview with Kate Woznow, February 19, 2010.

48. Author interview with Lhadon Tethong, February 3, 2010.

49. Students for a Free Tibet Report for August 1, 2007, to August 2, 2008.

50. Author interview with Lhadon Tethong, February 3, 2010.

51. Ibid.

Chapter 10

1. Lyndon Barnett, "Progress in New Republic of Nepal," *Sydney Star Observer*, June 16, 2009. Available at http://www.starobserver.com.au/opinion/soapbox-opinion /2009/06/16/progress-in-new-republic-of-nepal/13887 (accessed January 30, 2011).

2. Among members of the lesbian, gay, bisexual, transgender, and intersex (LGBTI) community, various terminology is used to refer to sexual minorities. In Jamaica, advocates often refer to lesbians, all-sexuals, and gays (LAG). The term "all-sexual" is used to acknowledge a sexual continuum where labels of "gay," "lesbian," and "bisexual" may not apply. In Nepal, advocates often use the term LGBTI to refer to lesbians, gays, bisexuals, transgender, and intersex persons. In Nepal, persons who do not conform to a specific gender are also known as "third gender," and transgender individuals (persons who are biologically one gender but dress and identify as another gender) are often referred to as *metis*. Advocates in both countries also refer to men who have sex with men and women who have sex with women to include persons who may not identify as gay or lesbian. In this chapter, all of these terms are used, but "LGBT" or "LGBTI" are used most often.

3. According to the International Lesbian, Gay, Bisexual, Trans, and Intersex Association, in 2011, seventy-six countries prosecuted individuals based on their sexual orientation, with five imposing the death penalty. Eddie Bruce-Jones and

Lucas Paoli-Itaborahy, *State-Sponsored Homophobia* (Brussels: International Lesbian, Gay, Trans and Intersex Association, May 2011). Available at http://old.ilga.org/Statehomophobia/ILGA_State_Sponsored_Homophobia_2011.pdf (accessed January 14, 2012).

4. Jyoti Thottam, "Why Asia's Gays Are Starting to Win Acceptance," *Time*, August 24, 2009. Available at http://www.time.com/time/magazine/article/0,9171,1916097,00 .html (accessed January 30, 2011). And Tim Padgett, "The Most Homophobic Place on Earth?," *Time*, April 12, 2006. Available at http://www.time.com/time/world /article/0,8599,1182991,00.html (accessed January 30, 2011).

5. "Jamaica: A Grim Place to Be Gay," *The Independent*, September 12, 2009. Available at http://www.independent.co.uk/news/world/americas/jamaica-a-grim-place -to-be-gay-1786273.html (accessed January 30, 2011).

6. Human Rights Watch, "Jamaica: Shield Gays from Mob Attacks," press release, January 31, 2008. Available at http://www.hrw.org/en/news/2008/01/31/jamaica -shield-gays-mob-attacks (accessed January 30, 2011).

7. Ibid.

8. Many sought refuge in the United States, where in 1994, former US attorney general Janet Reno expanded the grounds for asylum to include persecution based on sexual preference. Although gay asylum cases make up only a small fraction of asylum applications in the United States, a disproportionate number of these applicants originated from Jamaica. Immigration Equality, which works for immigration equality for the LGBT community, reported in 2009 that Jamaican cases made up about 20 percent of their caseload and accounted for more than the number of cases from the next three countries combined.

9. "Jamaican Activist Seeks Asylum in Canada," PinkNews.co.uk, February 14, 2008. Available at http://www.pinknews.co.uk/news/articles/2005–6852.html/ (accessed August 9, 2010).

10. Bruce-Jones and Paoli-Itaborahy, *State-Sponsored Homophobia*.

11. Offences against the Person Act, Article 76. The act defines "buggery" as anal intercourse between a man and a woman, or between two men. Most prosecutions under the act have been against men suspected of having anal sex.

12. Offences against the Person Act, Article 79.

13. *Nicholas Toonen v. Australia*, Human Rights Committee, 50th Session, Case no. 488/1992, UN doc. CCPR/C/50/D/488/1992 (April 4, 1994).

14. "Buggery Laws Firm: PM Says Life or 15 Years for Some Sex-Offense Breaches," *Jamaica Gleaner*, March 4, 2009. Available at http://jamaica-gleaner.com/ gleaner/20090304/lead/lead1.html (accessed January 30, 2011).

15. Ibid.

16. Anja Tranovich, "Fear and Loathing in Jamaica," *Passport Magazine*, January 2009. Available at http://www.passportmagazine.com/departments/Jamaica.php (accessed January 30, 2011).

17. See Amnesty International, "Battybwoys affi dead" [Faggots have to die]: Action Against Homophobia in Jamaica," May 17, 2004; Human Rights Watch, *Hated to*

Death: Homophobia, Violence and Jamaica's HIV/AIDS Epidemic (New York: Human Rights Watch, 2004).

18. Ministry of Health, "Jamaica National HIV/STI Programme, Country Progress Report to the Secretary-General of the United Nations," March 31, 2010, 9. Available at http://data.unaids.org/pub/Report/2010/jamaica_2010_country_progress_report_en.pdf (accessed August 9, 2010).

19. Joint UN Programme on HIV/AIDS (UNAIDS) and World Health Organization (WHO), *2009 AIDS Epidemic Update* (Geneva: UNAIDS, 2009), 53–56.

20. UNAIDS, "A Global View of HIV Infection, 2007." Available at http://www.unaids.org/en/KnowledgeCentre/HIVData/GlobalReport/2008/2008_Global_report.asp (accessed July 31, 2010).

21. Rebecca Schleifer, quoted in Human Rights Watch, "Jamaica: Police Violence Fuels AIDS Epidemic," press release, November 15, 2004. Available at http://www.hrw.org/en/news/2004/11/15/jamaica-police-violence-fuels-aids-epidemic (accessed January 30, 2011).

22. Tranovich, "Fear and Loathing in Jamaica."

23. Constitution, Section 24(3).

24. IGLHRC, "Jamaica: Support the Inclusion of Sexual Orientation as a Protected Category in the Jamaican Constitution," action alert, September 9, 2000. Available at http://www.glapn.org/sodomylaws/world/jamaica/jaalert001.htm (accessed January 30, 2011).

25. Amnesty International, "Battybwoys affi dead."

26. Author interview with Maurice Tomlinson, legal counsel, J-FLAG, August 6, 2010.

27. Author interview with Jason McFarlane (a pseudonym), program manager, J-FLAG, September 1, 2010.

28. Outrage!, "Dancehall Dossier," February 2004. Available at http://outrage.org.uk/wp-content/uploads/2010/05/Dancehall-Dossier-FULL.pdf (accessed August 5, 2010).

29. Tranovich, "Fear and Loathing in Jamaica."

30. Outrage!, "Dancehall Dossier."

31. Canadian Jewish Congress, "Letter to Hon. Diane Finley, Minister of Citizenship and Immigration," September 26, 2007. Available at http://www.egale.ca/smm/docs/070926_JewishCongressLetter.pdf (accessed July 30, 2010).

32. Center for Research-Action on Race Relations, "Letter to Mr. Dave Burwick, President and CEO, Pepsi-Canada," October 5, 2007. Available at http://www.egale.ca/smm/docs/071005_RaceRelations.pdf (accessed July 30, 2010).

33. Alexis Petridis, "Pride and Prejudice," *The Guardian* online, December 10, 2004. Available at http://www.guardian.co.uk/music/2004/dec/10/gayrights.popandrock (accessed July 30, 2010).

34. Ibid.

35. Peter Tatchell, "Buju Banton Says Boom Bye Bye to Homophobia," press release, July 23, 2007. Available at http://www.petertatchell.net/popmusic/bujubantonbyebyehomophobia.htm (accessed August 5, 2010).

36. IGLHRC, "Jamaica: Reggae Stars Renounce Homophobia," press release, June

13, 2007. Available at http://iglhrc.org/cgi-bin/iowa/article/takeaction/partners/434.html (accessed January 30, 2011).

37. Tatchell, "Buju Banton Says Boom Bye Bye to Homophobia."

38. "Murder Music: Two-Face Reggae Stars Sign, then Reneg on, Pledge to Stop Hate Songs," *Gay City News*, July 26, 2007. Available at http://direland.typepad.com/direland/2007/07/murder-music-tw.html (accessed January 30, 2011).

39. Ibid.

40. "Prime Minister of Jamaica Orders Forum on X-Rated Songs," *Jamaica Gleaner*, February 10, 2009. Available at http://jamaica-gleaner.com/gleaner/20090210/lead/lead6.html (accessed January 30, 2011).

41. Author interview with Jason McFarlane, September 1, 2010.

42. Tony Grew, "Jamaican Gays Reject Tourist Boycott over Homophobia," *PinkNews*, March 3, 2008. Available at http://www.pinknews.co.uk/news/articles/2005-7013.html (accessed January 30, 2011).

43. Matt Mills, "Dispatches from Kingston: Three Days in One of the Most Homophobic Place on Earth," *Extra!* Canada's Gay and Lesbian News, May 12, 2008. Available at http://www.xtra.ca/public/National/Dispatches_from_Kingston_Jamaica-4763.aspx (accessed July 31, 2010).

44. Krishna Rau, "Jamaica Boycott Called Off: Official Response from the Island Government Is a Step Forward, Says Stop Murder Music Canada," *extra.ca*, May 21, 2008. Available at http://www.xtra.ca/public/viewstory.aspx?AFF_TYPE=1&STORY_ID=4808&PUB_TEMPLATE_ID=9 (accessed January 30, 2011).

45. US State Department, "Jamaica," in *2008 Country Reports on Human Rights Practices*, February 25, 2009. Available at http://www.state.gov/g/drl/rls/hrrpt/2008/ (accessed January 17, 2011).

46. Sonia Mitchell, "Gays in US 'Boycott Jamaica,'" *Jamaica Gleaner*, April 1, 2009. Available at http://www.jamaica-gleaner.com/gleaner/20090401/news/news2.html (accessed July 31, 2010).

47. Jason MacFarlane, "Jamaica: Don't Boycott Us!," April 12, 2009, published by IGLHRC. Available at http://iglhrc.org/cgi-bin/iowa/article/takeaction/partners/888.html (accessed January 30, 2010).

48. Shamette Hepburn, "Red Stripe Pulls Plug on Live Music Events," *The Jamaica Star*, April 5, 2008. Available at http://jamaica-star.com/thestar/20080405/ent/ent1.html (accessed January 30, 2011).

49. Ibid.

50. Michael Petrelis, "'Gay Omission:' Red Stripe Beer Pulled Support of Homo-Hating Concerts in Jamaica," The Petrelis Files, April 13, 2009. Available at http://mpetrelis.blogspot.com/2009/04/gay-omission-red-stripe-beer-pulled.html (accessed August 1, 2010).

51. Author interview with Maurice Tomlinson, August 6, 2010.

52. Ibid.

53. Ibid.

54. Ibid.

55. Ibid.

56. Ibid.

57. AIDS-Free World, ""Walk for Tolerance" Calls for End to Bigotry in Jamaica," press release, April 8, 2010. Available at http://www.aidsfreeworld.org/Our-Issues/Homophobia/Walk-for-Tolerance-Calls-for-End-to-Bigotry-in-Jamaica.aspx (accessed January 30, 2011).

58. "J-FLAG Calls for CARICOM to End Gay Discrimination," *UK Gay News*, July 5, 2010, Available at http://www.ukgaynews.org.uk/Archive/10/Jul/0502.htm (accessed August 1, 2010).

59. Author interview with Maurice Tomlinson, August 6, 2010.

60. Ibid.

61. Ibid.

62. Author interview with Jason McFarlane, September 1, 2010.

63. Ibid.

64. See http://www.youtube.com/watch?v=JhH6UhfEI-E (accessed January 12, 2012).

65. Concluding observations of the Human Rights Committee, Unedited Advance Version, HRC 103rd Session, Geneva, October 17–November 4, 2011, para. 8.

66. J-FLAG, "J-FLAG Celebrates 13 Years of Promoting Tolerance for Gays," press release, December 9, 2011. Available at http://www.jflag.org/2011/12/ (accessed January 14, 2012).

67. Human Rights Watch, "Nepali Police Attack Transgender People: Pattern of Abuse Highlights Broader Threat to Civil Society," press release, April 18, 2005. Available at http://www.hrw.org/en/news/2005/04/17/nepal-police-attack-transgender-people (accessed January 30, 2011). "Brutal Start to Nepali New Year as Police Beat Metis," *UK Gay News*, April 14, 2005. Available at http://www.ukgaynews.org.uk/Archive/2005april/1401.htm (accessed January 30, 2011).

68. IGLHRC, "Nepal: IGLHRC Condemns Violence and Arbitrary Arrests," press release, August 12, 2004. Available at http://www.iglhrc.org/cgi-bin/iowa/article/pressroom/pressrelease/538.html (accessed January 30, 2011).

69. David Rohde, "Nepal: Concern at Detention of 39 Gay Men," *New York Times*, August 19, 2004. Available at http://query.nytimes.com/gst/fullpage.html?res=9E04E5D91E3FF93AA2575BC0A9629C8B63 (accessed January 30, 2011). IGLHRC, "Nepal: IGLHRC Condemns Violence and Arbitrary Arrests," press release, August 12, 2004. Available at http://www.iglhrc.org/cgi-bin/iowa/article/pressroom/pressrelease/538.html (accessed January 30, 2011).

70. "First Gay Weekly to Be Launched in Nepal," *Indo-Asian News Service*, January 2, 2005. Available at http://www.mail-archive.com/gay_bombay@yahoogroups.com/msg02553.html (accessed January 30, 2011). "Gay Rights in High Places," *SFWeekly.com*, March 16, 2005. Available at http://www.sfweekly.com/2005-03-16/news/gay-rights-in-high-places/ (accessed January 30, 2011).

71. Blue Diamond Society, "The Kathmandu Statement on Sexual Orientation, Gender Identity and Human Rights," February 20, 2004.

72. Doug Ireland, "Nepal's First Gay MP Speaks: Nation's Two largest Political

Parties Embrace LGBT Rights," *Gay City News*, May 8, 2008. Available at http://direland.typepad.com/direland/2008/05/nepals-first-ga.html (accessed January 30, 2011).

73. Barnett, "Progress in New Republic of Nepal."

74. "Interview with Sunil Pant," *Trikone Magazine*, June 2003. Available at http://www.trikone.org (accessed January 30, 2011).

75. Henry Chu, "Gay Activist in Nepal Campaigns Against Discrimination," *Los Angeles Times*, June 30, 2008. Available at http://www.csmonitor.com/World/Asia-South-Central/2008/0630/p04s03-wosc.html (accessed January 30, 2011).

76. Richard Ammon, "Gay Nepal: A Struggle Against History," www.globalgayz.com, December 2003, updated July 2007. Available at http://www.globalgayz.com/country/Nepal/view/NPL/gay-nepal-a-struggle-against-history (accessed January 30, 2011).

77. Blue Diamond Society website, available at www.bds.org.np (accessed August 4, 2010).

78. Blue Diamond Society, "The Kathmandu Statement on Sexual Orientation, Gender Identity and Human Rights," February 20, 2004.

79. IGLHRC, "A Celebration of Courage: Nepal's Blue Diamond Society Receives International Recognition for LGBT Human Rights Work," press release, January 17, 2007. Available at http://www.iglhrc.org/cgi-bin/iowa/article/support/coc2007/402.html (accessed January 30, 2011).

80. Individuals who identify as neither male nor female.

81. Supreme Court of Nepal, "Initial Note of the Decision," December 21, 2007. Available at http://www.bds.org.np/decision.html (accessed August 5, 2010).

82. Ibid.

83. According to the International Lesbian, Gay, Bisexual, Trans, and Intersex Association, in 2010 seven countries allowed same-sex marriage: Belgium, Canada, the Federal District in Mexico, the Netherlands, Norway, Spain, South Africa, Sweden, and parts of the United States. Daniel Ottosson, *State-Sponsored Homophobia*.

84. Blue Diamond Society, "Great Victory of Nepalese LGBTI!" press release, November 17, 2008. Available at http://www.iglhrc.org/cgi-bin/iowa/article/takeaction/partners/322.html (accessed January 30, 2011).

85. Diwas Kc, "The State of Homosexuality," *Himal Magazine*, March 2008. Available at http://www.himalmag.com/The-state-of-homosexuality_nw2139.html (accessed August 4, 2010).

86. Barnett, "Progress in New Republic of Nepal."

87. "Nepal Readies to Recognize Third Gender Voters," *Hindustan Times*, December 14, 2009. Available at http://www.hindustantimes.com/Nepal-readies-to-recognise-third-gender-voters/Article1-477674.aspx (accessed January 30, 2011).

88. IGLHRC, "IGLHRC and Lambda Legal Consulting with Nepali Government on LGBTI Rights Protections," press release, December 21, 2009. Available at http://www.iglhrc.org/cgi-bin/iowa/article/pressroom/pressrelease/1053.html (accessed January 30, 2011).

89. "Nepali Gay Men Contesting Poll Hope to End Taboo," *Reuters*, February

26, 2008. Available at http://www.reuters.com/article/2008/02/26/idUSDEL226231 (accessed January 30, 2011).

90. Ireland, "Nepal's First Gay MP Speaks."

91. "Nepal's Highest Court Confirms Full Rights for LGBT People," *PinkNews,* November 17, 2008.

92. Thottam, "Why Asia's Gays Are Starting to Win Acceptance."

93. See the Blue Diamond Society website, www.bds.org.np.

94. Speech to Legislature-Parliament by Finance Minister Dr. Babu Ram Bhattarai, September 19, 2008. Available at http://www.mof.gov.np/publication/speech/2008_1/index.php# (accessed August 4, 2010).

95. Ministry of Tourism and Civil Aviation, "2008 Annual Report of Nepal Tourism Statistics," July 2009. Available at http://www.tourism.gov.np/pdf/Final%20Book%20NTS_2008.pdf (accessed August 4, 2010).

96. Letter from Nepal Minister of Tourism and Civil Aviation to the International Conference on Gay and Lesbian Tourism, October 28, 2009. Available at http://www.bds.org.np/images/Tourism.jpg (accessed August 4, 2010).

97. Pink Mountain Travels and Tours. Available at http://www.pinkyatra.com.

98. Author interview with Sunil Pant, founder, Blue Diamond Society, April 11, 2011.

99. Kyle Knight, "New York City LBGT Center an Inspiration a World Away," November 28, 2011, Huffington Post. Available at http://www.huffingtonpost.com/kyle-knight/new-york-city-lgbt-center_2_b_1110475.html (accessed January 14, 2012).

100. Ibid.

101. "Nepal Readies to Recognize Third Gender Voters," *Hindustan Times.*

102. IGLHRC, "IGLHRC and Lambda Legal Consulting with Nepali Government on LGBTI Rights Protections."

103. Author interview with Maurice Tomlinson, August 6, 2010.

104. Author interview with Jason McFarlane, September 1, 2010.

105. "Government Says No to Gay Rights Advocates," *Jamaica Observer,* January 22, 2002. Available at http://www.jamaicaobserver.com/news/20109_Gov-t-says-no-to-gay-rights-advocates (accessed January 30, 2011).

106. UN Office on Drugs and Crime, "Homicide Statistics, Criminal Justice Sources—Latest Available Year (2003–2008). Available at http://www.unodc.org/unodc/en/data-and-analysis/homicide.html (accessed August 4, 2010). In 2008, the homicide rate in Jamaica was 59.5 per 100,000 people, while in Nepal, the rate for 2007 was 2.2 per 100,000.

107. Chu, "Gay Activist in Nepal Campaigns Against Discrimination."

108. Jamaica Ministry of Tourism, Entertainment, and Culture, "Cultural Heritage Must be Viewed as an Investment," August 23, 2006. Available at http://www.jis.gov.jm/indus_tourism/html/20060822t100000-0500_9798_jis_cultural_heritage_must_be_viewed_as_an_investment___assamba.asp (accessed July 31, 2010).

109. "Nepal to Offer Everest Weddings to Attract More Gay Tourists," *New York Times,* March 15, 2010. Available at http://intransit.blogs.nytimes.com/2010/03/15/

nepal-to-offer-everest-weddings-to-attract-more-gay-tourists/ (accessed January 30, 2011).

110. Lisa Dazols, "Nepal Supergay: Sunil Pant," blog post, November 22, 2011. Available at http://www.outandaround.com/nepal-supergay-sunil-pant/2011/11# (accessed January 14, 2012).

111. Author interview with Sunil Pant, April 11, 2011.

112. AIDS-Free World, "'Walk for Tolerance' Calls for End to Bigotry in Jamaica," press release, April 8, 2010. Available at http://www.aidsfreeworld.org/Our-Issues/Homophobia/Walk-for-Tolerance-Calls-for-End-to-Bigotry-in-Jamaica.aspx (accessed January 30, 2011).

113. "Nepal's Highest Court Confirms Full Rights for LGBT people," *PinkNews*, November 17, 2008.

Chapter 11

1. Author interview with Debi Hodge, member, CARES for Youth, July 21, 2010.

2. Campaign for Fair Sentencing of Youth. Available at http://www.endjlwop.org/ (accessed July 22, 2010).

3. Amnesty International et al., Amicus Curiae Brief filed in *Graham v. Florida*, 130 S. Ct. 2011 (2010). Available at http://www.endjlwop.org/wp/wp-content/uploads/2010/02/Graham-Sullivan-Amnesty-International-Amicus.pdf (accessed December 31, 2011).

4. Human Rights Watch, "2009 JLWOP Figures," May 7, 2009. Available at http://www.hrw.org/en/news/2009/05/07/us-end-life-sentences-youth-offenders (accessed July 22, 2010).

5. Human Rights Watch and Amnesty International, *Rest of Their Lives: Life Without Parole for Child Offenders in the United States* (New York: Human Rights Watch and Amnesty International, 2005).

6. Ibid.

7. Honorable James B. Linn, Associate Justice, Circuit Court of Cook County, *People v. Miller* 202 Ill 2d 328, 781 N.E. 2d, 300, 269Ill Dec. 503 (2002), cited in Illinois Coalition for the Fair Sentencing of Children, *Categorically Less Culpable: Children Sentenced to Life Without Parole in Illinois* (Chicago: Illinois Coalition for the Fair Sentencing of Children, 2008), 14.

8. Honorable Thomas Dwyer, Associate Judge, Circuit Court of Cook County, Brief of Petitioner at 10, *People v. Allen*, No 92 CR 08607–02 (December 13, 2002), cited in Illinois Coalition for the Fair Sentencing of Children, *Categorically Less Culpable,* 10.

9. Human Rights Watch, *"When I Die, They'll Send Me Home": Youth Sentenced to Life Without Parole in California* (New York: Human Rights Watch, 2008).

10. Cases were chosen that were at least four years old, to increase the chances that their appeals were concluded, in order to avoid potential interference with their cases.

11. Human Rights Watch, *"When I Die, They'll Send Me Home."*

12. Ibid.

13. Ibid.

14. California Penal Code 190.5, enacted by Proposition 115 passed by California voters in 1990.

15. Later amended to resentencing after fifteen years of incarceration.

16. Among the criteria to be considered: the defendant did not commit a felony with significant potential for personal harm prior to the current conviction; the defendant committed the offense with at least one adult codefendant; prior to the offense, the defendant had insufficient adult support or supervision and had suffered from psychological or physical trauma; the defendant suffers from cognitive limitations due to mental illness, developmental disabilities, or other factors that did not constitute a defense, but influenced the defendant's involvement in the crime; the defendant has performed acts that indicate rehabilitation or potential for rehabilitation; the defendant has maintained family ties or has eliminated contact with individuals outside of prison who are currently involved with crime; the defendant has had no violent disciplinary violations in the last five years.

17. Leland Yee, "Bill Introduced to Reform Life Sentences for Minors," press release, February 26, 2009. Available at http://dist08.casen.govoffice. com/index.asp?Type=B_PR&SEC=%7BEFA496BC-EDC8-4E38-9CC7- 68D37AC03DFF%7D&DE=%7B5261BD8C-68AF-4E55-86F1-5D6DF00899E7%7D (accessed July 22, 2010).

18. See http://www.fairsentencingforyouth.org/get-the-facts/fiscal-impact/.

19. Author interview with Elizabeth Calvin, senior advocate, Human Rights Watch, June 12, 2009.

20. Author interview with Debi Hodge, July 21, 2010.

21. Author interview with Brandy Novak, member, CARES for Youth, July 22, 2010.

22. Author interview with Debi Hodge, July 21, 2010.

23. Ibid.

24. Author interview with Brandy Novak, July 22, 2010.

25. "California's Prison Population Falls for Second Straight Year," *Los Angeles Times*, March 17, 2010. Available at http://articles.latimes.com/2010/mar/17/local/ la-me-prisons17–2010mar17 (accessed July 22, 2010).

26. Author interview with Elizabeth Calvin, January 12, 2010.

27. Sasha Abramsky, "When Prison Guards Go Soft," *Mother Jones,* July/August 2008. Available at http://motherjones.com/politics/2008/07/when-prison-guards-go- soft (accessed July 22, 2010).

28. Author interview with Elizabeth Calvin, January 12, 2010.

29. Miriam Aroni Krinsky, Ernie Pierce, and Jeanne Woodford, "Youthful Offenders Deserve a Second Chance," *Los Angeles Times*, June 2, 2010. Available at http://arti- cles.latimes.com/2010/jun/02/opinion/la-oe-krinsky-sentences-20100602 (accessed January 30, 2011).

30. Author interview with Elizabeth Calvin, January 12, 2010.

31. Author interview with Javier Stauring, director, Healing Justice Coalition, January 20, 2010.

32. See www.fcfcla.org.

33. Holy Family Productions, "God Cries When We Sentence Youth to Die in Prison," YouTube, May 19, 2009. Available at http://www.youtube.com/watch?v=Mg jLY97LStM (accessed January 30, 2011).

34. Author interview with Javier Stauring, January 20, 2010.

35. California Catholic Conference, "Backgrounder: SB 399." Available at www .cacatholic.org (accessed January 30, 2011).

36. Faith Communities for Families and Children, available at www.fcfcla.org (accessed January 30, 2011).

37. Faith Communities for Families and Children, "JJWF 2010 Stories," website. Available at http://www.fcfcla.org/index.php?option=com_content&task=view &id=55&Itemid=99 (accessed July 22, 2010).

38. Ibid.

39. Fair Sentencing for Youth, "When I Die, They'll Send Me Home," video. Available at www.fairsentencingforyouth.org (accessed January 30, 2011).

40. Free Sara Kruzan, http://www.facebook.com/group.php?gid=135555313406 &ref=ts (accessed July 22, 2010).

41. "Opening a Horizon for Juvenile Lifers," editorial, *Sacramento Bee,* May 27, 2009.

42. "Sentenced as Minors to Life: Young Lives Can Be Redeemed," editorial, *Ventura County Star,* June 28, 2009. Available at http://www.vcstar.com/news/2009 /jun/28/sentenced-as-minors-to-life/ (accessed January 30, 2011).

43. "Don't Throw Away the Key on Juvenile Offenders," editorial, *San Francisco Chronicle,* June 1, 2009. Available at http://articles.sfgate.com/2009-06-01/opin-ion/17208582_1_young-killers-parole-yee (accessed January 30, 2011). See also "Redemption and Rehabilitation," editorial, *San Francisco Chronicle,* January 18, 2008; "When 'Life' Is Cruel," editorial, *Los Angeles Times,* January 14, 2010; "Locking up Kids for Life," editorial, *Los Angeles Times,* January 16, 2008. Selected editorials are available at http://www.fairsentencingforyouth.org/supporters/newspapers -across-california-support-an-end-to-jlwop/ (accessed January 30, 2011).

44. Five justices joined the majority opinion; Chief Justice John G. Roberts voted with the majority that the sentence in the specific case under consideration was so harsh that it violated the US Constitution, but supported a case-by-case approach to such sentencing, rather than a blanket prohibition.

45. *Roper v. Simmons* (2005).

46. *Graham v. Florida* (2010). Available at http://www.supremecourt.gov/opinions /09pdf/08-7412.pdf (accessed January 30, 2011).

47. "Why 'Throw Away Key' for Juveniles?" *Sacramento Bee,* May 21, 2010. Available at http://www.fairsentencingforyouth.org/wp/wp-content/uploads/2010/10/ editorial-jwop-sacbee-5-20-10.pdf (accessed January 30, 2011).

48. "Life Sentences Without Parole: Too Cruel for the Young," *Los Angeles Times,* May 18, 2010. Available at http://articles.latimes.com/2010/may/18/opinion/la-ed-ju-veniles-20100519 (accessed July 26, 2010).

49. "Bill Would End Life-Without-Parole for Some Teen Killers," *San Francisco Chronicle,* April 18, 2007. Available at http://articles.sfgate.com/2007-04-18/bay-area/17240784_1_parole-sentence-yee (accessed January 30, 2011).

50. Fair Sentencing for Youth, "SB 399 Fails to Pass in Assembly—But—All is Not Lost for the Bill," June 30, 2009, Available at http://www.fairsentencingforyouth .org/2009/07/sb-399–fails-to-pass-in-assembly%E2%80%94but%E2%80%94all-is-not-lost-for-the-bill/ (accessed January 30, 2011).

51. Email communication from Elizabeth Calvin, September 2, 2010. Author's files.

52. Ibid.

53. Author interview with Elizabeth Calvin, September 7, 2010.

54. Author interview with Brandy Novak, July 22, 2010.

55. Heritage Foundation, "California Public Safety Committee Votes to Revictimize Victims," blog post, January 13, 2010. Available at http://blog.heritage. org/?p=23806 (accessed July 24, 2010).

56. Author interview with Javier Stauring, January 20, 2010.

57. Author interview with Elizabeth Calvin, September 7, 2010.

58. Author interview with Javier Stauring, January 20, 2010.

59. Author interview with DK (name withheld by request), member, CARES for Youth, July 24, 2010.

60. Author interview with Brandy Novak, July 22, 2010.

61. Author interview with DK (name withheld by request), July 24, 2010.

62. Author interview with Elizabeth Calvin, June 2009.

63. Author interview with DK (name withheld by request), July 24, 2010.

64. Author interview with Javier Stauring, January 20, 2010.

65. Author interview with Kim McGill, organizer, Youth Justice Coalition, May 28, 2011.

66. Author interview with Elizabeth Calvin, September 7, 2010.

67. Letter from individual serving life without parole (name withheld) to Human Rights Watch, September 2010.

Lessons for the Future

1. Author interview with Cristina Barbaglia, September 16, 2010.

2. Author interview with DK (name withheld by request), July 24, 2010.

3. Marcelina Bautista, secretary general, CONLACTRAHO, cited in Mather, Respect and Rights, 40a.

4. Author interview with Lhadon Tetong, February 3, 2010.

5. Author interview with Eric Witte, January 3, 2012.

6. Author interview with Rachel Brett, December 15, 2010.

7. Lisa Dazols, "Nepal Supergay: Sunil Pant," blog post, November 22, 2011. Available at http://www.outandaround.com/nepal-supergay-sunil-pant/2011/11# (accessed January 14, 2012).

8. Author interview with Eric Witte, January 3, 2012.

9. Author interview with Alan Keenan, December 17, 2010.

10. Letter from individual serving life without parole (name withheld) to Human Rights Watch, September 2010.

Further Reading and Additional Resources

Transnational Activism and the Origins of the Human Rights Movement

Clark, Ann Marie. *Diplomacy of Conscience: Amnesty International and Changing Human Rights Norms*. Princeton, NJ: Princeton University Press, 2001.

Keck, Margaret, and Kathryn Sikkink. *Activists Beyond Borders*. Ithaca, NY: Cornell University Press, 1998.

Lauren, Paul. *The Evolution of International Human Rights: Visions Seen*. Philadelphia: University of Pennsylvania, 2003.

Moyn, Samuel. *The Last Utopia: Human Rights in History*. Cambridge and London: Belknap Press of Harvard University Press, 2010.

Roth, Kenneth. "Human Rights Organizations: A New Force for Social Change." In *Realizing Human Rights*, ed. Samantha Power and Graham Allison. New York: St. Martin's Press, 2000.

Tarrow, Sidney. *The New Transnational Activism*. New York: Cambridge University Press: 2006.

Human Rights Advocacy: Strategies and Practice

Gready, Paul. *Fighting for Human Rights*. London and New York: Routledge, 2004.

Gready, Paul, and Brian Phillips, eds. *Journal of Human Rights Practice*. New York: Oxford University Press, ongoing.

Hurwitz, Deena, Margaret Satterthwaite, and Doug Ford, eds. *International Human Rights Advocacy Stories*. New York: Thomson Reuters/Foundation Press, 2009.

Joyce, Mary, ed. *Digital Activism Decoded: The New Mechanics of Change*. New York and Amsterdam: International Debate Education Association, 2010.

New Tactics in Human Rights. *New Tactics in Human Rights: A Resource for Practitioners*. St. Paul, MN: New Tactics in Human Rights, a project of the Center for the Victims of Torture, 2004.

VeneKlasen, Lisa, with Valerie Miller. *A New Weave of Power, People and Politics: The Action Guide for Advocacy and Citizen Participation*. Warwickshire, UK: Practical Action Publishing, 2008.

Campaigns and Coalitions

Amnesty International. *Campaigning Manual.* London: Amnesty International, 2001. Available at http://web.amnesty.org/pages/campaigning-manual-eng.

Hamilton, Rebecca. *Fighting for Darfur: Public Action and the Struggle to Stop Genocide.* New York: Palgrave Macmillan, 2011.

Moyes, Richard, and Thomas Nash. *Global Coalitions: An Introduction to Working in International Civil Society Partnerships.* London: Action on Armed Violence, 2011. Available at www.globalcoalitions.org.

Williams, Jody, Stephen D. Goose, and Mary Wareham. *Banning Landmines: Disarmament, Citizen Diplomacy, and Human Security.* Lanham, MD: Rowman and Littlefield, 2008.

Online Resources

DigiActive. www.digiactive.org. Contains an archive (through 2010) of posts on digital activism tools, campaigns, and tactics from around the world, including guides on using Twitter, Facebook, and mobile phones for activism.

Global Voices Advocacy. http://advocacy.globalvoicesonline.org/. Includes guides describing techniques and tools for online advocacy campaigns.

Meta-Activism Project. www.meta-activism.org. Resources and blogs on digital activism, including a Global Digital Activism Data Set (GDADS), a coded case-study list of more than a thousand digital action cases from more than one hundred countries around the world.

New Tactics in Human Rights. www.newtactics.org. Interactive website providing access to a database of more than 190 specific and successfully implemented human rights tactics and peer-to-peer dialogues with human rights practitioners in more than 130 countries.

Child Soldiers

Child Soldiers International. Available at www.child-soldiers.org.

Coalition to Stop the Use of Child Soldiers. *Child Soldiers Global Report 2008.* London: Coalition to Stop the Use of Child Soldiers, 2008. Available at www.child-soldiers.org.

Hubert, Don. "Humanitarian Advocacy Campaigns: Lessons on Government Civil Society Collaboration." In *Civil Society and Government Cooperation on Conflict Prevention and Peacebuilding,* ed. Paul van Tongeren et al. The Hague: European Centre for Conflict Prevention, 2007.

Wessels, Michael. *Child Soldiers: From Violence to Protection.* Cambridge, MA: Harvard University Press, 2007.

Domestic Workers

International Domestic Worker Network. Available at www.domesticworkerrights.org.

International Domestic Worker Network's Blog During the ILO Convention Negotiations. Available at http://idwnilo.wordpress.com/.

International Labor Organization. *Decent Work for Domestic Workers, Report IV(I)*. Geneva: International Labor Office, 2009.

Langevin, Louise, and Debra Parkes, eds. "Regulating Decent Work for Domestic Workers." Special issue, *Canadian Journal of Women and the Law* 23, no. 1. Toronto: University of Toronto Press, 2011.

Mather, Celia. *Respect and Rights: Protection for Domestic/Household Workers!* Tilberg and Geneva: IRENE and IUF, 2008.

UN Human Rights Council

Human Rights Watch. *Keeping the Momentum: One Year in the Life of the UN Human Rights Council*. New York: Human Rights Watch, 2011.

Moss, Lawrence. "Opportunities for Nongovernmental Advocacy in the Universal Periodic Review Process at the UN Human Rights Council." *Journal of Human Rights Practice* 2, no. 1 (2010): 122–50.

NGO Coalition for an Effective Human Rights Council. Available at http://www.hrw.org/sites/default/files/features/hrc2010/index.html.

Office of the High Commissioner for Human Rights. "The Human Rights Council." In *Working with OHCHR: A Handbook for NGOs*. Geneva: OHCHR, 2010. Available at http://www.ohchr.org/Documents/Publications/NGOHandbooken.pdf.

UN Special Rapporteurs

Nowak, Manfred. "Fact-Finding on Torture and Ill-Treatment and Conditions of Detention." *Journal of Human Rights Practice* 1, no. 1 (2009): 101–19.

Office of the High Commissioner for Human Rights. "Special Procedures." In *Working with OHCHR: A Handbook for NGOs*. Geneva: OHCHR, 2010. Available at http://www.ohchr.org/Documents/Publications/NGOHandbooken.pdf.

Piccone, Ted. *Catalysts for Human Rights: The Unique Contribution of the UN's Independent Experts on Human Rights, Final Report of the Brookings Research Project on Strengthening UN Special Procedures*. Washington, DC: The Brookings Institution, 2010.

Violence Against Children

Pinheiro, Paulo Sérgio. *World Report on Violence Against Children*. Geneva: United Nations Secretary-General's Study on Violence Against Children, 2006. Available at www.unviolencestudy.org.

Special Representative of the Secretary-General on Violence Against Children. Available at http://srsg.violenceagainstchildren.org/.

Bringing Charles Taylor to Justice

Global Policy Forum. Charles Taylor. Relevant documents and article archive related to Charles Taylor and his trial, available at http://www.globalpolicy.org/international -justice/rogues-gallery/charles-taylor.html.

Lanegran, Kimberly. "The Importance of Trying Charles Taylor." *Journal of Human Rights* 6 (2007): 165–79.

Open Society Justice Initiative. The Trial of Charles Taylor. A log of courtroom updates from the trial of Charles Taylor, including daily, weekly, and monthly summaries, available at http://www.charlestaylortrial.org/.

The Special Court for Sierra Leone. Available at www.sc-sl.org.

United Nations, Panel of Experts on Sierra Leone Diamonds and Arms. "Report of the Panel of Experts appointed pursuant to Security Council resolution 1306 (2000)," S/2000/1195, December 20, 2000.

Justice for the Abu Salim Prison Massacre

Human Rights Solidarity. *Abuslim*. Geneva: Human Rights Solidarity, 2009.

Human Rights Watch. *Truth and Justice Can't Wait: Human Rights Developments in Libya Amid Institutional Obstacles.* New York: Human Rights Watch, 2009.

Accountability for War Crimes in Sri Lanka

International Crisis Group. *War Crimes in Sri Lanka*, Asia Report no. 191. Brussels: ICG, 2010.

United Nations. *Report of the Secretary-General's Panel of Experts on Accountability in Sri Lanka.* New York: UN, 2011.

Weiss, Gordon. *The Cage: The Fight for Sri Lanka and the Last Days of the Tamil Tigers.* London: The Bodley Head, 2011.

Campaign for a Free Tibet

Beijing Wide Open. A blog initiated during the Beijing Olympics campaign. Available at http://beijingwideopen.org.

Rozeboom, Annelie. *Waiting for the Dalai Lama: Stories from All Sides of the Tibetan Debate.* Hong Kong: Blacksmith Books, 2011.

Smith Jr., Warren W. *China's Tibet? Autonomy or Assimilation.* Lanham, MD: Rowman and Littlefield, 2008.

Students for a Free Tibet. Available at www.studentsforafreetibet.org.

Organizing Against Homophobia and Antigay Violence in Jamaica and Nepal

An Activist's Guide to the Yogyakarta Principles on the Application of International Human Rights Law in Relation to Sexual Orientation and Gender Identity (2010).

Available at http://www.ypinaction.org/files/02/85/Activists_Guide_English
_nov_14_2010.pdf.

Blue Diamond Society. Available at www.bds.org.np.

Dubel, Ireen, and André Hielkema, eds. *Urgency Required: Gay and Lesbian Rights Are Human Rights.* The Hague: Hivos, 2010.

Jamaica Aids Support for Life (JASL) et al., *Submission by Stakeholder LGBTI, Sex Workers and PLWHIV Coalition for the Universal Periodic Review of Jamaica.* UN Human Rights Council Ninth Session (November 2010). Available at http://lib.ohchr.org/HRBodies/UPR/Documents/Session9/JM/JASL_JamaicaAidsSupportforLife_JS.pdf.

Jamaica Forum of Lesbians, All-Sexuals and Gays. Available at www.jflag.org.

Abolishing Sentences of Life Without Parole for Juvenile Offenders

Amnesty International and Human Rights Watch. *Rest of Their Lives: Life Without Parole for Child Offenders in the United States.* New York: Human Rights Watch and Amnesty International, 2005.

Fair Sentencing for Youth. Available at www.fairsentencingforyouth.org.

Human Rights Watch. *"When I Die, They'll Send Me Home": Youth Sentenced to Life Without Parole in California.* New York: Human Rights Watch, 2008.

Glossary of Key Terms

Additional or Optional Protocol—a legally binding agreement negotiated by states to supplement a previously agreed treaty. A protocol can amend the previous treaty or add additional provisions. Parties to the original treaty are not required to adopt the protocol.

Commission on Human Rights—an intergovernmental UN body created in 1946 that was concerned with the promotion and protection of human rights. In 2006 it was replaced by the Human Rights Council.

Convention—a legally binding multinational treaty, usually negotiated by governments; International Labor Organization conventions are negotiated by representatives of governments, workers (trade unions), and employers organizations.

Human Rights Council—an intergovernmental UN body created in 2006 in order to strengthen the promotion and protection of human rights around the globe. It has forty-seven member states that are elected by the members of the UN General Assembly and replaced the Commission on Human Rights.

Immunity– provisions in law that prohibit criminal or civil action against perpetrators of abuses.

Impunity—failure to bring perpetrators of human rights violations to justice through criminal, civil, or disciplinary proceedings.

Mandate—authority or scope of responsibility established by an intergovernmental body, for example, the mandate of a special rapporteur established by the UN Human Rights Council.

Member State—a state (country) that is a member of an international organization, such as the United Nations.

Ratification—Formal consent by a national government to accept the legal obligations of an international treaty or convention. In many countries, approval by the national legislature is required for ratification of an international treaty. For ratification of human rights treaties to be complete, an instrument of ratification must be deposited with the UN secretary-general. *Ascension* is the ratification of a treaty that has already gone into effect.

Security Council—a fifteen-member body of the UN General Assembly responsible for international peace and security; the permanent members are China, France, Russia, the United Kingdom, and the United States. Other members are chosen by region and serve for two-year terms.

Special Procedures—the term given to the mechanisms established by the UN Human Rights Council to address either specific country situations or thematic issues in all parts of the world. Special procedures can be either an individual (called "Special Rapporteur," "Special Representative of the Secretary-General," or "Independent Expert"), or a working group usually composed of five members (one from each region).

Special Rapporteur—an individual expert fulfilling a mandate created by the UN Human Rights Council to monitor and report on either the human rights situation in a specific country or territory (a "country mandate"), or on a particular type of human rights violations worldwide (a "thematic mandate").

Special Representative of the Secretary-General—an expert appointed by the UN secretary-general to address key human rights or other issues. The mandate of an SRSG is usually established by the UN General Assembly. Unlike a special rapporteur, an SRSG is usually salaried and may have a small staff.

State Party—a country that has ratified a particular treaty or convention.

Treaty—a legally binding international agreement negotiated by two or more governments.

Acknowledgments

THE BEST PART OF WRITING THIS BOOK was interviewing dozens of inspiring activists who have devoted themselves to the struggle for dignity, justice, and human rights. I am deeply grateful to each person who spoke with me and shared insights about their work: Brad Adams, Philip Alston, Ayodele Ameen, Tania Baldwin-Park, Cristina Barbaglia, Rachel Brett, Mara Bustelo, Elizabeth Calvin, Roberta Cecchetti, "DK," Cookie Diokno, Corinne Dufka, Yolanda Foster, Edriss El Hassy, Giumma El Omami, Dokhi Fassihian, Cecilia Flores-Oebanda, Nathan Freitas, Jeannine Guthrie, Deborah Hodge, Jonathan Hulland, Sulaiman Jabati, Elise Keppler, Vicky Kanyoka, Alan Keenan, Jason MacFarlane, Martin MacPherson, Lilibeth Masamloc, Stuart Maslen, Kim McGill, Eric Mongelard, Heba Morayef, Lawrence Moss, Peter Newell, Brandy Novak, Manfred Nowak, Sunil Pant, Andreas Rister, Ellen Sana, Elizabeth Sepper, Javier Stauring, Rachel Stohl, Lhadon Tethong, Aloysius Toe, Maurice Tomlinson, Myrtle Witbooi, Eric Witte, and Kate Woznow.

I'm indebted to colleagues who generously reviewed and provided valuable comments on portions of the book, including Elizabeth Calvin, Corinne Dufka, Giumma El Omami, Elise Keppler, Kyle Knight, Sophie Richardson, Maurice Tomlinson, and especially Jim Ross. Samantha Barthelemy provided helpful research assistance for the chapter on special rapporteurs. My editor at Stanford University Press, Kate Wahl, supported the project from the beginning and provided excellent guidance. The index was created by J. Naomi Linzer Indexing Services.

Finally, thanks to my students at Columbia's School of International and Public Affairs for inspiring this project; my husband, Jan Hesbon, for his patience and support; and my incomparable colleagues at Human Rights Watch for their inspiration and encouragement.

Index

Stones of Hope: How African Activists Reclaim Human Rights to Challenge Global Poverty
Edited by Lucie White and Jeremy Perelman
2010

Judging War, Judging History: Behind Truth and Reconciliation
Pierre Hazan
2010

Localizing Transitional Justice: Interventions and Priorities After Mass Violence
Edited by Rosalind Shaw and Lars Waldorf, with Pierre Hazan
2010

Surrendering to Utopia: An Anthropology of Human Rights
Mark Goodale
2009

Human Rights for the 21st Century: Sovereignty, Civil Society, Culture
Helen M. Stacy
2009

Human Rights Matters: Local Politics and National Human Rights Institutions
Julie A. Mertus
2009